Essentials of Economics

The Addison-Wesley Series in Economics

Abel/Bernanke
Macroeconomics

Bade/Parkin
Foundations of Economics

Bierman/Fernandez
Game Theory with Economic Applications

Binger/Hoffman
Microeconomics with Calculus

Boyer
Principles of Transportation Economics

Branson
Macroeconomic Theory and Policy

Bruce
Public Finance and the American Economy

Byrns/Stone
Economics

Carlton/Perloff
Modern Industrial Organization

Caves/Frankel/Jones
World Trade and Payments

Chapman
Environmental Economics: Theory, Application, and Policy

Cooter/Ulen
Law and Economics

Downs
An Economic Theory of Democracy

Ehrenberg/Smith
Modern Labor Economics

Ekelund/Tollison
Economics

Fusfeld
The Age of the Economist

Gerber
International Economics

Ghiara
Learning Economics

Gordon
Macroeconomics

Gregory
Essentials of Economics

Gregory/Stuart
Russian and Soviet Economic Performance and Structure

Hartwick/Olewiler
The Economics of Natural Resource Use

Hubbard
Money, the Financial System, and the Economy

Hughes/Cain
American Economic History

Husted/Melvin
International Economics

Jehle/Reny
Advanced Microeconomic Theory

Klein
Mathematical Methods for Economics

Krugman/Obstfeld
International Economics

Laidler
The Demand for Money

Leeds/von Allmen
The Economics of Sports

Lipsey/Courant/Ragan
Economics

Melvin
International Money and Finance

Miller
Economics Today

Miller
Understanding Modern Economics

Miller/Benjamin/North
The Economics of Public Issues

Miller/Benjamin
The Economics of Macro Issues

Mills/Hamilton
Urban Economics

Mishkin
The Economics of Money, Banking, and Financial Markets

Parkin
Economics

Perloff
Microeconomics

Phelps
Health Economics

Riddell/Shackelford/Stamos/Schneider
Economics: A Tool for Critically Understanding Society

Ritter/Silber/Udell
Principles of Money, Banking, and Financial Markets

Rohlf
Introduction to Economic Reasoning

Ruffin/Gregory
Principles of Economics

Sargent
Rational Expectations and Inflation

Scherer
Industry Structure, Strategy, and Public Policy

Schotter
Microeconomics

Stock/Watson
Introduction to Econometrics

Studenmund
Using Econometrics

Tietenberg
Environmental and Natural Resource Economics

Tietenberg
Environmental Economics and Policy

Todaro/Smith
Economic Development

Waldman
Microeconomics

Waldman/Jensen
Industrial Organization

Weil
Economic Growth

Williamson
Macroeconomics

Essentials of Economics

Sixth Edition

Paul R. Gregory

University of Houston

Boston San Francisco New York
London Toronto Sydney Tokyo Singapore Madrid
Mexico City Munich Paris Cape Town Hong Kong Montreal

Editor-in-Chief: Denise Clinton
Acquisitions Editor: Adrienne D'Ambrosio
Editorial Assistant: Kirsten Dickerson
Director of Development: Sylvia Mallory
Managing Editor: James Rigney
Senior Production Supervisor: Katherine Watson
Project Coordination and Electronic Page Makeup: Electronic Publishing Services Inc., NYC
Manufacturing Buyer: Hugh Crawford
Design Manager and Cover Design: Regina Hagen Kolenda
Cover Photo: ©Getty Images

Printed in the United States of America

ISBN 0-321-24852-X

1 2 3 4 5 6 7 8 9 10—PHH—08 07 06 05 04

CONTENTS

PART 3 MICROFOUNDATIONS OF MACROECONOMICS 131

PREFACE

Economics has the power to explain economic events as they unfold. As we approach the mid-mark of the first decade of the twenty-first century, the decade-long economic expansion is a distant memory after the recession of 2000 to 2001. Clear signs of a strong economic recovery are beginning to emerge. The prices of stocks that collapsed during the recession are approaching their previous highs. The U.S. Congress approved tax cuts that Democrats characterize as massive and Republicans characterize as prudent and the 2004 presidential campaign has begun, whose outcome will largely hinge on the strength of the economy. Russia has emerged from economic ruin aided by the high price of oil. Blackouts of electricity and other economic problems in California have resulted in the recall of its governor and his replacement by a popular movie star. The U.S. president has initiated talks for a hemisphere-wide free trade zone encompassing North and South America. China, the world's most populous country, continues its advance to superpower status. Europe continues its move toward a single European market of almost 400 million persons by admitting twelve new countries to the European Union. Europe's move to a single currency has been completed, and the euro is rising relative to the dollar.

The sixth edition of *Essentials of Economics,* through coverage of the basic principles of modern micro- and macroeconomics, shows how economic theory can be used to explain these events. If students are to learn both micro- and macroeconomics in one course, it is better to learn the essentials well than to be overwhelmed by an excessive amount of over-specialized materials. This book is designed for a one-semester course, but it can be used in two semester micro-macro sequences in combination with assigned readings.

The sixth edition has taken on a new organization that recognizes the growing connection between micro- and macroeconomics. Part I provides the basic concepts of supply, demand, and markets, thereby acquainting students with the basic vocabulary of economics. It adds a new chapter on the economics of the Internet. Part II presents the core of microeconomics, focusing on the costs of production, the behavior of competitive enterprises, and the behavior of noncompetitive enterprises. Part III, *Microfoundations of Macroeconomics,* supplies the microeconomic building blocks of macroeconomics; namely, consumption, saving, interest rates, and public finance. Part IV provides the core of macroeconomics: aggregate supply and demand, national income, economic growth, inflation, and unemployment. Part V deals with the globalization of the world economy and describes the world economy of "Haves" and "Have-Nots," trade theory, and the international monetary system.

Essentials of Economics provides a strong pedagogical exposition of basic micro- and macroeconomic theory in a blend of both traditional topics and new theories. In the macro area, it integrates modern aggregate supply and demand analysis, expectations theory, contracting, and the natural rate hypothesis. It analyzes the different views of aggregate supply in the short and long runs and discusses the activism—nonactivism policy debate. The macro portion has been shortened by going to aggregate demand and aggregate supply directly rather than through the detour of the aggregate expenditure model. Theories of unemployment consumption, investment and interest rates are covered, once and only once, in the micro-foundation part. The microeconomics chapters cover the most modern topics in economics: information theory, network externalities, Nash equilibrium, peakload pricing, lifecycle consumption, moral hazard, investment bubbles, and contemporary industrial organization and provide a comprehensive treatment of traditional microeconomics.

Because essentials covers core economic topics, it is also important to be clear and accessible in explanation of theory. Theoretical concepts are explained in direct intuitive terms. The vocabulary of modern economics is carefully developed, and key terms and ideas are set in margins for easy reader reference. The theoretical concepts are introduced in both graphs and prose explanations without overwhelming the reader with excessive figures and graphs. Each chapter shows its real-world relevance. The micro chapters provide a number of boxed applications and examples that include electricity blackouts, stock markets, e-commerce, the Microsoft case, telecommuting, and Moore's Law. The macro chapters reinforce theoretical concepts with real-world data and policy examples. The goal of this book is to demonstrate that economics is a lively field of study that, if properly examined, will allow students to understand the real world.

Essentials of Economics is accompanied by a complete support package. The Online Student Study Guide presents the strongest problem-solving orientation of any one-term principles study guide, with numerous problem sets and analytical multiple-choice questions. The Companion Web site, www.aw-bc.com/gregory, contains additional student and instructor resources; an online Test Bank is also available for instructor support.

A number of persons made valuable suggestions to the earlier editions of this book. They are Claire H. Hammond, Wake Forest University; Gena F. Hampton, Gainesville College; Robert Kerr, College of Lake County; John Neal, Lake Sumter Community College; Charles A. Rambeck, Saint John's University; Steven Husted, University of Pittsburgh; Jerry Knarr, Hillsborough Community College; William John Mason, San Francisco State University; W. Douglas Morgan, University of California, Santa Barbara; Nic Nigro, Cogswell College; Mark Rush, University of Florida; Anthony Stair, Frostburg State University; Richard A. Zuber, University of North Carolina at Charlotte; Richard L. Tontz, California State University at Northridge; and Paul A. Stock, Tarleton State University. I would also like to thank William Carlson, St. Olaf College; Laurence Malone, Hartwick College; Mark Aldrich, Smith College; Rhona Free, East Connecticut State University; Michael K. Wohlgenant, North Carolina State University; Marlene Kim, University of Massachusetts, Boston; and Mark Healy, William Rainey Harper College for their valuable suggestions for this sixth edition.

Finally, I thank the staff at Addison-Wesley for their editorial and production expertise.

PART ONE

INTRODUCTION TO ECONOMICS

CHAPTER 1

SCARCITY, CHOICE, AND OPPORTUNITY COSTS

Chapter Preview

We take for granted the electricity that heats and air-conditions our homes, cooks our food, and runs our factories and businesses. Electricity blackouts are supposed to be catastrophes that plague "other people" in underdeveloped countries of Africa or Asia. The blackouts that plagued California, the most populous state in the United States, from 2001 to 2003 serve as a reminder that all economic resources are scarce, that they must be allocated among competing ends, and that there is "no such thing as a free lunch." When we use economic goods for one purpose, they are not available for alternative uses. We use the example of one single product—electricity—to illustrate scarcity and choice in this first chapter.

Definition

Economics studies how we use our scarce resources to specialize in production and to exchange and consume goods and services according to the prevailing economic system.

Economics studies how economic agents—households, businesses, and governments—use their scarce resources to specialize in production and to exchange and consume goods and services according to the prevailing economic system.

The main actors on the economic stage are households, businesses, and governments. They must choose among alternative actions within the limits imposed by finite resources. Economic actors, who specialize in different economic activities, must exchange or trade with one another. Production and exchange culminate in the consumption of the goods and services that determine our material standard of living. The economic system comprises the legal, political, and social institutions that organize exchange.

Concepts and Themes

Because so much information is packed into our definition of economics, we must explain its key concepts: economic agents, scarce resources, choice, specialization, exchange, and economic systems.

Economic Agents

Economic agents engage in production, exchange, specialization, and consumption.

Economic agents are those individuals and organizations that engage in production, exchange, specialization, and consumption. They can be individuals in households, businesses, nonprofit organizations, or governments. Because economics concentrates on private economic activity, the main agents we study are businesses and households, but we are also interested in how voters and government institutions make economic decisions.

How many economic agents are there in the American economy? There are roughly 100 million single- and multiple-person households and 15 million businesses. There are some 80,000 governmental units.

Who are the economic agents that participate in the electricity market? There are more than 10,000 generating units operating hydro, steam, gas turbine, and nuclear plants. These units produce electricity for 114 million residential customers, 15 million commercial establishments, and 575,000 industrial users (www.eia.doe.gov).

Scarce Resources

Scarce resources are land, labor, and capital resources the demands for which exceed the supply if they were given away free.

Resources are the land and natural resources, labor, and capital that can be combined to produce goods and services. They are also called the **factors of production.**

Scarcity exists when the amount of the good or resource offered is less than what users would want if it were given away free.

To understand **scarce resources,** we must define both **resources** and **scarcity.** Resources are the land and natural resources, labor, and capital (plants, equipment, and inventories) that are combined to produce goods and services.

Productive resources are also called **factors of production.** They represent economic wealth because they ultimately determine how much output we can produce. We classify resources into the three general categories of land and natural resources, labor, and capital. Land can vary from productive farmland to garbage dumps. Capital can range from a hydroelectric dam to an 80-story office building to a plow. Labor ranges from a skilled surgeon to a ditchdigger. Resources, especially labor, must be considered in both quantitative and qualitative dimensions. One person may possess superb athletic ability; another may be a gifted talker; another may have had years of professional training. In addition to its power plants and labor, the electricity industry uses scarce resources to produce electricity. In 2003, it used a billion tons of coal, almost 7 trillion cubic feet of natural gas, and 190 million barrels of petroleum liquids to produce electricity. These resources could have been used in other ways.

The term **scarcity** is used differently in economics than in everyday language. Scarcity exists whenever the amount of the good or resource offered to users is less than they would want if it were given away free. Scarcity has little to do with wealth or poverty. It exists in both rich and poor societies. The only requirement is that there be an imbalance between what is available and what people would want if the good were free. Goods consumed by the rich, such as Rolls-Royces, pleasure cruises, and Manhattan penthouses, can be just as scarce as goods consumed by the poor (city bus rides, canned meats, and mobile homes). In both cases, the amounts people would want to have at a zero price exceed the amounts available.

Not all resources are scarce. Some natural resources, such as oxygen and the sun's rays (without which no production could take place), are available in such abundance that the amount available exceeds the amount users would want at a zero price. Such nonscarce goods, or free goods, do not require complicated choices. They are simply available to anyone who wants them.

Choice

Scarcity forces economic agents to make choices. The factors of production are limited; we cannot produce infinite quantities of goods and services. Households must choose how to spend their limited income on the things they want. Businesses must choose among alternate combinations of scarce resources and among different goods to produce. Manufacturers must decide whether to use assembly-line workers or industrial robots. Automobile producers must choose among compact cars, SUVs, and trucks. Governments must choose whether to spend more on defense or on education. If we had infinite resources, we would not be faced with choices because scarcity would not exist. There would be more than enough to go around for everyone.

Electricity producers have chosen to produce 70 percent of our electricity by steam generation, 20 percent by nuclear generators, and 10 percent by hydro power. Consumers must choose between spending their money on electricity, natural gas, or other goods. These are all economic choices.

Specialization and Exchange

Specialization is the use of resources to their best advantage.

Economic agents specialize. **Specialization** is the use of resources to their best advantage. Some people sell; others program computers. Some people specialize in law; others in medicine. Iowa farmland is used for corn; Kansas farmland for wheat. Japan specializes in electronics and compact cars; the United States in commercial aircraft and wheat. Individuals, businesses, and countries cannot afford to be jacks-of-all-trades. They increase their material well-being by doing what they do relatively better than others can.

Adam Smith, the founder of modern economics, explained in his 1776 book *The Wealth of Nations* that specialization and exchange are the sources of economic prosperity. Smith used the now-classic example of a pin factory to show that 10 people working in a mechanized factory at specialized tasks could produce 100 or 1000 times as much output as the same 10 people working alone. (See Example 1.1.)

Exchange is the trading of goods and services produced through specialization.

Specialization dictates **exchange.** Without exchange, specialization would be of no benefit because economic agents would be left only with their own goods. Without exchange, Japan would have its electronic products and compact cars but little food; a doctor could look after his or her own health but would be without legal services, food, clothes, and auto repair services.

Specialization and exchange raise material well-being.

In the case of electricity, most households and businesses obtain their power through exchange. They buy electricity from the power company, even though they could have installed a windmill (or a gas-driven generator) to generate their own. But nonutility power producers—large companies, university power plants, and windmill owners—generate some 150 billion kilowatt-hours (of the total of over three trillion). In these rare cases, electricity consumers choose not to specialize but to produce the product themselves.

Economic Systems

If societies are to function, they must make their choices in an orderly fashion. Different societies use different institutions to make their economic choices. Some use

EXAMPLE 1.1 SPECIALIZATION AND TOYOTA'S JUST-IN-TIME MANUFACTURING

Toyota's "Just-in-Time" manufacturing system is a contemporary illustration of Smith's principle of specialization. In the early postwar years, Toyota had to be as cost-effective as American giants, such as Ford and General Motors, even though it produced a smaller number of cars and trucks. Toyota competed by producing batches of similar goods from its assembly lines and inventories rather than large numbers of identical goods, which was the American approach—Toyota's *batch production* process (as opposed to custom production or mass production). Toyota uses its tools intensively, like a custom production plant, but its plant layout is similar to a mass production process. Toyota's production lines operate like a river with raw material inventories and receiving docks serving as the sources, parts fabrication and subassembly operations as the tributaries, and final assembly as the main channel. Work centers pull inventory from supplying work centers when needed, just as shoppers pull groceries from grocery shelves. Each parts container has an exact identifying card for the supplier work center and for the user. If the supplying center runs out of cards or if its cards accumulate, this signals that the supply chain is out of balance. Parts are being supplied either too slowly (running out of cards) or too many parts are on hand (cards build up). The goal is to have "just-in-time manufacturing," where parts arrive just as they are needed. Moreover, Toyota's parts can be used interchangeably in its various models. Toyota's just-in-time manufacturing approach is now widely used. For example, Airbus Industrie, the European manufacturer of commercial passenger jets, uses just-in-time inventories (delivered by huge freighter aircraft) and interchangeable parts (each of its aircraft has the same cockpit) to compete with its archrival, Boeing Aircraft.

Source: JIT Manufacturing: The Toyota System, http://recursionist.org/wealth_appendix.html

The arrangements and institutions that deal with scarcity are called an **economic system.**

Under **capitalism,** resources are privately owned and people make their own economic decisions. Under **socialism,** the state owns the resources and makes the decisions.

private ownership and market allocation; others use public ownership and government allocation. Most use an economic system that is a combination of private and public ownership and of market and government allocation. The set of organizational arrangements and institutions that are established to deal with scarcity is called an **economic system.**

Societies have experimented with different economic systems. This book is about **capitalism** or *market economies,* in which there is private ownership of resources and people are largely free to make their own economic decisions. The major alternative is **socialism,** in which the government owns most of the resources and the state makes the major economic decisions. With the collapse of the Soviet Union in 1991, capitalism emerged victorious, but debate continues on how large the economic role of government should be.

Ownership of the resources used to produce economic goods is a prime determinant of the economic system. Most economies are mixed ownership systems in which the government owns some of the resources and the rest are owned privately.

In the United States, privately owned producers generate 80 percent of the electricity, and government-owned producers generate 20 percent. In France, on the other hand, most electricity is generated by state companies. For most other products, the government-produced share is quite small.

Limited Resources versus Unlimited Wants

The **economic problem** is how to choose what products to produce; how they are to be produced; and for whom.

Wants are what people would wish to have if the price were zero.

The imbalance between limited resources and unlimited wants is the source of the **economic problem** that all economic systems must face. Because resources are scarce, we must choose *what* products to produce, *how* these products are to be produced, and *for whom.* The economy cannot produce enough goods and services to meet everyone's wants.

Wants are the goods and services we would wish to have if there were no costs (if the price were zero). If we were to tally everyone's wants, the result would stagger the imagination. One individual's wish list (remember, everything is free) might include two or three luxury cars (a Mercedes-Benz, a Jaguar, and a Rolls-Royce thrown in for good measure), a 20-bedroom home in the best part of town plus a ski lodge in Colorado, a staff of servants, Maine lobster every day, and a 20-carat diamond ring for each day of the year. In the United States alone the combined wish list might equal 100 million Mercedes-Benz cars; 10 million tons of Maine lobster per week; 50 million domestic servants; and 100 million penthouse apartments overlooking Manhattan's Central Park.

If we then look at society's ability to meet these wants, not enough land, labor, and capital resources are available. There is not enough land overlooking Central Park, virtually the entire adult population would have to be domestic servants, and the waters off Maine would not yield enough Maine lobster.

The **law of scarcity** states that wants always exceed our ability to meet these wants.

The **law of scarcity** states that wants will always exceed our ability to meet them. There will never be enough resources. Therefore, choices must be made.

What?

What refers to what goods and services to produce.

The first choice is *what?* What goods should society produce with its limited resources? Should it produce trucks or buses, full-sized or compact cars, guns or butter, single-family houses or apartments? Should cities improve the school system, build rapid-transit systems, or hire more police officers? By deciding *what,* society decides which wants will be satisfied.

How?

How refers to how to combine resources to produce output.

Once an economy decides what to produce, it must determine *how* to produce. Which combinations of land, labor, and capital resources will be used to produce the cars, trucks, computers, houses, and other products? Goods are not produced according to rigidly prescribed recipes. Assembly lines can use more industrial robots and fewer

EXAMPLE 1.2 HOW TO ORGANIZE THE "ECONOMIC SYSTEM" OF ELECTRICITY PRODUCTION (AND AVOID BLACKOUTS)

The largest-ever electricity blackout in August 2003 focused attention on how we should organize the production and distribution of electricity. Our "economic system" of providing electricity to businesses and households has changed dramatically over time. Starting in the 1930s, local or regional electricity companies were given exclusive franchises, establishing each as a sole provider of electricity to its region. In return, electric companies were regulated by local or state commissions. These regulatory commissions allowed electric companies to set their prices equal to their costs plus a percentage profit margin (say, 8 percent). Each electric company generated its own electricity using fuels at hand; most had little interest in holding down costs, which could be passed on to the consumer in the form of higher prices. Because companies supplied only their own markets, regional electricity grids were not interconnected, and electric companies could not buy or sell electricity to other regions. Companies with abundant fuels (such as natural gas) produced electricity more cheaply than others, such as those that had to rely on coal. The "regulated" economic system provided no opportunity for specialization and exchange. Each company had to produce its own electricity.

The late 1990s saw the partial deregulation of electricity. (*Deregulation* means that prices and other terms are no longer set by regulatory commissions.) With deregulation, electric companies were allowed to buy and sell electricity from one another. Electricity produced in Texas could be sold to California by the companies themselves or by a new breed of energy traders, such as the now defunct Enron Corporation. Each state deregulated its electricity market according to its own rules and timetable. California, for example, continued to regulate the retail price of electricity (holding retail prices steady) while allowing the wholesale price to vary. When the costs of producing electricity rose in the summer of 2000, California was forced to sell electricity to retail customers below the wholesale price, driving California electric utilities and the state itself into debt. Other states deregulated the electricity market with less dramatic effects.

The partial deregulation of electricity meant that huge volumes of electricity had to be transmitted over an inadequate infrastructure of long-distance power lines from one regional grid to another. Transmitted electricity encountered critical choke points as it passed from one grid system to another. The transmission infrastructure had not kept pace with deregulation. It remained unclear who owned and should operate the system, and there were substantial delays in building new transmission capacity. (People don't want high-voltage lines going through their neighborhood, especially with rumors of rampant brain cancer near such lines.)

In mid-August 2003, a massive power outage hit from Ottawa, Canada, to the East Coast and into Detroit as summer temperatures soared and the demand for electricity spiked. Not enough electricity could pass through bottlenecks in the transportation system, and the system itself failed in the form of a massive blackout that lasted two days or more. Critics of deregulation argued that this failure was a result of deregulation; advocates of free market allocation argued that the blackout was the result of the failure to completely deregulate. The shape of the electricity industry will be addressed in the energy bill before Congress in 2004.

people; farmers can use more weed killer and fewer farmhands; homebuilders can use bricks, wood, adobe, or plastics on the exterior of homes. Governments can produce national defense with submarine-launched missiles, antiballistic weapons located in outer space, or conventional weapons.

For Whom?

For whom refers to how output is divided among people.

How will the economy's output be divided among the members of society? Will everyone get an equal share? Will a few get most of the output? Will differences in wealth be allowed to persist over generations? The law of scarcity teaches a hard lesson: All wants cannot be satisfied, and therefore there will be both winners and losers in the struggle for goods.

In 2004, electricity producers in the United States generated more than one trillion kilowatt-hours (*what*), using steam, nuclear, and hydroelectric facilities (*how*). The one hundred million American households (*for whom*) used more than one-third of this electricity production to heat, cool, and light their homes and to cook their food. Plants and factories (*for whom*) used slightly less than one-third of this production to run their machinery, and commercial establishments (*for whom*) consumed the remaining kilowatt-hours to run their computers and light their facilities.

Solving the Economic Problem

The economic system **allocates scarce resources** among competing ends.

Allocation is the apportionment of resources for a specific purpose or to particular persons or groups.

There is no single formula for allocating scarce resources. Scarcity requires that choices be made. The imbalance between wants and the ability to meet them has forced all societies at all times to use their economic systems to **allocate scarce resources.** Social order requires an economic system to provide for the orderly allocation of scarce resources. Otherwise, anarchy would prevail as we fight among ourselves for scarce resources.

Allocation is the apportionment of resources for a specific purpose or to particular persons or groups. The next chapter explains how capitalist, or market, economies use the price system to allocate scarce resources among competing ends. Since the collapse of communism, markets are the major means of allocating scarce resources in the world's economies. Example 1.3 explains the allocation of electricity.

Opportunity Costs

The **opportunity cost** is the loss of the next-best alternative.

Choice means that when one action is taken, another must be sacrificed. Costs are measured by these sacrificed alternatives. The **opportunity cost** of an action is the loss of the next-best alternative.

Every time a *what, how,* or *for whom* choice is made, alternative courses of action must be sacrificed. If you buy a new home, you have sacrificed other opportunities: With the same money you could have bought an oceanfront condominium, invested in the stock market, or bought a luxury sports car. The opportunity cost of the new home is, therefore, the cost of the next-best alternative forgone. If you would have spent the money on an oceanfront condominium as your next-best alternative, this particular forgone alternative is the opportunity cost of the home.

The opportunity cost of a young person joining the armed forces is the next-best alternative sacrificed, whether it is taking a civilian job or continuing a college education. If a business that owns prime land chooses to use that land for a corporate headquarters, the opportunity cost is the next-best alternative use of this land—selling it, renting it to another company, or holding it for future use.

Opportunity costs identify scarce goods. If a good is available in sufficient supply so that there is more than enough to go around, its opportunity cost is zero. If one more bucket of Sahara desert sand is taken, there is still more than enough to go around. No one has been deprived of that extra bucket of sand. No alternative has had to be sacrificed. Goods that have zero opportunity costs are **free goods. Scarce goods** have a positive opportunity cost. In order to have more of a scarce good, an alternative must be sacrificed. Every choice involving the allocation of scarce goods involves opportunity costs.

Free goods have a zero opportunity cost. Users can have more without others having to give up some of the good.

Scarce goods have a positive opportunity cost. In order to have more of a scarce good, an alternative must be sacrificed.

Electricity is a scarce good. Valuable labor, capital, and material resources must be used to produce it. We could have used the billion tons of coal, the seven trillion cubic meters of natural gas, and the 190 million barrels of petroleum to produce other things. As the opportunity costs of this electricity, think how many miles we could have driven using the gasoline or the many petrochemical products that could have been refined from the 190 million barrels of petroleum.

Production Possibilities and Opportunity Costs

Economies produce millions of different commodities, but economists deliberately deal with simplified models because they are easy to understand and the lessons they teach apply generally. The **production possibilities frontier (PPF)** is used to illustrate scarcity, opportunity cost, and efficiency.

The **production possibilities frontier (PPF)** shows the economic choices available when the factors of production are utilized to their full potential.

Suppose an economy produces only two goods: tanks and wheat. Figure 1.1 gives the amounts of tanks and wheat that this hypothetical economy can produce with its limited resources and technical knowledge. If our hypothetical economy produces no tanks, it could produce a maximum of 18 tons of wheat from the resources at its disposal (*a*). If the economy produces no wheat, it could produce a maximum of 5000 tanks (*f*). The curved PPF line connecting *a* and *f* shows all the maximum combinations of wheat and tanks that the economy can produce with its available resources and technology. Point *c*, for example, shows that if 2000 tanks are produced, the maximum number of tons of wheat is 15. While six points have been labeled, any point on the PPF is possible. The production possibilities frontier (PPF) shows the combinations of goods and services available when the factors of production are utilized to their full potential. The PPF therefore shows the economic choices open to an economy producing at full potential. The PPF shows both attainable and unattainable output combinations. Any output combination on, such as *c*, or inside the PPF, such as *h*, is attainable. Any output combination that lies beyond the frontier, such as *g*, cannot be attained with available resources and existing technology.

For an economy to operate on its PPF, it must utilize its resources with maximum efficiency. If the economy produces any output combination that lies on the PPF, the economy is **efficient.** It is not possible to produce more of one good without cutting back on another good. If the economy is operating at *h* (inside the PPF), it is inefficient. It is possible to produce more of both goods without expanding available resources. In effect, potential output is being wasted.

The economy is **efficient** when no resources are unemployed and when no resources are misallocated.

EXAMPLE 1.3 AUCTIONING BROADCAST FREQUENCIES: $4.4 MILLION FOR CHANNEL 38

Since 1994, the Federal Communications Commission (FCC) has conducted auctions of licenses for electromagnetic spectra for radio, TV, and cell phone frequencies. These auctions are open to any eligible company or individual that submits an application and upfront payment, and is found to be a qualified bidder by the Commission. FCC auctions are conducted electronically and are accessible over the Internet. Qualified bidders can place bids from the comfort of their home or office, and anyone with a Web browser can follow the progress of an auction and view the results of each round. Prior to 1994, the Commission mainly relied upon comparative hearings and lotteries to select a single licensee from a pool of mutually exclusive applicants. Broadcast frequencies are a scarce good. The FM band is constrained from expanding above 107.9 MHz by the presence of aeronautical operations on 108 MHz to 136 MHz, and is also prevented from expanding below 88.1 MHz by Channel 6 television operations on 82.0 through 88.0 MHz. The scarcity of broadcast frequencies is reflected in the magnitude of the winning bids to obtain broadcasting rights. For example, the winning bid for the TV38 market of Corpus Christi, Texas, in auction #54 of July 2003 was for $4.4 million.

Source: http://wireless.fcc.gov/auctions/about/index.html

An economy is inefficient when resources are standing idle or are misallocated. If there is excessive unemployment, or if machines are not being used, output is being wasted. Resource misallocation—not using resources to their best advantage—yields the same result. If Kansas wheatland is used to grow bananas, if a skilled auto mechanic works as a ditchdigger, or if a 12-wheeler truck is used as a taxicab, resources are misallocated. The output of the economy could be increased if these resources were put to their best use.

The Law of Increasing Costs

The PPF is curved like a bow instead of being a straight line. In our example we have a hypothetical economy that produces only two goods, tanks and wheat. The opportunity cost of increasing the production of one good is the amount of the other good that must be sacrificed. At *a* in Figure 1.1, the economy produces 18 tons of wheat and no tanks. The opportunity cost of increasing tank production from 0 to 1000 is the 1 ton of wheat that must be sacrificed in moving from *a* to *b*. The opportunity cost of 1000 more tanks (moving from *b* to *c*) is 2 tons of wheat. As more tanks are produced, their opportunity cost increases, as more production of wheat

FIGURE 1.1 The Production Possibilities Frontier (PPF)

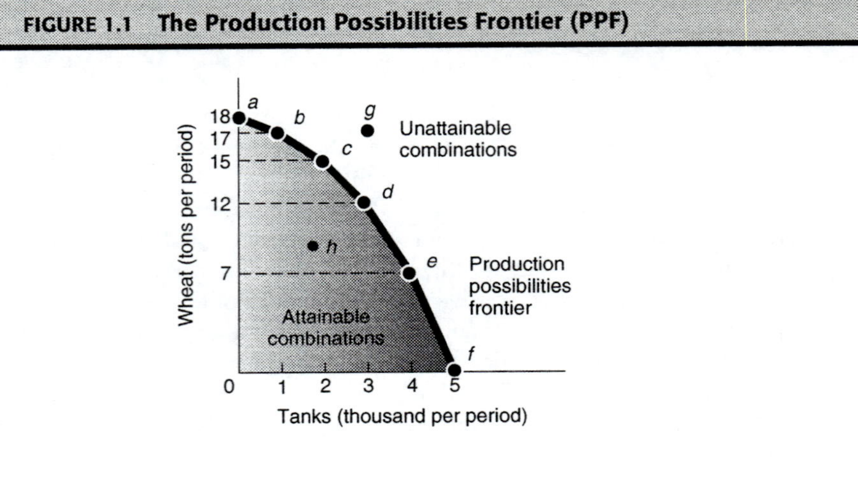

Combination	Tanks (thousands)	Wheat (tons)	Opportunity Cost of Tanks (tons of wheat)
a	0	18	0
b	1	17	1
c	2	15	2
d	3	12	3
e	4	7	5
f	5	0	7

The PPF shows the combinations of outputs of two goods that can be produced from society's resources when these resources are utilized to their maximum potential. Point *a* shows that if 18 tons of wheat are produced, no tank production is possible. Point *f* shows that if no wheat is produced, a maximum of 5000 tanks can be produced. Point *d* shows that if 3000 tanks are produced, a maximum of 12 tons of wheat can be produced. Point *g* is above society's PPF. With its available resources the economy cannot produce 17 tons of wheat and 3000 tanks. Points like *h*, which are inside the PPF and are therefore attainable, represent an inefficient use of the society's resources. Figure 1.1 is based on the accompanying table.

must be sacrificed. The opportunity cost of the fifth thousand unit of tanks (moving from *e* to *f*) is a higher 7 tons of wheat. The opportunity cost rises with the production of tanks.

The **law of increasing costs** states that opportunity cost per unit will increase as production increases.

The **law of increasing costs,** which states that as more of a particular commodity is produced its opportunity cost will increase, explains the bowed-out shape of the PPF. Why would opportunity costs rise as more of the commodity is produced? Suppose the country is at peace, producing only wheat (point *a*). War breaks out, and the economy must move along its PPF to point *d*. Some factors of production will be as well suited to tank production as to wheat production; they can be shifted to tank production without raising opportunity costs. Thus at low levels of tank production the opportunity cost of an extra tank will be relatively low. But as tank production increases, it becomes more and more difficult to shift resources into tank production without raising opportunity costs. Factors that are well suited to wheat production but poorly suited to tank production must be shifted to tank production. Agricultural specialists who have never operated precision machine tools find themselves working in tank factories; farm tractors are used to move semifabricated tank parts from one plant to another. As tank production continues to expand, ever-increasing amounts of ill-suited resources must be shifted from wheat to keep tank production expanding at a constant rate. Hence, the law of increasing opportunity costs simply reflects the situation in the real world.

Macro and Micro

Economics provides powerful tools to analyze the real world. The large issues, such as inflation, unemployment, the business cycle, economic growth, and balance of international payments, attract the most attention. They influence presidential elections, when we buy new cars and homes, whether we are laid off from jobs, and whether we view the future with optimism or pessimism. The study of the economy in the large is called **macroeconomics.** Macroeconomics treats the economy as a whole. It studies the determinants of total output and its growth, total employment and unemployment, and the general movement in prices.

Macroeconomics studies total output and its growth, total employment and unemployment, and the general movement in prices.

Economists study the small issues as well—how individual businesses behave in different competitive environments; how we choose to use our time; how prices of individual commodities are determined; whether a farmer plants wheat or rye. Although these routine decisions seemingly have a less dramatic effect, they determine the way we live our daily lives. The small issues determine how our television sets and automobiles are built; the prices we pay for cable television; whether soft drinks are sweetened with sugar or corn syrup; whether shoe leather is cut by hand or by lasers; and whether the prices of airline tickets rise or fall. This study of the economy in the small is called **microeconomics.** Microeconomics looks at the behavior of the economy's small parts—business firms and households.

Microeconomics studies the economic decisions of the individual participants in the economy.

Economic Theories

The economy generates an immense number of facts—millions of distinct prices, interest rates, millions of goods produced in different locations. Gathering all the facts would be impossible, even if the facts could speak for themselves. Instead of fact gathering, we use economic theories to make sense out of the complicated world, to show which facts are relevant and how and why these facts are related.

An **economic theory** is a coherent and plausible explanation of how economic facts are related. Economic theory isolates the factors that are most important in explaining economic behavior. Economic theories yield hypotheses (or predictions) about how things are related.

An **economic theory** isolates the factors that are most important in explaining an economic phenomenon and yields hypotheses (or predictions).

Consider how we use theories to make sense out of our complicated world. Say we wish to understand new-home construction. A simple theory might be that interest rates are a significant determinant of how many new homes are built. At low interest rates, more families can afford new homes. Nothing more than simple logic is involved. If mortgage rates are rising, it is logical to expect home construction to drop.

Theories are valuable only if they are supported by facts. Data on new-home construction and mortgage interest rates are displayed in Figure 1.2. Figure 1.2 supports the theory because periods of high construction activity tend to be associated with periods of low interest rates. When interest rates rose in the early 1970s and mid-1980s, housing starts fell. When interest rates fell in the early 1980s, late 1980s, and early 2000s, housing starts rose. Note that our theory does not say that interest rates alone determine housing starts. Other factors play a role as well. Hence, we can find some exceptions, such as flat housing starts in the mid-1970s, when interest rates were rising. Only if we find that lower interest rates actually appear to spur home construction can we say that the theory is consistent with the facts. If the facts are not consistent with the theory, the theory must be revised. A new logical theory must be formulated and tested against the facts. Economic theories are good only if they work; if they do not work, they must be discarded.

FIGURE 1.2 Testing a Theory: Interest Rates and New Housing Units Started

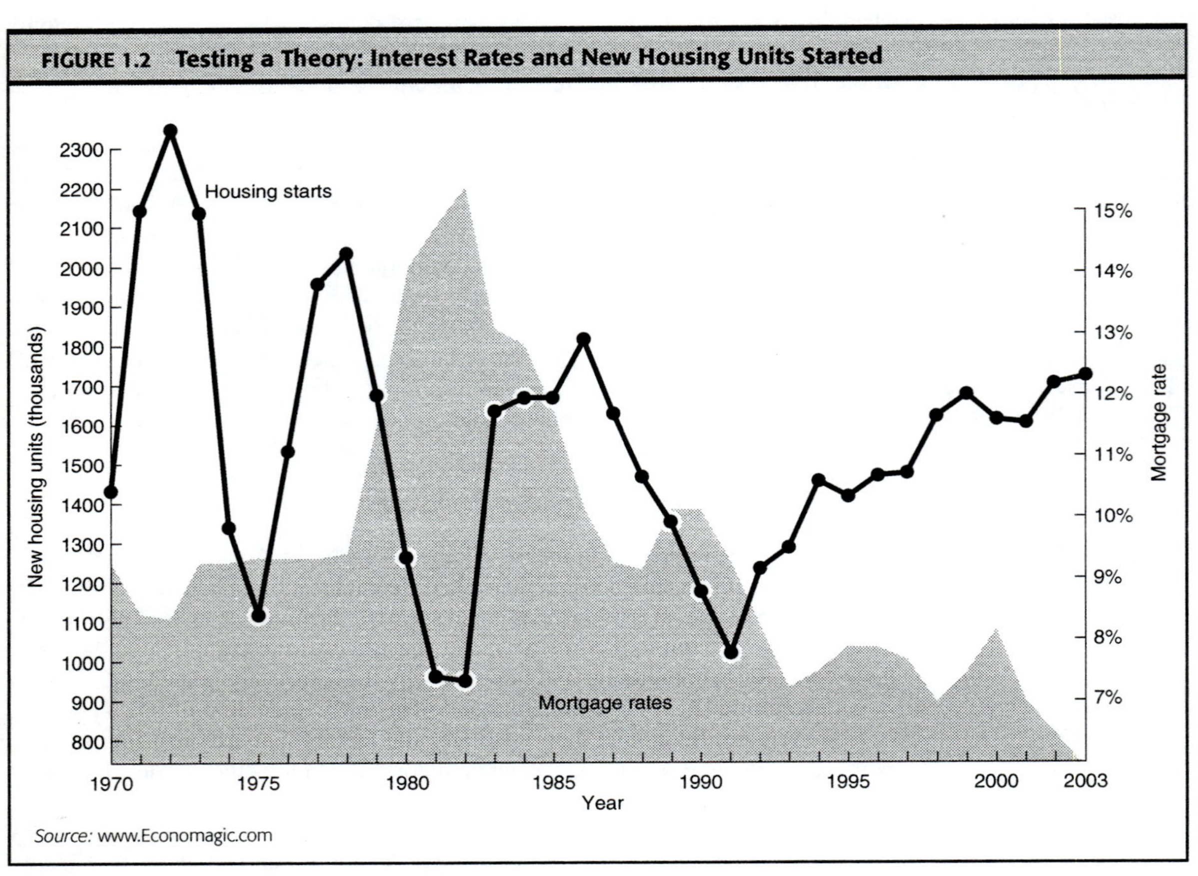

Source: www.Economagic.com

Positive versus Normative Economics

Positive economics studies what is in the economy.

Normative economics studies what ought to be in the economy.

Economics deals both with what *is* and what *should be.* **Positive economics** studies *what is.* It explains how the facts stick together. If the price of product *X* falls relative to other prices, what will happen to its sales? If the money supply rises, what will happen to the inflation rate? Positive economics seeks to formulate and test theories that explain relationships among economic factors.

Normative economics deals with the way the economic world *should be.* Should we have a more equal distribution of income? Should we sacrifice more inflation for less unemployment? Should we spend public dollars on welfare or on national defense?

Like everybody else, economists disagree about how the world ought to be. They may agree, for example, that increases in the money supply cause inflation, but they may violently disagree about whether the money supply should be increased.

Economists are more likely to agree on issues of positive economics: There is more of a consensus on how the economy functions, although there are still important controversies on how the macroeconomy functions. The major disagreements are in normative economics. We cannot expect professionals in any scientific discipline to agree on how the world ought to be.

Summary

1. Economics is the study of how economic agents use their scarce resources to specialize in production and to exchange and consume goods and services according to the prevailing economic system.
2. Economic agents engage in the acts of production, specialization, and exchange.
3. Scarce resources—for example, land and natural resources, labor, and capital—are resources in which the amount that economic agents would want free of charge exceeds the amount available. Resources are also called the *factors of production.*
4. Scarcity dictates choice; it means that we cannot have everything.
5. Economic agents specialize. Specialization dictates exchange.
6. The economic system is the set of arrangements that economic agents use to deal with scarcity.
7. The economic problem is how to allocate scarce resources among competing uses. Societies must decide what is to be produced, how to produce, and for whom. The economic problem is caused by the friction between unlimited wants and scarce resources.
8. Costs are measured in terms of opportunity costs—the loss of the next-best alternative.
9. The production possibilities frontier (PPF) shows the economic choices open to an economy producing at full potential. The economy is efficient if it is operating on the frontier; it is inefficient if it operates inside the frontier.
10. The law of increasing costs states that as more of a commodity is produced, its opportunity cost per unit will increase.
11. Economics studies both the economy in the large—macroeconomics—and the economy in the small—microeconomics. Macroeconomics deals with inflation,

unemployment, growth, and changes in the level of business activity. Microeconomics studies the behavior of the individual participants in the economy.

12. Economic theories explain how economic facts are related. Economic theories isolate the most important factors that explain an economic phenomenon. Economic theories must be consistent with the facts.
13. Positive economics studies what is; normative economics studies what ought to be. Most disputes among economists are over normative issues.

Questions and Problems

1. Consider a world populated by only three people. If one becomes a farmer, the second a cattle rancher, and the third a homebuilder, explain why exchange would be essential.
2. Is air a scarce resource? How about sand in the Sahara Desert? Farmland in Texas? Discuss.
3. Explain the following quotation from the chapter: "Scarcity dictates choice."
4. Develop an economic theory to explain how many pounds of beef you (or your family) buy per week. What facts are relevant? How can you tell whether the theory is correct?
5. Identify each of the following statements as an example of either normative or positive economics:
   - **a.** Interest rates are too high. The government should do something.
   - **b.** Whenever interest rates rise, sales of homes fall.
   - **c.** Inflation is caused by too much money.
   - **d.** Mr. Jones is too rich. He should give more to charity.
6. If interest rates affect home construction negatively while personal income affects home construction positively, explain why it would be difficult to separate the two effects when interest rates and personal income are both changing.
7. Why is it important to define correctly the meaning of *wants* when we say that there is an imbalance between scarce resources and wants? What is the difference between wanting a car and being willing to buy a car, for example?
8. "Air will always be a free good. More is available than people could ever want." Evaluate this statement. Can you conceive of situations where this statement would not be true?
9. Consider an island cut off from communication with the outside world. The island economy produces only dairy products and oranges. Use the law of increasing cost to explain what would happen to the opportunity cost of oranges if the production of oranges were cut in half. Why?

10. Consider the following data on a hypothetical economy's PPF:

Thousands of Plows	*Tons of Milk*
16	0
14	8
10	20
6	28
2	32
0	37

a. Graph the PPF.
b. Explain its shape.
c. Calculate the opportunity cost of the first 8 tons of milk. Calculate the opportunity cost of the first 2000 plows. Does the PPF illustrate the law of increasing costs?
d. If the economy produces 10,000 plows and 15 tons of milk, what would you conclude?

11. You have five apples and there are 20 people in your class who like apples. Consider the different ways you might allocate the five apples among the 20 people.

12. Explain what is meant by *what, how,* and *for whom.*

13. During economic downturns, enrollment in the armed services rises as does enrollment in universities and colleges. Using the notion of opportunity costs, explain why this is so.

14. Use the terminology of economics to explain the difference between the fact that I'd like to have a new car every year but I actually buy a new car once every five years.

15. Evaluate the following statement in terms of what you have learned in this chapter about specialization and exchange: "It is very bad that the U.S. economy is so dependent on imported oil."

APPENDIX CHAPTER 1

WORKING WITH GRAPHS

Graphs efficiently display statistical information and reveal whether relationships are positive or negative. In microeconomics, graphs are used to explain the behavior of consumers and firms in the marketplace. In macroeconomics, graphs are used to display macroeconomic data and to develop theories of output, employment, and inflation.

Positive and Negative Relationships

A **positive** (or **direct**) **relationship** exists if an increase in the value of one variable leads to an increase in the value of the other.

Two positively related variables are graphed as an **upward-sloping curve.**

A **negative** (or **inverse**) **relationship** exists if an increase in the value of one variable leads to a reduction in the value of the other.

When two variables are negatively related, the graph of the relationship is a **downward-sloping curve.**

Graphs reveal whether two variables are positively or negatively related. A **positive** (or **direct**) **relationship** exists between two variables if an increase in the value of one variable is associated with an increase in the value of the other variable.

An increase in horsepower will increase the maximum speed of an automobile. In Panel A of Figure A.1, the vertical axis measures the maximum speed of the car from the 0 point (called the *origin*), and the horizontal axis measures the horsepower of the engine. When horsepower is 0 (the engine has broken down), the maximum speed the car can attain is obviously 0; when horsepower is 300, the maximum speed is 100 miles per hour. When a line is drawn through all the intermediate values of horsepower (between 0 and 300), the resulting curved line shows the effect of horsepower on maximum speed. Since the line goes from low to high speeds as horsepower increases, it is an upward-sloping curve. When two variables are positively related, the graph of their relationship is an **upward-sloping curve.**

A **negative** (or **inverse**) **relationship** exists between two variables if an increase in the value of one variable is associated with a reduction in the value of the other variable.

As the horsepower of the automobile increases, the gas mileage (for given driving conditions) will fall. In Panel B of Figure A.1, horsepower is still measured on the horizontal axis, but now gas mileage is measured on the vertical axis. Since the curve goes from high to low values of gas mileage as horsepower increases, it is a downward-sloping curve. When two variables are negatively related, the graph of their relationship is a **downward-sloping curve.**

FIGURE A.1 Graphing Positive and Negative Relationships

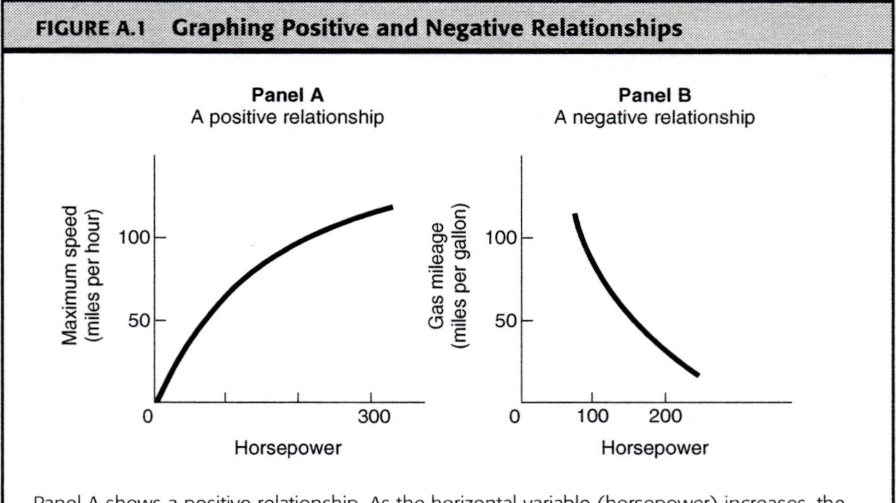

Panel A shows a positive relationship. As the horizontal variable (horsepower) increases, the value of the vertical variable (maximum speed) increases. The curve rises from left to right. Panel B shows a negative relationship. As the horizontal variable (horsepower) increases, the vertical variable (mileage) decreases. The curve falls from left to right.

If there is a change in relationships, the entire graph can shift. For example, if a new fuel-efficient engine is discovered, the gas mileage–horsepower curve will shift up, as shown in Figure A.2. Economists work frequently with relationships that shift, so it is important to understand shifts in graphs.

FIGURE A.2 Shifts in Curves

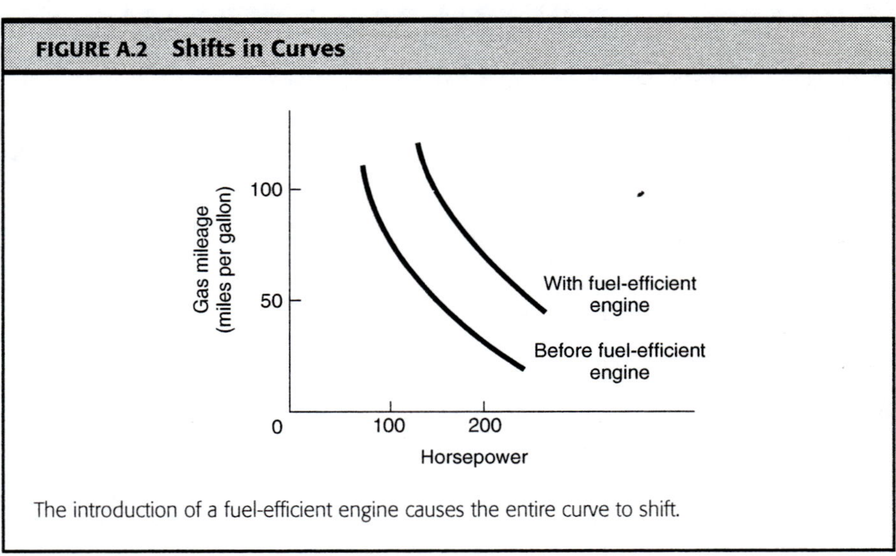

The introduction of a fuel-efficient engine causes the entire curve to shift.

Slope

The relationship between two variables can be represented by a curve's slope. Many central concepts of economics depend on an understanding of slope.

To understand slope, consider the straight-line relationship between the two variables X and Y in Panel A of Figure A.3. When $X = 5$, $Y = 3$; when $X = 7$, $Y = 6$. When variable X is allowed to *run* (to change horizontally) from 5 units to 7 units, variable Y *rises* (increases vertically) from 3 units to 6 units. The **slope** of a straight line is defined as the ratio of the rise (or fall) in Y over the run in X. Thus, the slope of the line in Panel A of Figure A.3 is

The **slope** of a straight line is the ratio of the rise (or fall) in *Y* over the run in *X*.

$$\text{Slope} = \frac{\text{Rise in } Y}{\text{Run in } X} = \frac{3}{2} = 1.5$$

A *positive value* of the slope signifies a *positive relationship* between the two variables.

This formula works for negative relationships as well. In Panel B of Figure A.3 when X runs from 5 to 7, Y *falls* from 4 units to 1 unit. Thus, the slope is

$$\text{Slope} = \frac{\text{Fall in } Y}{\text{Run in } X} = \frac{-3}{2} = -1.5$$

A *negative value* of the slope signifies a *negative relationship.*

Let ΔY (delta Y) stand for the change in the value of Y and ΔX (delta X) stand for the change in the value of X:

$$\text{Slope} = \frac{\Delta Y}{\Delta X}$$

This formula holds for positive or negative relationships.

FIGURE A.3 Positive and Negative Slope

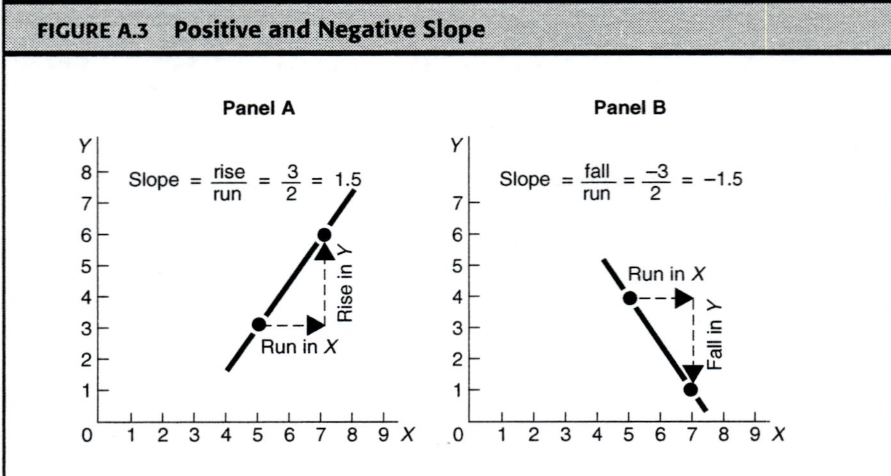

Positive slope is measured by the ratio of the rise in *Y* over the run in *X*. In Panel A, *Y* rises by 3 and *X* runs by 2, and the slope is 1.5. Negative slope is measured by the ratio of the fall in *Y* over the run in *X*. In Panel B, the fall in *Y* is –3, the run in *X* is 2, and the slope is –1.5.

The points in Figure A.3 are connected by straight lines. Such relationships are called *linear relationships.*

Slopes can also be measured when the relationship between X and Y is *curvilinear* (Fig. A.4). When X runs from 2 units to 4 units ($\Delta X = 2$), Y rises by 2 units ($\Delta Y = 2$); between *a* and *b* the slope is $2/2 = 1$. Between *a* and *c,* however, X runs from 2 to 6 ($\Delta X = 4$), Y rises by 3 units ($\Delta Y = 3$), and the slope is $3/4$. In the curvilinear case, the value of the slope depends on how far X is allowed to run. Between *b* and *c,* the slope is $1/2$. The slope changes along a curvilinear relationship. In the linear case, the value of the slope will *not* depend on how far X runs because the slope is constant.

There is no single slope of a curvilinear relationship. The slope can be measured between two points (say, between *a* and *b* or between *b* and *c*) or at a particular point (say, at point *a*). Insofar as the slope depends on the length of the run, a uniform standard is to use tangents to determine the slope at a particular point. A **tangent** is a straight line that touches the curve at only one point.

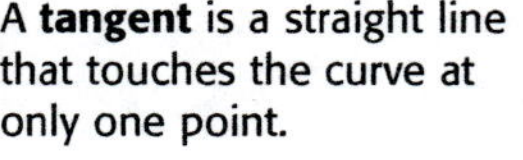
A **tangent** is a straight line that touches the curve at only one point.

If the relationship is really curved at *a,* there is only one straight line that just barely touches *a* and only *a.* Any other line will cut the curve at two points or none. The tangent to *a* is drawn in Figure A.4. The slope of a curvilinear relationship at a particular point is defined as the slope of the straight-line tangent at that point. Because the tangent is a straight line, the length of the run does not matter. For a run from 2 to 4 ($\Delta X = 2$), the rise (ΔY) equals 3 (from 5 to 8), yielding a tangent of 1.5.

Figure A.5 shows two curvilinear relationships that have distinct high points or low points. In Panel A, the relationship between X and Y is positive for values of X less than 6 units and negative for values of X more than 6 units. The exact opposite holds for Panel B. The relationship is negative for values of X less than 6 and positive for

FIGURE A.4 Calculating Slopes of Curvilinear Relationships

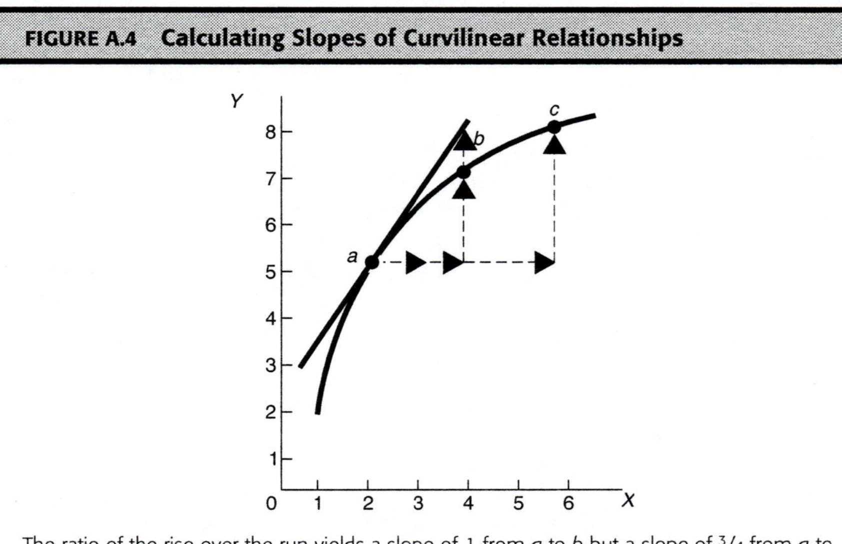

The ratio of the rise over the run yields a slope of 1 from *a* to *b* but a slope of $3/4$ from *a* to *c.* From *b* to *c* the slope is $1/2$. To compute the slope at point *a,* the slope of the tangent to *a* is calculated. The value of the slope of the tangent is $3/2$.

FIGURE A.5 Maximum and Minimum Points

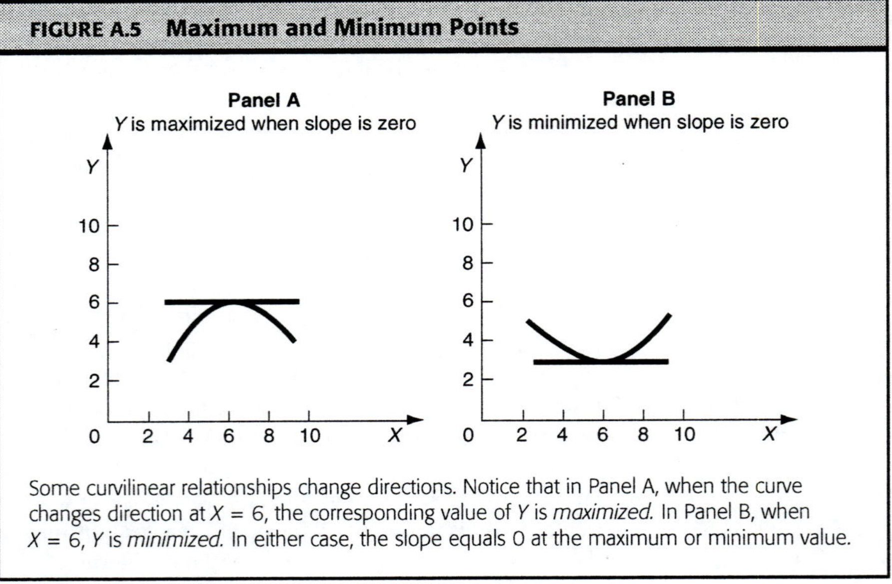

Some curvilinear relationships change directions. Notice that in Panel A, when the curve changes direction at $X = 6$, the corresponding value of Y is *maximized.* In Panel B, when $X = 6$, Y is *minimized.* In either case, the slope equals 0 at the maximum or minimum value.

X greater than 6. Notice that at the point where the slope changes from positive to negative (or vice versa), the slope of the curve will be exactly 0; the tangent at point $X = 6$ for both curves is a horizontal straight line that neither rises nor falls as X changes.

When a curvilinear relationship has a 0 slope, the value of Y reaches either a high point—as in Panel A—or a low point—as in Panel B—at the value of X where the slope is 0.

Economists pay considerable attention to the maximum and minimum values of relationships—as when they examine how a firm maximizes profits or minimizes costs. Suppose, for example, that X in Panel A represents the production of automobiles by General Motors (GM) (in units of 1 million) and that Y represents GM's profits (in billions of dollars). According to this diagram, GM should settle on $X = 6$ million units of automobile production because GM's profits would be higher at $X = 6$ than at any other production level.

Suppose that in Panel B the Y axis measures GM's costs of producing an automobile while X still measures automobile production. Production costs per automobile are at a minimum at $X = 6$. In other words, GM will produce cars at the lowest cost per car if GM produces 6 million cars.

Areas

Panel A of Figure A.6 shows the area of a rectangle, and Panel B shows the area of a triangle. In Panel A, a firm sells 8 units of its product for a price of $10, and it costs $6 per unit to produce the product. How much profit is the firm earning? The firm's profit is the area of the rectangle *abcd.* To calculate the area of a rectangle,

FIGURE A.6 Calculating Areas of Rectangles and Triangles

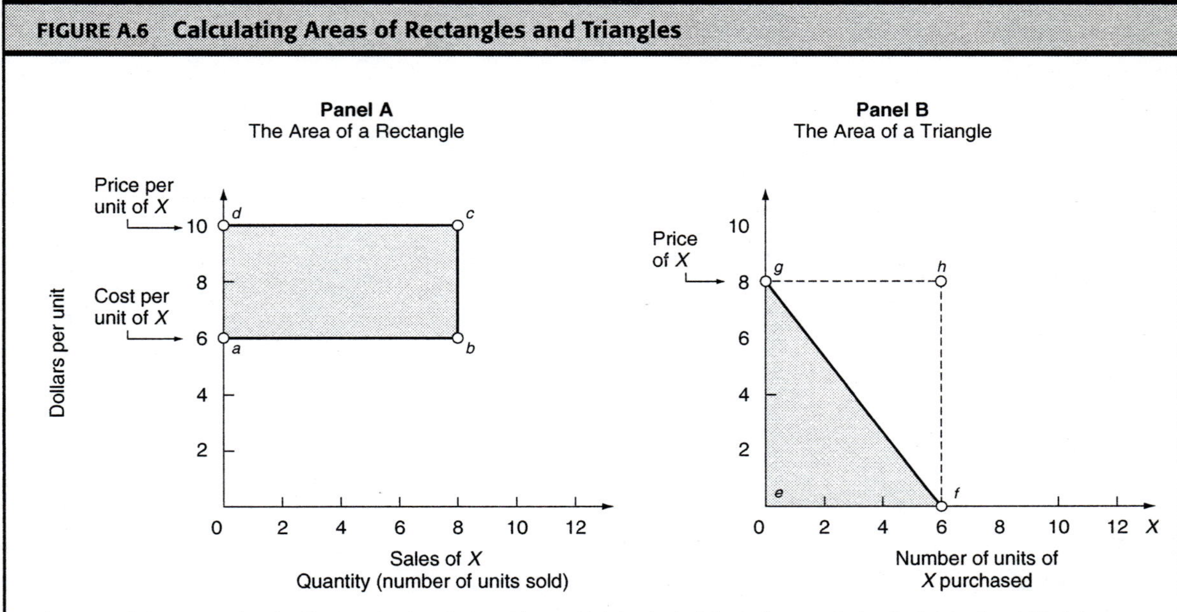

The area of the rectangle *abcd* in Panel A is calculated by multiplying its height (*od* or, equivalently, *bc*) by its width (*ab* or, equivalently, *dc*). The height equals $4, and the width equals 8 units; therefore the area of the rectangle equals $32. Thus, $32 is the amount of this firm's profits. The area of the triangle *efa* in Panel B is one-half the area of the corresponding rectangle *efgh.* The area of the rectangle is 8 × 6 = 48. The area of the triangle *efg* is therefore 0.5 × 48 = 24.

we must multiply the height of the rectangle (*ad* or *bc,* or $10 − $6 = $4 per unit) by the width of the rectangle (*ab* or *dc,* 8 units). The area of the rectangle is $4 per unit times 8 units, or $32 of total profit.

Panel B of Figure A.6 shows the area of triangle *efg.* Because this triangle accounts for one-half the area of the rectangle *efgh,* we must first determine the area of the rectangle (which equals 8 × 6 = 48) and multiply it by 1/2. In this example, the area of the triangle is 0.5 × 48 = 24.

Relationships, Trends, and Scatter Diagrams

A **time series** is a measurement of one or more variables over a designated period of time, such as months, years, or quarters.

Much of economics is about relationships among economic variables. Do housing starts increase when mortgage interest rates fall (a negative relationship)? Does household spending increase when household income increases (a positive relationship)? A whole branch of economics, called *econometrics,* studies how to measure these relationships. Most economic variables are measured over time. A **time series** is a measurement of one or more variables over a designated period of time, such as months, years, or quarters. Figure A.7 graphs time series of industrial electricity consumption (100 million kilowatt-hours) and industrial electricity prices (cents per kilowatt-hour) for the period 1977 to 2000. The relationship between the two variables appears to be negative:

FIGURE A.7 Time Series of Industrial Electricity Consumption and Price Paid

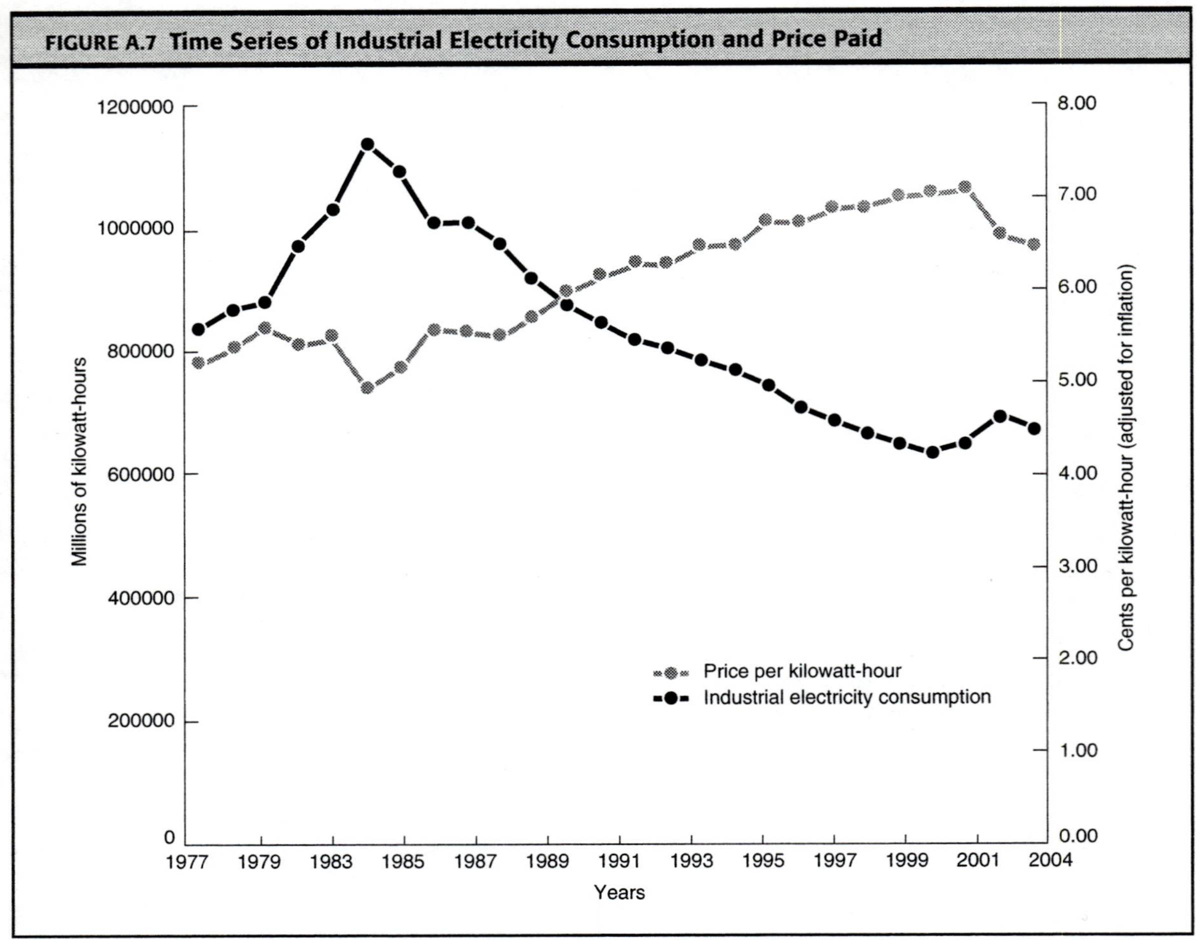

A **scatter diagram** plots the values of one variable against the values of another variable for a specific time interval.

Throughout most of the period, the price was falling while industrial electricity consumption was rising. Often we can see whether a pattern is positive or negative by plotting the data in **scatter diagrams.** A scatter diagram plots the values of one variable against values of another variable for a specific time interval.

In Figure A.8, industrial electricity prices are measured along the horizontal axis, and industrial electricity use is measured along the vertical axis. Each of the dots on the scatter diagram shows the combination of usage and prices for a particular year. The pattern of dots provides visual information about the relationship between the two variables. If the dots show a pattern of low prices and high usage but high prices and low usage, the scatter diagram suggests a *negative relationship,* indicated by a generally declining pattern of dots from left to right. A generally rising pattern of dots from left to right shows a *positive relationship.* If there were no relationship, the dots would be distributed randomly.

FIGURE A.8 Scatter Diagram of Industrial Electricity Consumption versus Price Paid (1997–2002)

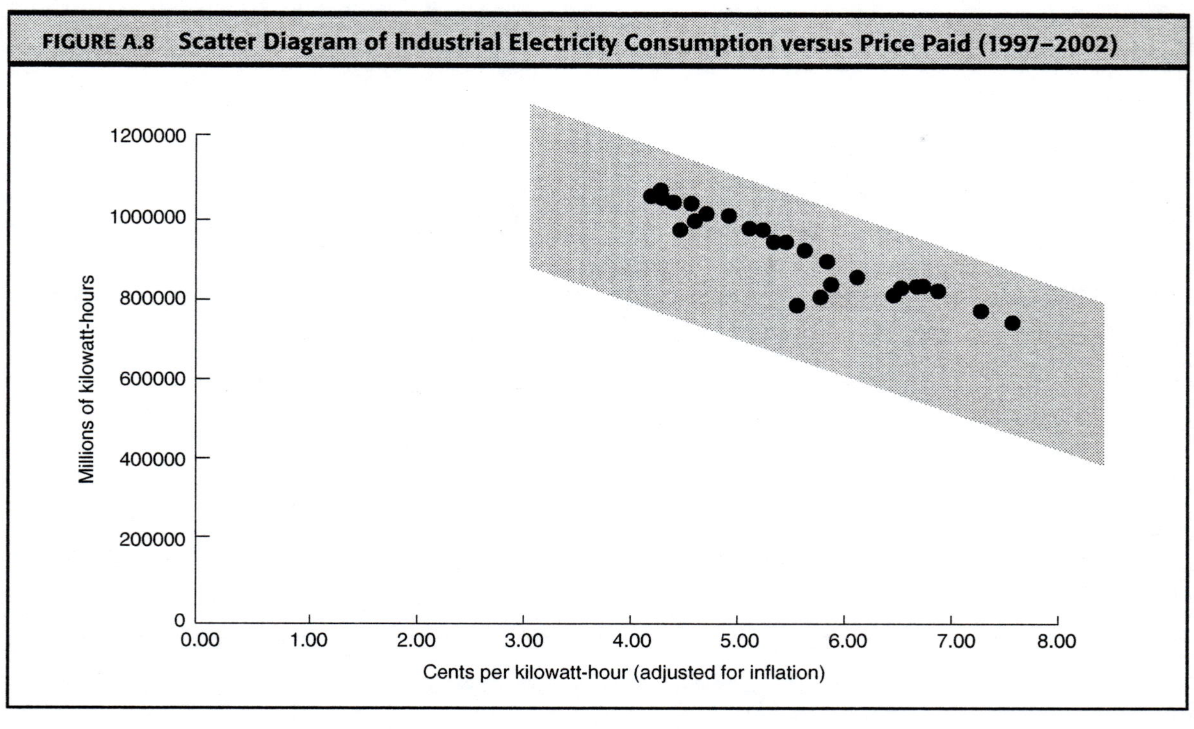

Figure A.8 shows a negative relationship between prices and usage. The broad, negatively sloped band traces the general pattern of declining dots. Such a pattern makes sense: Electricity usage should drop when the price rises.

A **time trend** is the tendency of variables to rise generally, or to fall generally, with the general rise in the economy.

Frequently in economic time series, both variables tend to rise because the economy grows over time. A **time trend** is the tendency of variables to rise generally, or to fall generally, with the general rise in the economy. Time trends make it difficult to determine whether two variables are really related or are simply reacting to common time trends. Figure A.9 shows a common approach to determining relationships when both variables are subject to time trends. It plots first differences—the difference between each variable in successive years. For example, the price in 1977 was 5.6 cents; in 1978, it was 5.8 cents. The first difference is +0.2 cents, which is one of the dots in the figure. First differences, obviously, can be either positive or negative. By working with first differences, we remove time trends and are in a better position to determine whether the relationship is truly positive or negative. Although the dots in Figure A.9 form a less clear pattern of positive price changes being associated with falling usage, the general pattern still appears to be negative.

Note that some dots in Figure A.9 are located far from the trend line. These points are called *outliers*. Outliers suggest that some extraordinary event occurred often in that year that affected the outcome.

FIGURE A.9 A Scatter Diagram of Industrial Energy Consumption versus Price Paid—First Differences

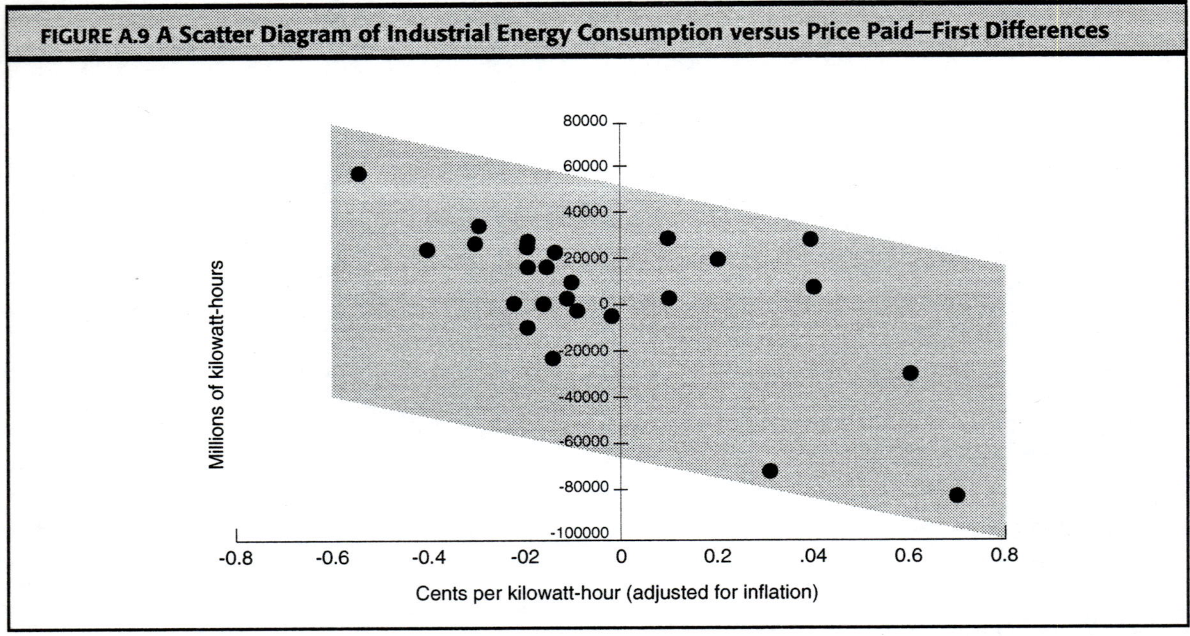

Summary

1. Graphs are useful for presenting relationships between two variables.
2. A positive relationship exists between two variables if an increase in one is associated with an increase in the other; a negative relationship exists between two variables if an increase in one is associated with a decrease in the other.
3. For a straight-line curve, the slope is the ratio of the rise in *Y* over the run in *X*. The slope of the curvilinear relationship at a particular point is the slope of the straight-line tangent at that point. When a curve changes slope from positive to negative as the *X* values increase, the value of *Y* reaches a maximum when the slope of the curve is 0; when a curve changes slope from negative to positive as the *X* values increase, the value of *Y* reaches a minimum when the slope of the curve is 0.
4. The area of a rectangle is height times width. The area of a triangle is half the area of the associated rectangle.
5. Scatter diagrams plot the value of one variable against the value of another variable. The pattern of the dots allows us to detect positive or negative relationships.
6. We study time series to detect relationships among variables over time. Time series are often subject to time trends. We use first differences to remove these time trends.

Problems

Go to www.eia.doe.gov and obtain data for consumption of another type of fuel and for the price of that fuel (such as gasoline consumption versus its price). From this database, prepare a time series chart, a scatter diagram, and a scatter diagram of first differences. Then answer the following questions:

a. Is the relationship between fuel consumption and price positive or negative?
b. Are there significant outliers?
c. Which type of diagram provides better information on whether the relationship is positive or negative?

CHAPTER 2

HOW A MARKET ECONOMY WORKS: THE PRICE SYSTEM

Chapter Preview

This chapter explains how profit-seeking business enterprises respond to relative prices in making their input and output decisions. Consumers use relative price information to substitute relatively cheap goods for relatively expensive goods. Private property rights motivate economic agents to use their resources to maximize their welfare. The "invisible hand" of markets leads to the elimination of shortages and surpluses and causes participants to process information efficiently. This chapter also explains the circular flows of goods and services and of factors of production between businesses and households.

Markets and Business Organizations

A **market** brings buyers and sellers together to determine conditions for exchange.

Markets bring buyers and sellers together for the purpose of determining conditions of exchange, such as quantities of purchase and prices. Markets exist in a wide variety. There are markets for commodities (wheat and soybeans), manufactured goods (television sets and cars), services (plumbers and dentists), and the factors of production.

Some markets are small, with only a few participants. There may be fewer than ten buyers and sellers of ancient biblical manuscripts in the entire world. Other markets are large. On any day in New York, Chicago, and London, millions of buyers and sellers participate in the major stock and commodity exchanges, such as the New York or NASDAQ stock exchanges. Modern telecommunications allow millions of buyers and sellers to know instantaneously the prices of stocks, bonds, gold, silver, and wheat.

Some markets bring together buyers from a limited geographical area. Only residents of the local community buy and sell homes in that community. Even if homes are relatively cheap in Detroit, residents of San Francisco want to buy homes only in the San Francisco Bay area. Buyers and sellers of labor services typically operate in markets defined by a reasonable commuting distance to work, although telecommuting is creating labor markets without geographic boundaries. Some markets bring

Virtual markets bring buyers and sellers together in cybers pace via personal computers.

buyers and sellers together in **virtual markets,** in which buyers and sellers engage in transactions in cyberspace via personal computers. One familiar example is eBay. Buyers and sellers of highly perishable, nontransportable items (such as fresh Gulf red snapper) come together in local or regional markets.

Buyers usually outnumber sellers, although there are some exceptions. One large company, for example, may be the sole employer of labor in a small town. One large international company, DeBeers of South Africa, is the dominant wholesale diamond buyer. But in most markets, there is a much larger number of buyers than sellers. When we rent videos and DVD disks, we are among the thousands of local consumers of these products. In a medium-sized city, there may be 20 automobile dealerships but thousands of potential buyers of cars and trucks. On any particular day, there are literally hundreds of thousands of buyers in commodity markets such as wheat or soybeans.

The number of sellers in a market can have substantial impact on the conditions of exchange. A market in which there is one producer will behave differently from one in which there is a large number. Producers organize themselves into businesses, which can range from one-person operations to large international concerns. Businesses are distinguished by how they are owned and operated.

Forms of Businesses

There are three broad types of ownership of business: sole proprietorships, partnerships, and corporations.

The **sole proprietorship** is owned by one individual who makes all the business decisions, receives all the profits, and bears sole financial responsibility.

The **sole proprietorship** is owned by one individual who makes all the business decisions, receives all the profits, and bears sole financial responsibility for losses. Minimal legal work is required to set up a proprietorship, although the owner will often seek legal and accounting advice. The proprietor is responsible for deciding who should be hired, what products to produce, how much to advertise, and where to locate. The proprietor must observe the law and honor legal contracts. Otherwise, he or she is free to make wise or foolish decisions.

A **partnership** is owned by two or more partners who make all the business decisions, share the profits, and bear financial responsibility jointly.

A **partnership** is owned by two or more partners who, like the sole proprietor, make all the business decisions, share the profits, and bear financial responsibility for losses. Partnerships are based on agreements that spell out ownership shares and the duties of each partner. Partners may contribute equal or different amounts of financial capital; one partner may specialize in finance, another in sales. One partner may make all business decisions while the other partner may provide financial capital. Partnerships range in size from small apartment houses to nationally known law firms or brokerage houses.

A **corporation** is owned by stockholders; it is authorized by law to act as a legal person. The stockholders elect a board of directors, which appoints the management.

A **corporation** is owned by stockholders; it has the legal status of an individual, and it is authorized by law to act as a legal person. The stockholders elect a board of directors, which appoints the management. Management carries out the actual operation of the corporation. The owners of a corporation have limited liability. If the corporation cannot pay its debts, the shareholders are not personally liable for these debts. The worst thing that can happen is that the value of their shares can drop to zero, causing them to lose their investment.

A corporate charter is required to set up a corporation, which is then incorporated in a specific state and becomes a legal person, subject to the laws of that state. The corporation's stockholders own shares in the corporation. A stockholder's share of the corporation equals the number of shares he or she owns divided by the total number of shares outstanding. Owners of stock have the right to vote on corporate matters. Corporations often have a large number of stockholders. AT&T, for example, is owned by over 3 million individuals. Unlike the sole proprietor or partner, there is usually a separation of ownership and management. Corporate stockholders do not participate in the day-to-day running of the company unless they own a substantial portion of outstanding stock. Management, appointed by the board of directors, makes the decisions that run the corporation. The management remains in office as long as the stockholders and the board judge its performance to be satisfactory. Stockholders can, however, exercise indirect control over management by selling their shares. Widespread sell-offs of stock will depress its price and invite a takeover by another corporation. (See Example 2.1 on the relative size of each form of ownership.)

EXAMPLE 2.1 A PROFILE OF AMERICAN BUSINESS

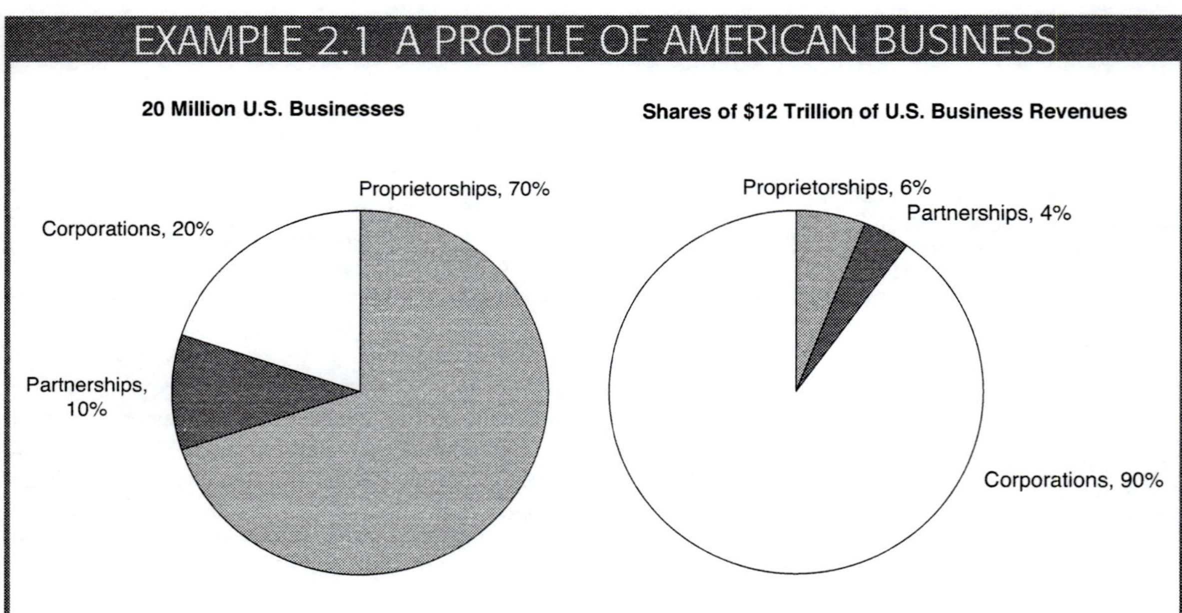

The American economy is made up of almost 20 million businesses. About 12 million of them are very small, most employing only a few persons. In some cases, the owner is the only employee. There are almost 2 million partnerships. Most of them are small, with two or three partners and a handful of employees, but some partnerships grow to be relatively large companies. Corporations can range from small S-corporations, which have fewer than 20 shareholders, to the world's largest industrial giants, such as ExxonMobil, Microsoft, and General Electric. Although corporations account for only 20 percent of U.S. businesses, they earn 90 percent of all business revenues.

Property rights are the rights to use and exchange property.

In a capitalist society, most property and business are owned by private individuals who exercise property rights. **Property rights** are the rights of an owner to use and exchange property. The legal system protects owners from theft, unlawful damage, and unauthorized use of their property and defines who has property rights. The owner of private property has the legal right to sell the property at terms mutually agreed on by the buyer and seller. The legal system can, however, restrict the use of private property. Chemical plants are not allowed to dump toxic chemicals; shops in residential areas must close at a designated hour; owners of homes must observe deed restrictions and zoning laws.

Private owners are guided by relative prices. The owner of an oil refinery will use relative prices to determine whether to produce gasoline, fuel oils, or kerosene; the owner of a truck will use relative prices to determine whether to move furniture or haul vegetables; we look at relative wages in different occupations to determine where to seek employment. Private property rights ensure that owners will use private property to maximum personal advantage. In the case of privately owned businesses, private property rights will be exercised to maximize profits.

The Circular Flow of Economic Activity

Economic activity is circular. Households buy goods and services with the incomes they earn by furnishing labor, land, and capital to business firms. The money spent by households comes back to them as income from the sale of the factors they own.

The Circularity of Economic Activity

The **circular-flow diagram** summarizes the flows of goods and services from enterprises to households and the flows of the factors of production from households to business firms.

Product markets are markets in which goods and services are bought and sold.

Factor markets are markets in which the factors of production are bought and sold.

The **circular-flow diagram** in Figure 2.1 shows the circularity of economic activity. The flows between households and firms are conducted through two markets: the market for goods and services, the **product market,** and the market for the factors of production, the **factor market.** The circular-flow diagram consists of two circles: The outer circle shows the physical flows of goods and services and productive factors; the inner circle shows the payments for goods and services and for productive factors. The physical and money flows go in opposite directions. When households buy goods and services (the top half of the outer circle), physical goods flow to households but the sales receipts flow to the business sector (the top half of the inner circle). When households supply labor to business firms, productive factors flow to businesses (the bottom half of the outer circle) while the resulting labor income flows to the household sector (the bottom half of the inner circle).

Intermediate Goods

The circular-flow diagram captures the movements of goods and services to households. However, a large number of transactions take place within the business sector as firms exchange intermediate goods. Steel, aluminum, and plastics producers sell their products to automobile manufacturers, who use them to produce cars for the circular flow.

FIGURE 2.1 The Circular Flow of Economy Activity

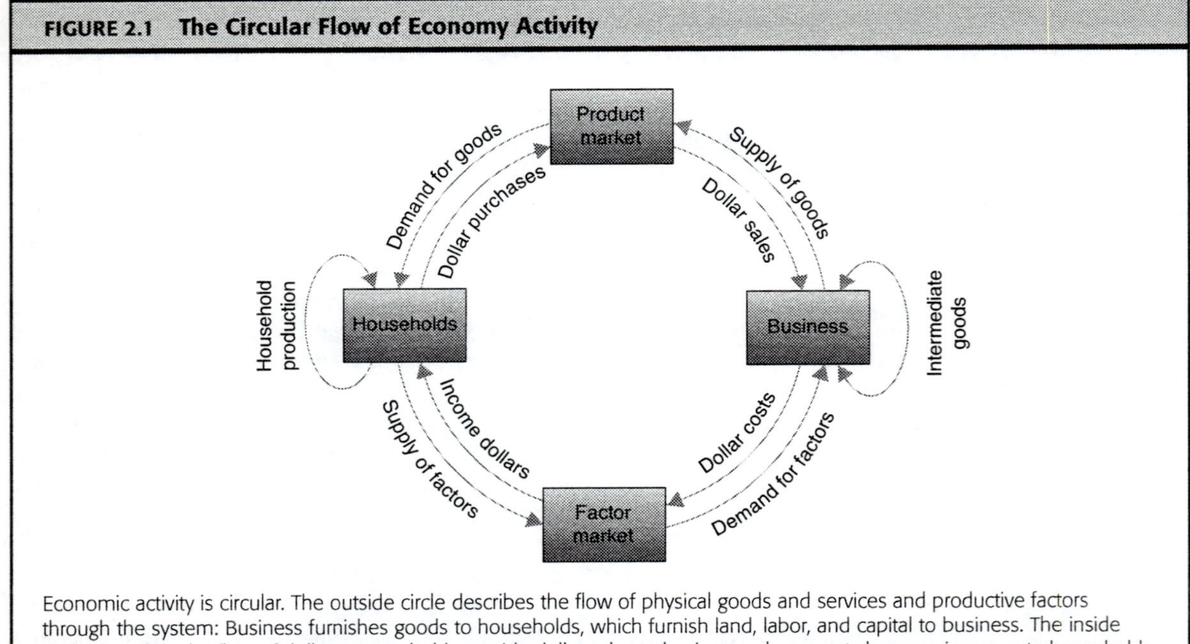

Economic activity is circular. The outside circle describes the flow of physical goods and services and productive factors through the system: Business furnishes goods to households, which furnish land, labor, and capital to business. The inside circle describes the flow of dollars: Households provide dollar sales to business, whose costs become incomes to households. These circles flow in different directions. Intermediate goods and household production do not enter the circular flow.

Intermediate goods and **household production** do not enter the circular flow.

Although intermediate goods do not enter the circular flow, they affect the flows between businesses and households. The efficiency with which the business sector uses intermediate goods determines the size of the flows of goods and services to households.

Household Production

Goods and services produced and used within the household also do not enter the circular flow. Homemakers provide cooking, cleaning, transportation, and other services to other family members. These services are both produced and consumed within the household and, accordingly, do not enter the circular flow. If the same services are purchased from a business firm (eating in a cafeteria instead of at home), they then enter the circular flow.

The Price System

The circular-flow diagram brings home economic interdependency. Hundreds of thousands of business firms produce millions of different goods and services for millions of households. The households, in turn, supply labor, capital, and land to the business sector. Complex flows of intermediate goods take place within the business sector. How are all these actions coordinated? Will not the complexity of the resource allocation task lead to chaos and anarchy? Market allocation systems use relative prices and private property rights to solve the resource allocation problem.

Relative Prices

The price system solves the economic problems of *what, how,* and *for whom* in market economic systems. By the *price system,* we mean relative prices, not money prices. A **money price** is a price expressed in monetary units (such as dollars, yen, or pesos). A loaf of bread may cost 85 cents. A movie ticket may cost $7.50. A barrel of oil may cost $25. These are some of the millions of money prices in an economy. A **relative price** is a price expressed in terms of other commodities.

A **money price** is a price expressed in monetary units.

A **relative price** is a price expressed in terms of other commodities.

Money prices, by themselves, do not play a meaningful role in resource allocation because they do not provide information on what goods are "cheap" and what goods are "expensive." Is crude oil cheap or expensive at a money price of $25 per barrel? Is a high-definition TV cheap or expensive at $850? Is a loaf of white bread cheap or expensive at 85 cents? We cannot answer these questions unless we know how these prices relate to other prices. Crude oil is cheap at $25 per barrel if alternate fuels to produce the same amount of energy cost $50. A high-definition TV is cheap at $850 if the average worker earns $100 per hour. A loaf of white bread is expensive at 85 cents if a loaf of wheat bread costs 25 cents, but it is cheap if wheat bread costs $1.50.

The **price system** is the entire set of relative prices.

The **price system** is the entire set of millions of relative prices. Relative prices are constantly changing and can move in directions opposite to the general level of money prices. Even when money prices are generally rising, some relative prices are falling. For example, Figure 2.2 shows the money prices and the relative price of regular and cell phones. It shows a substantial fall in the relative price of cell phones: The relative price of cell phone service fell from almost 2.5 to 1.5 times that of a regular phone. The price of new autos doubled over the past 30 years while money prices, in general, more than tripled. Although the money price of autos rose, their relative price fell. Changes in relative prices provide important signals. The fall in the relative price of autos signals consumers that autos have become a "better buy." The fall in the relative price of cell phones in the early 2000s signaled consumers that they were becoming "cheaper."

The Principle of Substitution

Relative prices signal which goods are cheap and which are expensive.

A relative price is the ratio of two money prices. If the price of white bread is $2 and the price of wheat bread is $1, the white bread's relative price is 2. This says that white bread is twice as expensive as wheat bread.

Consumers spend their incomes on different things. Producers have options as to what to produce and how. Consumers and producers substitute or trade off one good for another as relative prices change. The **principle of substitution** states that practically no good is irreplaceable. We substitute one good for another as relative prices change.

The **principle of substitution** states that we substitute one good for another as relative prices change.

Virtually no good is fully protected from the competition of substitutes. Aluminum competes with steel; charter jets compete with first-class air travel; pay-per-view

FIGURE 2.2 Money versus Relative Prices, Regular versus Cell Phones (1997–2002)

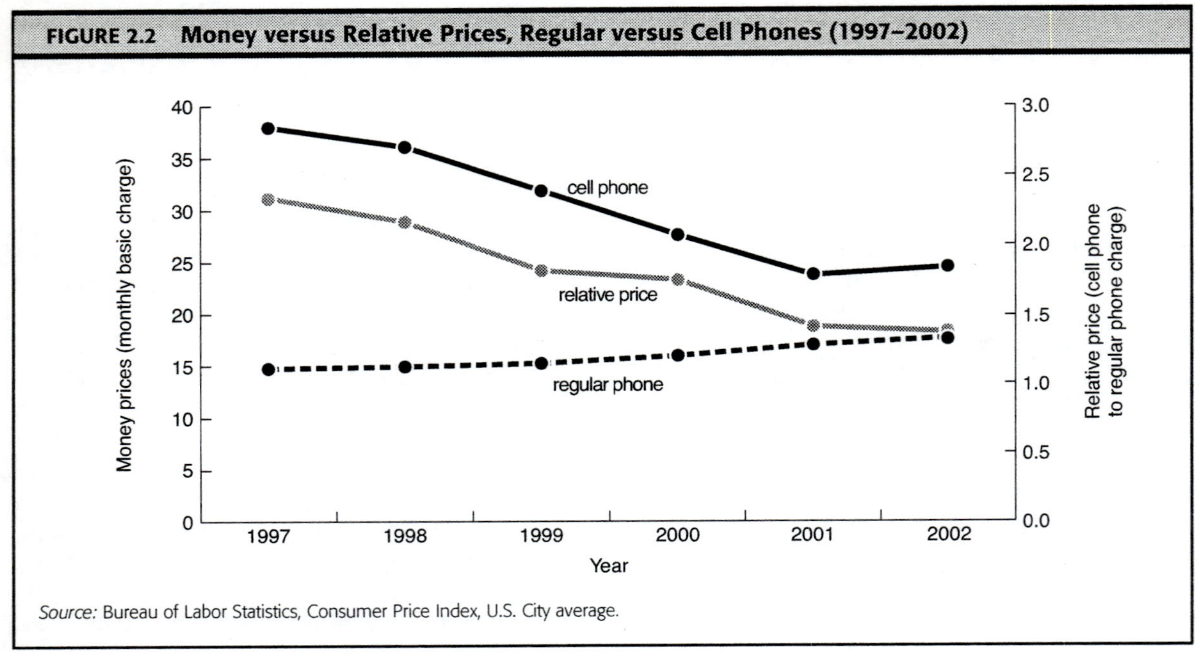

Source: Bureau of Labor Statistics, Consumer Price Index, U.S. City average.

TV competes with cable television, which competes with regular television and with theater movies; natural gas competes with electricity. The only goods that are impervious to substitutes are such goods as minimal quantities of water, salt, and certain lifesaving medications.

To say that there is a substitute for virtually every good does not mean there is an *equally good* substitute. A compact Ford is a good substitute for a compact Chevrolet but a poorer substitute for a Cadillac limousine. The compact Ford is an even poorer substitute for a private jet or yacht. An Airbus 340 is a good substitute for a Boeing 747, while an ocean liner is a relatively poor substitute for an intercontinental jet. (See Example 2.2.)

Increases in relative prices motivate economic agents to seek out substitutes.

Relative prices signal users to make substitutions. Rising relative prices motivate us to seek out substitutes. If the price of one good rises relative to its substitutes, users switch to relatively cheaper substitutes. The decline in relative energy prices in the 1980s caused a resurgence in sales of full-sized cars. The advent of fast-food chains caused families to switch from home-cooked meals to eating out more often. The decline in the relative price of cellular phones caused us to substitute them for our regular telephones.

Equilibrium and the Invisible Hand

Adam Smith, the father of modern economics, puzzled over how the price system solves the economic problem of resource allocation. Writing in his 1776 masterwork, *The Wealth of Nations,* Smith stated his solution as follows:

EXAMPLE 2.2 SUBSTITUTIONS AND HOW WE COMMUNICATE

A short 20 years ago, we had few choices when we wanted to communicate with one another: We could send letters through the U.S. Postal Service, make telephone calls on the fixed telephone lines of the Bell System, or send telegrams through Western Union. Through the unleashing of competition and vast changes in technology, we now have a much broader range of choices. We can substitute cellular for fixed telephone services, faxes for mail, e-mail for faxes, one long-distance provider for another, and the various overnight mail delivery services for the U.S. Postal Service. We can even use our computers for "free" long-distance telephone calls to foreign countries.

With all the choices, how we communicate depends on relative prices. If the U.S. Postal Service raises its rates, we use more UPS or Federal Express. If AT&T raises its long-distance rates, we switch to Sprint or MCI. If airlines raise their business fares, we substitute picture-phone conference calls for business meetings.

The availability of these substitutes places pressure on businesses to keep their prices low. If they raise their prices, their customers will make substitutions in favor of their competitors.

> Every individual endeavors to employ his capital so that its produce may be of greatest value. He generally neither intends to promote the public interest, nor knows how much he is promoting it. He intends only his own security, only his own gain. And he is led by an *invisible hand* to promote an end which was no part of his intention. By pursuing his own interest he frequently promotes that of society more effectively than when he really intends to promote it.[1]

The **invisible hand** states that a capitalist economy can function well without government direction by using the signals of the price system.

Smith's invisible hand works through the price system. The millions of relative prices that make up the price system inform buyers and sellers what goods are cheap and what goods are expensive. As businesses use this information to gain profits and buyers use this information to determine their best buys, the economy runs itself without direction or planning from government.

We shall see in later chapters that, while the invisible hand usually works well, there are instances where it breaks down. But for now, let us see how the invisible hand prevents lasting shortages and surpluses. If automobile manufacturers produce more cars than buyers want to buy at the asking price, excess inventories of unsold cars will build up. Dealers must pay their bills and cannot live on unsold inventories. Therefore, they must lower their prices. As the relative price of cars falls, consumers begin to substitute more new-automobile purchases for substitutes like home entertainment equipment, kitchen remodeling, or used cars. The decline in the relative price of cars signals auto manufacturers to produce fewer cars and turn to truck production or defense contracts to produce tanks.

The **equilibrium price** is that price at which the amount of the good people are prepared to buy equals the amount offered for sale.

As buyers and sellers adjust to the change in relative prices, eventually a balance is struck between the number of cars people are prepared to buy (the quantity demanded) and the number offered for sale (the quantity supplied). The price at which this balance is struck is the **equilibrium price.**

---

[1]Adam Smith, *The Wealth of Nations*, ed. Edwin Cannon (New York: Modern Library, 1937), p. 423.

The economy's search for equilibrium takes place in markets simultaneously. As the price of autos is changing, so are the prices of other goods, including those goods and services that substitute for automobiles. As relative prices change, so do buying and selling decisions, and the reactions of buyers and sellers to these changes move each market toward equilibrium.

Table 2.1 returns to the electricity market discussed in the first chapter. It shows the equilibrium balance struck between the production and use of electricity and the prices that created this equilibrium.

The Price System and *What, How,* and *For Whom*

The price system solves *what, how,* and *for whom* by itself. No individual is required to be concerned about the economy as a whole; we need only worry about our own self-interest. Government is not required to coordinate economic activities. In fact, some government actions such as price controls can interfere with the market's checks and balances.

Dollar votes show the willingness of people to buy particular goods at specified prices.

The *what* problem is solved by consumers and producers responding to relative prices. What is produced is determined by the dollar votes cast by consumers. **Dollar votes** are simply the willingness of consumers to buy at a specified price. If many dollar votes are cast for a particular good, this means that buyers are willing to pay a high relative price for it. If production costs are equal among goods, producers will produce those goods with high relative prices.

The price system solves the *how* problem through relative price signals. Business firms produce goods by combining resources in the least costly way. If the relative price of farmland increases, farmers will use more labor, chemical fertilizers, and tractors to work the land more intensively. If the relative price of copper rises, homebuilders will use aluminum wiring. If business firms fail to use

TABLE 2.1 Equilibrium in Electricity Market

	Uses (billion kilowatt-hours)				
	Residential	*Commercial*	*Industrial*	*Other*	*Total*
Quantity	909	785	808	84	2586
		Production (billion kilowatt-hours)			
		Electric Utilities	*Nonutility Power*		*Total*
Quantity		2300	585		2885
Minus Transmission losses					299
Price					2586
Cents/kwh	8.2	7.2	4.4	6.7	

Source: Energy Information Administration, http://www.eia.doe.gov.

lowest-cost combinations, the competition of other firms will reduce their profits and, possibly, drive them out of business.

The price system also resolves the *for whom* problem. The market assigns relative prices to the resources owned by each household. The distribution of income among households therefore depends on the relative prices of the factors of production and on the distribution of property rights to scarce land, labor, and capital. People who are fortunate enough to be able to provide high-priced labor services (brain surgeons, gifted athletes, presidents of large corporations) receive a large share of output. The poor are those who own few resources, which command low relative prices, and who furnish low-priced labor services to the market.

Imperfections: Public Goods and Externalities

In the real world, the invisible hand has imperfections. The price system does not guarantee a satisfactory solution of the *for whom* problem. The invisible hand may lead to an unfair distribution of income. It may not work well when firms gain monopoly control over markets. The invisible hand may also fail to deal with externalities, such as pollution. In addition, it may produce business cycles—booms and busts of employment and inflation.

Laissez-faire is the doctrine that the government should limit its activities to essential state functions.

The basic policy conclusion of the invisible hand is laissez-faire. **Laissez-faire** is the doctrine that the government should limit its activities to essential state functions such as national defense, a legal system, public roads, and police protection. In fact, economists agree that private markets cannot supply public goods such as national defense; they must be supplied by government.

Public goods are characterized by two features: More can be consumed by one consumer without less being available for other consumers, and nonpayers cannot be excluded from using the product.

Public goods are characterized by two features: More can be consumed by one consumer without less being available for other consumers, and nonpayers cannot be excluded from using the product by those who actually pay. The amount of protection I get from a missile defense system (which covers the entire country) does not lessen the protection that you get. If my house lies in a flood zone, the protection afforded my house by a flood-control project does not lessen the protection afforded to other houses. If I do not pay my share for flood-control projects, my neighbors who do pay cannot prevent my house from being protected. These two features make it difficult for private markets to provide public goods. Since public goods cannot be sold, there is no incentive to "pay one's share" voluntarily. Most would try to ride free, sitting on the sidelines hoping that others will pay. One solution is for the government to provide such goods, paying for them with tax revenues.

An **external cost** is an unpriced cost that is imposed on others.

Another problem with the invisible hand is that we impose external costs on others that are not reflected in our private economic calculations. An **external cost** is an unpriced cost that is imposed on others. If my factory pollutes the river and raises the water-purification costs of downstream factories or reduces the number of fish for fishers, I do not take these external costs into account when I make my own private decisions regarding the factory. Accordingly, I would produce more output, and hence more pollution, than I would if I had to pay these external costs. The presence of external costs creates another potential role for government: namely, to use government programs to make sure that those who impose these external costs include them as part of their private calculations.

Summary

1. Markets bring buyers and sellers together to determine conditions of exchange.
2. Forms of business include proprietorships, partnerships, and corporations.
3. The circular-flow diagram shows the flows of goods and services and the factors of production between businesses and households. Each physical flow has a corresponding money flow in the opposite direction. When goods and services flow from businesses to households, money receipts for these purchases must flow back to the business sector. The circular flow does not show the transactions of intermediate goods that take place entirely within the business sector, nor does it show household production.
4. Relative prices tell consumers what is cheap and what is expensive. Substitutes exist for virtually every good, and changes in relative prices signal that substitutions should take place. Property rights are held predominantly by private owners in capitalist societies, and people are motivated to use their property rights to best advantage.
5. Business firms can be organized as sole proprietorships, partnerships, or corporations.
6. The invisible hand ensures that markets will move toward equilibrium. An equilibrium price is established when the amount of the good people are prepared to buy equals the amount businesses are prepared to sell.
7. The price system solves the *what* problem by consumers and producers responding to relative prices. The *how* problem is solved by business firms using relative prices to combine resources in a least-cost fashion. The *for whom* problem is resolved by the relative resource prices established in factor markets.
8. Imperfections in the operation of the invisible hand are business cycles, the possibility of an unfair distribution of income, externalities, monopoly, the inability of private markets to supply public goods, and the problem of external costs.

Questions and Problems

1. The circular-flow diagram shows flows of receipts to business enterprises from households and the flow of factor income from businesses to households. Speculate about the relationship between the sizes of each flow.
2. "Economists should not emphasize relative prices so much. I base my decisions on the money price of each good, not on its relative price." Comment.
3. Give an example, based on your own observations, of a commodity whose relative price has risen and a commodity whose relative price has fallen.
4. In the first chapter we defined *scarcity.* In this chapter we talk about how the price system deals with shortages. What is the difference between scarcity and shortage?
5. "I need to eat. I need transportation, and I need clothing. I'll need these things even if relative prices are rising. The principle of substitution does not work when it comes to life's necessities." Comment.

6. "The price system comprises millions of relative prices. There is no way anyone can function effectively in a market economy. People are required to know too much information." Comment.
7. Explain why it would be very hard to have the giant business concerns of today without some form of limited liability.
8. Discuss the positive and negative features of the separation of ownership and management.
9. The statistics on sole proprietorships reveal that they are, on average, smaller than partnerships and that partnerships are smaller, on average, than corporations. From what you know about the features of business organizations, explain why.
10. Explain why external costs may require government action.
11. Two decades ago there were few personal computers per household. Now virtually every household has a PC. Use what you have learned in this chapter to explain why.
12. Assume that I open a plant to sell t-shirts labeled "I am the world's smartest person." Because this t-shirt is unique, I decide I'll sell it for $85. What will tell me whether this price is right?
13. Would a renter or a home owner be more inclined to take good care of the home? Why? If we asked the same question about a business owned by the government versus one owned by a private individual, what would your answer be?
14. Explain why national defense is a public good.

CHAPTER 3

MARKET DEMAND, SUPPLY, AND ELASTICITY

Chapter Preview

This chapter explains the law of demand and draws the distinctions between shifts in demand and supply curves and movements along supply and demand curves. It also shows the effects of shifts in supply and demand on prices and quantities and how elasticities affect price changes.

Ceteris Paribus

Economic theory zeroes in on the most important factors that explain an economic phenomenon. If more than one explanatory factor is involved, it can be difficult to sort out what has caused what. When a number of factors are involved, it is important to isolate the effect of any one factor on what you are trying to explain.

Ceteris paribus describes the relationship between two factors when all other relevant factors do not change.

Economists use the **ceteris paribus** assumption in much the same way that physicists use the vacuum. While physical theories describe how particles would behave in a perfect vacuum, economic theories explain how two factors are related if all other relevant factors remain the same. *Ceteris paribus* is a Latin term meaning "other things being equal." If the theory says that a rise in the price of hamburgers causes people to buy fewer hamburgers, this means that this relationship holds ceteris paribus—only if all other things that affect hamburger purchases remain the same.

Market Demand

People **demand** that quantity of a good they are actually prepared to buy with their limited income at prevailing prices.

Markets bring together buyers and sellers. Buyers who "want" goods are not necessarily prepared to buy them. *Wants* refers to the goods and services that people would take if those goods and services were given away free. The amounts of goods we want are quite different from the amounts that we actually demand. We **demand** that quantity of a good we are actually prepared to buy with our limited income at prevailing prices. *Demand* refers to what economic agents actually do when confronted with opportunity costs and limited income, where having more of one good means having less of another.

The Law of Demand: Income and Substitution Effects

The **law of demand** states that there is a negative (inverse) relationship between the price of a good and the quantity demanded, ceteris paribus.

The **law of demand** states that there is a negative (inverse) relationship between the price of a good and the quantity demanded, ceteris paribus. The quantity demanded is the amount of a good or service that we are willing and able to buy at the prevailing price. The law of demand states that quantity demanded increases as the price is lowered. (See Example 3.1.)

Two factors explain the law of demand. First, there is the principle of substitution. As the price of a good falls, ceteris paribus, its relative price falls. It has become cheaper relative to its substitutes, and we, finding it a better buy, purchase more of the good.

Second, as the price of the good falls, consumers can buy the goods and services they used to buy plus more. A decrease in price is like an increase in income because it frees income to purchase more goods, including the good whose price has fallen. The change in purchases of the good attributable to the increase in income's buying power is called the income effect.

When the price of a good falls, people buy more because its relative price has fallen (the **substitution effect**), and the resulting increase in purchasing power leads to greater purchases of goods, including the good itself (the **income effect**).

When the price of a good falls, we tend to buy more of it because its relative price has fallen (the **substitution effect**), and the price reduction increases the purchasing power of income, which normally leads to greater purchases of goods, including the one whose price has fallen (the **income effect**).

Substitution and income effects explain the law of demand—why we buy more of a good whose relative price has fallen. Just as individuals tend to buy more of a good at a lower price, the market as a whole—made up of all individuals who are prepared to buy the good at different prices—does the same.

In most cases, the income effect is not strong. When the price of beef falls, not that much extra income is freed up for more purchases. If the average family spends $15.00 per week on beef at $1.50 per pound and the price of beef drops to $1.00 per pound (a very substantial drop), the family can now purchase the same amount of beef as before for $10.00, and an extra $5.00 per week of income is released. The extra $5.00 will be used to purchase more goods and services, but the extra $5.00 will likely have only a small effect on beef purchases. The substitution effect from the drop in the relative price of beef will have a more substantial impact because now beef has become cheaper relative to chicken, fish, and pork.

EXAMPLE 3.1 M&MS AND THE LAW OF DEMAND

The law of demand states that the quantity demanded will increase as the price is lowered as long as other factors that affect demand do not change. In the real world, factors that affect the demand for a particular product change *frequently.* Tastes change, incomes rise, and prices of substitutes and complements change. The makers of M&M candy conducted an experiment that illustrates the law of demand, holding the necessary demand-affecting conditions constant. Over a 12-month test period, the price of M&Ms was held constant in 150 stores while the content weight of the candy was increased. By holding the price constant and increasing the weight, the price (per ounce) was lowered. In the stores where the price was dropped, sales rose by 20 to 30 percent almost overnight. As predicted by the law of demand, a reduction in price causes the quantity demanded to rise, ceteris paribus.

In some cases, the income effect can be substantial. Changes in interest rates, for example, can unleash a substantial income effect. A family with a $100,000 mortgage pays $6000 per year in interest when the mortgage interest rate is 6 percent. If the mortgage rate falls to 4 percent, the annual interest payment on a $100,000 mortgage falls to $4000, freeing up an extra $2000. This extra income may enable the family to purchase a more expensive home, increasing substantially the quantity of credit demanded.

The Demand Curve

The **demand curve** shows the quantities of the good demanded at different prices, all other factors held constant.

The relationship between quantity demanded and price is shown by the **demand curve** when graphed, or equivalently, by the demand schedule when in tabular form. The ceteris paribus relationship between price and quantity demanded is negative because of the law of demand. As price goes up, the quantity demanded goes down.

A hypothetical demand curve for corn is shown in Figure 3.1. When price is $5, quantity demanded is 20 million bushels per month (point *a*). When price is a lower $4, the quantity demanded is a higher 25 million bushels per month (point *b*). The curve drawn through points *a* through *e* connects the quantities demanded by the market at each price. Along the demand curve (*D*), the price and quantity are negatively related due to the law of demand.

The market demand curve shows that the price must be lowered in order to sell more. If buyers of corn are purchasing 20 million bushels of corn per month at a price of $5 per bushel, the price must fall to $4 if corn farmers are to sell 25 million bushels to consumers. As long as the price stays at $5 per bushel, only 20 million bushels will be sold per month. If the telephone company wishes to increase long distance phone calls, it must offer a lower price. If the gas company wishes its customers to use less natural gas per month, it must raise the price of natural gas.

Shifts in Demand

Demand increases when the demand curve shifts to the right. Demand falls when the demand curve shifts to the left.

Factors other than the current price can change the quantity of the good people are prepared to buy. When this happens, the demand curve shifts. (Remember the curve shift example in the Chapter 1 Appendix.) When the demand curve shifts to the right, people are now prepared to buy more of the good at every possible price than before. Demand has increased. When the demand curve shifts to the left, people are now prepared to buy less at any price than before. Demand has fallen.

Factors other than the current price affect the quantities buyers are prepared to purchase. There are five factors that cause shifts in demand.

Two goods are **substitutes** if the demand for one rises when the price of the other rises. Two goods are **complements** if the demand for one rises when the price of the other falls.

Prices of Related Goods Goods can be related in two ways: Two goods are **substitutes** if the demand for one rises (the demand curve shifts to the right) when the price of the other rises or if demand falls when the price of the other falls. Examples of these are Coca-Cola and Pepsi, tea and coffee, stocks and bonds, natural gas and electricity, and cell phones and regular phones. Some goods, such as Coca-Cola and Pepsi, are very close substitutes, and others, like telephones and carrier pigeons, are very distant ones.

FIGURE 3.1 Demand Curve for Corn

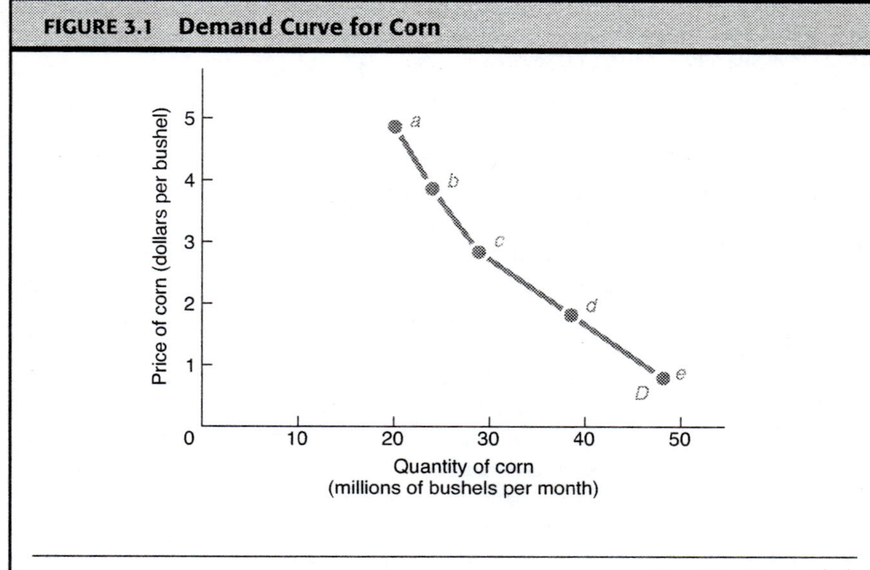

	Price (dollars per bushel)	Quantity Demanded (millions of bushels per month)
a	$5	20
b	4	25
c	3	30
d	2	40
e	1	50

This figure describes how the quantity of corn demanded responds to the prices of corn, holding all other factors constant. It is based on the accompanying table. At *a*, when the price of corn is $5 per bushel, the quantity demanded is 20 million bushels per month. At *e*, when the price of corn is $1, the quantity demanded is 50 million bushels. The downward-sloping curve (*D*) drawn through these points is the demand curve for corn. It shows the amounts of corn consumers would be willing to buy at different prices in the specified time period.

Two goods are **complements** if the demand for one rises (the demand curve shifts to the right) when the price of the other falls or when the demand for one falls when the price of the other rises. Examples of complements are automobiles and gasoline, bread and butter, dress shirts and neckties, and computer games and home computers. When goods are complements, the two goods are used jointly (automobiles plus gasoline equals automobile transportation). An increase in the price of one good increases the price of the joint product, causing less of the joint product to be demanded. As the price of gasoline rises, automobile transportation becomes more expensive. As people cut back on automobile transportation, the demand for automobiles falls.

Income Consumer income affects demand because, as income rises, people tend to spend more on most, but not all, goods and services. Prior to graduation, a young

The demand for a normal good increases (its demand curve shifts to the right) as income rises.

The demand for an inferior good falls (its demand curve shifts to the left) as income rises.

couple's combined income was $6000 per year, and now it is $60,000 per year. The dramatic rise in income will cause a substantial increase in their purchases of goods and services; they may buy a new car, better cuts of meat, and new wardrobes. Purchases of some goods and services would actually fall with the rise in income. Instead of riding a city bus, they now drive to work in a new car. Instead of eating macaroni and cheese at home, they eat out.

Goods are classified as *normal* or *inferior* depending on what happens to their demand as income rises. The demand for a normal good increases (its demand curve shifts to the right) as income rises. The demand for an inferior good falls (its demand curve shifts to the left) as income rises. For example, the demand for catfish falls as income increases, while the demand for salmon rises as income increases.

Preferences *Preferences* are what people like and dislike without regard to budgetary considerations. Preferences show the structure of wants when goods are given away free. One person may prefer a high-rise apartment to a single-family home; another may prefer an American luxury car to a European luxury car. You may like ice cream but detest frozen yogurt; you will detest frozen yogurt at both a low and a high price.

Demand changes as preferences change. When smoking was declared dangerous to health, the demand for cigarettes fell. If fashion dictates that men have long hair, the demand for barber services falls (the demand curve shifts to the left). If there is social pressure in the suburbs for every family to own an SUV, the demand for SUVs rises.

The Number of Potential Buyers If more buyers enter a market, demand will rise. Populations grow; relaxed immigration laws allow more people to enter the country, or people may move from the Northeast to the Southwest. The number of potential buyers can also be increased by the removal of barriers to trade. An agreement to sell grain or computers to Russia increases the number of potential buyers; lowering the legal age for alcoholic beverage purchases increases the number of buyers of beer and wine.

Expectations The law of demand states that the quantity demanded is negatively related to the current price of the good. People's expectations of how the price will behave in the future can also affect demand. The expectation that the price of a good will rise can increase the demand for the good (shift the demand curve to the right), even if there is no change in the current price. If people fear that home prices will rise in the future, they may speed up their purchases of homes in order to buy while prices are still reasonable. Conversely, if people expect personal computer prices to fall, they may delay their purchases in anticipation of lower prices. Consumers must determine when to buy and must weigh the opportunity costs of buying now or later. If much higher prices are expected in the future, the opportunity costs of buying now are lowered.

Shifts in Demand Curves versus Movements Along a Demand Curve

The amount of a particular good people are prepared to purchase can change for two general reasons:

1. The price of the good can change.

2. Other factors that affect purchases in addition to the good's current price can change.

An increase in demand occurs when the demand curve shifts to the right. Consumers are now willing to purchase more of the good at each price.

Because both effects result in increased sales, they are easily confused. Figure 3.2 shows that corn sales can rise from 25 to 30 million bushels per month either because the price of corn falls from \$4 to \$3 per bushel (the movement from *b* to *c*) *or* because average family income rises sufficiently to raise purchases from 25 to 30 bushels (the movement from *b* to *b′*). There is a fundamental difference between these two changes. In the first case, there has been an increase in the quantity demanded because of a lowering of the price. Graphically, there has been a downward movement along the stationary demand curve (from *b* to *c*). In the second case, there has been a change in a factor other than current price—income—that affects demand, shifting the entire demand curve to the right (from point *b* on *D* to point *b′* on *D′*). As shown in the previous section, a change in the factors that affect demand, other than current price, causes the demand curve to shift. In Figure 3.2, the rightward shift in the demand curve from *D* to *D′* has been caused by an increase in income.

An increase in quantity demanded occurs when the price of the good falls and there is a movement down the demand curve.

An increase in demand occurs when the demand curve shifts to the right. Consumers are now willing to purchase more of the good at each price. An increase in quantity demanded occurs when the price of the good falls and there is a movement down the demand curve.

FIGURE 3.2 Increase in Demand Versus Increase in Quantity Demanded

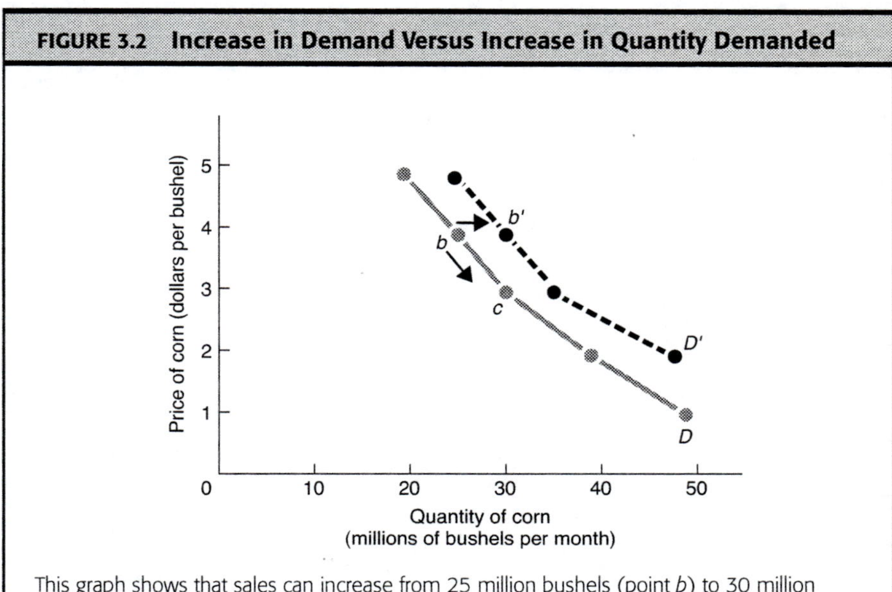

This graph shows that sales can increase from 25 million bushels (point *b*) to 30 million bushels either because of a fall in price from \$4 to \$3 or because of an increase in demand (from *D* to *D′*). The increase in quantity demanded because of a lower price is shown as the movement from *b* to *c*, and the increase in demand is shown as the movement from *b* to *b′*.

Market Supply

The **quantity supplied** of a good or service is the amount offered for sale at a given price.

Although we cannot speak of a universal *law* of supply, typically the higher the price, the greater the quantity supplied, ceteris paribus. The **quantity supplied** of a good or service is the amount offered for sale at a given price.

The ceteris paribus relationship between price and quantity supplied is normally positive—the higher the price, the greater the quantity supplied. The reasons for this positive relationship are explored in the chapter on costs of production. For now we can say that a higher price will cause producers, who must choose between producing this product and another, to produce more of this product. A farmer who produces corn, oats, and rye will produce more corn and less oats and rye as the price of corn rises. The manufacturer of cars and trucks will produce more trucks as the price of trucks rises.

The Supply Curve

The hypothetical supply curve for corn in Figure 3.3 shows the normal case of a positive relationship between price and quantity supplied. A positive relationship means that more is supplied at a higher price.

The **supply curve** shows the quantities of a good supplied at different prices, all other factors that affect supply being held constant.

The **supply curve** shows the quantities of a good supplied at different prices, all other factors that affect supply being held constant. As with demand curves, price is on the vertical axis and the quantity supplied is on the horizontal axis. When the price is $5 per bushel, farmers are prepared to supply 40 million bushels per month (point *a*). At a price of $4 per bushel, the quantity supplied falls to 35 million bushels (point *b*). The smooth curve drawn through points *a* through *e,* labeled *S,* is the supply curve. It demonstrates that higher prices are required to induce producers to offer more units for sale. The only way to get corn farmers to offer more units for sale is to have a higher price of corn.

Shifts in Supply

As the prices of other goods increase, the supply of the good should fall (its supply curve shifts to the left).

Four factors can cause changes in the quantity of the good or service firms are prepared to supply at prevailing prices.

Prices of Other Goods Firms must weigh the opportunity costs of producing one good versus another. As the production possibilities frontier showed, productive resources are limited and choices among outputs must be made. Such choices depend on relative prices. A farmer with farmland suited for both corn and soybeans must decide how much of each crop to plant. As the price of soybeans falls, more land will be planted in corn. Oil refiners will be guided by the relative prices of fuel oil, gasoline, and kerosene in deciding how much of each to refine. A higher price of fuel oil tends to lower the supply of other refined oil products. Firms must also compare today's prices with those expected in the future.

An increase in input prices causes a reduction in supply (the supply curve shifts to the left).

Prices of Inputs Goods and services are produced by combining land, labor, and capital resources. As the prices of these resources change, the supply curve shifts.

FIGURE 3.3 Supply Curve for Corn

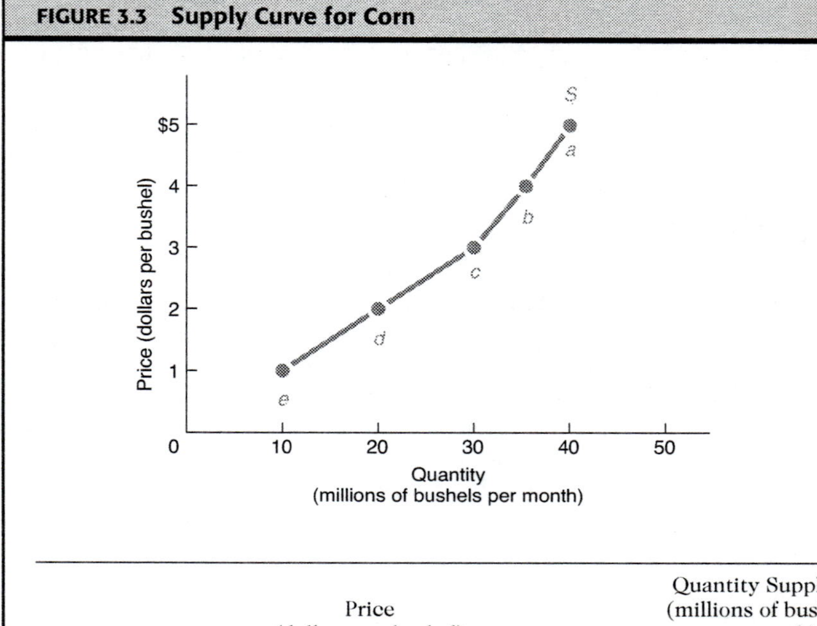

	Price (dollars per bushel)	Quantity Supplied (millions of bushels per month)
a	$5	40
b	4	35
c	3	30
d	2	20
e	1	10

This graph depicts how the quantity of corn supplied responds to the price of corn. It is based on the accompanying table. In situation *a*, when the price of corn is $5 per bushel, the quantity supplied by farmers is 40 million bushels per month. In the last situation, *e*, when the price is $1 per bushel, the quantity supplied is only 10 million bushels per month. The upward-sloping curve (*S*) drawn through these points is the supply curve of corn.

Suppose corn farmers were willing to supply 35 million bushels per month at a price of $4 per bushel when they were renting farmland for $300 per acre per month. If the rent were to double to $600 per acre, they would now be prepared to supply less at the $4 price. To give a second example, an increase in lumber prices raises the cost of building a home. Homebuilders would be prepared to build fewer homes at the same price as before when lumber prices were lower. Thus, an increase in the firm's costs shifts the supply curve to the left.

Technology is accumulated scientific and technical knowledge about how to produce specific goods and services.

Technology Changes Costs of production are determined by resource prices and by the efficiency with which resources are used. This efficiency is dictated by the state of **technology,** the accumulated scientific and technical knowledge about how to produce specific goods and services.

As technology advances, more goods and services can be produced from the same volume of resources. In effect, a technological improvement is like a reduction in input prices. Costs of production fall, and firms are willing to supply more of the good or service at the same price as before. Automobile manufacturers were not able to supply cars at a price affordable to the masses until Henry Ford developed the technology of mass assembly-line car production. The invention of the transistor paved the way for the mass production of televisions, radios, and personal computers offered to consumers at relatively low prices. Technological advances shift the supply curve to the right.

Improvements in technology cause supply to increase (the supply curve shifts to the right).

An increase in the number of sellers causes supply to increase (the supply curve shifts to the right).

Number of Sellers As more sellers enter the market, larger quantities of goods are offered to buyers at the same price as before. As later chapters show, the number of producers typically increases when high profits are being earned. For example, the profits of Apple Computer in the late 1970s encouraged a large number of new personal computer manufacturers to enter the market; the high profits of a few video game producers in the early 1990s encouraged the entry of many more companies that produce video games.

Shifts in Supply Curves versus Movements Along a Supply Curve

An increase in supply occurs when the supply curve shifts to the right. Sellers are now willing to offer more for sale at each price.

The amount of a particular product good offered for sale can increase for two reasons:

1. The price of the good can rise.
2. A factor other than current price can change to cause an increase in the amount offered for sale.

An increase in quantity supplied occurs when the price of the good rises, and there is a movement up the supply curve. More is offered for sale, but the supply curve has not budged.

In Figure 3.4, the amount of corn offered for sale increases from 30 million bushels per week to 35 million bushels per week. In the first case, the increase in quantity is because of an increase in the price of corn from \$3 to \$4 per bushel (the movement from *c* to *b* on the supply curve *S*). This is an *increase in quantity supplied.* There has been no "increase in supply." The supply curve has not budged; there has been a movement up the supply curve due to the higher price. In the second case, the increase in quantity is because of a fall in the price of soybeans, which causes farmers to switch to corn (the movement from *c* on *S* to *c′* on *S′*). This is an *increase in supply;* the supply curve has shifted to the right. More is now offered at each and every price as before. An increase in supply occurs when the supply curve shifts to the right. Sellers are willing to offer more for sale at each price than before.

Independence of Supply and Demand

Shifts in supply do not cause shifts in demand, and vice versa. The factors that increase the demand for a good are different from the factors that change the supply of that good. Increases in consumer income raise the demand for new cars. However, increasing income does not change the technology of car production, input prices, or the relative prices of cars versus trucks. There is no reason to expect rising income to increase the supply of new cars. On the other hand, an improvement in the technology of automobile production, which increases the supply of new cars, would not be expected to shift the demand curve for new cars.

FIGURE 3.4 Causes for Increases in Goods Offered for Sale

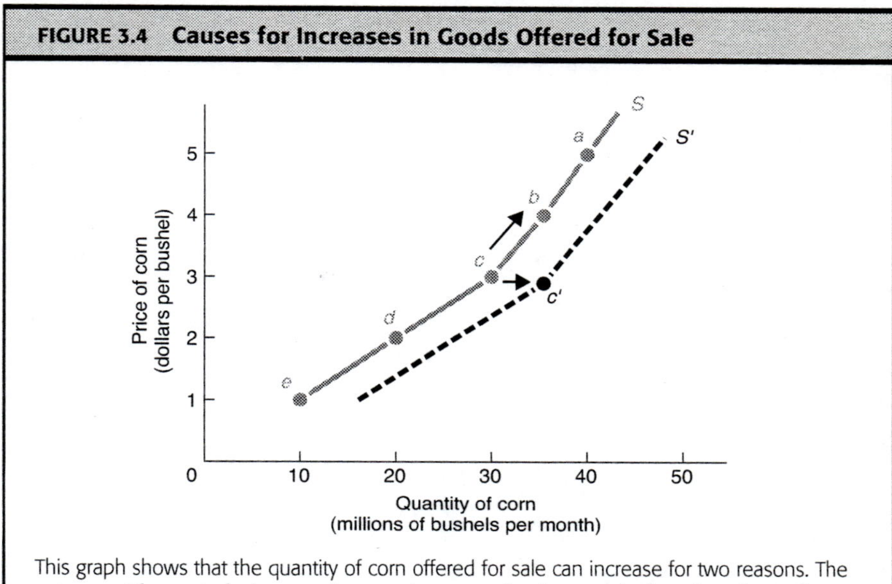

This graph shows that the quantity of corn offered for sale can increase for two reasons. The movement from *c* to *b* shows an increase because of an increase in the price of corn (from $3 to $4 a bushel). The movement *c* to *c'* shows a movement caused by an increase in supply because of a reduction in the price of soybeans. In this case, the supply curve shifts from *S* to *S'*.

The different factors that cause demand and supply curves to shift are summarized in Table 3.1.

Equilibrium: Supply and Demand Together

The market demand curve tells us what consumers are prepared to buy at different prices; the supply curve tells us what producers are prepared to sell at different prices. Figure 3.5 puts together the demand and supply curves.

Shortages and Surpluses

A **shortage** results if the quantity demanded exceeds the quantity supplied at the prevailing price.

To understand why markets settle at an equilibrium price, one must first understand why the market rejects other prices. Suppose the price of corn happens to be $2 per bushel. At a $2 price, consumers will want to buy 40 million bushels, but producers will be willing to sell only 20 million bushels. This means that at a price of $2 there is a **shortage** of 20 million bushels.

What will happen in such a shortage situation? Some corn buyers find they cannot get corn at a $2 price. They discover, however, if they offer a higher price, they can bid corn away from other buyers. A bidding war breaks out among buyers. Accordingly, shortages cause buyers to bid up the price, and the price will increase.

TABLE 3.1 Factors That Cause Shifts in the Demand and Supply Curves

Factor	*Example*
Demand Curve	
Change in price of substitutes	Increase in price of coffee shifts demand curve for tea to right.
Change in price of complements	Increase in price of coffee shifts demand curve for sugar to left.
Change in income	Increases in income shift demand curve for automobiles to right.
Change in preference	Announcement that cigarettes are hazardous to health shifts demand curve for cigarettes to left.
Change in number of buyers	Increase in population of City *X* shifts demand curve for houses in City *X* to right.
Change in expectations of future prices	Expectation that prices of canned goods will increase substantially over the next year shifts demand curve for canned goods to right.
Supply Curve	
Change in price of another good	Increase in price of corn shifts supply curve of wheat to left.
Change in price of resource	Decrease in wage rate of autoworkers shifts supply curve of autos to right.
Change in technology	Higher corn yields due to genetic engineering shift supply curve of corn to right.
Change in number of sellers	New sellers entering profitable field shift supply curve of product to right.

The increase in the price of corn will both discourage consumption and encourage production. Some buyers who are prepared to buy at $2 will not buy at $3; some sellers who are not willing to sell at $2 will sell at $3. The increase in the price of corn, through the actions of independent buyers and sellers, will lead to market decisions that reduce the shortage of corn.

Why would the market reject a $4 price? At a price of $4 per bushel, consumers want to buy 25 million bushels, but producers want to sell 35 million bushels. There is a **surplus** of 10 million bushels; the price is too high to equate the quantity demanded with the quantity supplied.

A **surplus** results when the quantity supplied exceeds the quantity demanded at the current price.

At a $4 price, some willing sellers cannot find buyers; their corn inventories pile up. Sellers find, however, that by lowering the price, they can attract buyers away from other sellers. The competition among sellers will cause the price to fall. The fall in the price of corn will encourage consumption and discourage supply. Some buyers unwilling to purchase at $4 per bushel will now buy at $3. Some sellers willing to sell at $4 will not sell at $3. Through the automatic fall in the price, the surplus will disappear. (See Example 3.2.)

Equilibrium

The **equilibrium** or **market-clearing price** is the price at which the quantity demanded equals the quantity supplied by producers. It is called the *equilibrium price* because there is no automatic tendency to move away from it.

The **equilibrium** (or **market-clearing**) **price** is the price at which the quantity demanded by consumers equals the quantity supplied by producers. This price is called the *equilibrium price* because there is no automatic tendency to move away from this price. Markets will seek this equilibrium price unless there are legal or other restriction.

According to the supply and demand curves of Figure 3.5, there will be no shortage or surplus when the price of corn is $3 per bushel. At this price, consumers want to buy 30 million bushels and producers want to sell 30 million bushels. The equilibrium price is $3; the equilibrium quantity is 30 million bushels.

FIGURE 3.5 Market Equilibrium

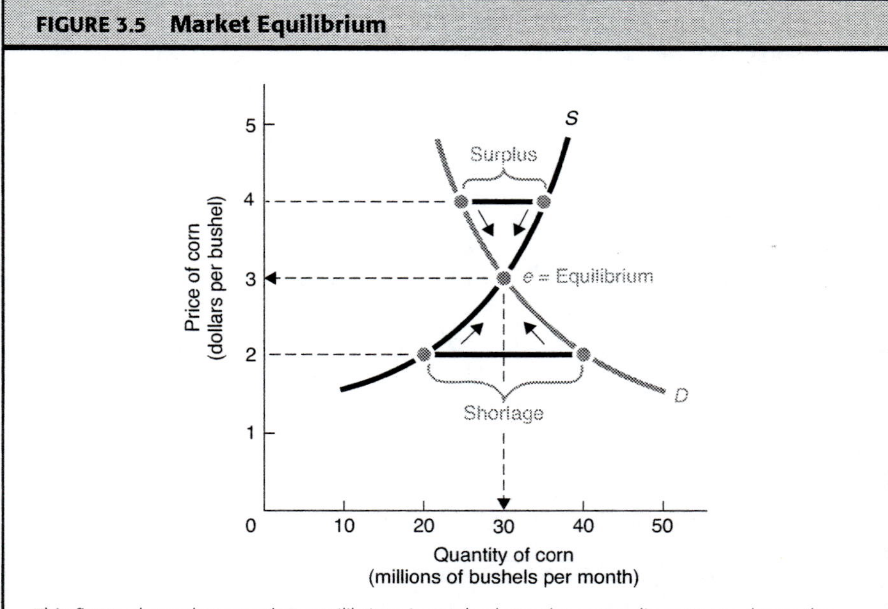

This figure shows how market equilibrium is reached. On the same diagram are drawn the demand and the supply curves for corn. When the price of corn is $2, the quantity demanded is 40 million bushels, but the quantity supplied is only 20 million bushels. The result is a shortage of 20 million bushels of corn. Unsatisfied buyers will bid the price up. Raising the price will reduce the shortage.

When the price of corn is raised to $4 per bushel, the quantity demanded is 25 million bushels while the quantity supplied is 35 million bushels. The result is a surplus of 10 million bushels of corn. This surplus will cause the price of corn to fall as unsatisfied sellers bid the price down to get rid of excess inventories of corn. As the price falls the surplus will diminish.

The equilibrium price is $3 because the quantity demanded at that price equals the quantity supplied. The equilibrium quantity is 30 million bushels.

EXAMPLE 3.2 ELECTRICITY CONSERVATION, PRICE, AND SHORTAGE

Example 1.2 discussed the electricity blackout of August 2003 in terms of the "economic system" of delivering electricity to homes and business. It showed how high summer temperatures could create a peak demand that would activate supply bottlenecks that could cause the system to fail in large parts of the country. This chapter teaches that the demand for products is determined by the price and that during periods of high demand the price tends to rise, thereby cutting back on the quantity demanded. Unlike other products, the price of electricity usually does not change with demand. We pay the same price for electricity throughout the day or week, irrespective of whether the demand is high or low. For example, the demand for electricity is higher during the day than at night, but the daytime price is the same as the nighttime price, although complex metering technology exists that would allow electric companies to charge higher prices for peak load periods. Without the flexibility to charge higher prices for peak load periods, the electricity supply system must be constituted to be able to meet the highest possible demand without raising the price. On those rare occasions where this is not possible, electric supplies must be cut to users. Cuts take the form of rolling blackouts, brownouts, or, in the worst cases, system failure.

Economists have long argued that we can avoid blackouts simply by allowing prices to adjust to changes in demand. The accompanying figure contrasts the current system of pricing with that proposed by many economists.

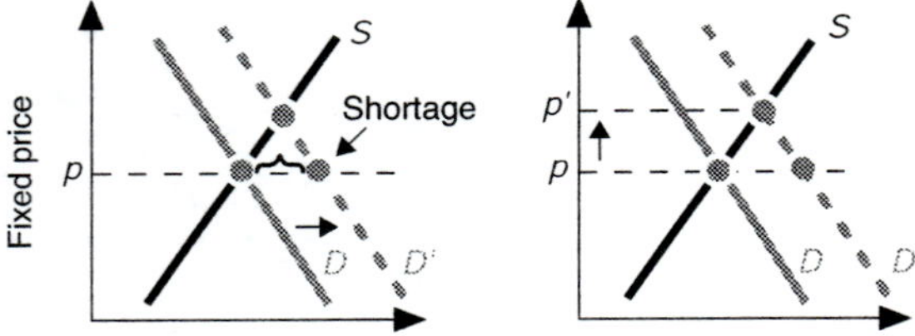

FIGURE 3.6 Increases in Electricity Demand with Fixed and Flexible (Peak Load) Prices
Explanation: In both cases, there is an enormous increase in the demand for electricity, say, due to high temperatures. In the left-hand diagram, prices cannot increase and a shortage of electricity exists, taking the form of rolling blackouts or system failure. In the right-hand case, the price rises (due to peak load pricing) so that the shortage is avoided. Instead of being without electricity, we pay more.

The equilibrium of supply and demand is stationary in the sense that price will tend not to change once the equilibrium price is reached. Movements away from the equilibrium price will create either shortages or surpluses, and the price will be returned to equilibrium by the bidding of excess buyers or sellers in the market place. The equilibrium price is like a rocking chair at rest; give it a gentle shove, and the original position will be restored after a little while. If, however, something happens to shift either the supply or the demand curve, a new equilibrium price will be established.

Changes in Equilibrium

An equilibrium price equates quantity demanded with quantity supplied. It is stable in the sense that movement away from the equilibrium price creates the shortages and surpluses that automatically return the market to equilibrium. Yet prices are always changing. Sometimes prices go up, and sometimes they go down. In relative price terms, prices go down as often as they go up. Prices change because of shifts in supply and demand curves.

Let's see how this occurs.

Changes in Demand

Increases in demand (rightward shifts in demand curves) cause both the equilibrium price and quantity to increase. Reductions in demand (leftward shifts in demand) cause both the equilibrium price and quantity to fall.

When the prices of substitutes rise, the prices of complements fall, preferences change in favor of the product, the number of buyers expands, or higher prices are expected in the future, the demand curve shifts to the right (demand increases). Movements of these factors in the opposite directions will cause the demand curve to shift to the left.

In Figure 3.7 we show the effect of an increase in demand on the equilibrium price. Say restrictions against U.S. corn imports are dropped, allowing the Japanese to purchase

FIGURE 3.7 An Increase in the Demand for Corn

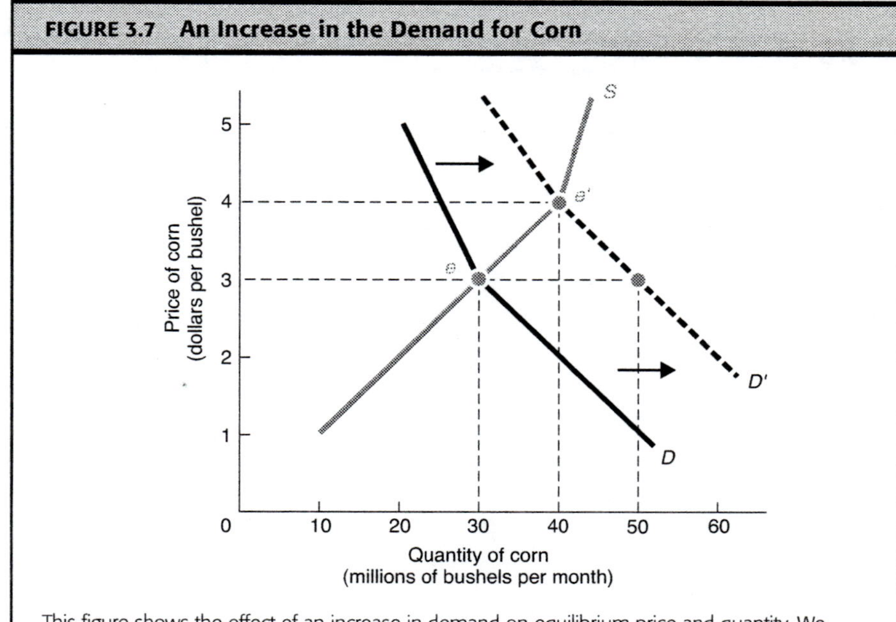

This figure shows the effect of an increase in demand on equilibrium price and quantity. We begin with the market for corn in equilibrium at *e* at a price of $3 per bushel and a quantity of 30 million bushels per month. Suppose demand increases because the number of buyers increases due to the dropping of Japanese trade restrictions against U.S. corn (the demand curve shifts from *D* to *D′*). $3 is no longer an equilibrium price because quantity demanded (50 million) exceeds quantity supplied (30 million). The price rises, and there is a movement up the supply curve to the new equilibrium at *e′* where the price is $4 and the equilibrium quantity is 40 million. The increase in demand causes both equilibrium price and quantity to increase.

American corn. Because additional buyers are in the market, demand increases from D to D'. The rightward shift of the demand curve has created a shortage at the original price. This shortage will cause buyers to bid up the price. As the price rises, there is a movement up the supply curve until a new equilibrium price is reached. At the new equilibrium, there are both a higher price and a higher equilibrium quantity.

Changes in Supply

An increase in supply causes the equilibrium price to fall and the equilibrium quantity to rise. A decrease in supply causes the equilibrium price to rise and the equilibrium quantity to fall.

The factors that cause increases in supply are reductions in the price of other products, reductions in prices of relevant resources, increases in the number of sellers, and technological improvements. Movements of these factors in the opposite direction reduce supply. In Figure 3.8 we illustrate the effect of an increase in supply (rightward shift of the supply curve) on the equilibrium price and quantity. In this case, let us say that the price of soybeans falls by 50 percent and farmers switch to the production of more corn and less soybeans. The supply of corn rises (the supply curve shifts to the right from S to S'). What happens to equilibrium price and quantity? At the original price of \$3 buyers are still prepared to buy 30 million bushels (nothing has happened to demand), but sellers are now prepared to sell 40 million bushels. The increase in supply has created a surplus of corn. Sellers of corn, unable to find customers, will bid down the price of corn. As the price falls, there is a movement

FIGURE 3.8 An Increase in the Supply of Corn

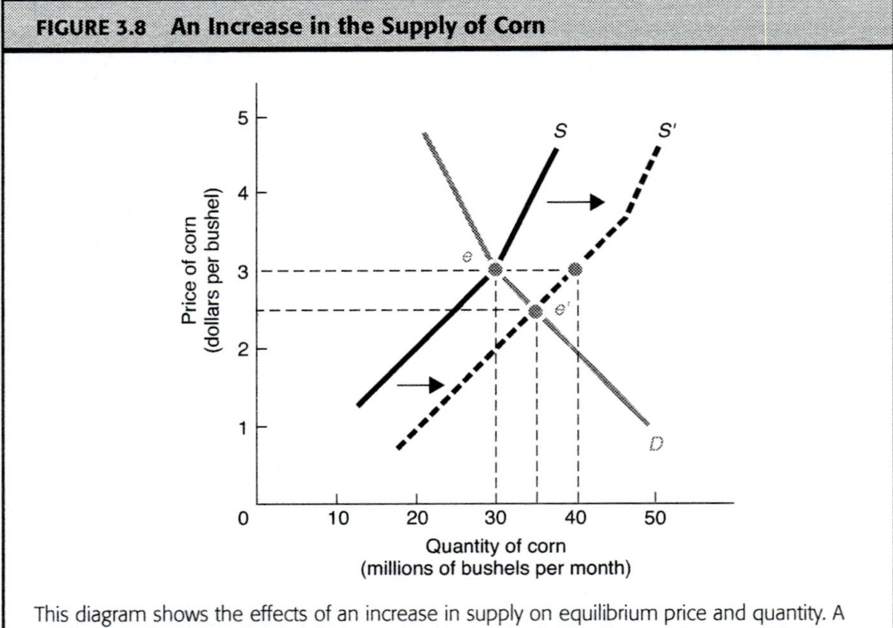

This diagram shows the effects of an increase in supply on equilibrium price and quantity. A reduction in the price of soybeans increases the supply of corn (the supply curve shifts from S to S'). The original price of \$3 is no longer an equilibrium price because the quantity supplied now exceeds the quantity demanded. The price is bid down, and there is movement down the demand curve until the new equilibrium at a price of \$2.50 and a quantity of 35 million is reached. The increase in supply increases quantity and lowers price.

down the demand curve *D* until a new equilibrium price is achieved. At the new equilibrium, the price is lower ($2.50) and the quantity (35 million bushels) is higher.

Example 3.3 uses honey prices to illustrate changes in prices due to shifts in supply and the resulting substitutions that such price changes cause.

EXAMPLE 3.3 HONEY PRICES, DUMPING, CHINESE ANTIBIOTICS, AND SUMMER DROUGHTS

For decades, the price of honey in the United States has been around $.50 per pound, but in midsummer 2003 the price reached $1.75 per pound, a "golden era" price that pleased honey producers from the South, Midwest, and Great Plains. The high 2003 honey price can be explained by supply and demand factors. On the demand side, honey consumption tends to grow as the population expands. The supply side, on the other hand, depends on weather conditions and on the number of foreign suppliers. The lack of rain in the Midwest and Great Plains depressed the production of honey in both 2002 and 2003. Also starting in the summer of 2001, the U.S. Department of Commerce agreed that two major importers (China and Argentina) were dumping their honey on the U.S. market at below-production costs and assessed new tariffs (taxes on imports). Imports from China were further depressed when it was discovered that China was using an unapproved antibiotic in its honey production.

This chapter teaches that higher relative prices cause consumers to switch to substitutes. Indeed, a spokesperson for the Grocery Manufacturers of America stated that some food makers were changing their honey use. Three major users of honey in breakfast cereals, Kellogg, General Mills, and Kraft, were being closely watched to see if they were switching from honey to syrups to keep their production costs steady.

The accompanying graph uses supply and demand to illustrate the increase in the price of honey.

FIGURE 3.9

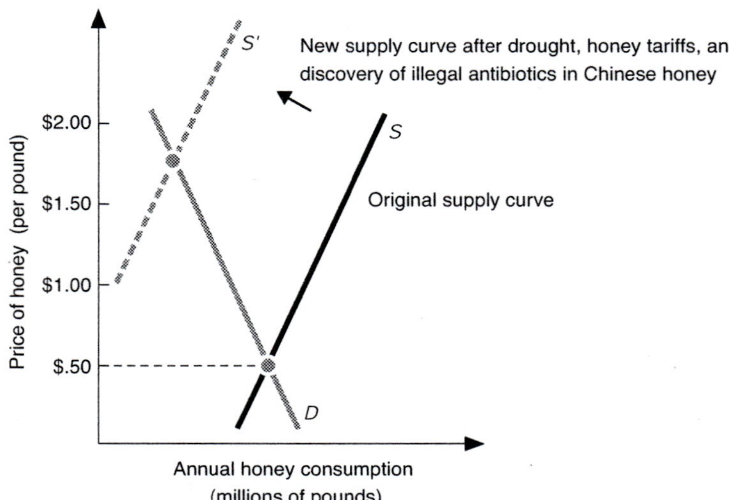

Source: "Pressure on Honey Prices May Sting Beekeepers in the U.S.," *Wall Street Journal,* 8 August 2003, P. C1.

Generalizations Figures 3.7 and 3.8 show what happens to prices and quantities when either demand or supply increases. Increases in demand raise prices and quantities, ceteris paribus. Increases in supply lower prices and raise quantities, ceteris paribus.

Figure 3.10 shows the effects of all possible combinations of supply and demand changes on equilibrium prices and quantities.

FIGURE 3.10 Summary of Effects of Supply Curve and Demand Curve Shifts

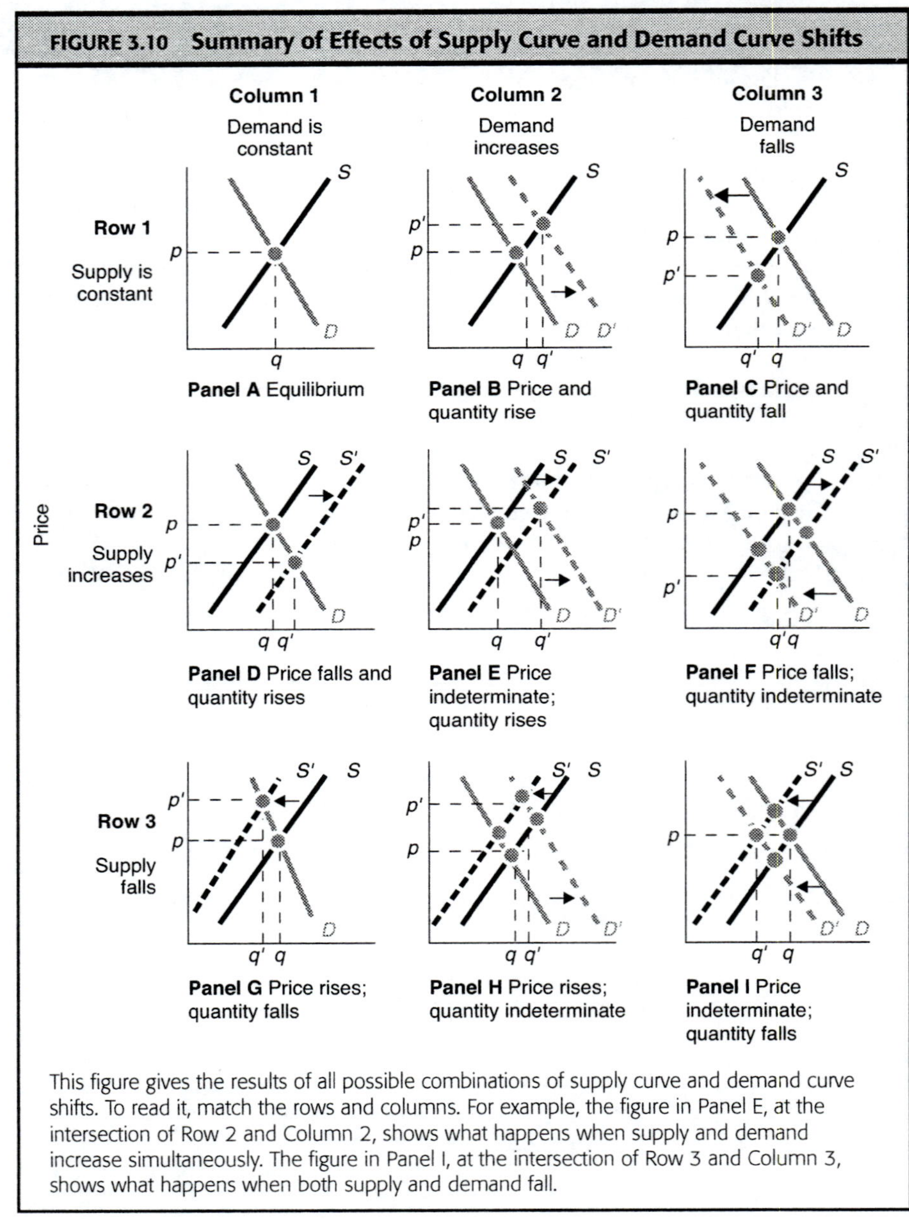

This figure gives the results of all possible combinations of supply curve and demand curve shifts. To read it, match the rows and columns. For example, the figure in Panel E, at the intersection of Row 2 and Column 2, shows what happens when supply and demand increase simultaneously. The figure in Panel I, at the intersection of Row 3 and Column 3, shows what happens when both supply and demand fall.

Elasticity and Price

Elasticity measures responsiveness to price changes.

Elasticities measure the degree of responsiveness to price changes of quantity demanded and supplied. If firms do not increase quantity supplied when the price rises, an increase in demand will push up the price substantially. People want to buy more at each price level, but firms are not supplying more. Something has to give, and the "give" is a much higher equilibrium price. If people are not prepared to buy more at a lower price, an increase in supply will translate into much lower prices. Firms are prepared to supply more at each price, but people are not prepared to buy more. Again something must give, and that "give" is a much lower equilibrium price.

Price Elasticity of Demand

The **price elasticity of demand** is the absolute value of the percentage change in quantity demanded divided by the percentage change in price.

The **price elasticity of demand** is the absolute value of the percentage change in quantity demanded divided by the percentage change in price.

Because of the law of demand, if the price rises, the quantity demanded falls. If the price of airplane tickets rises 10 percent and the quantity demanded falls 5 percent, the percentage change in quantity divided by the percentage change in price for airline tickets is –0.5. But, for the sake of simplicity, we ignore the negative sign by using the absolute value.

The price elasticity of demand can vary from 0 (absolutely no response to price changes) to an infinitely large response. Elasticities are divided into three categories:

1. When price elasticity of demand is greater than 1, demand is elastic.
2. When price elasticity of demand is equal to 1, demand is unitary elastic.
3. When price elasticity of demand is less than 1, demand is inelastic.

As a rule of thumb, an elastic demand curve can be shown as having a less steep slope than an inelastic demand curve. (See Figure 3.11.)

Price elasticity of demand depends on substitutes, importance in the budget, and time for adjustment.

Determinants of Price Elasticity of Demand The three determinants of the price elasticity of demand are (1) the availability of substitutes, (2) the relative importance of the good in the budget, and (3) the amount of time required to adjust to the price change.

The greater the number of substitutes, the more elastic is the demand. If a large number of good substitutes exist for a product, an increase in its price causes buyers to abandon that product for its substitutes. If tourist prices in Hawaii rise, people can readily substitute Caribbean or Florida vacations. However, if the price of prescripton medications goes up, people will be hard pressed to substitute, and the response of quantity demanded should be small.

Goods that make up a small fraction of the consumer's budget, such as salt, tooth picks, and drinking water, are more inelastic in demand than products that make up a large portion of the budget, like gasoline, mortgage payments, and fuel oil. An increase in the price of salt from $0.20 to $0.25 per package might raise the average family's cost of living by only $0.10 per year. A similar percentage increase in the price of gasoline might raise the average family's cost of living by $350 per year. Consumers would scarcely notice the price increase of salt, but they definitely would notice the gas price increase and so would respond more strongly than in the case of salt.

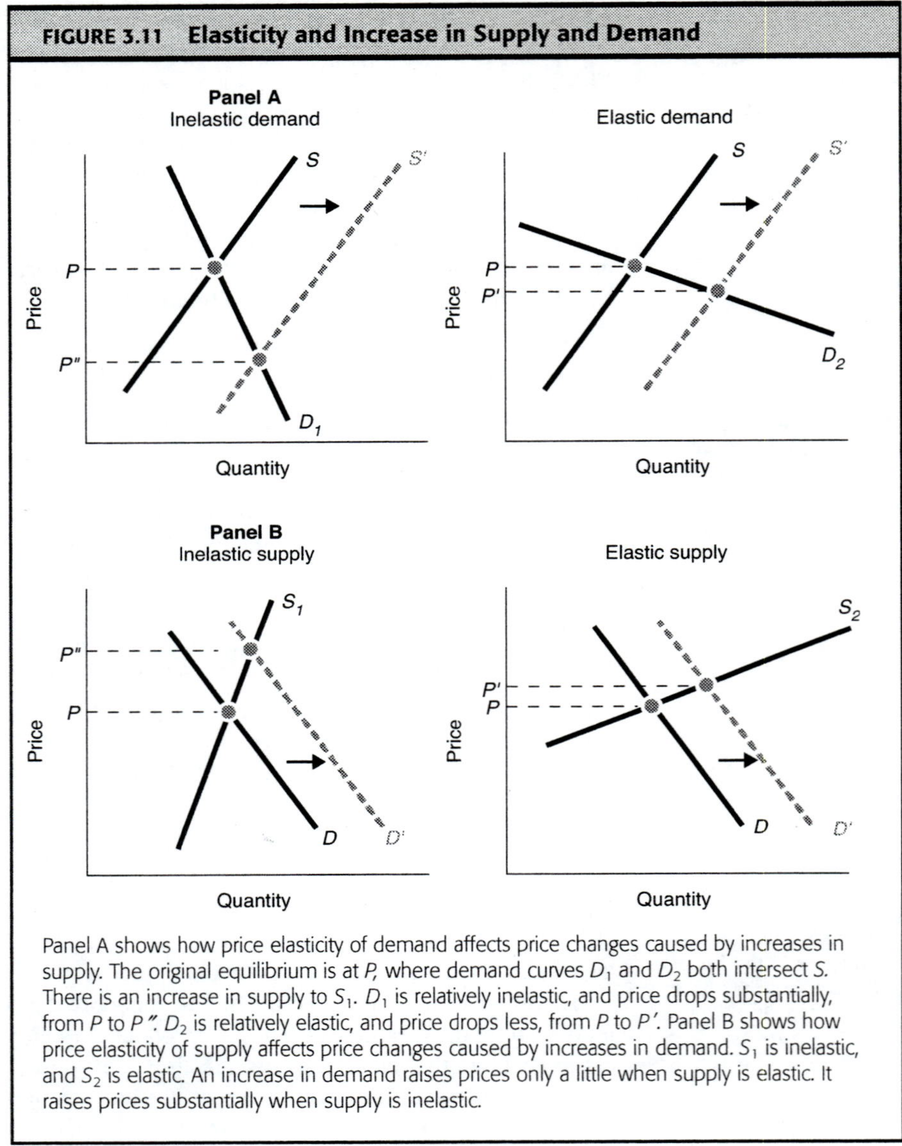

FIGURE 3.11 Elasticity and Increase in Supply and Demand

Panel A shows how price elasticity of demand affects price changes caused by increases in supply. The original equilibrium is at *P*, where demand curves D_1 and D_2 both intersect *S*. There is an increase in supply to S_1. D_1 is relatively inelastic, and price drops substantially, from *P* to *P″*. D_2 is relatively elastic, and price drops less, from *P* to *P′*. Panel B shows how price elasticity of supply affects price changes caused by increases in demand. S_1 is inelastic, and S_2 is elastic. An increase in demand raises prices only a little when supply is elastic. It raises prices substantially when supply is inelastic.

The longer the time period people have to adjust to price changes, the more elastic is the demand. Consider the response to higher electricity prices. Immediately after the price increase, consumers can do little more than lower their heating thermostats. As time passes, however, they can install more insulation, buy more energy-efficient heating systems, and substitute gas heating systems for electrical systems. With time, they can also break habits. For example, if a family is accustomed to having fresh fruit daily and the price of fresh fruit rises, it may take time to break the habit.

EXAMPLE 3.4 ELASTICITIES AND SMOKING: WHO PAYS AND WILL HIGHER TAXES STOP SMOKING?

Cigarette taxes are used to raise government revenues and to reduce smoking. The federal cigarette excise tax was $0.39 per pack in 2002, and state excise taxes varied from $0.025 per pack in Virginia to $1.50 in Massachusetts. Federal and state government collect almost $20 billion annually from cigarette taxes. Elasticities allow us to study who ultimately pays for cigarette taxes, how much revenue they raise, and whether such taxes cut back on smoking.

The figure shows the elasticity of demand for cigarettes in a short-run scenario (Panel A), in which smokers cut back very little when cigarette prices rise (an inelastic demand), and a longer-run scenario (Panel B), where smokers do cut back considerably in response to higher prices (a more elastic demand).

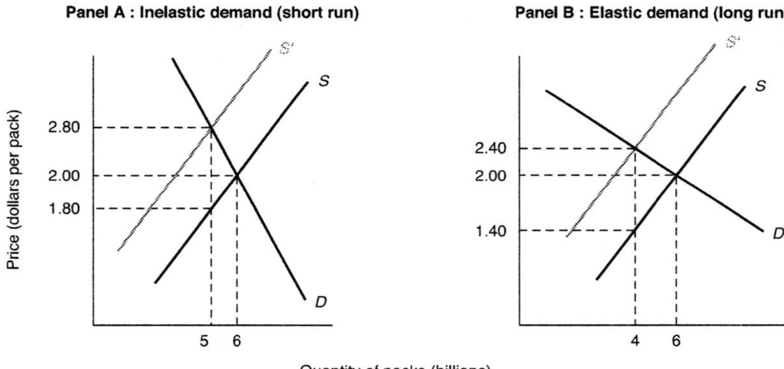

In both panels, *S* refers to the supply curve before a $1 tax increase. The tax increase shifts *S* up vertically by $1. As less is supplied than before at each *P*, the price rises. In A, smokers don't cut back; therefore the price rise is substantial and reaches $2.80. In B, smokers cut back considerably and the price rises to $2.40. In A, smokers pay for 80 percent of the tax via the 80-cent price increase. In B, smokers pay for 40 percent of the tax in the form of a 40-cent price increase. When demand is inelastic, a tax increase on cigarettes is paid for predominantly by the smokers themselves. If demand is elastic in the long run, more of the burden of the tax falls on cigarette manufactures, who cannot pass the tax to smokers as higher prices. Note the effect of elasticities on tax revenues. In A, the quantity sold is 5 billion for a $5 billion tax. In B, the quantity sold is 4 billion for a $4 billion tax.

Price Elasticity of Supply

The **price elasticity of supply** is the percentage change in quantity supplied divided by the percentage change in price.

The elasticity of supply measures the responsiveness of producers to price changes. The **price elasticity of supply** is the percentage change in the quantity supplied divided by the percentage change in price. Because supply curves are normally positively sloped, price and quantity supplied move in the same direction and the price elasticity of supply is positive. Like elasticity of demand, the price elasticity of supply is broken down into elastic (elasticity of supply greater than 1), inelastic (elasticity of supply less than 1), and unitary elastic (elasticity of supply equals 1) categories.

In general, the more time the producer has to adjust to price changes, the greater the elasticity of supply.

Although there are a number of determinants of elasticity of supply, the most important is the amount of time producers have to adjust to price changes. In general, the more time the producer has to adjust, the greater the elasticity of supply.

As the price rises, the producer may have limited flexibility to respond. If the price of wheat rises after the crop has been planted, the wheat farmer can use more fertilizer or hire more labor to weed, but the major response must wait until the next growing season, when the farmer can plant more wheat. As the price of compact cars rises, automobile manufacturers must retool existing plants and build new plants before they can increase their output of compact cars by more than a modest amount. As time passes, adjustments to price changes have been completed, and the supply response to price changes becomes more elastic.

When supply or demand curves shift, the size of the resulting price change depends on the elasticities of demand and supply. In the top part of Figure 3.11 we show how the price effect of an increase in supply (from S to S') depends on the price elasticity of demand. One demand curve is relatively inelastic; the other is more elastic. The increase in supply lowers the equilibrium price more for the inelastic demand curve. The bottom part of the figure shows that a similar rule holds for demand increases. The more inelastic the supply, the greater the price increase resulting from demand increases. (See Example 3.4 for an application of elasticities to smoking.)

Summary

1. Demand is that amount of a good that people are actually prepared to buy at prevailing prices and income. The demand curve shows the quantities demanded at different prices, ceteris paribus.
2. The law of demand states that there is an inverse relationship between quantity demanded and price. The law of demand is explained by income and substitution effects.
3. Demand curves shift when there are changes in prices of related goods, consumer income, preferences, the number of buyers, or expectations. Demand increases when the curve shifts to the right. An increase in purchases because of a rightward shift of the demand curve is called an *increase in demand.* An increase in purchases because of a lowering of price is called an *increase in the quantity demanded.*
4. The supply curve shows the quantities of a good offered for sale at different prices. Under normal circumstances, the supply curve is positively sloped.
5. The supply curve shifts with changes in relevant factors such as the prices of other goods, prices of resources, technology changes, and number of sellers. Increases in supply occur when the supply curve shifts to the right because of changes in these other factors. An increase in the quantity supplied occurs when there is a movement up the supply curve because of a higher price.
6. The equilibrium price is the one at which the quantity demanded equals the quantity supplied. If the price is above the equilibrium price, a surplus will result—quantity supplied exceeds quantity demanded. If the price is below the equilibrium, a shortage will result—quantity demanded exceeds quantity supplied.

7. The price remains at equilibrium unless there is a shift in supply or demand.
8. Increases in demand cause both the equilibrium price and the quantity to increase. Increases in supply cause the equilibrium price to fall and the quantity to rise.
9. Price elasticities measure the responsiveness of quantity supplied or quantity demanded to price changes. The price elasticity of demand is the absolute value of percentage change in the quantity demanded divided by the percentage change in price. The price elasticity of supply is the percentage change in quantity supplied divided by the percentage change in price. Elasticities are divided into three categories: elastic, unitary elastic, and inelastic.
10. The determinants of price elasticity of demand are availability of substitutes, relative importance in the budget, and adjustment time. Elasticities determine by how much equilibrium prices and quantities change when the equilibrium is disrupted. Elasticity of supply depends on adjustment time.

Questions and Problems

1. *Wants* and *demand* can be defined exactly in economics; *needs* cannot. Explain why this is so.
2. Give an example of a good or service where a reduction in price would set in motion a substantial income effect. Give a counterexample of a good or service where an increase in price would create a minuscule income effect.
3. On January 1, consumers are observed buying 10,000 widgets per day at a price of $5 per unit. On January 2, they are observed buying 8000 widgets per day at a price of $5 per unit. Is this a decrease in demand or a decrease in quantity demanded?
4. Construct an example that gives a simultaneous increase in demand and in quantity demanded.
5. "As a consequence of higher milk prices, dairy farmers are producing less cheese." Is this a reduction in supply or a reduction in quantity supplied?
6. Which of the following goods are likely to be inferior goods? Explain your answers.

   a. Margarine
   b. Hot dogs
   c. Dog food
   d. Apartments

7. Plot the supply and demand curves from the data given in the accompanying table.

Price (dollars)	*Quantity Demanded*	*Quantity Supplied*
$10	10	50
8	20	40
6	30	30
2	40	20
0	50	10

a. What equilibrium price/quantity combination would this market establish?
b. Is this a scarce good? Explain.
c. If the price of a substitute rose and people now want to buy twice as much as before at each price, what would happen? Why?
d. If this is a normal good, income rises, and there is an improvement in the technology required to produce this good, what will happen to equilibrium price and quantity?

8. Which of the following statements uses incorrect terminology? Which one uses correct terminology?

a. The price cutting among personal computer manufacturers has increased the demand for personal computers.
b. The reduced price of Japanese imports has reduced the demand for American automobiles.

9. Explain what will happen to the equilibrium price/quantity combination when there is a simultaneous reduction in demand and supply.
10. If you were an American manufacturer of shoes, what would your attitude be toward laws that make it more difficult for foreign-made shoes to enter the United States? Why?
11. From the data in Question 7, calculate at least two elasticities of supply and two elasticities of demand.
12. From the following pairs of goods and services, explain which should have a higher price elasticity of demand:

a. Matches/automobiles
b. Local telephone service/long-distance telephone service

13. The price of Product *X* falls from $100 to $50 and the number of units sold increases by 500 units. From this information, what can you conclude about price elasticity of demand?
14. Price changes do not bring about any change in the quantity demanded of Product *X*. Price changes do bring about an increase in the quantity supplied of Product *X*. What is the price elasticity of demand? Who will bear the burden of a tax per unit of output, the consumer or the producer?
15. Use Figure 3.8 to explain what happens to price and quantity when demand increases and supply increases, and when supply falls and demand increases.
16. In the following pairs of products, pick the one that would have the higher price elasticity of demand and explain why.

Salt–meat
Insulin–aspirin
Trucks–Ford trucks

CHAPTER 4

INFORMATION, THE INTERNET, E-COMMERCE, AND FINANCIAL MARKETS

Chapter Preview

Markets require information. In order for transactions between a buyer and seller to take place, buyers and sellers must be able to communicate, and they must have information about products, prices, and assortments of products. The previous chapter pointed out that markets bring buyers and sellers of a particular product together to determine conditions of exchange, such as prices, quantities, delivery dates, guarantees, and so on. This chapter studies how markets use information in various forms; how various information specialists bring buyers and sellers together and earn returns from such activities; and how the technologies of information generation and distribution evolve and thereby change, often fundamentally, how markets operate. The earliest markets, for example, brought buyers and sellers face to face at market fairs or village markets to which buyers and sellers traveled by primitive means of transport. Early-twentieth-century markets, via the telegraph or teletype, brought buyers and sellers together regardless of location. Today's markets, which use personal computers operating through the World Wide Web (the Web) to bring buyers and sellers together, allow them to buy and sell stocks (the NASDAQ stock exchange) and books (Amazon.com) and to pay bills through online checking. A buyer in Malaysia can buy shares of stock electronically almost as quickly as a buyer sitting next door to the NASDAQ building in New York City.

Information and Prices

Frederick Hayek, a Nobel laureate in economics, writes about the efficiency with which markets process information "to secure the best use of resources known to any member of society, for ends whose relative importance only these individuals know."

Hayek further writes of the price system: "The marvel is that in a case like that of a scarcity of one raw material, without an order being issued, without more than perhaps a handful of people knowing the cause, tens of thousands of people whose identity could not be ascertained by months of investigation, are made to use the material or its products more sparingly."[1]

[1]Frederick A. Hayek, "The Use of Knowledge in Society." *American Economic Review* 35. no. 4 (Sept. 1945): 519– 530.

Each agent specializes in economic information that is personally relevant. Workers know wage rates, relative prices of consumer goods, and interest rates on home mortgages. The computer manufacturer knows prices of competing manufacturers, the prices of microchips, and the costs of advertising. The professional investor specializes in the relative prices of stocks, bonds, and real estate.

Economic agents need only know the prices of the things that are significant to them.

Information is a scarce good. Some people make their living from information. Real estate brokers know the locations and prices of homes. Investment bankers know where to find investors for companies that need capital.

Information Costs

Information costs are the costs in time and money of acquiring information on prices today and in the future and on product qualities.

People are not perfectly informed about prices today or in the future; they do not know exactly the qualities of the products they buy. Information is a scarce and valuable commodity. Information is costly because we have limited capacities to process, store, and retrieve facts about prices, qualities, and locations of products. **Information costs** are the costs, in time and money, of acquiring information on prices today and in the future and on product qualities.

"Time is money," and we must spend time, on the telephone and in the car, gathering price information. We must read consumer reports and scour the newspapers for sale information. On major commercial purchases, paid consultants are hired to evaluate purchase contracts; gasoline must be purchased to drive from one auto showroom to another; stock market investors subscribe to investment newsletters.

We must choose among alternatives—we cannot have all the goods and services we want. Similarly, we cannot have all the information we want. We must decide whether to obtain information ourselves or pay people who are specialists in economic information.

Information and the Internet

Buyers and sellers require information, and the costs of acquiring information affect how markets function. Markets characterized by limited and expensive information, such as illicit international arms sales or insurance against rare and catastrophic events, are populated by few buyers and sellers, and the prices that are paid must cover the high cost of gathering and processing information. In some cases, the costs of acquiring information are so high that the market cannot function and the product is not offered at all; one such product is private insurance against unemployment. As technology improves, the cost of information falls. Prior to the telegraph, the Pony Express (mail delivery by mounted riders who changed horses at intervals) was able to deliver mail over the 2000-mile route from Missouri to California in ten days at an average speed of ten miles per hour (http://www.americanwest.com/pages/ponyexp1.html). The Pony Express went out of business when the telegraph route was completed in October 1861. The teletype machine was introduced in 1907 and reached its maturity in the 1920s, replacing the telegraph as the primary means of communicating information over long distances. The fax machine was invented in 1843 by a Scottish inventor, seven years after Samuel Morse invented the telegraph, but it was not until 1924 that the first fax photos were sent long distance for newspaper publication. The modern fax machine dates to the early 1970s when new equipment made fax machines available at a reasonable size and price.

The Internet, or "the Net," as it is called, was created in the 1960s by scientists working for the U.S. Defense Department's Advanced Research Projects Agency (now called DARPA) and research universities including the Massachusetts Institute of Technology (MIT), the University of California, Los Angeles (UCLA), and Stanford. The first Internet system comprised just four large government and university computers (http://www.isoc.org/internet/history/brief.shtml), but the advent of low-priced personal computers in the mid-1980s eventually placed computers in virtually every home, office, and classroom by the turn of the century. Moreover, new telephone and cable transmission technology brought high-speed data transmission into the home and workplace, which allowed the sending and receipt of vast amounts of information over long distances (even from continent to continent) at relatively low prices. Just as important was the creation of standard operating systems, such as Windows and MAC, which enabled computers to exchange electronic files efficiently.

The **Internet** is a global network of networks that enables computers of all kinds to directly and transparently communicate and share services throughout much of the world.

The **Internet** is a global network of networks that enables computers of all kinds to directly and transparently communicate and share services throughout much of the world. The Internet constitutes a shared global resource of information, knowledge, and means of collaboration and cooperation among individuals and organizations throughout the world (http://www.isoc.org/internet).

A **virtual market** brings buyers and sellers together in cyberspace via the Internet to make transactions and determine conditions of exchange.

For those who do not have personal computers, the Internet is available in the classroom and the public library. With hundreds of millions of the world's population connected to the Internet, a vast new technology brings together informed buyers and sellers in virtual markets. A **virtual market** brings buyers and sellers together in cyberspace via the Internet to make transactions and determine conditions of exchange.

Paying for the Internet

The Internet requires billions of dollars of investments in switching technology, mainframe computers, Web browsers, satellites, fiber-optic cables, large-capacity exchange points, routers, and capacity circuits. Although the federal government funded the early stages of development of the Internet, it is privately owned and operated. The costs of the Internet, like any other economic resource, must either be paid by someone or disappear.

Public goods were defined in Chapter 2 as goods whose use by one consumer does not reduce the use of other consumers and where nonpayers (free riders) cannot be excluded from using the product. The Internet meets the first criterion of a public good. Its capacity is so vast that users can use as much of it as they wish without reducing the consumption of others. (The traffic on some Web sites is so intense that congestion results, but such cases are rare.) The Internet does not clearly meet the second criterion, however, because technology makes it possible to screen out nonpayers.

There are a number of options of paying for the Internet:

The first option is to charge consumers for information downloaded from the Internet. If I wish to download an article in economics or science, I could be made to pay a fee (say, via credit card) before I could do so. There are indeed a large number of cases where Internet users do buy information from Web sites, but, to date, such financing covers only a small fraction of the cost of the Internet. Any number of commercial publishing ventures that sought to sell print material online, the most notable being the failed *Slate* magazine, did not succeed because not enough customers were prepared to buy online material. The major exception is online pornography, which brings in more than $2 billion in revenues annually from an estimated more than one million Web sites worldwide.

The second financing option is advertising. Just as American television and radio broadcasting have traditionally paid for themselves via advertising, the Internet today is largely financing itself through advertising in the form of irritating spam mail and pop-ups as well as more legitimate advertising. The principle of Internet advertising is the same as that of television and radio. If a Web site can generate a sufficient audience (as measured by the number of hits per day), advertisers will be willing to pay that Web site to post its messages. The more successful the Web site is in attracting viewers, the higher its advertising revenues (see Example 4.1 on Google). Currently, online advertisers spend $3.2 billion on Web advertising.

The third financing option is for the government to charge a monthly fee to Internet users, probably as a surcharge on phone or cable lines on which Internet use is detected. The collected fees would then be distributed by the government to "deserving" Web site operators or other businesses that contribute resources to the Internet. This third option is the one used in much of Europe to finance television broadcasting, such as the monthly fee charged to British television users.

A **virtual market** brings buyers and sellers together in cyberspace via the Internet to make transactions and determine conditions of exchange.

Virtual Markets

A **virtual market** brings buyers and sellers together in cyberspace via the Internet to make transactions and determine conditions of exchange. Although there existed

EXAMPLE 4.1 ADVERTISING ON GOOGLE

A Web browser is a search engine that permits Internet users to search the billions of bits of information available on the World Wide Web. Although there are a large number of Web browsers, some developed by Internet giants such as Microsoft, the dominant Web browser is Google, which has gained dominance by offering the most efficient search engine on the Web. Internet users browsing the World Wide Web for information have concluded that Google is better than other search engines at identifying the Web sites they seek. Currently, Internet users use Google more than 200 million times per day. This astonishing statistic says that sellers who advertise on Google have an opportunity to expose their products to potential consumers 200 million times per day! The Google Web site explains its advantages to potential advertisers. Through Google, advertisers can reach more potential customers than through conventional television, radio, or print media. Moreover, Google can prompt advertising messages to appear when browsers enter certain key words that identify them as potential buyers of the good or service. Advertisers are charged on a cost-per-click billing formula. *Cost-per-click* means advertisers are charged only when users click on the ad. Users throughout the world can enjoy the enormous benefits of using an efficient search engine without footing the bill. Rather, Google is paid for by advertisers.

Although Google's advertising revenues are not published, Web advertisers spend about $300 million per year on search-engine advertising. As the most used search engine, Google would get a substantial percentage of this sum.

electronic markets that brought the orders of buyers to sellers in computerized markets before the Internet (such as the NASDAQ Stock Exchange), a virtual market brings together buyers who place their orders via the Internet with sellers who offer their goods and services via the Internet. Such virtual markets that operate in cyberspace are also called *e-commerce* or *online shopping*.

Virtual markets differ in dramatic respects from traditional brick-and-mortar stores, where the shopper must be physically present in order to gain information on the assortment, prices, and quality of goods. In the case of traditional shopping, the buyer must incur costs in time, transportation, and money. Insofar as such information gathering is expensive, different customers will purchase using differing amounts of information. One buyer may buy the same good for a much higher price than another customer in a store just a few blocks away. Although virtual shoppers still incur costs of gathering information, such as the need to browse a number of e-commerce sites, presumably the expense, primarily the time expense, should be much lower. Hence, different buyers will make their purchases with approximately the same amounts of information. E-commerce merchandisers who demand higher prices should therefore lose customers unless they lower their prices to equal those of their competitors. Accordingly, the prices paid by virtual market buyers should be basically the same for the same product.

Another advantage of e-commerce is that virtual markets increase the number of buyers who can participate in the market. For sellers, virtual markets offer the prospect of higher prices because the greater the number of buyers, the higher the price, ceteris paribus. Heterogeneous, rare, and otherwise unusual products typically required specialized auction houses (such as Sotheby's) to gather together in one market a sufficient number of potential buyers. Virtual markets, such as eBay (see Example 4.2) can gather potential buyers from all parts of the globe in cyberspace to bid on goods and services offered by sellers.

E-commerce, despite its advantages, still accounts for a relatively modest (2 percent) share of the total $4 trillion of retail sales. Buyers who rely on e-commerce tend to be more sophisticated Internet users, such as broadband customers. Virtual markets also have a number of institutional details to perfect, such as guarantees of delivery, danger of Internet hackers, and general issues of reliability and reputation (see the example to see how eBay has dealt with such problems). E-commerce has been most successful in book sales (Amazon.com), airline ticket sales (Travelocity), and, surprisingly, movie and concert tickets, which host about 20 million visitors per month. Although e-commerce remains a small share of the total market, it is growing faster than traditional retail sales, so its percentage of total sales should rise in the future.

Intermediaries

In business transactions there must be a buyer and a seller. In order for transactions to take place, the parties must be aware of each other's existence. In other words, they must have information concerning the fact that the other party is a potential participant in a business deal.

Most firms produce goods and services. Some firms produce "information" that enables business firms and consumers to conduct their transactions. Such firms are run by intermediaries who specialize in information concerning exchange opportunities.

EXAMPLE 4.2 eBAY

eBay is one of the most successful e-commerce businesses. Unlike Amazon.com, it does not need expensive warehouses and storage facilities. eBay earns its revenues by charging a small fee to sellers who list their products on eBay for sale. While other dot-com companies have suffered losses in recent years, eBay has been consistently profitable, earning almost $150 million in annual profits. eBay exists in all major countries (eBay Germany, eBay Austria, eBay Canada, and so on). eBay operates a worldwide virtual auction market in which registered sellers can list products and registered buyers can enter bids for them. Participants in this virtual market can follow the progress of bids online as each auction progresses. (Usually an ending time of each auction is listed.) Products auctioned on eBay range from the ordinary to the unique or exotic. On a given day, wooden crates of rough jade ($15.95), a Tibetan bronze Buddha ($88), a 1913 Catholic dictionary ($204), a 1725 bible ($348), and an 1895 U.S. Navy steam launch engine ($2025) can be found on auction. Although hackers have broken into the accounts of eBay participants, such cases have been rare. eBay deals with problems of dishonesty by maintaining bulletin boards of comments submitted by eBay subscribers, organized by the identification number of eBay buyers and sellers. These ratings provide information on records of past honesty and reliability. A "cheating" buyer or seller would not be able to buy or sell on eBay after disclosure of negative comments.

eBay offers enormous advantages to buyers and sellers. The seller can gain access to a large number of potential buyers of unusual products by paying a small fee to eBay. Buyers have the opportunity to bid on thousands of products and services without leaving the comfort of their homes. Historically, exotic products such as Rembrandt paintings and Kennedy presidential memorabilia were auctioned by prestigious auction houses such as Sotheby's, which typically collected fees of 15 percent or more. It appears only a matter of time until rare and expensive items will be auctioned on eBay.

Intermediaries specialize in information either to bring together the parties to a transaction or to buy in order to sell again.

Intermediaries specialize in information either to bring together the parties to a transaction or to buy in order to sell again.

Real estate brokers, grocery stores, department stores, used-car dealers, auctioneers, stockbrokers, insurance agents, and travel agents are all intermediaries. All these professionals *mediate*, or stand between, ultimate buyers and sellers in return for a profit.

Why are firms and people willing to pay for information from information specialists? Suppose that a company is willing to sell its multimillion-dollar corporate jet for no less than $23 million and that somewhere a potential buyer is willing to pay at most $25 million for such an airplane. Someone with information about this opportunity could act as an intermediary. It would be possible for the seller to get $23 million, for the buyer to pay $25 million, and for the intermediary to charge as much as $2 million for the service of bringing the two together. The intermediary could either collect the difference in the form of a fee or buy the jet for $23 million and then resell it for $25 million. In both cases, the intermediary is receiving a fee for information.

Transactions arranged by intermediaries take place all the time. Realtors bring together the buyers and sellers of residential homes. Stock-market brokers bring together buyers and sellers of a particular stock. Auction houses bring together sellers of rare works of art with potential buyers.

Many people believe that intermediaries do not "earn" their fees. Yet parties to transactions can, in most situations, avoid paying the intermediary fee. We could drive to farmers' markets and to wholesale distributors of meats and dairy products instead of buying from the grocery store. The seller of the corporate jet could try to seek out a buyer without an intermediary. The intermediary, by specializing in bringing together buyers and sellers, is able to provide the service at a lower cost. As long as we voluntarily pay for intermediaries, the intermediary is supplying information at a lower cost than the user of information services could have gained.

Intermediaries, by specializing in bringing together buyers and sellers, are able to provide the service at a lower cost.

We pay for intermediaries not only for bringing buyers and sellers together. They also certify quality. The consumer is confronted with a confusing array of goods, some of which are so complicated that the buyer has much less information about product quality than the seller. In such circumstances, the intermediary certifies the quality of the good.

Intermediaries certify the quality of complicated goods.

The customer is prepared to pay a price for this service in the form of a markup over costs. The person who buys a used car from a reputable used-car dealer pays a higher price than someone who buys from a fly-by-night dealer. The buyer is paying a fee to the reputable dealer in return for certification of quality. Customers of major grocery chains and of major department stores know that if a purchased product is defective, their money will be returned. Safeway and Sears would like you to return to buy more of their products.

Manufacturers also certify quality by identifying their products with brand names. If consumers cannot distinguish the product of one manufacturer from that of all other manufacturers, there is little incentive for the manufacturer to produce products of reasonable or uniform quality. Brand names like Sara Lee, Levi's, Maytag, Apple, and Xerox serve as certifiers of product quality.

Product Liability

Firms do not want dissatisfied customers; they do not want lawsuits. Firms that want to stay in business seek to produce products that meet consumer expectations.

Nevertheless, buyers often end up with such defective products as "lemon" cars, shrinkproof dresses that shrink, and new homes with cracked foundations. Drivers are injured or even killed in vehicles with defective tires, and infants are burned in flame-resistant clothing. Who should be liable for such defects?

The two approaches to the assigning of liability are *caveat emptor* ("let the buyer beware") and *caveat venditor* ("let the seller beware"). In the case of **caveat emptor** buyers assume liability for products they purchased. In the case of **caveat venditor**, the seller assumes liability.

In **caveat emptor** ("let the buyer beware") the buyer assumes liability for defective or dangerous products.

In **caveat venditor** ("let the seller beware") the seller assumes liability for defective or dangerous products.

When consumers purchase cars, television sets, and home computers, they are typically at an information disadvantage relative to the seller. When the costs of acquiring information are very high to the buyer, it is cheaper to assign liability to the producer (caveat venditor). If the washing machine does not wash or the car does not work, the seller is responsible for setting it right.

Caveat emptor, even in the case of complex products, has advantages. First, it provides consumers with an incentive to gather information about product quality, durability, and safety. If consumers are not liable for damages, they may not be as careful in choosing products. Second, if the seller were liable for all damages, the cost of the product could become excessive. If, for example, manufacturers of sulfuric acid were liable for all personal injuries, little sulfuric acid would be supplied, and only at a high price. It is more efficient to require the manufacturer to label the product as poisonous. Third, manufacturers cannot anticipate all uses to which the product will be put. Consider a letter, received by the Clorox Company, that began: "Dear Clorox, we love your bleach. In fact we use it all the time—to brush our teeth." Clearly, it may be prohibitively expensive to design a product that is safe in all uses. An automobile manufacturer who is liable for brake failure that occurs at 150 miles per hour would be forced to produce a car that would cost the buyer more because it would have technical characteristics that are of little use to the average buyer.

Speculators

Speculators buy now to sell at a higher price.

Speculators are intermediaries who buy now to sell at a higher price either immediately or in the future. Speculators are pictured as scavengers who buy flood-damaged homes at distress prices, remove farmland from cultivation for shopping center development, or buy and sell foreign currencies or gold to make a quick profit. Crop-killing frosts, wars, and plagues all appear to provide the professional speculator with opportunities to make a profit. In reality, speculators play a positive role in the economy if they guess right.

Simple arbitrage is buying in a market where a commodity is cheap and reselling it in a market where the commodity is more expensive.

Arbitrage equalizes prices in different markets.

A speculator engages in **simple arbitrage** by buying in a market where a commodity is cheap and reselling where it is expensive. Arbitrage serves to equalize prices in different markets. For example, arbitrageurs, persons who engages in arbitrage, buy wheat in Chicago at $5.00 per bushel and resell it for $5.10 the next minute in Kansas City. By doing so, they keep the price of wheat in Chicago and Kansas City equal.

Simple arbitrage is not very risky since prices in Chicago and Kansas City can be obtained instantly by computer. Arbitrageurs must act quickly and have sharp pencils and keen minds if they are to prosper.

Arbitrage through time is buying a commodity at a time when it is cheap and reselling at a time when it is expensive.

Unlike the arbitrageur, who buys in one location and resells in another, the speculator engages in arbitrage through time. **Arbitrage through time** is buying a commodity at a time when it is cheap and reselling it at a time when it is expensive. The speculator buys goods at one time and resells at another time. Speculation is a risky business because tomorrow's prices cannot be known with certainty.

The speculator wishes to make a profit by buying low and selling high. When the speculator is making a profit and when there are enough speculators, speculation will drive prices up when they are low and down when they are high, and thus stabilize both prices and production.

Profitable speculation stabilizes prices and consumption by reducing fluctuations in prices and consumption over time.

Profitable speculation stabilizes prices and consumption over time by reducing fluctuations in prices and consumption over time. Profitable speculation is illustrated in Figure 4.1. The supply of wheat in the first period is S_1, or 4 million bushels. The supply of wheat in the second period is S_2, or 2 million bushels. Assuming that demand will not change in the two periods, if there were no speculation the price of wheat would be $3 in Period 1 and $5 in Period 2. Thus, without speculation, the prices and consumption of the two periods would vary dramatically.

FIGURE 4.1 Profitable Speculation

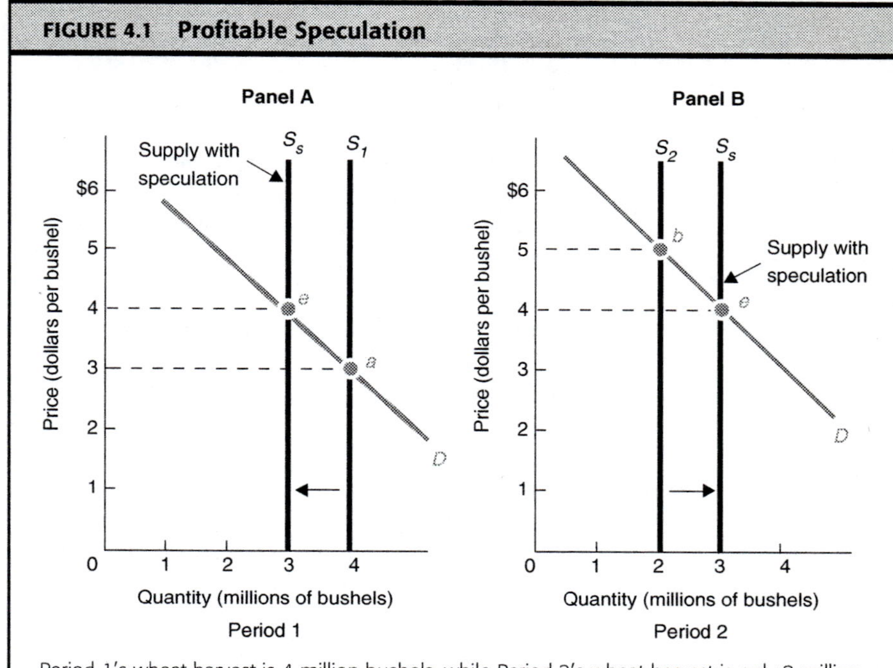

Period 1's wheat harvest is 4 million bushels, while Period 2's wheat harvest is only 2 million bushels. If there were no speculation, the price would be \$3 in Period 1 and \$5 in Period 2. Perfect speculation will cause 1 million bushels of wheat to be purchased and stored by speculators in Period 1, to be sold in Period 2. As a result, the price is driven up to \$4 in Period 1 and driven down to \$4 in Period 2. Both prices and consumption are stabilized by speculation in this case.

Profitable speculation shifts supplies from periods of relative abundance to periods of relative scarcity.

If speculators correctly anticipate the next year's wheat crop to be small, they can make handsome profits by buying at \$3 and selling in the second year at \$5. As speculators begin to buy the first year's wheat, they withdraw it from the market by placing it in storage, and the supply of wheat is reduced. If speculation is "perfect," one million bushels will be bought by speculators in the first period, driving the price up to \$4. Speculators resell this wheat in the second period. The price remains stable at \$4 in both periods, and the quantity of wheat sold on the market remains at 3 million bushels despite substantial differences in the wheat harvest in the two periods. Profitable speculation shifts supplies from periods of relative abundance to periods of relative scarcity and stabilizes prices and consumption over time.

Unprofitable speculation is destabilizing because it shifts supplies from periods of relative scarcity to periods of relative abundance and amplifies movements in prices and consumption over time.

Unprofitable speculation occurs when the speculator guesses wrong, buys at a high price, and must sell at a low price. When this occurs, speculation destabilizes prices and consumption over time. When prices would otherwise be high, speculators are buying and driving prices even higher. When prices would otherwise be low, speculators are selling and driving prices even lower. Unprofitable speculation is destabilizing because it shifts supplies from periods of relative scarcity to periods of relative abundance and amplifies movements in prices and consumption over time.

Speculators must make guesses about the future; the future is uncertain, and often they guess wrong. On balance, does society benefit from speculation? The business of speculation is populated by a core of expert, professional speculators and a revolving door of amateurs. Since decisions must be made about uncertain future events, it is probably better for such decisions to be made by the best-informed specialists rather than by amateurs. The professional speculator who survives in the business must have a knack for guessing right. Otherwise, persistent losses will drive him or her out of business. As long as the speculator guesses right, society benefits with more stable prices and consumption.

Intermediaries and the Internet

The income earned by intermediaries depends on the value of their information. If information about the availability of products, the location of buyers and sellers, and product quality and reliability is widely available, intermediaries will be paid low prices or will disappear from the scene. The Internet can provide buyers and sellers with massive amounts of information cheaply. Web sites are widely available that provide pictures and characteristics of new and used homes listed for sale; airline customers can go directly to an airline's own Web site or to a Web site of large reservation systems (such as America Airline's Sabre, Orbitz, and Travelocity) to search for the most convenient flight at the best price. Families shopping for home mortgages can browse Web sites that compare mortgage rates.

Economic theory suggests that the Internet will substantially reduce the incomes of intermediaries by providing buyers and sellers with alternate sources of information at a much lower cost. In fact, the Internet is becoming a giant electronic intermediary populated by a large number of competing Web sites offering information to all who can log on. Experience shows that buyers and sellers continue to use intermediaries in most cases, but in some cases (such as travel agencies, as in Example 4.3) the Internet has threatened their very existence. We continue to use intermediaries because the buying and selling of some products is simply too complex (such as residential homes and their financing) or because we continue to need a reliable certifier of quality.

Financial markets are markets in which financial instruments, such as stocks and corporate or government bonds, are bought and sold.

Shares of stock represent ownership shares of corporations. Once these shares have been issued, they are bought and sold (traded) on stock exchanges.

Bonds represent the debt of the issuing agency. They promise to pay the owner a rate of interest over the period of the bond's existence, called its *maturity*.

Information About the Future: Financial Markets

Financial markets are markets in which financial instruments, such as shares of stock and corporate or government bonds, are bought and sold. **Shares of stock** represent ownership shares of corporations. Once these shares have been issued (sold for the first time to the public), they are bought and sold (traded) on stock exchanges, such as the New York Stock Exchange and the NASDAQ Exchange. **Bonds** represent the debt of the issuing agency (a corporation or a government entity, such as the U.S. Treasury). They promise to pay the owner a rate of interest over the period of the bond's existence, called its *maturity*. For example, the buyer of a 15-year $100,000 corporate bond, purchased at a 5 percent rate of interest, would receive $5,000 in interest every year for 15 years, and at the end of the period would receive a principal payment of $100,000. Once these bonds are sold to the public, they are also traded in financial markets.

EXAMPLE 4.3 TRAVEL AGENTS VERSUS BUYING E-TICKETS ONLINE

Just ten years back, most airline tickets were paper tickets purchased from independent travel agents who earned their revenues by charging the airline a fee—usually around 15 percent of the ticket price. Passengers were free to buy directly from the airline by visiting its ticket office or having the ticket mailed, but they generally chose the convenience of neighborhood travel agencies. Airlines benefited from this system because travel agencies allowed them to limit the number of reservationists and ticket office locations. As the number and sophistication of Internet users expanded, airlines jumped on the opportunity to issue electronic tickets (e-tickets) themselves. They invested large amounts in the simplification of their own online reservation system and in their frequent flyer programs, which ensured that loyal customers would use electronic ticketing to earn frequent flyer miles. To encourage electronic ticketing, airlines even began adding a surcharge for paper tickets.

The airlines have conducted a protracted campaign against travel agencies, both traditional and online. Delta and United Airlines stopped paying commissions to traditional travel agents in 1995, and in 2003 Northwest and KLM announced that they would not pay commissions to online travel agencies such as Expedia and Travelocity. The only remaining way for small travel agents to earn money from ticket sales was to charge the passenger a direct surcharge (usually in the range of $25 per ticket). Large travel agencies, however, could continue to buy large blocks of tickets from airlines that needed to fill seats and then sell them for whatever price they could get. In the long run, it is expected that small travel agencies will no longer sell airlines tickets; rather, they will specialize in tours or cruises, or, more likely, go out of business.

The demise of the travel agency does deprive passengers of a key certifier of quality. When airline tickets were sold largely through travel agencies, the travel agency could transmit passenger complaints about poor service, canceled flights, and other problems directly to the carrier, and the carrier, not wishing to alienate a large intermediary, would seek to redress the problem to the customer's satisfaction. Now, with e-tickets purchased directly, the passenger's only recourse is to go directly as a single buyer to the airline, and the chances of redress are much lower.

By their very definitions, stocks and bonds are forward-looking. We buy shares of Microsoft because we believe that their value will rise in the future. We buy bonds of the U.S. Treasury or of AT&T because we hope either that the interest rate they pay will offer us reasonable compensation or even that they too will rise in value. Thus, buyers of stocks and bonds are speculators, even if they are small individual buyers earning modest incomes.

Whether we will earn profits from our financial investments is unsure because the future itself is uncertain. Shares of Microsoft will rise in value in the future if Microsoft continues to be a good innovator capable of outcompeting its rivals. They could fall in value in the future for a number of reasons; perhaps a fatal flaw may be discovered in Microsoft Windows or the Justice Department will rule that Microsoft is an unfair competitor that must be broken up into pieces. Our investment in AT&T bonds could prove disastrous if AT&T falls on hard times and is unable to repay its debt upon maturity.

Speculation in financial markets takes place on the major stock and bond exchanges, where current owners of stocks and bonds consider whether to sell, and at what price, and potential buyers consider whether to buy, and at what price. In order for a transaction to take place—for example, for 1000 shares of Microsoft to change hands—there must be an owner of 1000 shares willing to sell at that price and a buyer willing to buy at that price. The share price, like any other market price, is the price that equates the number of sellers willing to sell at that price with the number of buyers willing to buy at that price, as shown in Figure 4.2.

There are some general principles that determine stock and bond prices. In this chapter, we focus only on stock prices and use the most general explanation possible. We buy shares of stock of corporations only if we believe that the corporation will earn profits either now or in the future. If we take the hypothetical XYZ Corporation, which has one million shares of stock outstanding, no one would wish to own that stock if it were clear that it would never earn a profit. With no profits in sight, XYZ Corporation would never have any earnings to distribute to shareholders as dividends or to reinvest in the company so that its future profits would be even higher. Thus, the value of one share of XYZ Corporation stock depends on its current and future profits.

Earnings per share equals profits divided by the number of shares.

Let us say that XYZ is currently earning a profit of $10 million, which means that its **earnings per share** (profits divided by the number of shares) is $10. Let us now say that the consensus view of the financial market on which XYZ Corpora-

FIGURE 4.2 The Demand and Supply of Shares of XYZ Corporation

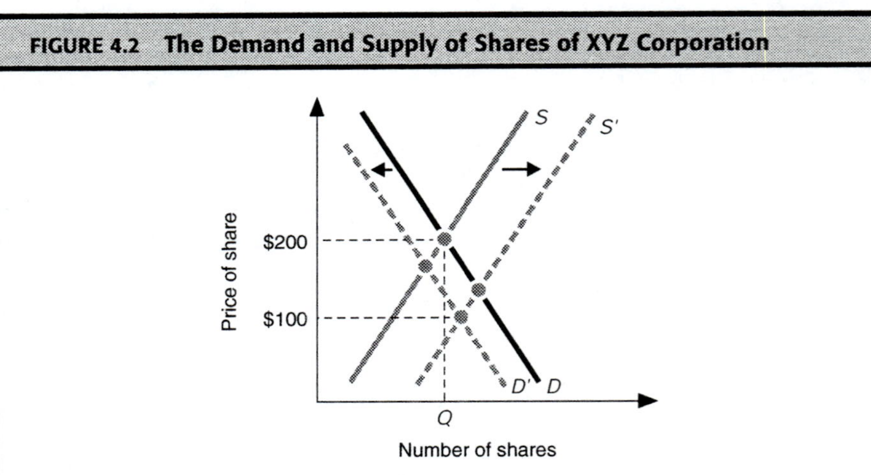

Explanation: The initial demand curve (*D*) shows the number of shares that potential buyers of XYZ stock are prepared to buy at different prices. The initial supply curve (*S*) shows the number of shares that current owners of XYZ stock are prepared to supply (sell) at different prices. The initial equilibrium price is the price at which the number of shares offered for sale equals the number of shares purchased. At this equilibrium price ($200), the marginal buyer and seller agree that earnings per share will remain at $10 forever and the interest rate is 5 percent. D′ and S′ show shifts in supply and demand as a consequence of, say, a corporate scandal within the ranks of top XYZ corporation management. Now buyers wish to buy fewer shares at the same price as before and potential sellers wish to sell more shares at the same price as before. Accordingly, the equilibrium price falls.

tion shares trades is that XYZ's profits will remain at $10 per share per year forever! (This is a useful initial simplification to help explain what is going on.) In effect, owners of one share of XYZ stock "own" the $10 of profit that will be earned each year. How much would a rational buyer be willing to pay for this $10 to be earned forever? It would be the amount of money that would have to be placed in a savings account (the principal sum being left there forever) in order to earn interest of $10 per year. The formula to calculate this principal sum is a simple one:

Principal sum = annual earning/interest rate

If the interest rate is 5 percent, you would have to deposit $200 in an interest-earning account (and leave it there) in order to earn $10 per year. According to this logic, one share of stock of XYZ Corporation should trade at $200 per share at an interest rate of 5 percent (Chapter 9 discusses how interest rates are determined). Note that if annual earnings were to rise, the share price should rise as well. If the interest rate were to fall, the share price should also rise.

Our example of XYZ Corporation, which is expected to earn the same profit, year in and year out, forever, is, of course, not realistic. Its future is uncertain; so no one knows what its future earnings will be. Some potential buyers and sellers will be pessimistic; others will view XYZ Corporation's future through rose-colored lenses. No one knows what interest rates will be in the future. Some will guess that they will rise; others that they will fall. Emotions will play a major role in determining the degree of optimism or pessimism. If a terror strike hits a major U.S. city, or if a massive power outage (of a magnitude of August 2003) hits the Northeast, people will become pessimistic. If everything appears to be going well, people will swing to a mood of optimism. If XYZ Corporation happens to be in an expanding industry, people will be optimistic about its future profits. If an accounting or management scandal is announced on the front pages of the financial press, people will want to get rid of XYZ shares before matters get worse.

Figure 4.2 shows these swings in mood relating to the shares of stock of XYZ Corporation. The leftward shift of the demand curve shows potential buyers becoming more pessimistic about future profits of XYZ Corporation. The rightward shift of the supply curve shows current owners becoming more pessimistic and wishing to sell their shares as fast as possible.

Financial markets tell us what people think of the future. A rising stock market means that we are growing more optimistic about our future. A falling stock market shows that a mood of pessimism is spreading. Movements in financial markets may be more meaningful than other measures of sentiment. When we buy or sell financial instruments we are betting with our own money, and we take the time and effort to make the best choices possible. We do not want to throw away our money. On the other hand, if we merely are asked by a pollster whether we are becoming more optimistic or pessimistic, we stand to lose nothing, and our answer will be less informed and less valuable as a purveyor of information about the future (See Example 4.4 on the proposed terrorism futures market).

Financial markets tell us what people who are willing to risk their money think of the future. Expectations are constantly changing. In fact, stock prices tend to change not when corporate profits themselves change but rather when corporate profits are different from the level that was anticipated by financial markets. Hence, XYZ

EXAMPLE 4.4 DARPA'S TERRORISM FUTURES MARKET

The Defense Advanced Research Projects Agency (DARPA) was one of the developers of the Internet and has the reputation for thinking outside the envelope. In the summer of 2003, DARPA proposed a futures market for terrorist activities that would allow bettors to bet on the likelihood of terrorist events. Speculators could bet in DARPA's Policy Analysis Market on specific events happening within a designated period of time, such as the overthrow of the king of Jordan, the assassination of Yasser Arafat, or a missile launch by North Korea. The idea of the Policy Analysis Market was inspired by the fact that the Iowa Election Market, set up by University of Iowa economists, in which speculators bet on political elections, outperformed polling organizations. It appears that we can obtain better predictors of some events through a market in which people are actually risking their money.

The notion of creating such a futures market in terrorism was quickly dropped after it set off a firestorm of protest. One senator blasted the plan for offering profit potential to anonymous bidders in the case of catastrophes. Another commentator speculated that the Pentagon dropped its plan when it learned that a very active market in terrorism futures has already existed for some time. Tradesports is a live (i.e., real money at risk) marketplace where futures are traded on, among other things, future security alert levels and the likelihood of Osama bin Laden's capture (www.interesting-people.org/archives/interesting-people/200307/msg00165.html).

Corporation's stock would not fall upon news that its profits had declined *if* potential buyers and sellers of XYZ stock had anticipated the decline in profits. Financial markets respond when something unexpected happens.

Summary

1. Information is a scarce good. There are costs of acquiring information on prices today and in the future and on product quality. Because information is costly, buyers and sellers do not possess perfect information.
2. The high cost of information requires economic agents to specialize in the information that is relevant to them. Information is distributed among the population in bits and pieces. Some people—intermediaries and speculators—even specialize in the business of information. An intermediary buys in order to sell again, or simply brings buyers and seller together. Rarely is anyone forced to use the services of an intermediary; therefore, intermediaries must provide information at a lower cost than if the individuals involved had to gather the information themselves.
3. The Internet is a global network of computers that can speak with one another. It is largely paid for by private advertising, although it has some characteristics of a public good. The Internet has created virtual markets (also called e-commerce) that bring potential buyers and sellers together in cyberspace and has

markedly lowered the costs of information. E-commerce has also decreased the earnings of many intermediaries.

4. The two views of product liability are *caveat emptor*, "let the buyer beware," and *caveat venditor*, "let the seller beware." Caveat emptor works well when buyers possess as much information about the product as sellers do. Even when the seller has more information than the buyer, caveat emptor still has some advantages.
5. Speculators engage in arbitrage through time. Profitable speculation stabilizes prices and quantities through time. Unprofitable speculation destabilizes prices and quantities.
6. Financial markets, in which stocks and bonds and other financial instruments are traded, provide information about the future. Stock prices are based on projected earnings per share and on interest rates. Because expectations concerning future profits can change quickly, stock prices change frequently as well.

Questions and Problems

1. Using the concept of scarcity developed in earlier chapters, explain why information is a scarce good.
2. In the case of ladder manufacturers, which liability doctrine—caveat emptor or caveat venditor—would appear to you to be more appropriate?
3. In a survey of five local grocery stores, would you expect to find more price dispersion for coffee or for tea? Why?
4. A realtor may earn $50,000 for arranging the sale of a million-dollar home. Has the realtor performed a service that is actually worth this amount of money?
5. Coffee speculators buy coffee in 2004 upon hearing of bad weather in the major coffee-growing regions of the world. In 2005 the weather in these regions is even worse than the year before. Is this speculation stabilizing or destabilizing?
6. Consider what will happen to prices and quantities if speculators guess wrong and sell in periods of abundance and buy in periods of scarcity.
7. If news is released that suggests that the earnings of Microsoft Corporation will fall, what should be the effect on the price of the stock?
8. Explain why betting markets may yield more accurate predictions than other means of gathering information about the future.

PART TWO

ESSENTIALS OF MICROECONOMICS

Supply and demand are the most important analytical tools of economics. They explain how prices of goods and services, wage rates, and interest rates are determined. They show how interference with the invisible hand of supply and demand causes shortages, and they explain who will actually bear the burden of a tax when it is levied on products like cigarettes.

Microeconomics goes "behind the scenes" of supply and demand curves by examining the behavior of buyers and sellers. The demand curve shows the behavior of all buyers who make up a particular market. Individual buyers are the households that spend their money wisely, or "rationally," to get the most satisfaction possible from their limited income. Sellers are the business enterprises—the proprietorships, the partnerships, and the corporations—that also manage their resources rationally. When applied to enterprises, *rationality* means that sellers are striving to earn as large a profit as possible.

The next three chapters present the core of microeconomics. The first focuses on costs of production. Since profits equal revenues minus costs, we begin with costs in order to understand how enterprises go about earning profits. The second chapter analyzes how enterprises behave when they are faced with a great deal of competition and lack market power. The third chapter explains how enterprises that face little or no competition behave.

Adam Smith emphasized the importance of competition in his *The Wealth of Nations.* He felt it was competition that made the invisible hand work. In these chapters we examine this proposition. Why is competition a good thing and the lack of competition a bad thing?

CHAPTER 5

COSTS AND PRODUCTIVITY

Chapter Preview

This chapter focuses on business firms and the cost side of the profit equation. Business decisions are based on the firm's revenues and costs. Making a profit depends on a careful weighing of the costs and benefits of business decisions at the margin. These decisions concern the revenues that are earned through the sale of goods and services; the costs are the costs incurred in hiring the factors of production to produce goods and services.

Opportunity Costs

The **opportunity cost of any action** is the value of the next-best alternative lost.

The correct measure of the costs of any action is what has been given up by taking that action instead of another. The **opportunity cost of any action**—consumption, production, leisure, government spending—is the value of the next-best alternative. The opportunity cost of a new urban fixed-rail transit system is the value of the next most highly valued local government spending program that must be given up, such as an increase in the number of city buses. Opportunity cost is precisely defined not by *any* alternative but by the *next-best* alternative.

Business costs are measured by the next-best use of the firm's resources. The opportunity cost of expanding Microsoft's operations into Asia may be the sacrifice of a valuable opportunity to expand its operations in Europe. The cost to a small business of renting an expensive telephone switchboard may be the sacrifice of a badly needed secretarial position.

To produce goods, scarce resources must be acquired. A plant must be constructed, machinery and materials must be purchased, and managers and blue- and white-collar workers must be hired.

Because there are alternative uses for these scarce resources, a high enough price must be paid to prevent needed resources from being used elsewhere. If the firm tried to hire skilled mechanics at $2 per hour, there would be no response if mechanics can earn $25 per hour from other firms. Any prospective employer who fails to offer the same wage, or more, that skilled mechanics can earn elsewhere in a comparable job will not be able to hire them. (See Example 5.1.)

That workers must be paid what they can earn elsewhere in their next-best alternative applies to all owners of resources. The **opportunity cost of any resource**—land, labor, capital, materials—is what that resource would receive in its next-best alternative use. The opportunity cost of using an acre of land near a busy freeway for a furniture store is what that land could have earned in its next-best alternative use. If its next-best alternative were as a used-car lot at $5000 per month rent, the furniture store owner must offer at least that much to acquire the lease to the land. If the next-best use of a used Boeing 727 is to transport mail and packages at $50,000 per month, a charter airline would have to pay at least that amount to obtain the lease to the plane.

The **opportunity cost of any resource**–land, labor, capital, materials–is the payment that that resource would receive in its next-best alternative use.

Explicit and Implicit Costs

Typically, when a firm acquires resources, it makes payments for the resources. The skilled mechanic gets a weekly paycheck; the utility company's bills and lease payments must be paid. An **explicit cost,** also called an *accounting cost,* is incurred when an actual payment is made for a resource.

An **explicit cost** is incurred when an actual payment is made for a resource.

Firms also incur implicit costs in acquiring and using resources. In the case of implicit costs, no actual payments are made; no money changes hands, but these are real costs to the firm. An **implicit cost** is incurred when an alternative is sacrificed by the firm using a resource that it owns.

An **implicit cost** is incurred when an alternative is sacrificed by the firm using a resource that it owns.

Implicit costs are incurred when the firm's owner devotes his or her time and energy, which are worth money in alternate uses, to running the business. Whether or not the firm writes a paycheck to the owner, these services are still an opportunity cost. If the firm owns outright the land upon which it conducts its business, its implicit cost is the rent the land would have earned in the next-best use.

Economic Profits

A firm's costs are measured by its opportunity costs, whether they are explicit or implicit. If the firm does not include a charge for the owner's management services

EXAMPLE 5.1 WHY ACCOUNTING AND LAW PROFESSORS ARE PAID MORE

In universities and colleges, accounting and law professors earn the highest average salaries (not counting salaries of athletic coaches). English professors and professors of foreign languages earn the lowest average salaries. These wage differences are explained by opportunity costs. Accounting and law professors can earn relatively high salaries working for private industry as accountants or as corporate lawyers. If universities do not pay them their opportunity costs (which take into consideration the added amenities of being a college teacher), persons with advanced degrees in accounting and law will go elsewhere. English and language professors, on the other hand, do not have the outside earning opportunities of accountants and lawyers; therefore, they are paid less.

or for the firm's own land on which the business is operated, it is not calculating all its costs.

Economic profit equals the firm's revenues minus its total opportunity costs (explicit plus implicit costs).

Economic profits equal the firm's revenues minus its total opportunity costs (explicit plus implicit costs).

If revenues do not cover total opportunity costs, the owner will not be willing to commit entrepreneurial resources and financial capital on an ongoing basis. Resources cannot be attracted into a business activity (in the long run) unless revenues at least cover total opportunity cost.

A **normal profit** is earned when total revenues equal total opportunity costs. An economic profit is earned when total revenues exceed total opportunity costs.

A **normal profit** is earned when total revenues equal total opportunity costs. An economic profit is earned when total revenues exceed total opportunity costs. A normal profit is that profit just sufficient to persuade the owner to commit capital and entrepreneurial resources to the enterprise. A normal profit includes normal returns to committed capital and entrepreneurial effort.

The Short Run and Long Run

In the next two chapters, the operation of a profit-maximizing firm are explored. The optimal (profit-maximizing) level of output depends, in part, on how opportunity costs change with the level of output. Business firms expand their volume of output by hiring or using additional resources. As more resources are employed, the opportunity costs of production increase. The opportunity costs of the resources used to produce output depend on their prices and their productivity. The higher the resource prices, the higher the opportunity costs of production. The lower the productivity of resources, the higher the opportunity costs of production.

Variable inputs increase with output.

Time plays a role in determining resource costs. Some resources can be increased or reduced more rapidly than others. These are called **variable inputs.** Firms can augment or reduce the number of hours worked by adjusting overtime, layoffs, and the length of the workweek. Additional materials are often only a telephone call and a truck delivery away.

Fixed inputs cannot be changed in the relevant time frame.

Other resources cannot be varied within the relevant time frame. The installation of a new assembly line may require one year. The construction of a new plant may take several years. Resources with input levels that cannot be increased or reduced in the relevant time frame are called **fixed inputs.**

The **short run** is a period of time too short for plant or equipment to be varied.

Economists distinguish between the short run and long run when considering the time necessary to change input levels. The **short run** is a period of time too short for existing plant or equipment to be varied. Additional output can be produced only by increasing the variable inputs, usually labor and materials. The short run is too short a time for new businesses to enter or for established firms to permanently leave the industry. However, a firm can temporarily cease production.

The **long run** is a period of time long enough to vary all inputs and for firms to enter and leave the industry.

The **long run** is long enough to vary all inputs and for firms to enter and leave the industry. The long run is not a predetermined amount of calendar time. A new assembly line may be installed in a few weeks; building a fast-food restaurant may require three months from start to finish. A new steel furnace, on the other hand, may require several years to complete, a nuclear power plant 15 to 20 years. Engineering complexity generally determines whether the long run is a matter of weeks or of years.

Diminishing Returns

The English economist David Ricardo first wrote in the nineteenth century about the law of diminishing returns. Ricardo noted that agricultural land was in fixed supply in nineteenth-century England, and, even though other factors of production, like labor, could be increased, there were limits to the growth of agricultural output. As more and more variable inputs were added to the fixed amount of input, land, eventually these variable inputs would yield smaller and smaller additions to output. Why? Eventually, as the fixed input became overcrowded with variable inputs, as more farmhands were added to already overcrowded farmland, their extra contribution to output would become smaller and smaller.

An illustration of diminishing returns in a more modern setting is a business firm that is operating in the short run with a fixed amount of capital and a variable amount of labor. What will happen to output as the variable input, labor, increases? Of particular interest is how much extra output each successive unit of labor produces, that is, the marginal product of labor.

The **marginal product of labor** or of any variable factor is the increase in output that results from increasing the input by one unit.

The **marginal product of labor**—or of any other variable factor—is the increase in output that results from increasing the input by one unit. Figure 5.1 shows a firm that is increasing its level of output by expanding its variable factor, labor, while its stock of capital remains fixed. The first unit of labor adds 100 units to output, which rises from 0 to 100, so its marginal product (*MP*) is 100. The second unit of labor adds 150 units (output expands from 100 to 250), so the *MP* of the second unit of labor is 150. Beginning with the third unit and beyond, the *MP* of successive units of labor drops.

The **law of diminishing returns** states that as ever larger inputs of a variable factor are combined with fixed inputs, eventually its *MP* will decline.

The decline in marginal product as output expands is explained by the **law of diminishing returns,** which states that as ever larger inputs of a variable factor are combined with fixed inputs, eventually the *MP* of the variable input will decline.

Why would we expect the law of diminishing returns, applied originally to an agricultural economy, to apply to modern industrial firms? With some factors of production fixed in the short run, there will be an optimal combination of the fixed and variable inputs. At very low levels of variable input, the firm will be below this optimal combination. At some very high level of variable input, the firm will be above this optimal combination. Just like Ricardo's farm economy, eventually the fixed factor will become crowded with the variable factor. If a large steel mill were staffed by only three people, obviously the marginal product of an additional worker would be very high, because there would be too few workers for such a large plant. On the other hand, if this one plant were called upon to meet the entire world demand for steel and attempted to do so by hiring more and more workers, eventually the marginal product of additional workers would become very low. Each worker would have to share an overcrowded plant and equipment with thousands of other workers. (See Example 5.2.)

Short-Run Costs

The behavior of costs in the short run reflects the law of diminishing returns.

FIGURE 5.1 Total Output and Marginal Product

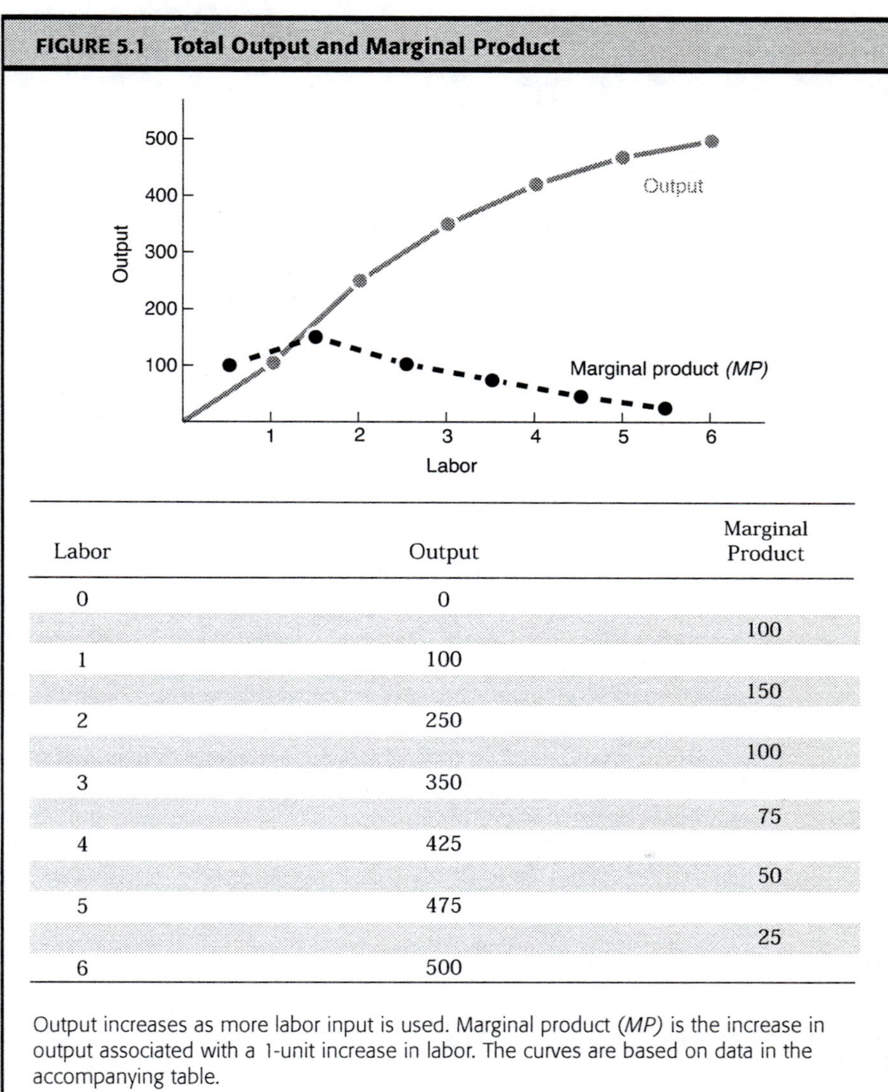

Labor	Output	Marginal Product
0	0	
		100
1	100	
		150
2	250	
		100
3	350	
		75
4	425	
		50
5	475	
		25
6	500	

Output increases as more labor input is used. Marginal product *(MP)* is the increase in output associated with a 1-unit increase in labor. The curves are based on data in the accompanying table.

Fixed and Variable Costs

Fixed costs *(FC)* do not vary with output; **variable costs *(VC)*** do. **Total costs *(TC)*** are fixed costs plus variable costs: *TC* = *FC* + *VC*.

In the short run, some factors (such as plant and equipment) are fixed in supply; even if the firm wanted to increase or reduce them, it would not be possible in the short run. The costs of these fixed factors are **fixed costs (*FC*).** The firm pays these costs even if it produces no output. In the short run, greater output is obtained by using more of the variable inputs (such as labor and raw materials); the costs of these variable factors are **variable costs (*VC*).** The sum of variable and fixed costs is **total costs (*TC*).**

EXAMPLE 5.2 WHY WINE IS PRODUCED ALMOST EVERYWHERE: DIMINISHING RETURNS

The best wine-producing land is located 30 to 60 degrees north and south of the equator, where the mean daily temperature is 10 degrees C in the spring and 20 degrees C in the summer months. Spring frosts, which can destroy fragile grape crops, must be rare, and soil conditions must be just right. Europe provides the ideal climate and soil for wine production, and countries ranging from Germany in central Europe to Italy, Portugal, and Greece in southern Europe are noted for their fine wines. People have been drinking wine for more than two millennia, and some of the vineyards of Europe have been under cultivation for that long. Currently, Europe produces and consumes about three-quarters of the world's wines.

The law of diminishing returns explains why Europe, which has the best natural conditions, does not produce virtually all of the world's wine, and, in fact, is falling with respect to its share of world wine output and exports. Since the early 1990s, the export shares of wine by the United States, Australia, New Zealand, Argentina, Chile, and South Africa have risen from 4 percent to almost 20 percent and are projected to rise further. In the traditional wine-producing countries of Europe, the share of vineyards of total cultivated land ranges from 5 to 10 percent. In the new wine-producing regions of the world, it is well below 1 percent. The high cultivation rates in Europe tell us that the good wine-producing land is already under cultivation; the only way to expand Europe's wine production is to move into land that is inferior for the purpose. If one travels through the wine-producing region of Germany's Neckar Valley, for example, one sees that the vineyards are planted to the very tops of the hills. Virtually every square meter available for cultivation has been used. In the language of average and marginal product, the average product of Europe's vineyards is still higher than that of new wine-producing regions, but its marginal product is lower.

Even in the United States, a relative newcomer to wine production, diminishing returns are seen in the traditional wine-producing regions, such as California and New York, causing wine production to spread into new areas, such as Indiana and Texas. In the United States alone there are now 2200 vineyards, and each state has at least one.

In the long run, all costs are variable and fixed costs are zero. In the short run, some costs are fixed.

The short run may also be defined as a period of time in which some costs are fixed. As the time horizon expands, more and more inputs can be varied. In the long run, all inputs are variable and so all costs are variable and fixed costs are zero.

In the short run, there is no way to change fixed costs; fixed resources have no alternative use. They are fixed and cannot be used elsewhere. Output can be expanded only by an increase in variable inputs and hence in variable costs.

Marginal and Average Costs

The behavior of costs depends on the law of diminishing returns. Indeed, productivity and costs are inversely related. The higher productivity, the lower costs; the lower productivity, the higher costs.

Marginal Costs Total cost equals variable costs plus fixed costs. Since fixed costs are constant, as output increases both total cost and variable cost increase by the same amount. Suppose, for example, that when a shrimping boat increases its output of shrimp by two bushels per day, total (and variable) costs rise by $10. The change in its costs divided by the change in its output is **marginal cost (*MC*).** In this example, *MC* = $5 = (10/2). *MC* is the increase in cost per unit increase in output. If the increase in output is only one unit, *MC* is the increase in costs associated with this increase in output by one unit. If the increase in output is larger than one, the increase in costs must be divided by the increase in output. Marginal cost can be determined for any increase in output—one unit, two units, or any number.

Marginal cost (*MC*) is the change in total cost (or, equivalently, in variable cost) divided by the increase in output—or, alternatively, the increase in costs per unit increase in output (*Q*): $MC = \Delta TC/\Delta Q = \Delta VC/\Delta Q$.

Average Costs While marginal costs look at the change in costs per unit change in output, average costs spread total, variable, or fixed costs over the entire quantity of output. **Average variable cost (*AVC*)** equals variable costs divided by output. **Average fixed cost (*AFC*)** equals fixed costs divided by output. **Average total cost (*ATC*)** equals total cost divided by output. Alternatively, *ATC* is the sum of *AFC* and *AVC*.

Average variable cost (*AVC*) is variable cost divided by output.

Average fixed cost (*AFC*) is fixed cost divided by output.

Average total cost (*ATC*) is total cost divided by output, which also equals the sum of average variable cost and average fixed cost.

The Cost Curves

Figure 5.2 provides cost and output information about a firm that produces a single product. The firm is operating in the short run because fixed costs are present.

Figure 5.2 shows total costs (*TC*), variable costs (*VC*), and fixed costs (*FC*) in Panel A. Panel B shows average total cost (*ATC*), average variable cost (*AVC*), and marginal cost (*MC*).

The table of cost curves provides two sets of marginal costs. Column 5a shows the marginal cost of producing one more unit of output. For example, the extra cost of producing the first unit is $20; the extra cost of producing the second unit is $10, the seventh unit $20. Note that these marginal cost figures are placed *between* the rows. The $20 marginal cost of going from zero to one unit of output is placed between 0 and 1. Column 5b provides a second way to measure marginal costs that permits us to place the marginal cost figure on the *same line* as the output figures. The marginal cost of going from zero to one unit of output is $20; marginal cost falls by $10 if we go back from two to one. Hence, the marginal cost of the first unit of output is $15—the average of the two between-the-lines marginal cost figures in 5a. We plot in Figure 5.2 the marginal cost figures in Column 5b.

MC first falls and then rises. Marginal costs first fall because as the first few units of output are produced, the variable inputs produce higher and higher marginal physical products as they specialize in different aspects of production. But eventually the law of diminishing returns sets in and marginal product falls. At this point, it takes a larger increase in the variable inputs to produce a given increase in output. The law of diminishing returns dictates that marginal costs must eventually rise as output increases. As diminishing returns set in, marginal costs rise.

The law of diminishing returns dictates that marginal costs must eventually rise as output expands.

AFC (not illustrated in the figure) declines throughout because the same fixed cost is being spread out over more and more units of output. Because *ATC* = *AVC* + *AFC*, the vertical distance between the *AVC* and *ATC* curves is *AFC*. As a given

FIGURE 5.2 Short-Run Cost Curves

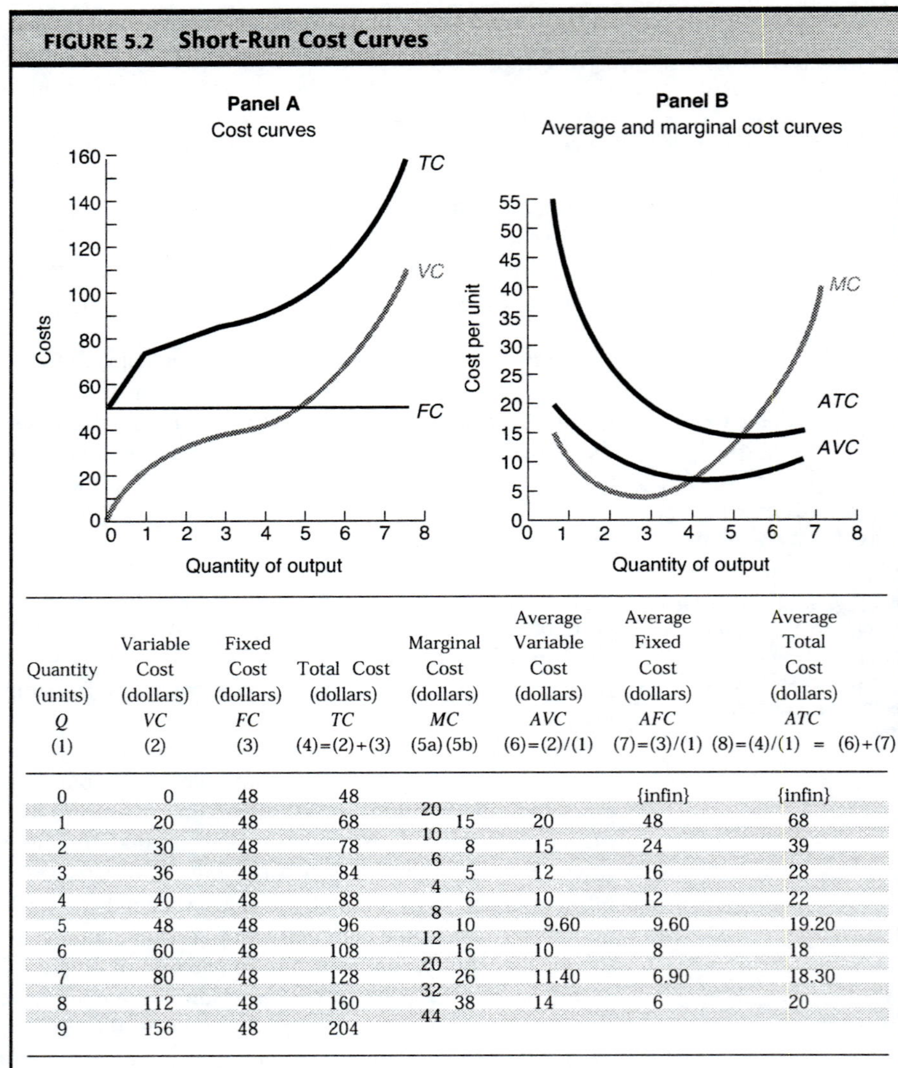

Quantity (units) Q (1)	Variable Cost (dollars) VC (2)	Fixed Cost (dollars) FC (3)	Total Cost (dollars) TC (4)=(2)+(3)	Marginal Cost (dollars) MC (5a)	(5b)	Average Variable Cost (dollars) AVC (6)=(2)/(1)	Average Fixed Cost (dollars) AFC (7)=(3)/(1)	Average Total Cost (dollars) ATC (8)=(4)/(1) = (6)+(7)
0	0	48	48				{infin}	{infin}
1	20	48	68	20	15	20	48	68
2	30	48	78	10	8	15	24	39
3	36	48	84	6	5	12	16	28
4	40	48	88	4	6	10	12	22
5	48	48	96	8	10	9.60	9.60	19.20
6	60	48	108	12	16	10	8	18
7	80	48	128	20	26	11.40	6.90	18.30
8	112	48	160	32	38	14	6	20
9	156	48	204	44				

In Panels A and B, the marginal and average figures (except for average fixed cost) are graphed from the data in the accompanying table. Average total cost is the sum of average variable cost and average fixed cost. *ATC* approaches *AVC* as output grows, and *MC* intersects both curves at their minimum points.

fixed cost is spread over a larger and larger output, *AFC* gets smaller and smaller. Thus, the *AVC* and *ATC* curves get closer together as output rises—but *AFC* can never equal zero, so the *ATC* and *AVC* curves never meet.

Marginal cost equals *ATC* and *AVC* at their minimum values.

Panel B of Figure 5.2 shows the graphical relationship between marginal cost and average variable cost and average total cost. When the marginal cost figure is below the corresponding average cost figure, average costs fall. When the marginal cost figure is above the corresponding average cost figure, average costs rise. When output increases from three to five units, *MC* is initially \$5 (less than both *ATC* and *AVC*), and *AVC* falls from \$12.00 to \$9.60 and *ATC* from \$28.00 to \$19.20. The marginal cost of \$5 is below *AVC* and *ATC* and pulls them both down. When output is five units, *MC* is slightly above *AVC* and so just begins to pull average variable costs upward. When output is larger than five units, *MC* exceeds *ATC* and pulls up average variable costs. When output is smaller than five units, *MC* falls short of *ATC* and pushes down average variable costs.

Panel B illustrates an important principle: The *MC* curve intersects the *AVC* and *ATC* curves at their minimums. The average cost figure increases if the marginal cost exceeds it; the average cost figure decreases if the marginal cost falls short of it. At the minimum point the average value is neither rising nor falling; therefore the marginal and average values must be equal.

Minimum *ATC* occurs after the minimum *AVC*. When *AVC* reaches its minimum, *MC* is equal to *AVC* and is still below *ATC*. When *AVC* is minimized, the *ATC* curve must still be falling. When the *ATC* curve reaches its minimum point, fixed resources are being operated at their most efficient level.

Long-Run Costs

In the long run, enterprises do not have any fixed costs; all costs are variable. The business is free to choose any combination of inputs to produce output. Once long-run decisions are executed (the company completes a new plant, the farming enterprise signs a ten-year lease for additional acreage), the enterprise again has fixed factors and fixed costs. In the long run, enterprises are free to select the cost-minimizing level of capital, labor, and land inputs. Long-run cost-minimizing decisions are based on the prices the firm must pay for land, labor, and capital.

Shifts in Cost Curves

Take the case of Acme Steel Company, which produces steel tubes. Acme Steel knows the average total cost curves it would face with different-sized plants. With a small plant and unspecialized machinery, Acme Steel would face the average total cost curve ATC_1 in Figure 5.3. Notice that with this cost curve, *ATC* reaches its lowest point at output level q_1. With a slightly larger plant and somewhat more specialized equipment, Acme Steel's average total cost would be lower for larger levels of output, such as at q_2. The average total cost curve associated with the larger plant and more specialized equipment is ATC_2. The remaining *ATC* curves show the average costs for even larger plants. The curve ATC_3 yields the most efficient plant size. At output level q_3, average total cost is lower than any other *ATC* for any other plant size.

The Long-Run Cost Curve

Figure 5.3 demonstrates that there is a different *ATC* curve for each level of fixed input. For every plant size there is a different average total cost curve. In the long run, all costs are variable; therefore, there is no distinction between long-run variable costs

FIGURE 5.3 Shifts in Cost Curves with Different Plant Size

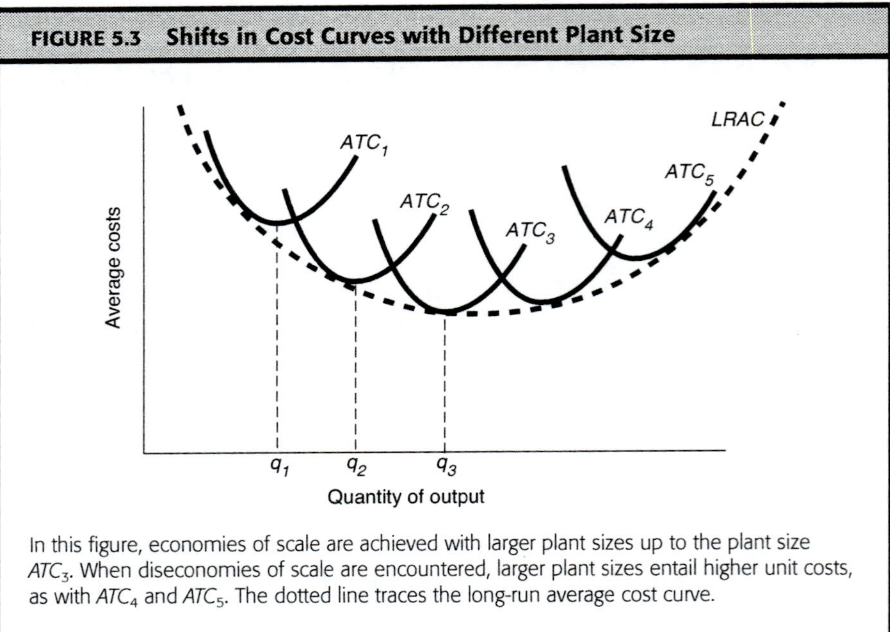

In this figure, economies of scale are achieved with larger plant sizes up to the plant size ATC_3. When diseconomies of scale are encountered, larger plant sizes entail higher unit costs, as with ATC_4 and ATC_5. The dotted line traces the long-run average cost curve.

Long-run average cost (*LRAC*) is the average cost for each level of output when all factor inputs are variable.

and long-run total costs—there is only long-run average cost (*LRAC*). **Long-run average cost (*LRAC*)** consists of the average cost for each level of output when all factor inputs are variable (and when factor prices and the state of technology are fixed).

In the long run, the enterprise is free to select the most effective combination of factor inputs because none of the inputs are fixed. The long-run cost curve *envelops* the short-run cost curves, forming a long-run curve that touches each short-run curve (*ATC*) at only one point, as shown by the dotted line in Figure 5.3.

Economies and Diseconomies of Scale

In the short run, the fact that some factors of production are fixed causes the short-run average total cost curve to be U-shaped. The law of diminishing returns does not apply to the long run because all inputs are variable. The long-run average cost curve will also be U-shaped, as shown in Figure 5.3. Why would long-run average costs (*LRAC*) first decline as output expands and then later increase as output expands even further? The reason is that firms experience first economies of scale, then constant returns to scale, and finally diseconomies of scale as output expands.

Economies of scale are present when an increase in output causes average costs to fall.

Economies of Scale The declining portion of the *LRAC* curve is due to economies of scale that arise out of the indivisibility of the inputs of labor and capital goods or equipment. In a large firm, workers are able to specialize in various activities, increase their productivity or dexterity through experience, and save time in moving from one task to another. It is difficult for one person to be one part mechanic, two parts supervisor, and three parts electrician and still remain as efficient as one who specializes in one of these tasks. The classic example of worker specialization is the assembly line of an automobile plant: One worker specializes in installing rear windows while another installs doors. The same principles apply to machines. A small firm might use general-purpose machine tools, whereas a large firm builds special equipment or machines that substantially lower costs when large quantities are produced.

Economies of scale occur because of the greater productivity of specialization in any of a variety of areas, including technological equipment, marketing, research and development, and management. The optimal rate of utilization for some types of machinery may occur at high rates of output. Some workers may not be able to perfect specialized skills until a high rate of output allows them to concentrate on specific tasks. As the output of an enterprise increases with all inputs variable, average costs will decline because of the economies of scale associated with increased specialization of labor, management, plant, and equipment.

Constant returns to scale are present when an increase in output does not change average costs of production.

Constant Returns to Scale Economies of scale will become exhausted at some point when expanding output no longer increases productivity. The evidence suggests that for a large range of outputs there will be constant returns to scale, where the average costs of production remain constant.

Diseconomies of Scale As the enterprise continues to expand its output, eventually all the economies of large-scale production will be exploited and long-run average costs will begin to rise. The rise in long-run average costs as output of the enterprise expands is the result of diseconomies of scale.

Diseconomies of scale are present when an increase in output causes average costs to increase.

Diseconomies of scale can be caused by various factors. As the firm continues to expand, managers must assume additional responsibility, and managerial talents are spread so thin that the efficiency of management declines. The problem of maintaining communications *within* a large firm grows, and additional rules, regulations, and paperwork requirements become commonplace. Large firms may find it difficult to correct their mistakes. Employees of large firms may lose their identity and feel that their contributions to the firm are not recognized. As the output of an enterprise continues to increase, average cost will eventually rise because of the diseconomies of scale associated with the growing problems of managerial control and coordination.

Minimum Efficient Scale

The **minimum efficient scale** is the lowest level of output at which long-run average costs are minimized.

Firms and industries differ in their patterns of *LRAC*. Firms have different **minimum efficient scales** of production, which is their lowest level of output at which long-run average costs are minimized. In Figure 5.4, Panel A, for example, the minimum efficient scale is reached at a fairly low scale of output. In Panel B, the minimum efficient scale is reached at a much higher scale of output.

Minimum efficient scale is an important determinant of industrial structure. In industries such as restaurants, commercial printing, and household furniture manufacturing, where firms reach their minimum efficient scale at low levels of output, the industry is populated by a large number of small firms. In industries such as automobiles and electricity generation, where minimum efficient scale is not reached until there are very high volumes of output, the industry is populated by a small number

FIGURE 5.4 Long-Run Average Cost: Two Examples

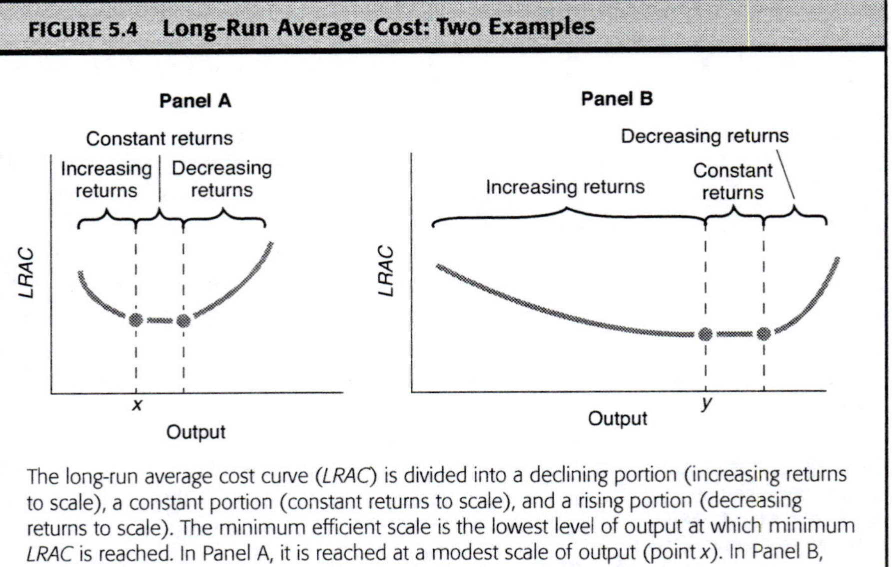

The long-run average cost curve (*LRAC*) is divided into a declining portion (increasing returns to scale), a constant portion (constant returns to scale), and a rising portion (decreasing returns to scale). The minimum efficient scale is the lowest level of output at which minimum *LRAC* is reached. In Panel A, it is reached at a modest scale of output (point *x*). In Panel B, the minimum efficient scale is reached at a high volume of output (point *y*).

of large firms. Thus, minimum efficient scale plays an important role in determining the amount of competition in the industry. (See Example 5.3.)

Summary

1. Opportunity cost is the appropriate measure of costs. The opportunity cost of any action is the next-best alternative sacrificed. Opportunity cost can be an explicit cost or an implicit cost.
2. Economic profit equals revenues minus total opportunity costs. A normal profit is achieved when revenues just equal total opportunity costs. A normal profit or above is required to attract resources.
3. The short run is a period of time short enough so that some factors of production are fixed. The costs associated with these fixed factors are fixed costs. In the short run, there are both fixed and variable costs. In the long run, all factors can be freely varied and there are no fixed costs.
4. Marginal product is the increase in output associated with the increase in a factor of production by one unit. The law of diminishing returns states that the marginal product of any input will eventually fall as output expands when other factors are fixed.
5. Marginal cost is the increase in variable cost associated with producing one more unit of output. The law of diminishing returns tells us that marginal costs eventually will rise as output expands. Marginal cost equals average variable and average total costs at their minimum points.

EXAMPLE 5.3 TWO VISIONS OF AVIATION IN THE TWENTY-FIRST CENTURY: AIRBUS VERSUS BOEING

The United States' Boeing Corporation and Europe's Airbus Industrie are the dominant producers of commercial aircraft. They have two quite different visions of commercial aviation in the twenty-first century. Boeing believes that the major growth will be in medium-sized markets, those serving flyers between such cities as St. Louis and Philadelphia to Stuttgart, Germany, and Manchester, England. Such markets require long-range aircraft that carry 300 or fewer passengers economically. Airbus believes, to the contrary, that the major growth will be in major markets, those serving such cities as New York, Los Angeles, Tokyo, London, and Paris. Such markets require long-range aircraft that will carry 600 passengers economically. The world's airlines must decide whether to order Boeing long-range aircraft (767, 777, 747), which carry from 250 to 400 passengers, or Airbus's new "superjumbo." Currently being developed, the superjumbo A380 will carry almost 600 passengers. Once the airlines buy one aircraft or the other, they have fixed their capital stock.

The Boeing *ATC* curve shows an aircraft that has minimum efficient scale at 400 passengers. If the Boeing vision of the future is correct, most long-range flights will carry this number, and the Boeing aircraft owner will be able to operate at a low average total cost (and, presumably, earn substantial profits). The hapless owner of the A380 will be carrying only 400 passengers on an aircraft suited for 600 and will be operating well below minimum efficient scale (and will not earn profits). If the Airbus vision of the future is correct, most long-range flights will carry 600 passengers; owners of A380s will operate at lower costs than owners of Boeing aircraft, and they will earn substantial profits.

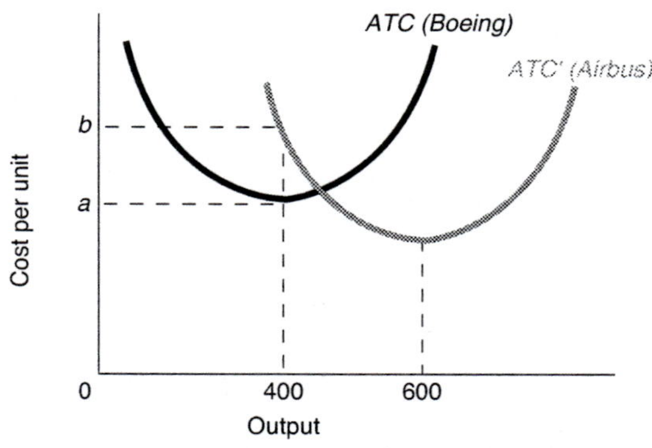

6. In the long run, economies and diseconomies of scale determine the shape of long-run average costs (*LRAC*). *LRAC* is the minimum cost of producing each level of output when all factor inputs are variable. *LRAC* declines when economies of scale are being experienced; *LRAC* is constant when there are constant returns to scale; and *LRAC* rises when there are diseconomies of scale.
7. Minimum efficient scale shows the minimum level of output at which *LRAC* is minimized. Minimum efficient scale has a large impact on the size and number of firms in an industry.

Questions and Problems

1. BMW and Mercedes-Benz advertisements emphasize economy by highlighting their cars' high resale value. Using opportunity costs, analyze the true costs of owning a $30,000 Mercedes that can be resold in five years for $30,000.
2. Explain why normal profits are required to attract resources to a particular firm. If a normal profit is just sufficient to attract resources to a firm or industry, speculate on the effect of economic profits to attract resources to a particular industry.
3. The marginal product of the third worker in a firm is 10 units of output. It costs $25 to hire that worker. What is the marginal cost associated with these 10 units of output?
4. Explain the differences between increasing marginal costs associated with the law of diminishing returns and increasing *LRAC* associated with the diseconomies of scale.
5. A firm increases its output by 50 units and finds that its costs, in the short run, increase by $200. What is its marginal cost of production over this range?
6. Suppose 30 units of labor produce 100 widgets, and 40 units of labor produce 200 widgets. If each unit of labor is paid $10, what is the marginal cost of producing widgets between those two output levels?
7. Using the information listed, plot all the short-run total cost and average cost curves discussed in this chapter. Do the cost curves have the expected shapes? Explain your answer.

Output (units)	*Fixed Costs (dollars)*	*Variable Costs (dollars)*
1	10	5
2	10	8
3	10	12
4	10	20
5	10	40

8. The United States is one of the world's largest producers of oil. If this is the case, why do we import so much oil?
9. One industry has five firms; another industry has 500. Is it possible that this difference is explained by long-run average costs?
10. A small store owner, who also has an advanced degree in engineering, makes an accounting profit of $20,000 per year. Is the owner making an economic profit? Explain your answer.
11. If it costs a manufacturer $100,000 to increase production by 20 units, what is the marginal cost?
12. The average total cost of producing 100 units of output is $100. If one more unit of output is produced, its marginal cost is $120. Explain what happens to average total costs as a consequence of producing one more unit.

CHAPTER 6

COMPETITIVE MARKETS

Chapter Preview

This chapter examines the two kinds of highly competitive markets. With perfect competition, the product is homogeneous and there is free access to its market by new firms. The workings of a competitive economy can be understood best by examining the theory of perfect competition in both the short run and the long run. In the second kind of highly competitive market, monopolistic competition, there is still free access by new firms, but the product is differentiated among the various firms.

Competitive Markets

The invisible hand of Adam Smith (as discussed in Chapter 2) describes how an economy works when there is competition among sellers and competition among buyers. The greatest degree of competition exists when no single buyer or seller has any control over price.

Perfect Competition

Perfect competition is a market with many sellers, perfect information, a homogeneous product, and freedom of entry.

A **price taker** has no control over the price.

In the real world, most sellers exercise some control over price, but the greater the competition, the less control the individual seller exercises over price. In the limiting case of **perfect competition,** the seller has absolutely no control over price. Each individual seller faces so much competition from other sellers that the market price is taken as given. When the price is given to the individual seller by the market, the seller is said to be a **price taker.** (See Example 6.1.)

The characteristics of perfect competition that result in price taking are the following:

1. The product's price is the same for each buyer and seller.
2. The product is homogeneous—one seller's product cannot be distinguished from another's.
3. Buyers and sellers have perfect information about prices and product qualities.
4. There are a large number of buyers and sellers.
5. There is complete freedom of entry into and exit from the industry.

EXAMPLE 6.1 PRICE TAKING AND HIGHLY LIQUID MARKETS: EXXONMOBIL

ExxonMobil is an integrated energy company that ranks as one of the world's largest companies. Its shares of stock are traded on the New York Stock Exchange. In late summer 2003, its share price was around \$37, and 6753 million shares were outstanding. If we multiply the share price times the number of shares, we get ExxonMobil's market value, or *market capitalization,* as it is called, of around \$250 billion. ExxonMobil's trading volume is the number of shares bought and sold per day. On a relatively slow day (20 August 2003), 8.1 million shares of ExxonMobil were traded (about one-third of a billion dollars). Large stock exchanges that trade the shares of large corporations are called *highly liquid stock markets* because of the large volumes of trade each day. Large percentages of the shares of major corporations are owned by mutual funds, such as Prudential or Vanguard, in which households invest their savings from 401k and other retirement accounts. One such large mutual fund is operated by CREF, the retirement fund of teachers. CREF owns some \$120 billion of stock in U.S. and foreign corporations. If CREF chose to place only 1 percent of its assets in ExxonMobil, it would own about 33 million shares, which would make it one of the largest single shareholders of ExxonMobil. If CREF wished to sell all its shares of ExxonMobil in one day, it would probably bid down the price. Even in a highly liquid stock market, it would be possible for a single owner to alter the price by buying or selling huge volumes. In this case, CREF would not be a price taker. Most likely, if CREF wished to sell its holdings of ExxonMobil, it would do so gradually and in such a manner that it could sell its shares without bidding down the price. By selling its shares gradually, CREF would be a price taker. CREF is an extreme example of a single owner with huge stock holdings. In virtually all other cases, single owners own such a small portion of outstanding shares that they can sell all they want without changing the price.

Monopolistic Competition

Monopolistic competition is a market with many sellers, freedom of entry, and perfect information but a differentiated product.

Monopolistic competition is a highly competitive market that has all the characteristics of perfect competition except for price uniformity (Characteristic 1) and product homogeneity (Characteristic 2).

Monopolistic competition allows each firm to have a slightly differentiated product because of such factors as location and costs of information. There may be a large number of fast-food restaurants in a large city, and there may be freedom of entry, yet each restaurant offers a slightly different product. Differentiation can be on the basis of location, price, speed of service, or variety of styles or colors.

This chapter describes how both perfect competition and monopolistic competition work.

The Firm and the Market: Perfect Competition

In perfect competition, all firms in the industry sell a homogeneous, or identical, product. No firm has an advantage over other firms in terms of quality, location, or other

FIGURE 6.1 The Demand Curve Facing the Perfectly Competitive Firm

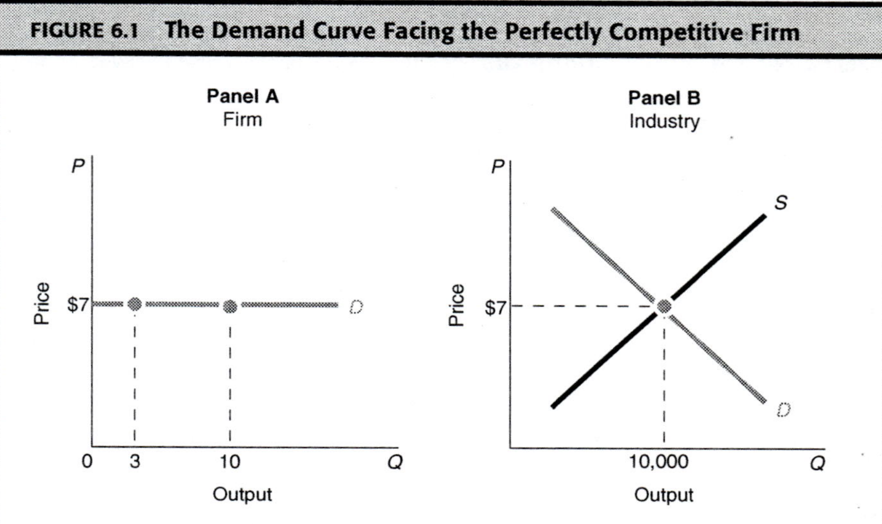

The perfectly competitive firm in Panel A must sell at the $7 price determined in the market. It is a price taker; it can sell all it wants at the prevailing price. Its demand curve is horizontal. For the industry as a whole (Panel B), the demand curve is negatively sloped. For the industry to sell more, a lower price is required. Note the differences in scale of the two diagrams. The firm's output 0.01 percent of the market.

product features. No rational buyer will buy from Firm A if it charges a higher price than Firm B. In a perfectly competitive market, buyers have perfect information about the prices different sellers charge; accordingly, every buyer would know if Firm B's price was lower than Firm A's price.

The difference between the perfectly competitive firm and the industry as a whole, called the *market,* is shown in Figure 6.1. Panel B shows the market demand curve *D* for the product. When the market price is $7, the quantity demanded in the market is 10,000 units. The individual firm, shown in Panel A, is such a small part of the market that it can sell all it wants at the going price of $7. Whether the firm sells three units or ten units, the market price is still $7. Thus, the demand curve facing the individual firm is perfectly elastic at the going market price.

The demand curve facing the perfectly competitive firm is horizontal, or perfectly elastic, at the market price.

If the price-taking firm can sell all it wants at the going market price, what prevents a single firm from supplying the entire market? The answer is costs.

The Competitive Firm in the Short Run

The last chapter defined the marginal cost curve. In a perfectly competitive market, marginal cost plays a major role in determining the supply curve, which shows how much the firm is willing to supply at different prices. The firm's supply behavior in the short run is the outcome of three forces: (1) its marginal cost curve, (2) the horizontal demand curve facing the firm, and (3) the desire to maximize profits or minimize losses.

Marginal Revenue

Marginal revenue (*MR*) is the increase in revenue from increasing output or sales by one unit.

Marginal revenue (*MR*) is the increase in revenue brought about by increasing output (sales) by one unit. If *MR* exceeds *MC*, and extra unit of output adds more to revenues than to cost. Thus, *MR* greater than *MC* implies that the profits of the firm can be increased, or its losses reduced, by producing one more unit of output. This principle is true for all firms, whether perfectly or imperfectly competitive. This logic tells us that firms will look at the relationship between *MR* and *MC* in making their decisions about how much output to produce.

For a firm in perfect competition, *MR* = *Price.*

In the case of a perfectly competitive firm, marginal revenue is simply the market price. If Kansas farmers sell one more bushel of wheat, their marginal revenue (*MR*) is the market price of that wheat. As long as the price of wheat exceeds the farmers' marginal cost, the extra cost of producing another bushel of wheat, farmers will want to produce more wheat. If the price of wheat is $4 and the marginal cost of wheat is $3, an extra bushel of wheat adds $1 to the farmers' profit. As more wheat is produced, marginal costs are driven upward by the law of diminishing returns. As a fixed amount of wheatland is used more intensively, marginal costs increase because the extra tractors and farmhands produce less and less additional wheat.

The Short-Run Supply Curve

In the short run, the firm's objective is to maximize profits or, if necessary, to minimize losses. Once the market price is set, it may be such that:

1. The firm makes economic profits.
2. The economic profit is zero.
3. The firm stays in business but produces at a loss.
4. The firm shuts down temporarily and hopes for the price to rise.

As these four outcomes illustrate, prices affect output decisions. At very low prices, the firm may have to shut down. At higher prices, it produces a positive amount of output. The quantity supplied at each price is simply the firm's profit-maximizing output (or its loss-minimizing output).

The firm's supply curve shows how much it is prepared to sell at each price.

Output will be pushed up to the point where price (*P*) = marginal cost. For a perfectly competitive firm, the profit-maximizing level of output occurs where *P* = *MC*. Any output short of *P* = *MC* means that too little is being produced; any output where *P* is less than *MC* means that too much is being produced. Competitive firms adjust output to the level at which price and marginal cost are equal.

Consider the competitive firm in Figure 6.2. The costs are the same as for the firm in the previous chapter. The firm's average variable costs (*AVC*) for different levels of output are shown in Column 2. The firm's average total costs (*ATC*) are shown in Column 3. Total costs are shown in Column 4, and the firm's marginal costs (*MC*) are shown in Column 5.

The minimum points on the *AVC* and *ATC* curves are important to keep in mind. Minimum average variable cost is $9.60—which occurs when output equals five units. Minimum average total cost is $18 and occurs when output equals six units.

FIGURE 6.2 The Profit-Maximizing Firm

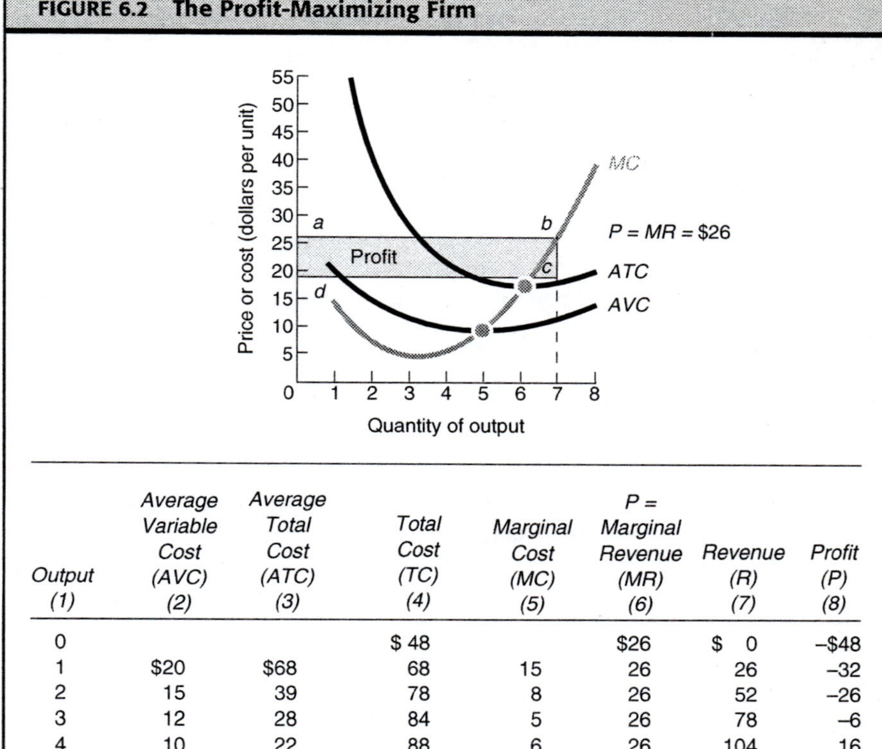

Output (1)	Average Variable Cost (AVC) (2)	Average Total Cost (ATC) (3)	Total Cost (TC) (4)	Marginal Cost (MC) (5)	P = Marginal Revenue (MR) (6)	Revenue (R) (7)	Profit (P) (8)
0			$ 48		$26	$ 0	–$48
1	$20	$68	68	15	26	26	–32
2	15	39	78	8	26	52	–26
3	12	28	84	5	26	78	–6
4	10	22	88	6	26	104	16
5	9.6	19.2	96	10	26	130	34
6	10	18	108	16	26	156	48
7	11.4	18.3	128	26	26	182	54
8	14	20	160	38	26	208	48
9	17.3	22.7	204				

The market price is $26. The firm maximizes profits at an output level of seven units (where $P = MC$). At $P = \$26$, price exceeds *ATC* by the distance *bc*. Total profit is the rectangle *abcd*. The curves are drawn from the accompanying table.

If the price exceeds minimum *ATC*, the firm can make an economic profit.

Whether the firm can make an economic profit or not depends on the price. The competitive firm can sell all it wants at the going price. If the price exceeds the minimum *ATC*, the firm can make an economic profit.

The Profitable Firm Let us start with a price of $26. Because the firm is perfectly competitive, $P = MR = \$26.00$. If the firm produces five units, where average total costs are $19.20, it can make a profit of $34.00. However, the firm can do better. When output is five units, *MC* equals $10.00. Since $MR = \$26.00$, the firm can increase its profit by producing more units. The increase in revenue exceeds the increase in costs.

If output is increased to six units, profit increases from \$34.00 to \$48.00 because the increase in revenue (\$26.00) exceeds the increase in costs (\$12.00) by \$14.00. As long as $MR > MC$, the firm can do better by producing more output. Profit will be maximized when $MR = MC$. This occurs when output equals seven units and total profit is \$54.00.

Perfectly competitive firms choose that level of output where $P = MC$, provided price is greater than the minimum level of *AVC*.

The $P = MR$ line shows the marginal revenue (which is the same as price) of the firm. At any point along this line, the firm's total revenue equals the price times the quantity at that point. Profit is maximized where the $P = MR$ line intersects the *MC* curve—which occurs, when $P = \$26$, at an output of seven units. The vertical difference between the price and the *ATC* curve at that point—the distance *bc*—shows profit per unit of output. Total profit is determined by multiplying this difference by the output of seven units. Total profit is measured by the rectangle *abcd.*

The Loss-Minimizing Firm Let us turn to the second case, where the market price is not high enough for the firm to make an economic profit. Since the minimum *ATC* is \$18, any lower market price must bring about losses. Consider a price of \$16. The firm cannot make an economic profit. Instead, it must worry about minimizing its losses. If the firm produced an output of 0, total costs would still be \$48—the firm's fixed costs do not go away if it shuts down. The firm's revenue would be 0, and its loss would be –\$48. If the firm shuts down, it still must pay its entire fixed costs.

If the firm's revenue exceeds its variable costs, something will be left over to cover some of its fixed costs. If the firm can pay even a small portion of its fixed costs, it is better off than if it shut down. The minimum *AVC* (\$9.60) occurs when output is five units. By producing five units, the firm's price exceeds *AVC* by \$6.40. According to the profit-maximizing rule, the firm's losses are minimized when the output is six units, where $P = MC$. In Figure 6.3, the firm's losses per unit of output are the distance *bc*, or $P - ATC = \$16 - \$18 = -\$2$. When it produces six units, the firm loses \$2 per unit. The difference between the price and *AVC* generates revenues to cover some of the fixed costs. The firm's total losses of –\$12 (the six units times the \$2 loss per unit) are shown by the rectangle *abcd.*

The Shutdown Case In both cases, the price of the product exceeded the minimum *AVC* of \$9.60. If the price falls short of the minimum *AVC,* the firm should temporarily shut down. If the price falls short of average variable cost, the firm's revenues fall short of variable costs. In this case, if the firm operates, it loses not only its fixed cost but also some additional part of its variable cost. Thus, the firm's **shutdown rule** holds that output should be 0 when the price is less than minimum average variable cost. In this example, the firm will shut down at any price below \$9.60.

The **shutdown rule:** If the firm's price at all levels of output is less than average variable costs, it minimizes its losses by shutting down.

The Industry Supply Curve

The three cases explain the competitive firm's supply curve. The supply curve shows the output that competitive firms are prepared to supply at each price. In each case, the profit-maximizing level of output increases as the price increases.

According to Figures 6.2 and 6.3, the competitive firm is prepared to supply seven units at a market price of \$26.00, six units at a market price of \$16.00, and zero units at any price below \$9.60. At each price, the firm selects its profit-maximizing level of output. The competitive firm's supply curve is its *MC* curve above the *AVC* curve. Because *MC* is positively sloped, the firm's supply curve is positively sloped.

FIGURE 6.3 The Loss-Minimizing Firm

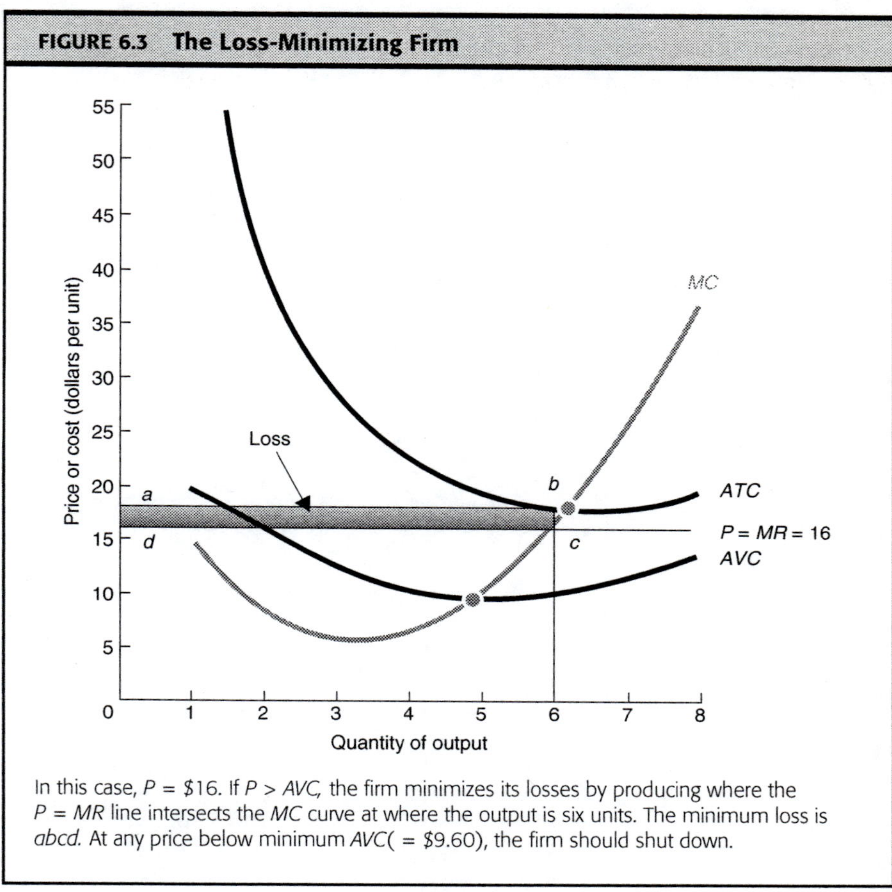

In this case, $P = \$16$. If $P > AVC$, the firm minimizes its losses by producing where the $P = MR$ line intersects the MC curve at where the output is six units. The minimum loss is *abcd*. At any price below minimum $AVC(= \$9.60)$, the firm should shut down.

In the short run, the market supply curve is the horizontal summation of the supply curves of each firm, which in turn are their *MC* curves above minimum *AVC*.

In the short run, the market supply curve is the sum of the profit-maximizing (or loss-minimizing) outputs of every firm at each price. Figure 6.4 shows the market supply curve in the case of 1000 identical firms, but the principles are the same for any number of firms. Each firm wishes to sell zero units at a price below \$9.60, six units at a price of \$16.00, and seven units at a price of \$26.00. The curve *S* shows the market supply curve for all 1000 firms.

The market supply curve is the horizontal summation of each firm's supply curve. With 1000 identical firms, no industry output is supplied at a price below \$9.60. At a price of \$16.00, 6000 units are supplied (the 1000 firms times six units each). At a price of \$26.00, the industry is prepared to supply 7000.

Short-Run Equilibrium

The market equilibrium is achieved when the market price equates the market supply with the market demand. Figure 6.4 shows how the short-run equilibrium price is determined. Panel A shows the individual firm and Panel B the industry consisting of 1000 such firms. The supply curve *S* in Panel B is the horizontal summation

FIGURE 6.4 Short-Run Equilibrium

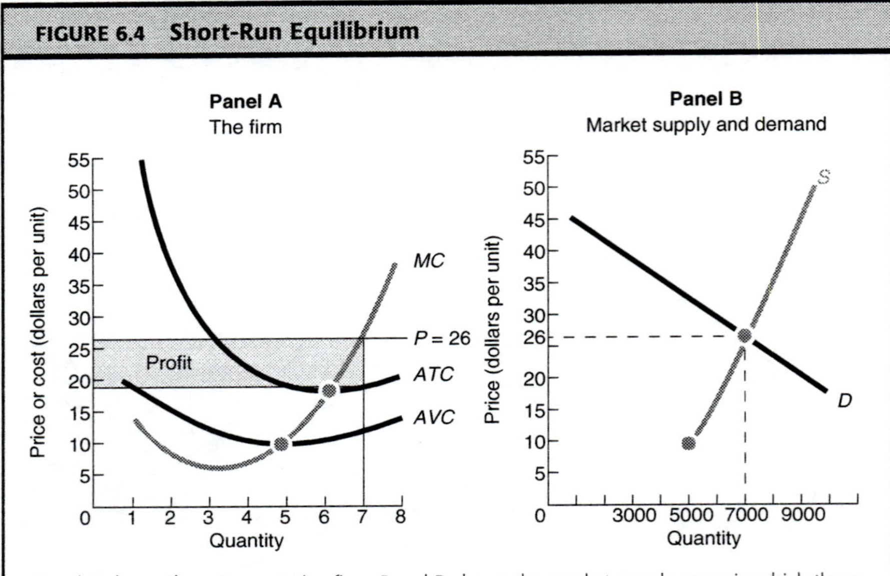

Panel A shows the representative firm; Panel B shows the market supply curve in which there are 1000 firms. In this case, the representative firm is making an economic profit. Note again the different scales of the two diagrams. The firm's output is only a small percentage of the market supply.

of each firm's *MC* curve above *AVC*. For example, at the price of \$26.00 each firm sells seven units and the industry sells 7000 units. The market demand curve, *D,* intersects the market supply curve at the price of \$26.00. At \$26.00, the quantity demanded equals the quantity supplied (7000). The \$26.00 market price becomes the firm's horizontal demand curve. In response to this price, the firm produces seven units of the output, where the *MC* curve intersects its *MR* curve. The profit-maximizing behavior of the individual firm is consistent with the profit-maximizing behavior of all the firms in the market.

Panel A shows a representative firm that is making an economic profit: *ATC* at the profit-maximizing output level of seven units is \$18.30; therefore, the firm is making a per-unit economic profit of \$7.70 (= \$26.00 − \$18.30) on each of the seven units for a total of \$54.00 economic profit.

Long-Run Adjustments

The effect of economic profits on perfectly competitive industries is felt primarily in the long run, when new firms can enter the industry and established firms can exit. As competitive firms respond to economic profits or losses, the industry short-run supply schedule shifts and prices change.

Economic Profit Attracts Resources

Economic profits equal revenues minus opportunity costs. Opportunity costs are the best alternatives sacrificed by the business firm when it engages in production. Included in these alternatives is the return that could be earned by the owner if the owner's money capital, labor, and managerial time had been used elsewhere. Economic losses are incurred when the return to the resources used in the business firm is less than the normal return they could earn in the next-best alternative. When economic profits are zero, the business firm is earning a normal profit.

A normal profit requires a normal competitive return on the resources used in the firm.

The persistence of economic profits ($P > ATC$) or economic losses ($P < ATC$) is not a long-run equilibrium for a competitive industry. If economic profits continue, there will be an incentive in the long run for new firms to enter the industry. New firms will cause the price to fall and economic profits to disappear. On the other hand, if there are economic losses, some firms will choose to exit from the industry. When long-term leases expire or an unprofitable plant can be sold, the firm no longer has these fixed costs and is free to leave the industry. The disappearance of firms will raise the price and eliminate the losses. Thus, economic profits and losses tend to move to the normal level. Only when a normal profit is being earned will the industry be at rest—in long-run equilibrium. *Long-run equilibrium occurs when firms no longer wish either to enter or to leave the industry.*

Long-run equilibrium occurs when firms no longer wish either to enter or to leave the industry.

Entry and Exit

When economic profits are being made in one industry, the resources used in that industry are being used more profitably than in other industries. Why? The returns in other industries are part of the opportunity costs of doing business in the first industry. New firms will be attracted to the more successful industry and away from others. By a similar token, when economic losses are being incurred, the resources used in that industry are being used less profitably than in other industries. Thus, resources will be attracted away to more profitable industries. At any given time there are *sunset industries* experiencing economic losses and *sunrise industries* earning economic profits.

Figure 6.5 shows how resources are attracted to industries making an economic profit. At $P = \$26$, each firm is making an economic profit—a return in excess of its opportunity costs. Economic profits encourage new firms to enter the industry. As the number of firms increases, market supply increases (as shown in Figure 6.5). The increase in supply drives down the market price. New firms will continue to enter as long as economic profits are being earned. Thus, the supply curve will settle at S' where the price equals $18 and no economic profits are being earned. Firms are just earning a normal profit.

If the market price were to fall below $18, firms would exit the industry and market supply would decrease. (See Example 6.2.)

Characteristics of Long-Run Equilibrium

Figure 6.5 shows a perfectly competitive market in long-run equilibrium. The industry is brought to a long-run equilibrium by entry in response to economic profits and exit due to losses. Consider the characteristics of this long-run equilibrium.

FIGURE 6.5 Long-Run Equilibrium: Adjustments That Eliminate Economic Profits

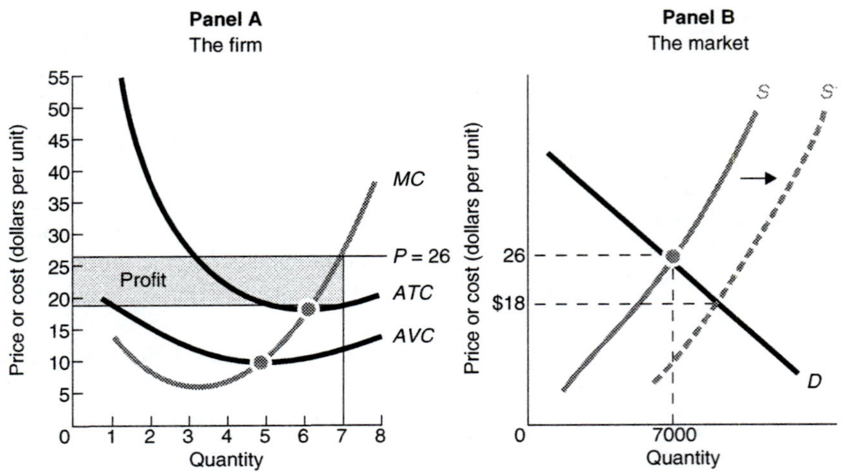

Panel A shows the representative firm; Panel B shows the market in which there are 1000 firms. In this case, the representative firm is making an economic profit at $P = 26$. The economic profit is shown by the rectangle. As time progresses, new firms enter the industry, the supply curve shifts to S', and the price falls to $18.

In the long run, the firm operates at an efficient scale of operation. When $P = MC$ and $P = ATC$ at the long-run equilibrium output, and when MC intersects ATC at its minimum point, the perfectly competitive firm is producing at the lowest average cost in the long run.

Long-run equilibrium occurs for the competitive industry when economic profits are zero and average costs are minimized.

Both forces together bring about efficient production, in which the good is being produced at the minimum cost to society. The firm in a competitive industry cannot be inefficient in the long run; the firm cannot select an inappropriate plant size.

Efficiency and Monopolistic Competition

There is usually some basis for distinguishing between the goods and services of different sellers, even though there may be a large number of sellers and freedom of entry. Product distinctions may be based on the physical attributes of the product (one pair of shoes is slightly different from other shoes), on location (one dry cleaner is located more conveniently than another), on type of service (one film developer takes one hour, the other one day), and even on imagined differences (one brand of aspirin may be perceived as being more effective than another). Figure 6.6 shows a firm operating in such a monopolistic competitive market.

Figure 6.6 tells an abbreviated story of the difference between a monopolistic competitive and perfectly competitive firm, after all long-run adjustments have been made.

EXAMPLE 6.2 COMPETITION, FREEDOM OF ENTRY, AND ONE-HOUR PHOTO PROCESSING

Twenty years ago, people had to wait overnight for film to be developed. In the early 1980s, French and Japanese manufacturers revolutionized the photo-processing industry by devising low-cost minilabs that could fit into a corner space in a pharmacy or any other small retail establishment. When introduced, these minilabs required an investment of $33,000. As technology was perfected, the price of the minilabs dropped.

The one-hour photo-processing business is characterized by minimal barriers to entry. Anyone who wants to enter the business can do so by buying the necessary equipment. The first entrepreneurs to offer one-hour processing made considerable economic profits. Later investors, attracted by these profits, entered the business and competed for customers without restriction.

Economic theory states that entry into competitive businesses will cease when all participants earn normal profits. The one-hour photo-processing industry reached this level of saturation in the early 1990s, when one-hour processing was available in virtually every pharmacy or copy shop, in addition to specialized outlets. Consumers benefited from this competition in terms of low prices and increased service. By the year 2003, photos could be processed while you waited; prints could be placed on computer disks; and photos could be cropped according to customer instructions. Small businesses could order cheap photosite toolkits that required only a PC and a high-quality printer. Yet even these low-cost businesses face a new form of competition. Now people can develop and print their own photos and display them on the Web simply by purchasing software and a color printer.

As was just shown, the perfectly competitive firm faces a horizontal demand curve (D'). The entry and exit of other firms ensures that economic profits (and losses) will eventually disappear, and that the perfectly competitive firm will operate at minimum efficient scale (minimum average total cost) with a zero economic profit. This occurs at point *a*. The monopolistic competitive result will be the same in terms of ending up with a zero economic profit. New firms will enter until economic profits disappear. The entry of new firms causes the demand curve to shift down and become more elastic (more horizontal). These changes in the demand curve of the monopolistic competitive firm continue until its economic profits disappear, which must occur where the price equals average costs (at point *b*, where the demand curve is tangent to the average cost curve). Point *b* will occur to the left of the minimum efficient scale because the demand curve will still have a slight negative slope due to product differentiation.

Figure 6.6 shows that, although monopolistic competitive industries also tend toward a normal, or zero, economic profit in the long run, they do not operate like their perfectly competitive counterparts at minimum efficient scale of operation. In fact, they tend to underutilize capacity by operating below minimum efficient scale. Monopolistic competition and product differentiation may make the economy some what less efficient, but their presence does make life more interesting in giving the consumer a broader variety of goods to choose from.

In the long run, monopolistically competitive firms produce where output falls short of minimum efficient scale.

Freedom of entry causes monopolistic competitive industries to more closely resemble perfect competition in the very long run. If existing firms are earning an

FIGURE 6.6 Monopolistic Competition versus Perfect Competition

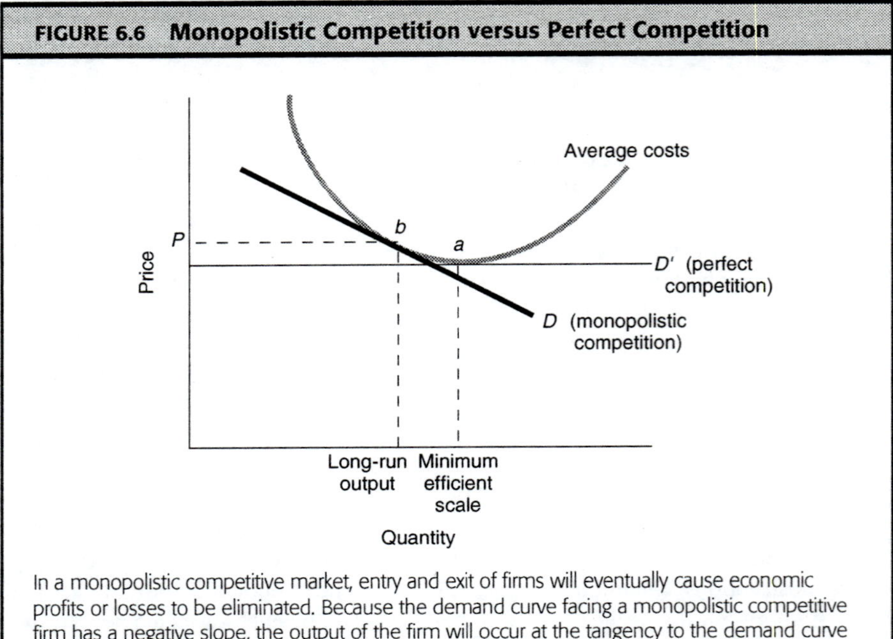

In a monopolistic competitive market, entry and exit of firms will eventually cause economic profits or losses to be eliminated. Because the demand curve facing a monopolistic competitive firm has a negative slope, the output of the firm will occur at the tangency to the demand curve and the average cost curve. Output will occur at less than minimum efficient scale.

economic profit, rival firms enter the industry offering products to lure away the customers of established firms. If a firm finds an innovative way to differentiate products, new entrants will copy this innovation. As more and more firms enter the market, the number of close substitutes grows; consumers become more indifferent to the firms they buy from. The amount of control producers have over price lessens and, eventually, the monopolistic competitive firm faces a demand curve that is, for all practical purposes, horizontal.

Policies to Promote Competition

Competitive industries produce output at minimum efficient scale. The entry and exit of firms push prices down to yield only normal profits for firms. Since the days of Adam Smith, economists have praised the virtues of competition.

There are a number of policies that can be pursued to increase the level of competition.

Removal of Trade Barriers

Countries can protect domestic firms by imposing tariffs and other restrictions on foreign competitors. As these restrictions are removed, there are more suppliers to the domestic market, competing more effectively with domestic firms. Relaxation of trade barriers reduces prices to consumers and lowers costs of production.

We have numerous examples of how competition increases when trade barriers are removed. Some states do not allow out-of-state banks or insurance companies to operate in their markets. When such barriers are removed, more companies compete in the market. The North American Free Trade Agreement (NAFTA) entered into force on 1 January 1994, removing barriers to trade within North America. Producers of food, appliances, vehicles, minerals, component parts, and so on in the United States, Canada, and Mexico could compete against each other on a level playing field. Their goods were no longer subject to import taxes as they crossed borders. The increased competition caused prices to fall generally in North America. Members of the European Union, which includes major countries like Germany, France, Italy, and the United Kingdom, no longer impose taxes on imports from one another, creating a single market larger than that of the United States. In spite of such agreements, however, proponents of trade barriers can still find innovative ways to erect them. (See Example 6.3.)

Deregulation

Deregulation is the elimination of government controls over a firm's prices, quantity, and quality of service.

Deregulation is the elimination of government controls over a firm's prices, quantity, and quality of service. The basic argument for deregulation is that, where the potential for competition exists, it is better to have professional managers make decisions about prices, fares, and services rather than government bureaucrats. In effect, deregulation introduces the forces of competition to industries previously controlled by government regulators.

In the late 1970s and early 1980s a number of U.S. industries were deregulated. In October 1978 President Jimmy Carter signed the landmark Airline Deregulation Act. This act allowed the airlines, rather than the Civil Aeronautics Board, to set their own fares and select their own routes. The Motor Carrier Act of 1980 curbed the Interstate Commerce Commission's control over interstate trucking. It allowed truckers greater freedom to set rates and change routes and eased the entry of new firms. The Staggers Rail Act of October 1980 gave the railroads more flexibility in setting

EXAMPLE 6.3 ARE MEXICAN TRUCKS UNSAFE?

Under the provisions of the NAFTA agreement, the U.S.–Mexico border is supposed to be open to trucking companies from both countries. Ten years after the NAFTA agreement, however, the United States still remains closed to Mexican truckers. The ban is a major irritant in U.S.–Mexican relations. Mexican goods must be trucked to the border and loaded onto American trucks, raising the costs of these goods when they are delivered in the United States. The ban continues because both Mexican truck drivers and Mexican trucks are said to be unsafe. The Teamsters Union, which represents most U.S. truck drivers, has led the battle against allowing Mexican rigs into the United States. As long as Mexican trucks are banned, there is less competition for U.S. truckers, and they can charge higher prices and earn higher wages. In fact, the Teamsters Union has made a continued ban on Mexican trucks a condition for their political support. The ban was not removed during the Clinton administration. It remains to be seen what the stance of the Bush administration will be.

rates, banned the industry's practice of collective rate setting, and allowed railroads to drop unprofitable routes. The year 1980 also saw the passage of the Depository Institutions Deregulation and Monetary Control Act, which eliminated interest rate ceilings on bank savings deposits and allowed savings and loans to provide more of the services offered by commercial banks. Since 1972, the Federal Communications Commission has been gradually deregulating the television broadcast industry by increasing the number of channels, removing barriers to direct satellite broadcasting, licensing new, low-power television stations, and removing some restrictions on cable television.

Deregulation has increased competition. Banks can now compete for customers by offering competitive interest rates; airlines are free to lower fares to attract customers. TV viewers now have a wide choice of channels and programs.

Deregulation has also revealed the consequences of competition. A number of airlines have disappeared; banks have failed. Competition creates winners and losers.

Based on the success of U.S. deregulation, other countries moved to deregulate their industries in the 1990s, and the European Union has agreed to deregulate most of Europe's regulated industries.

Antitrust Laws

Antitrust laws can set the legal rules of the game for businesses. They can forbid certain types of anticompetitive behavior (such as price fixing); they can prohibit specific forms of markets (such as markets with only one supplier); and they can prevent mergers and other acts that restrict competition.

Reducing Licensing Restrictions and Work Rules

Licensing agencies can lessen competition by restricting entry into a business. Unions determine which individuals can perform what tasks (plumbers cannot turn a screw or hammer a nail, for example). Licensing agencies determine who can be a truck driver, manicurist, or taxi driver. City governments may determine that only one taxicab company can service the municipal airport. While some restrictions may be required for public health and safety, others simply protect established companies and individuals and unnecessarily raise prices to consumers. Hence, eliminating unneeded licensing restrictions and work rules can help bolster competition.

Summary

1. Perfect competition exists when no single buyer or seller has any control over price. Perfect competition is also characterized by homogeneous products, perfect information, and freedom of entry.
2. The demand curve facing a perfectly competitive curve is horizontal—perfectly elastic. The firm can sell all it wants at the prevailing market price.
3. Profit-maximizing firms produce that quantity of output at which marginal revenue equals marginal cost. Because perfectly competitive firms can sell all they

want at the market price, price and marginal revenue are equal. Although perfectly competitive firms can sell all they want at the market price, rising marginal cost causes them to restrict production to that output at which $MR = MC$.

4. The marginal cost curve above *AVC* is the short-run supply curve of the competitive firm. Profits are maximized or losses are minimized when the firm produces the level of output such that $P = MC$.
5. In the long run, freedom of entry ensures that a zero economic profit (a normal profit) will be earned. Economic profits attract new firms until the price is driven down to yield a normal profit. Losses drive firms from the industry until the price rises to yield a normal profit. In the long run, the perfectly competitive firm operates where average costs are minimized.
6. Monopolistic competition closely resembles perfect competition, but firms have some very limited control over price because of product differentiation. In the long run, entry and exit will squeeze out economic profits. In long-run equilibrium, the monopolistic competitive firm operates below minimum efficient scale.
7. Policies to promote competition are relaxation of trade barriers, deregulation, and antitrust laws.

Questions and Problems

1. Consider a perfectly competitive market with a large number of buyers and sellers. A law is passed that prohibits new firms from entering the industry. Explain what would happen if:
   a. There were a significant reduction in long-run average costs because of some technological innovation.
   b. The number of buyers increased.
2. "How can the demand curve for corn be perfectly elastic? All studies show that the market demands less corn at a higher price." Clear up this problem.
3. Explain under which conditions a perfectly competitive firm would decide to shut down production temporarily.
4. "The law of diminishing returns explains why perfectly competitive firms produce a limited amount of production even though they can sell all they want at the market price." True or false? Why?
5. Explain the logic of the $MR = MC$ profit-maximizing rule. Explain also why this reduces to the $P = MC$ rule in the case of perfect competition.
6. The market price of a good is currently $20 per unit. The long-run average cost is $10. Predict what will happen in this industry:
   a. If it is perfectly competitive.
   b. If it is monopolistic competitive.
7. Explain what would happen in the short run to a perfectly competitive industry's price and output if the demand for the product suddenly fell due to bad publicity.
8. In Figure 6.2, fixed costs are $48. If fixed costs fell to $20, how would the supply schedule be affected in the short run? How would the supply schedule be affected in the long run?

9. A firm faces the following cost schedule.

Quantity (Q)	*Variable Cost (VC)*	*Fixed Cost (FC)*	*Total Cost (TC)*
0	$0	$5	$5
1	6	5	11
2	14	5	19
3	24	5	29
4	36	5	41

a. Calculate the firm's profit or loss for each level of output when the price is $5.99, when the price is $6.01, and when the price is $10.01.

b. How many units of output will the profit-maximizing or loss-minimizing firm produce at those three prices?

c. What is the firm's supply schedule?

10. You observe the (competitive) airline industry making economic losses. What do you expect to happen to ticket prices, to the quantity of airline passengers, and to the number of airline companies as time passes?

11. Explain why a reduction of trade barriers will increase competition.

12. You open a business. It is very successful and you earn an annual profit of one million dollars. What do you think will happen to that profit as time passes? Are there conditions under which you can keep the profit that high?

13. I employ 20,000 persons in a small, isolated town that has a population of 50,000. I pay each worker $15 per hour. I now need to expand my business and need to hire one thousand additional workers. What effect might this have on hourly pay? Now consider the same example but in the city of Chicago. Would your answer be the same?

CHAPTER 7

MONOPOLY, OLIGOPOLY, AND STRATEGY

Chapter Preview

In the previous chapter, the firms studied were small relative to the market, and new firms could compete with old firms without facing any significant obstacles. We now turn to firms that are large relative to the market. Such firms control, to some degree, the price of the product they sell and operate in markets that are difficult for new firms to enter. Firms that are large relative to the market are either monopolies, in which a single firm dominates the market, or oligopolies, where a handful of firms dominate.

Monopoly and Oligopoly

Price searchers face a downward-sloping demand curve.

A **monopoly** is one seller of a good that has no close substitutes, with considerable control over price and protection from competition by barriers to entry.

Perfectly competitive firms have no control over the prices they charge. Under monopolistic competition, the amount of control over price is minimal and short-lived. **Monopolists** and **oligopolists** exercise more control over price. They are not price takers; they are **price searchers,** who face a downward-sloping demand curve. If they want to increase sales, they must lower their price.

A **monopoly** is one seller of a good that has no close substitutes, with considerable control over price and protection from competition by barriers to entry. In a monopoly, there is a single firm facing no direct competition from other firms that produce the same, or a very similar, product. Water, electric, and gas companies have historically been good examples. Although there are substitutes, such as natural gas for electricity, there are no *close* substitutes. Pure monopolies come and go. Long-distance telephone service was a virtual monopoly of AT&T until the development of microwave and wireless transmission enabled companies like Sprint and MCI to offer alternative services. The railroads had a monopoly over long-distance transportation until the advent of trucking and air transportation. Today's "monopolies" are computer companies like Microsoft and Intel that dominate operating systems or microchip processing; if history is a guide, these "monopolies" will lose their dominant positions within a decade or two.

The **oligopolist** is a price searcher who must consider the reactions of competitors.

The most complex price searcher is the **oligopolist**—a firm that is sufficiently large to worry about the entire market for the product as well as the reactions of its rivals. Automobiles, breakfast cereals, refrigerators, and cigarettes are examples of oligopolistic industries.

Entry barriers are any conditions that put new firms at a disadvantage to old firms.

What differentiates one type of price searcher from another are the barriers to entry. **Entry barriers** are conditions that put new firms at a disadvantage to old firms. Examples are large minimum efficient scale, requiring huge capital investments; patents; monopoly ownership of critical raw materials; and government restrictions on entry such as licensing requirements (for example, TV stations or plumbers) or tariffs on imported products.

If entry barriers are weak and economies of scale are small, monopolistic competition is likely. As entry barriers increase, monopolistic competition shades into oligopoly. As barriers to entry grow, oligopolists act more boldly. Indeed, a group of oligopolists may get together and act like a single-firm monopoly. Pure monopoly requires absolute entry barriers and no close substitutes. It is difficult to find examples of pure monopolies in the world economy today.

Price Searching

A price-searching firm must lower its price to sell more.

The behavior of each price-searching firm is governed by certain general principles. First, a price searcher faces a downward-sloping demand curve. Unlike a perfect competitor, the price searcher cannot sell all it wants at the going market price. For the firm to sell more, it must lower its price. Second, the price searcher, like all firms in general, maximizes its profit by producing that output at which marginal revenue equals marginal costs.

Marginal revenue, *MR,* is the increase in revenue brought about by increasing output (sales) by one unit.

Figure 7.1 illustrates the difference between price takers and price searchers. The price taker's demand curve (Panel A) is perfectly elastic because the price is dictated by the market. In contrast, the price-searching firm (Panel B) must lower its price on all units sold in order to sell more. **Marginal revenue**, *MR,* is the increase in revenue brought about by increasing output (sales) by one unit. In the case of the price taker, when it increases sales from seven to eight, the firm can continue to charge the market price of \$6. Revenue rises by \$6 from \$42 to \$48. To the perfect competitor, $P = MR$. In the case of the price searcher (Panel B), to increase sales from seven to eight, the price must be reduced from \$6 to \$5. When the price is \$5, the firm loses \$1 per unit on the first seven units sold compared to the alternative of selling those seven units at \$6. The firm loses the shaded area, $c =$ \$7. The firm sells an extra unit at \$5 and thus gains the shaded area, $d =$ \$5. The net loss is the marginal revenue, $MR =$ Area $d -$ Area $c = -$\$2. As the example shows, price searchers can actually reduce revenues by producing more.

For the price searcher, price is greater than marginal revenue: $P > MR$.

For price searchers, the price does not equal marginal revenue. Instead, price is greater than marginal revenue: $P > MR$. In effect, selling more output "spoils the market" on the earlier units sold because their price is lower. (See Example 7.1.)

The Marginal Revenue Curve

The price searcher faces both a demand schedule and a marginal revenue schedule. To illustrate, imagine you own a mineral spring that faces the downward-sloping demand

FIGURE 7.1 The Relationship Between Price and Marginal Revenue

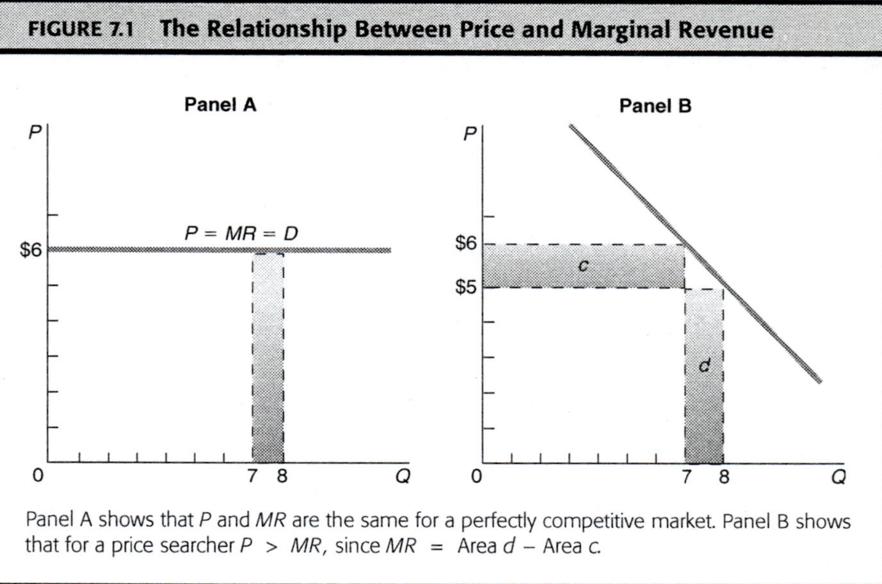

Panel A shows that *P* and *MR* are the same for a perfectly competitive market. Panel B shows that for a price searcher $P > MR$, since MR = Area d – Area c.

schedule in Figure 7.2. The *D* curve has a maximum price of $4 where zero units are sold and a maximum quantity of four units that can be sold at a zero price. At $4 per liter no water can be sold, but each $1 reduction in price increases quantity demanded by one liter. The total revenue schedule is price times quantity and is shown in column 3. Revenue is maximized when P = $2 and TR = $4. The *MR* schedule is in column 4. The *MR* of going from one unit to two units is $1, as revenue rises from $3 to $4. The *MR* of going from two units to three units is –$1. It is against the firm's interest to increase sales from two to three units, as the marginal revenue is negative. Why should the firm increase output if revenue falls as a consequence?

EXAMPLE 7.1 PRICE SEARCHING AND "SKIMMING THE MARKET"

A recognized marketing strategy is called *skimming the market.* Firms introduce new products by initially offering relatively small quantities. When first introduced to the market, the ballpoint pen, the transistor radio, the briefcase-sized typewriter, the color television set, the laptop computer, and the electronic organizer were produced in small production runs and were initially priced very high relative to their prices one year later. This marketing strategy aims at first "skimming off" the top of the market those consumers willing to pay the highest prices for the product. To achieve high prices, relatively small quantities must be supplied to prevent the price from being driven down. After the market is skimmed of the highest-paying customers, mass production takes place, and, in order to sell large volumes of output, the price must be dropped.

FIGURE 7.2 Marginal Revenue and Demand

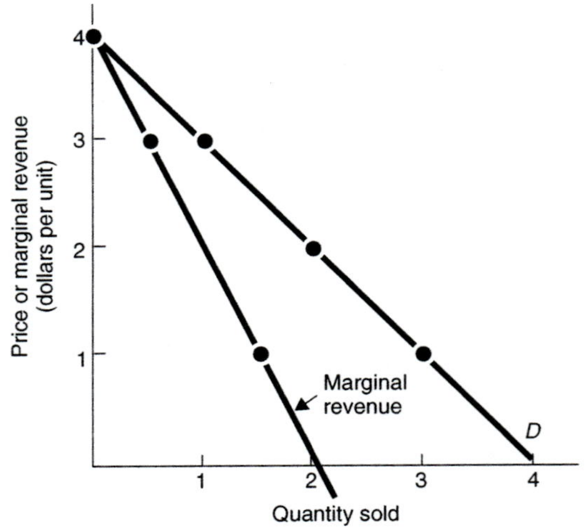

(1) Quantity Sold per Week Q	(2) Price P	(3) Total Revenue $TR = P \times Q$ (3) = (1) × (2)	Marginal Revenue MR (4a)	(4b)
0	$4	0		
			3	
1	3	3		2
			1	
2	2	4		0
			–1	
3	1	3		

Columns (1) and (2) are the demand curve. Column (3) is total revenue, the product of price time quantity. Column 4a shows the marginal revenue of going from 0 to 1, 1 to 2, etc., and is placed between the lines. Column 4b is the average of the between-the-lines *MR* and is placed on the same line as *Q*. Below we show that when the demand curve is a straight line, the marginal revenue curve is twice as steep. It intersects the horizontal axis at one-half the quantity when the demand curve intersects the horizontal axis.

Whether *MR* is positive or negative depends on whether demand is elastic or inelastic at the corresponding price. Remember from Chapter 3 that the price elasticity of demand is the percentage change in quantity demanded divided by the percentage change in price. If demand is elastic (greater than unity), a decrease in price causes the quantity demanded to increase faster than the price decreases, and so revenue rises.

When demand is elastic, therefore, a reduction in price raises total revenue so that *MR* is positive. When demand is inelastic, a reduction in price lowers total revenue, and *MR* is negative. For example, in Figure 7.2 demand is elastic between the prices of \$3 and \$4, and demand is inelastic between prices of \$2 and \$1. When *MR* is negative, the *MR* curve is below the horizontal axis.

With straight-line demand curves, the *MR* curve will be exactly halfway between the demand curve and the vertical axis.

Figure 7.2 illustrates a useful relationship between demand and marginal revenue curves. Whenever the demand curve is a straight line, *the* MR *curve will be exactly halfway between the demand curve and the vertical axis.* This rule is useful because it makes it easy to draw the *MR* curve associated with a straight-line demand curve.

Profit Maximizing by a Monopoly Producer

Like any profit-maximizing firm, the monopolist maximizes profit at that output where *MR* = *MC*. To keep the example simple, each unit of output costs \$4 to produce—that is, the marginal cost equals \$4. As output rises from 1 to 2 to 3, total costs rise from \$4 to \$8 to \$12. In this case, the average cost and marginal cost of production are both \$4 at each level of output. In Figure 7.3, the horizontal line labeled *MC* indicates that marginal (and average) cost is constant. The demand curve is *D*. The monopolist can sell nothing at a price of \$10, seven units at a price of \$3, and so on.

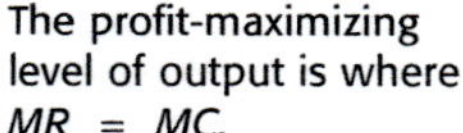
The profit-maximizing level of output is where *MR* = *MC*.

The demand curve determines the price, and where *MR* and *MC* intersect determines the quantity.

The demand curve facing the monopolist (*D*) is a straight line with a maximum price of \$10 and a maximum quantity of ten units. The *MR* curve intersects the *MC* curve at $Q = 3$ and the horizontal axis at $Q = 5$. The firm maximizes its profit at $Q = 3$ where *MR* = *MC*, since whenever *MR* exceeds *MC*, it pays the firm to expand output. *The demand curve determines the price, and where* MR *and* MC *intersect determines the quantity.* The price charged by the firm is \$7 because that is the highest price the firm

FIGURE 7.3 Profit Maximization: The Monopoly Firm

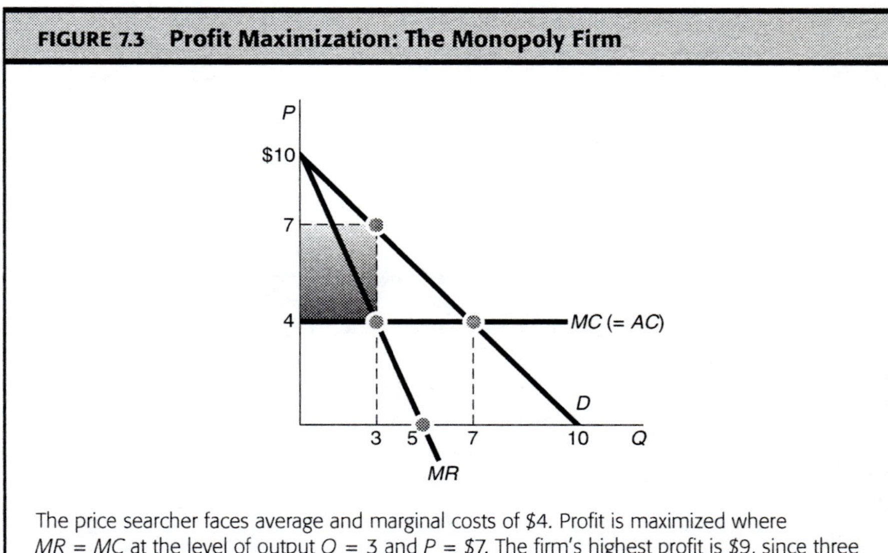

The price searcher faces average and marginal costs of \$4. Profit is maximized where *MR* = *MC* at the level of output $Q = 3$ and $P = \$7$. The firm's highest profit is \$9, since three units are sold at a per-unit profit of \$3.

can get when its output is three units (where $MR = MC$). The firm's profit is the light shaded area ($9), since the firm makes $3 per unit (Price − average cost) and sells three units. If the firm charged a higher price, it would sell fewer units and make smaller profits. For example, with the price of $8 it sells only two units. Its profit would then only be $8. Profits can be increased since at $Q = 2$, MR is higher ($6) than MC, indicating the firm can increase profit by increasing output.

The monopolist can set either the profit-maximizing price or the profit-maximizing quantity.

The monopolist maximizes profits either by setting the price at $4 and letting the market buy three units of output or by producing three units of output and letting the market establish a $7 price. *The monopolist can set either the profit-maximizing price or the profit-maximizing quantity.* Once it sets one, the market determines the other.

Some monopolists maximize profit by determining the profit-maximizing output. The DeBeers Company of South Africa, a syndicate that controls most of the sales of raw diamonds, maximizes profits by determining what quantity of raw diamonds to offer on the world raw-diamond market. Other monopolists set the monopoly price and then let the market determine the quantity. When AT&T had a monopoly over long-distance phone services, it set rates to motivate telephone users to demand the profit-maximizing quantity.

Oligopoly

Oligopoly is characterized by a small number of producers, barriers to entry, price searching, and mutual interdependence.

Oligopoly covers markets between monopoly and monopolistic competition. An oligopoly is an industry in which firms are price searchers and there are:

1. a relatively small number of firms
2. barriers to entry
3. recognized mutual interdependence

In an oligopoly, the number of firms is so small, relative to of the market, that each of the firms recognizes the interlinking of its fortunes. Oligopoly is more complicated than perfect competition, pure monopoly, or monopolistic competition because there is no one theory of oligopoly. In either perfect competition or monopoly, the firm need only equate marginal cost and marginal revenue. In the case of oligopoly, things are not that simple. The marginal revenue an oligopolist gains from a higher price depends on the reactions of rival firms, which might be difficult to predict.

Mutual Interdependence

Mutual interdependence characterizes an industry where it is recognized that the actions of one firm affect other firms in the industry.

There is a "relatively small" number of firms when each firm must take the reactions of rival firms into account. One firm must consider how a rival firm will respond to its actions, and vice versa. When firms must consider the responses of rival firms, the industry is characterized by **mutual interdependence.** Mutual interdependence is the most important feature of oligopoly. In making decisions concerning prices, quantities, and qualities of output, mutually interdependent firms must consider the reactions of rival firms. The rival firm, in reacting to the first firm, must consider how the first firm will react to its action.

In some oligopolistic industries, the pattern of reaction may be well understood by all participants; it may be dictated by custom or agreement. In other industries, the reactions of rival firms may be unpredictable, and participants must use strategic behavior to outguess and outmaneuver their rivals.

Strategic behavior occurs when oligopolistic rivals adopt strategies to outguess other firms.

Strategic Behavior Figure 7.4 provides an example of strategic behavior. **Strategic behavior** occurs when oligopolistic rivals adopt strategies to outguess other firms. Firm A and Firm B are mutually interdependent oligopolists. Each firm's profit depends on the price charged by the other. In this example, both firms earn exactly the same profit when they charge the same price. If one charges a slightly lower price, then it will make a large profit while the higher-priced firm makes a low profit.

Figure 7.4 shows a set of outcomes. Each firm has the option of choosing a price of either $20 or $19. Firm A's price choices are shown on the left side; Firm B's price choices are shown along the top. The profits earned by Firm A and Firm B are determined by the prices the two firms choose. Firm A's profits are shown in the lower left corner of each cell; Firm B's profits are shown in the upper right corner of each cell. When both charge $20, both earn $2500; when both charge $19, both earn $1500. When one charges $20 and the other charges $19, the lower-priced firm earns $3000 while the higher-priced firm earns only $1000.

One oligopolist stands to gain a high profit (at the expense of the other) by selecting the lower price if the rival selects the higher price. Both stand to earn a decent profit if both select the lower price. If both select the higher price, each earns a substantial profit. Yet each oligopolist must make a pricing decision not knowing what the other firm will do.

FIGURE 7.4 Profit Payoffs to a Two Firm Oligopoly

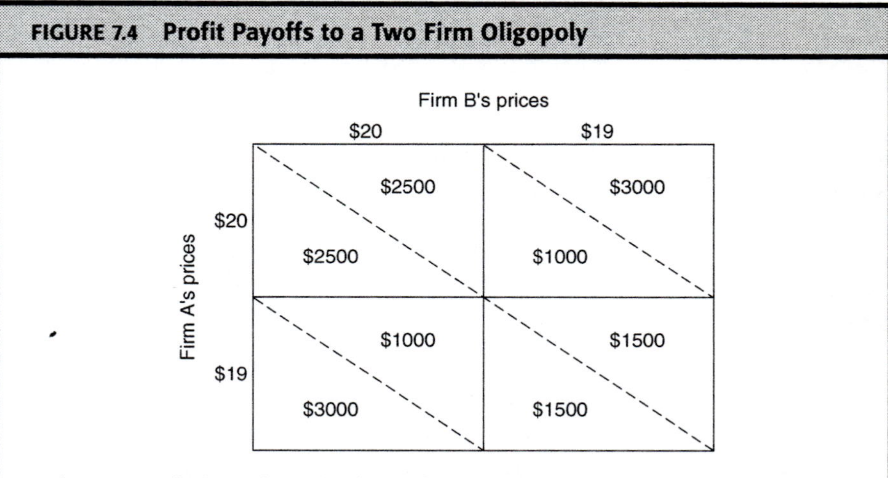

Each square (cell) shows the profits that each firm would earn when various combinations of prices are charged by the two firms. Firm A's profits are shown in the lower left-hand corner of each cell, and Firm B's profits are shown in the upper right-hand corner of each cell. If A charges $19 and B charges $20, A would earn a profit of $3000 and B would earn $1000. What strategy will each pursue? Both A and B are likely to charge $19, and thus each will earn $1500 profit. If one charged $20 and the other $19, the low-priced firm would earn $3000 and the high-priced firm only $1000. If A and B had to make pricing decisions repeatedly, they might learn to cooperate and each charge $20.

The oligopolist must guess how the rival firm will react. The reasoning would probably be as follows: "My rival probably won't risk charging the higher $20 price because of the fear that I will select the lower $19 price. I thus believe my rival will select the lower $19 price. If I were to select the higher $20 price, I will earn only $1000, whereas if I select the lower price I'll earn $1500. I'll therefore select the lower $19 price." If the rival firm uses the same reasoning and also decides to select the lower price, the two firms have correctly anticipated the actions of the other, and both have chosen the appropriate strategy.

In this situation, Firm A and Firm B each would select a price of $19 and pocket a profit of $1500. They are, however, aware that if both charged $20, each could earn a profit of $2500. If A and B made pricing decisions repeatedly over a long period of time, it is likely that Firms A and B somehow would learn that they are both better off charging higher prices. They might learn to cooperate and choose the strategy (a $20 price) that maximizes joint profits. There is another way they could settle immediately on a $20 price: They could reach an agreement that both would charge the higher price. For another "game," see Example 7.2.

Just as a concept of equilibrium applies to supply and demand in competitive markets, a concept of equilibrium applies to strategic behavior. A **Nash equilibrium**[1] is a set of strategies, one for each player, such that no player has an incentive to unilaterally change his or her action. Players are in equilibrium if a change in strategies by any one of them would lead the other player to earn less remaining with the current strategy.[2]

Notice that the strategic game described in Figure 7.4 is a Nash equilibrium. Both firms have chosen the $19 price, and each earns $1500 profit. If Firm A were to change its strategy and choose the $20 price, Firm B would not change its strategy. By continuing to charge $19, its profit would rise to $3000. The same would be true of Firm A if Firm B were to change its price to $20.

A **cartel** is an arrangement that allows the participating firms to coordinate their output and pricing decisions to earn monopoly profits.

Cartel Agreements The most direct way for an oligopoly to coordinate pricing and output decisions is to form a **cartel,** binding on all parties, to agree on prices or market shares. If successful, such agreements allow the oligopolistic firms to earn monopoly profits for the industry as a whole.

We can use Figure 7.3 to illustrate a cartel. Instead of one (monopoly) producer, we now have three. They can either engage in strategic behavior against each other or formally agree to all charge the monopoly price ($7) and to share the market equally (each sells one unit of output). As long as each adheres to the cartel agreement, each sells one unit for $7 while incurring a cost of $4 for a profit of $3. The price is well above the marginal cost.

Figure 7.3 shows why cartels are naturally unstable. Each of the three producers can produce an additional unit of output for $4. They could therefore increase their profits by lowering their price (perhaps through a secret deal with the customer)

[1]The Nash equilibrium is named after Nobel laureate mathematician John Nash (see www.gametheory.net/Dictionary/People/JohnNash.html), whose life was fictionalized in the popular movie *A Beautiful Mind.*

[2]This definition is taken from http://www.gametheory.net/Dictionary/NashEquilibrium.html.

EXAMPLE 7.2 THE PRISONERS' DILEMMA

The prisoners' dilemma game is a way to analyze a situation much like that often faced by oligopolistic producers. It explains why some oligopolists cooperate with rivals while others try to outmaneuver them. The setup is that two bank robbers have been apprehended by the police; they are being interrogated in separate rooms. If both talk, both go to prison for five years. If one talks and the other remains quiet, the one who talks is set free while the silent bank robber receives a 20-year jail sentence. If neither talks, both get only one year. Each prisoner is in a dilemma. Each knows that by keeping quiet both can get off with a light one-year sentence. But each has an incentive to talk—each can get off free if he or she confesses while the other keeps quiet. It pays each to confess given that the other does not; and thus both confess! In the prisoners' dilemma game both players benefit from cooperating, but each player has an incentive to cheat on the agreement.

Note that the prisoners' dilemma game is also a Nash equilibrium solution. If the first prisoner were to change strategy (remain silent), the second prisoner would not change strategy. He should still remain silent and go free.

Economists apply the prisoners' dilemma to many of today's oligopolists. Airlines could earn higher profits if they coordinated their prices, services, and markets, but they have to worry that their competitors will not cooperate. For example, if one airline unilaterally announces that it will offer more legroom in economy class, other airlines will probably have to do the same and industry profits will fall. Similarly, Coca-Cola and Pepsi would earn more profits if they did not spend so much on advertising, but each keeps on spending billions of dollars to protect itself against the other's advertising campaigns.

enough to steal that customer away from one of the other two firms. If, for example, the first firm can steal one customer away from the others at $6.75, the firm's profits will rise from $3 to $5.75. Although the cartel agreement specifically forbids such behavior, each firm must worry that other firms will cheat. As the concern becomes stronger, there will be pressure for one firm to cheat first. If it waits to be cheated, it might be too late.

In most countries, cartel agreements are against the law and must be kept secret. In the case of secret cartels, cheating is even more likely. In some cases, cartels are legal, but even in these instances, it is difficult to prevent cheating.

There are numerous historical examples of cartels. The member nations of the Organization of Petroleum Exporting Countries (OPEC) meet regularly, with full coverage by the world's press, to attempt to set the price of crude oil. The International Air Transport Association (IATA) also meets to set airfares for travel between countries.

Every cartel member can gain through the attainment of monopoly profits if each adheres to the agreement. Each member can gain by cheating on the agreement if the others do not cheat.

Most cartels have a history of instability because of the difficulty of enforcing collusive behavior. Most, like the ill-fated sugar, cocoa, tin, and coffee cartels, either disappear quickly or have no noticeable effect on prices. Greed leads firms to join cartels; greed also leads firms to break up cartels. Very few cartels are successful over the long run. The OPEC cartel, the most successful in history, has not been able consistently to enforce a strict monopoly price. There are many temptations for its members, especially those in need of cash, to cheat. In the 1980s and much of the 1990s, OPEC could not enforce discipline on its members. Although OPEC assigned its members production quotas, some members cheated by ignoring their quotas and producing above them.

With the long buildup to the Iraq war in early 2003, the loss of much Iraqi oil to the world market strengthened the hand of OPEC and particularly of its largest oil exporter, Saudi Arabia. With virtually all OPEC members producing at capacity, Saudi Arabia remained the only oil exporter that could either decrease or increase its production to affect world oil prices. In fact, during this critical period, Saudi Arabia increased its oil production whenever necessary to offset the loss of Iraqi oil.

Conscious Parallelism Informal agreements and conscious parallelism can also be used to coordinate oligopoly pricing and output decisions. In some industries, a price leader sets industry prices. Rival firms follow the price leader's price decreases and price increases. The price leader keeps a sharp eye on market demand and costs that are common to all firms. A price leader is a firm whose price changes are consistently imitated by other firms in the industry.

Examples of price leadership are plentiful. In the ready-to-eat breakfast cereal industry, whose "big three" corporations are Kellogg's, Post, and General Mills, Kellogg's leads for most product lines while General Mills and Post lead for their own best product lines.

Conscious parallelism occurs when oligopoly firms behave in the same way even though they have not agreed to act in a parallel manner.

Through conscious parallelism, the actions of producers can be coordinated without formal or even informal agreements.

Conscious parallelism is the most subtle form of collusion. **Conscious parallelism** occurs when oligopoly firms behave in the same way even though they have not agreed to act in a parallel manner. Examples are the submitting of identical bids and switching to high-season rates at the same time without any formal agreement to do so. All firms use their understanding of the industry to make their own decisions and anticipate the behavior of rival firms. Oligopolist firms are intimately acquainted with the way things work in their own industries. Business practices followed in the industry are well known—such as common percentage markups, the use of round numbers, the charging of prices like $4.95, and policies like "splitting the difference" or not offering discounts on international business-class tickets. As long as each oligopolist understands these standard practices, it can anticipate how rival firms will behave in given situations. If all firms in the oligopolistic industry use standard practices, they will behave in a parallel fashion, even without formal agreements.

Efficiency, Antitrust, and Network Externalities

There is **economic inefficiency** when it is possible to rearrange production so that the benefits to gainers outweigh the costs to the losers.

Monopoly is inefficient because it produces where $P > MC$.

In the case of monopoly, price *exceeds* marginal cost. In Figure 7.3, $P = \$7$ and $MC = \$4$. $P > MC$ implies economic inefficiency. There is **economic inefficiency** when it is possible to rearrange production so that the benefits to gainers outweigh the costs to the losers.

The economic inefficiency of monopoly follows directly from the fact that $P > MR$. Since the monopolist equates MR to MC, it must be that $P > MC$. But consumers buy until the marginal benefit to them equals the price. Hence, the price of the monopolized good is a measure of its marginal benefit to consumers. On the other hand, MC measures the marginal cost of the resources used to produce another unit. If marginal benefits to society exceed marginal costs to society, it follows that an extra unit of output of the monopolized good would add more to society's welfare than it would subtract. Thus, there would be a net gain to society from producing more of the monopolized good.

If this were a perfectly competitive industry, firms would expand output to where $P = MC$ and economic inefficiency is removed. If this were a competitive market, seven units of output would be produced at a price of $4 (where $D = MC$ in Figure 7.3). Stated simply, monopoly is costly to consumers and society because it raises prices by the artificial restriction of output to obtain the monopoly price.

There may be additional costs associated with gaining monopoly power. Owners of firms wish to have a monopoly because their profits are safe from competition. Thus, agents are willing to expend resources to "buy" monopoly profits, running in the millions or even billions of dollars. Monopolies can be achieved and maintained through government charters, franchises, regulations, quotas, or tariffs on foreign products. American automobile manufacturers and steel producers and their unions maintain staffs of lawyers, writers, and business economists to lobby Congress for protection from foreign imports. Most producers want government assistance aimed at reducing competition in their industry. This principle applies to industrial giants as well as to local firms lobbying for zoning laws. Scarce resources—lawyers, TV time for commercials, and so forth—are devoted to acquiring monopoly power. These costs are in addition to the costs imposed on society once the monopoly is achieved.

Monopoly rent-seeking is the expenditure of resources to gain monopoly rights from government.

Monopoly rent-seeking is the resources expended to gain monopolies from government and other agencies that can grant monopoly rights. (See Example 7.3.)

EXAMPLE 7.3 CAMPAIGN FINANCE AND MONOPOLY RENT-SEEKING

In its 2002 session, Congress passed campaign finance reform in the form of the McCain-Feingold Act (entitled the Bipartisan Campaign Reform Act). The McCain-Feingold Act imposed stricter rules governing campaign contributions, especially the use of "soft money" contributions from corporations and labor unions. (The McCain-Feingold Act has been challenged in the courts on the grounds that it illegally restricts free speech.) A number of economists argue that political contributions are ultimately intended to buy monopoly rents from the government. Labor unions make political contributions to gain "monopolies" for their members in the form of restrictions on immigration and protection from foreign imports. Corporations contribute to gain special provisions in the tax code. Sugar growers and dairy farmers contribute to encourage the government to give them high government-set prices. If the government was no longer in the business of granting monopolies in the form of tariffs, agricultural price supports, income tax exemptions, and licenses there would be no need for campaign finance reform. If we had free trade, a flat tax on income, fair auctions of licenses, and so on, people would no longer have to engage in rent seeking and would contribute to political parties for ideological reasons, not for personal gain.

Monopoly and Antitrust

The most notable monopolies of the past either were sole sources of long-distance transport (railroads), were dominant controllers of raw materials (Alcoa Aluminum), or were characterized by better innovation and technology (Eastman Kodak and IBM). These were created because of inventions covered by patents, the granting of franchises, or the control of a key raw material. Public distrust of monopoly peaked in the late nineteenth century during the era of the "robber barons" who appeared to control transportation and finance. Accordingly, antitrust legislation was enacted, beginning with the **Sherman Antitrust Act of 1890,** which, despite a number of later antitrust laws, remains the cornerstone of U.S. antitrust policy. The Sherman Act, which declared monopolies and the attempt to create monopolies illegal, was used to break up the American Tobacco and Standard Oil monopolies in 1913. Subsequently, a number of powerful companies—U.S. Steel, Alcoa, Eastman Kodak, IBM, and Microsoft—have been prosecuted by the Department of Justice for monopolistic business practices.

The **Sherman Antitrust Act of 1890** is the cornerstone of U.S. antitrust policy. It declared monopolies and the attempt to create monopolies illegal.

Antitrust laws raise a difficult legal and public policy issue. Some businesses will come to dominate their industry due to better innovation, management, or superior but fair competition. In such cases, antitrust laws should not be used to punish success. In other cases, companies may have become monopolies due to unfair competition or even illegal business practices. Another public policy issue is the fact that monopolies are transitory. Eventually, rival companies offer better products or more convenient substitutes at lower prices, and the once-mighty monopoly must compete just to stay in business. IBM was the dominant firm in the computer industry when it was charged with antitrust violations by the Department of Justice in 1969. By the time the suit was dismissed "without merit" in 1982, IBM was just one of many participants in the computer industry, having lost out in the race for the personal computer market. The Department of Justice's case against Microsoft Corporation bears many similarities to the IBM case (see Example 7.4).

Monopolies in the Long Run

When there is competition in an industry, the long-run entry and exit of firms ensures that economic profits will be squeezed out of the industry. In the case of the monopolist, the long-run/short-run distinction is not as important because barriers to entry prevent new firms from entering the industry and squeezing out monopoly profits. There is no automatic tendency for monopoly profits to be eliminated by the *entry of new firms.*

Unlike competitive economic profits, monopoly profits can persist for long periods.

In the United States economy today, it is difficult to find pure monopolies because of actual or potential substitutes and because *absolute* barriers to entry are rarely present. Exceptional monopoly profits have historically promoted the development of closer substitutes for the monopolist's product. As already mentioned, the railroads' monopoly over freight transportation was eventually broken by the development of trucking and air freight; the advent of microwave transmission broke AT&T's monopoly over long-distance telephone service. Cellular phone services are breaking the monopoly of local telephone companies over local service.

EXAMPLE 7.4 THE DEPARTMENT OF JUSTICE'S CASE AGAINST MICROSOFT

More than 90 percent of personal computers (PCs) operate with Microsoft's Windows operating system. Microsoft's licensing agreements with PC manufacturers required them to pay a fee on every computer they produced whether they used Windows or not. Microsoft's licensing agreements also allowed Microsoft to dictate the start-up screen, which permitted it to promote its own middleware products, most importantly its Web browser, MSN Explorer, over competitive products, such as Netscape's Navigator. In 1994 and then in 1995, the Department of Justice charged Microsoft with violations of antitrust laws on the grounds that it had a monopoly in operating systems, was attempting to create a monopoly in Internet browsers, and was denying consumers choice. Nineteen states joined the Department of Justice in its suit. On 3 April 2003, the presiding judge ruled that Microsoft's behavior was illegal. Among the remedies to be considered was the breaking up of Microsoft into separate companies. Microsoft appealed, claiming that it was being punished for superior innovation and product development. In August 2003, an agreement was reached between the Department of Justice and Microsoft in which Microsoft agreed to make available to certain competitors some of its closed-source codes and to give PC consumers more choice of Web browsers. Notably, the consent decree does not allow Linux, Microsoft's major competitor, which uses open-source software (as opposed to Window's closed-source software) to interoperate with its common Internet file system.

A search of the World Wide Web shows more than 100 established Web browsers in addition to the two market leaders, Microsoft Explorer and Netscape's Navigator. It is quite possible that one or more of these browsers will prove superior to the current leaders and come to dominate the market.

Although monopoly profits will not automatically be driven down to the normal return, there is a tendency for high monopoly profits to promote the development of substitutes in the very long run.

Currently, Microsoft Windows accounts for more than 90 percent of PC operating systems. Microsoft's domination was so strong as to promote an antitrust charges (as noted above). Linux, an open-source operating system, was created initially as a hobby by a student, Linus Torvalds, at the University of Helsinki in Finland in 1991. Programmers around the world are free to assist in the development of Linux's source codes, which are freely available to everyone. Companies and developers may charge money for it as long as the source code remains available. Linux may be used for a wide variety of purposes, including networking, software development, and as an end-user platform. Linux is often considered an excellent, low-cost alternative to more expensive operating systems, such as Windows. Linux has become popular worldwide, and a vast number of software programmers have adapted Linux to their individual needs. Currently, Linux has more than 20 million users worldwide (http://www.linux.org/info/index.html). With its unique concept of open-source software and software development by an army of volunteer programmers, Linux could pose a serious threat to Microsoft in the long run. Microsoft's major costs are those associated with developing new generations of Windows. If Linux can develop its higher-generation systems at basically a zero cost, it would be hard for Microsoft to remain competitive.

Monopoly and Network Externalities

Network externalities exist when the act of joining a network confers a benefit on all other members of the network.

The Internet and communications revolutions have created a new type of monopoly based on network externalities. **Network externalities** exist when the act of joining a network confers a benefit on all other members of the network.

Examples of networks are owners of fax machines, users of PCs that use a common operating system and can easily exchange files, and users of cell phones with text messaging. The greater the number of network members, the more valuable the network. (If you were the only fax machine owner, it would be of little value; if you were the only user of WordPerfect, you would find it difficult to exchange files with others.)

Monopolies can be created when network externalities exist because of the importance of common standards. When a new technology is first developed, there may be a number of competing standards, such as VHS or Beta standards for VCRs, or IBM and Macintosh standards for PCs. As the size of the network increases, however, it becomes advantageous to tip toward the standard that is expected to become the common one. Even if you prefer WordPerfect to Word, Beta to VHS, or Macintosh to Windows, new entrants to the network will choose the common standard, even if the alternative standard is in some sense superior. An example of tipping is the adoption of the qwerty standard for typewriter keyboards (qwerty is named for the first six characters on the upper left hand side of the keyboard) even though a different keyboard standard may allow for faster data entry. The qwerty standard, which was adopted in the era of manual typewriters to avoid the problem of keys sticking together, continues to be used on computer keyboards even though they pose no sticking problem. Once a technology standard has been chosen, the costs of switching to a different standard are substantial. They constitute a new type of barrier to entry and protect established producers.

Network externalities explain some of today's monopolies, such as the Microsoft Windows, the Intel monopoly of microprocessors (buyers look to see if the PC says "Intel inside"), and the monopoly of word processing by MS Word. Network externalities make it difficult for new entrants to compete with the established standard-setter, and it may lock industries in to inferior technologies due to the costs of switching to another standard.

Concentration Ratios

The ***x*-firm concentration ratio** is the percentage of industry output, accounted for by the largest *x* domestic firms in the industry.

The statistical tool commonly used to measure the extent of competition is the concentration ratio. The ***x*-firm concentration ratio** is the percentage of industry sales accounted for by the largest *x* firms in the industry. The four-firm concentration ratio, for example, is the percentage of industry sales accounted for by the four largest firms in the industry.

The higher the concentration ratio, the higher the presumed degree of monopoly power in that industry.

The higher the concentration ratio, the higher the presumed degree of monopoly power in that industry. If the four-firm concentration ratio is high (see Table 7.1), the price-searching power is presumed to be great.

Concentration ratios are an imperfect measure of the extent of oligopoly or monopoly for several reasons.

First, some markets are worldwide, such as automobiles and steel. Concentration ratios should really measure the percentage of the sales of the top x world firms of the world market rather than the share of the top x *domestic* firms of the domestic market. The concentration ratio in American automobile manufacturing belies the fact that the big three American automobile producers face intense competition from Japanese, German, Korean, and Italian automobile manufacturers.

TABLE 7.1 Concentration Ratios (Some Examples)

Industry	*Four-Firm Concentration Ratio*	*Number of Firms in the Industry*
Cigarettes	93	8
Malt beverages	90	160
Motor vehicles and car bodies	84	398
Aircraft	79	151
Cigars	74	25
Guided missiles and space vehicles	71	24
Potato chips and similar snacks	70	333
Tires and inner tubes	70	104
Internal combustion engines	56	250
Meat packing	50	1,296
Electronic computers	45	803
Semiconductors and related devices	41	823
Blast furnaces and steel mills	37	135
Bread, cake, and related products	34	374
Petroleum refining	30	131
Industrial and organic chemicals	29	489
Men's and boys' shirts	28	527
Pharmaceutical preparations	26	583
Fluid milk	22	525
Periodicals	20	4,390
Women's and misses' dresses	11	3,943
Plastics	5	7,605
Commercial printing	7	28,485
Industrial machinery	1	22,596

Source: U.S. Census of Manufacturers, MC92-S-2, http://www.census.gov.

Concentration ratios can give a false picture because of foreign competition and the existence of substitutes.

Second, concentration ratios can give a false picture of concentration within the relevant market. The four-firm concentration ratio in the pharmaceutical industry is low (22 percent), yet certain companies tend to dominate specific, narrowly defined, prescription drug markets. For example, Smith-Kline dominates the ulcer therapy market; Hoffmann–La Roche dominates the mild tranquilizer market. Should one count close substitutes as part of the market? Does aluminum foil constitute a single market, or should other flexible wrapping materials, such as waxed paper and plastic wrap, be included?

Third, concentration ratios may conceal the churning forces of competition. Industry X may have a four-firm concentration ratio of 80 percent, but every five years, the top four firms are new firms that have captured the markets of older, declining firms.

Trends in Concentration

There is a widespread impression that concentration has been increasing over time. This impression has been created by erroneously equating increases in the absolute size of firms with increases in their market shares. General Motors has grown substantially over the years, but its share of the American and world automobile industry has actually fallen.

In American manufacturing, the share of manufacturing output accounted for by highly concentrated industries, as measured by industries with four-firm concentration ratios of 50 percent or higher, has not changed for more than 50 years also, the largest 100 firms have accounted for the same percentage of manufacturing for almost a half-century (Table 7.2).

TABLE 7.2 Trends in Concentration in American Manufacturing: Two Measures

Year	*Percentage of Output by Firms with Four-Firm Concentration Ratio of 50 Percent or Above (1)*	*Percentage of Output of 100 Largest Firms (2)*
1947	24	23
1954	30	30
1958	30	32
1972	29	33
1977	28	33
1982	25	33
1994	24	32
2000	24	31

Sources: G. Warren Nutter, *The Extent of Enterprise Monopoly in the United States, 1899–1939* (Chicago: University of Chicago Press, 1951), pp. 35–48, 112–50; F. M. Scherer, *Industrial Market Structure and Economic Performance* (Boston: Houghton Mifflin, 1980), pp. 68–69; U.S. Department of Commerce, "Concentration Ratios in Manufacturing," *1977 Census of Manufacturers*, MC77-SR-9; *1982 Census of Manufacturing*, MC82-S-7. Figures updated by author: www.census.gov.

Although it is difficult to measure the degree of monopolization of an entire economy over time, the most common measures suggest that the economy is not becoming more monopolized. If anything, the statistics point to a remarkable stability of concentration. Moreover, these statistics do not capture the effects of growing international competition as a consequence of the globalization of the world economy.

Summary

1. Both monopolists and oligopolists are price searchers. A pure monopoly is one seller of a good that has no close substitutes, protected from competition by barriers to entry.
2. The price searcher faces a downward-sloping demand curve. The price searcher cannot sell all it wants at the prevailing price, so to sell more, it must lower its price. For price searchers, price is greater than marginal revenue.
3. Marginal revenue is positive when demand is elastic; it is negative when demand is inelastic. Price searchers, therefore, operate where demand is elastic.
4. Price-searching firms, like all profit-maximizing firms, produce that level of output at which $MR = MC$. At the profit-maximizing level of output, price exceeds marginal cost.
5. Price exceeding marginal cost is a sign of the economic inefficiency of monopoly. In addition, resources devoted to obtaining monopoly power (lobbying costs, for example) add to the efficiency losses of monopoly.
6. An oligopoly is an industry composed of a few interdependent firms with barriers to entry and price-searching ability.
7. Oligopolists use strategic behavior to anticipate the reactions of rivals. It is expected that oligopolists will learn to cooperate over time.
8. Nash equilibrium is a standard for determining equilibrium in a strategic game, such as the prisoners' dilemma.
9. Oligopolists can use formal agreements (cartels) and informal agreements (price leadership, conscious parallelism). A cartel is an arrangement that allows participating firms to operate the industry as a shared monopoly. The contradiction is that each member can gain by cheating if the others do not cheat. For this reason, cartels tend to be unstable.
10. Network externalities explain the creation of monopolies based on consumer networks or common standards.
11. The concentration ratio measures the percentage of industry sales accounted for by the largest firms in the industry. It is an imperfect measure of concentration because of world markets, the difficulty of defining the relevant market, and the existence of substitutes.
12. There has not been a long-run increase in the degree of concentration in American industry.

Questions and Problems

1. Cite an example of a pure monopoly that is *not* regulated by government.
2. Explain why price-searching power is limited when there are few barriers to entry.
3. A monopolist can sell 100 units at a price of $5 but must lower the price by $2 in order to sell 110 units. What is the marginal revenue of producing the 10 extra units?
4. Explain why $P > MC$ results in economic inefficiency.
5. Consider an industry comprising four equal-sized firms. Explain what factors determine whether it would be easy or difficult to collude. If the industry price is $10.00, would cheating on agreements be more likely if the average cost were $9.50 or $7.00?
6. Explain how some oligopolists can cooperate without formal agreements.
7. Explain the following statement: "Greed creates cartels, and greed destroys cartels."
8. Explain why an oligopolist's marginal revenue is difficult to calculate.
9. What does "a relatively small" number of producers mean in the context of oligopoly?
10. The four-firm concentration ratio in motor vehicles is 93 percent. The four-firm concentration ratio in petroleum refining is 31 percent. Explain why these figures could be misleading indicators of price-searching power.
11. Consider the following game between company X and company Y. Each has a choice of a high or low advertising budget. The diagram (Figure 7.5) shows X's and Y's payoffs from the two strategies (X's payoffs are shown in the left corner).
    a. What strategy would X and Y pick?
    b. Is this outcome a Nash equilibrium?

FIGURE 7.5

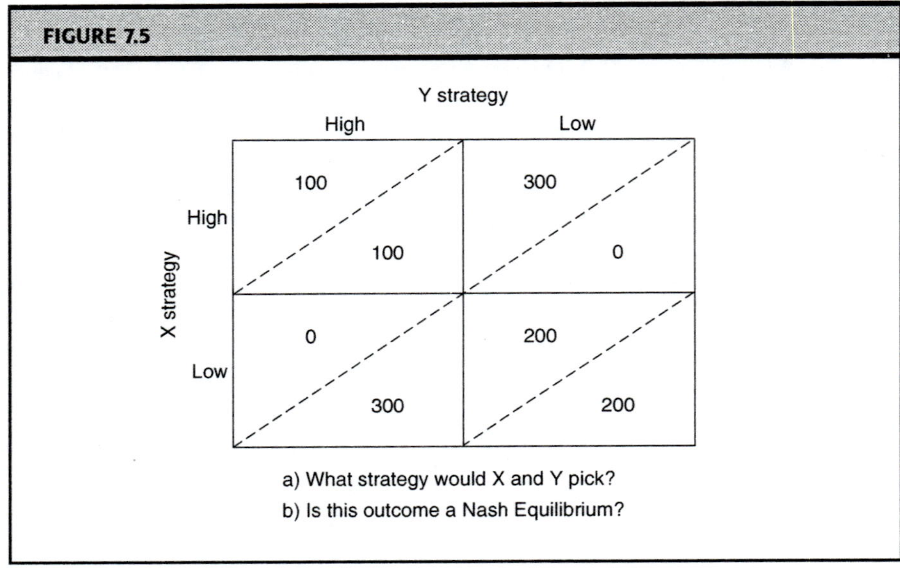

12. Jim and I both produce the only widgets in town. We can produce widgets at $1 per unit. We meet secretly and agree to sell widgets at a price no lower than $15. How stable would this agreement be?

13. Which of the following would be a network externality?

a. Jim subscribes for the first time to an Internet provider service.
b. I buy a box of cereal at the grocery store.
c. My company buys a video-conferencing center.
d. Anne buys a new Lexus.

14. I am thinking of raising my price, but I don't know what my competitors will do. What will my marginal revenue be in this case?

PART THREE

MICROFOUNDATIONS OF MACROECONOMICS

Microeconomics studies specific markets comprising businesses that operate under different types of competitive conditions. Macroeconomics studies the economy as a whole. This separation does not mean there are no subjects common to both specialties. The next three chapters focus on "micro" subjects that provide the foundations of macroeconomics. Macroeconomics studies economywide employment and unemployment, both of which are determined in the nation's labor markets. Hence, we must study the labor market in part and in full if we are to understand this aspect of macroeconomics. How we save and invest depends on interest rates, which are set in credit markets. Therefore, to understand economywide consumption, saving, and investment, we must study interest rates. In addition, how the government collects tax revenues and makes its expenditures affects not only the behavior of individuals but also the economy as a whole, thereby further tying together micro- and macroeconomics.

Only after completing these three microfoundation chapters will we turn to the study of macroeconomics proper—namely, to questions of growth of the economy, business cycles, inflation, and employment.

CHAPTER 8

THE LABOR MARKET: WAGES, EMPLOYMENT, AND UNEMPLOYMENT

Chapter Preview

The previous three chapters explained how business firms decide how much to produce and what prices to charge. We turn now to how these products are produced using the most important factor of production—labor. Labor constitutes the most significant production cost. This chapter explains how businesses decide how much labor to hire and how much to pay. We then generalize this knowledge to study how much employment and unemployment the economy creates.

Factor Markets

The circular-flow diagram presented in Chapter 2 showed that firms operate simultaneously in two types of markets. In the product market, they solve the *what* problem—what to produce and, if a price searcher, how much to charge. In the factor market, firms solve the *how* problem—how to combine the factors of production effectively to produce output.

A **factor (input) market** is one in which firms purchase land, labor, or capital inputs.

The prices of the factors of production are determined in **factor markets,** where firms purchase land, labor, or capital inputs. As in product markets, the purchasing firm can be either a price taker or a price searcher. The price-taking buyer, with a small share of total market, must simply pay the going market rate. The price-searching buyer, with a sufficiently large share of the market, can affect the price by buying more or less of it.

There is less price searching in factor markets than in product markets.

Price taking should prevail in factor markets. In factor markets, a firm must compete for inputs with all firms that use the same inputs. In New York City, universities, foundations, major corporations, brokerage firms, and television networks all compete against each other for secretaries, computer programmers, and office space. Whereas these organizations *do not* compete against each other in product markets, they do compete in factor markets.

Supply and Demand in Factor Markets

Just like prices in product markets, the prices of labor (wage rates), capital (interest rates), and land (rental rates) are determined by supply and demand. Just as there are market supply and demand curves for goods, so are there market supply and demand curves for the factors of production. This chapter is devoted to the labor market, but the general principles apply to all three factors of production.

The Supply of a Factor

The supply of all the factors of production—labor, land, and capital—depends on their opportunity costs. For example, the amount of unskilled labor offered at different wage rates depends on the alternatives sacrificed in other lines of employment. If the wage rate offered for garbage collection is low, fewer unskilled workers will conclude that garbage collection is superior to their next-best alternative.

The **supply curve of a factor** of production is the quantity offered at different factor prices, all other things remaining the same.

The higher the factor price (the wage), the larger the quantity of the factor typically supplied, ceteris paribus.

The Supply Curve The **supply curve of a factor** of production (like labor) is the quantity that is offered for sale (supplied) at different factor prices, all other things remaining the same. The opportunity cost principle reveals a normal shape to this supply curve. The higher the factor price, the greater the number of suppliers of that factor who conclude that this price equals or exceeds the next-best alternative use.

A factor supply curve for unskilled labor is drawn in Figure 8.1. At a wage of $4 per hour, 2000 worker-years of unskilled labor will be supplied; at a higher wage of $6 per hour, 3000 worker-years will be supplied. The factor supply curve has a positive slope.

The Demand for a Factor

The demand for the factors of production depends on the productivity of the factor and the demand for the product the factor is used to produce.

The **demand curve for a factor** shows the quantities of that factor that would be purchased (demanded) at different prices, ceteris paribus.

The Factor Demand Curve The **demand curve for a factor** of production shows the quantities of the factor that would be purchased (demanded) at different prices, ceteris paribus. In most general terms, this demand depends on two forces: the demand for the product the factor produces (derived demand) and the productivity of the factor.

Derived Demand Firms purchase inputs because they produce goods and services that can be sold. No matter how productive an input, it will not be hired unless it produces a good demanded in the marketplace. The garment industry buys sewing machines because they produce the suits, shirts, and dresses consumers buy.

Automobile workers are hired for the automobiles they produce. If the most productive tailor in the world made only three-armed shirts, the demand for the tailor's services would be zero. (See Example 8.1.)

FIGURE 8.1 The Factor Supply Curve (Unskilled Labor)

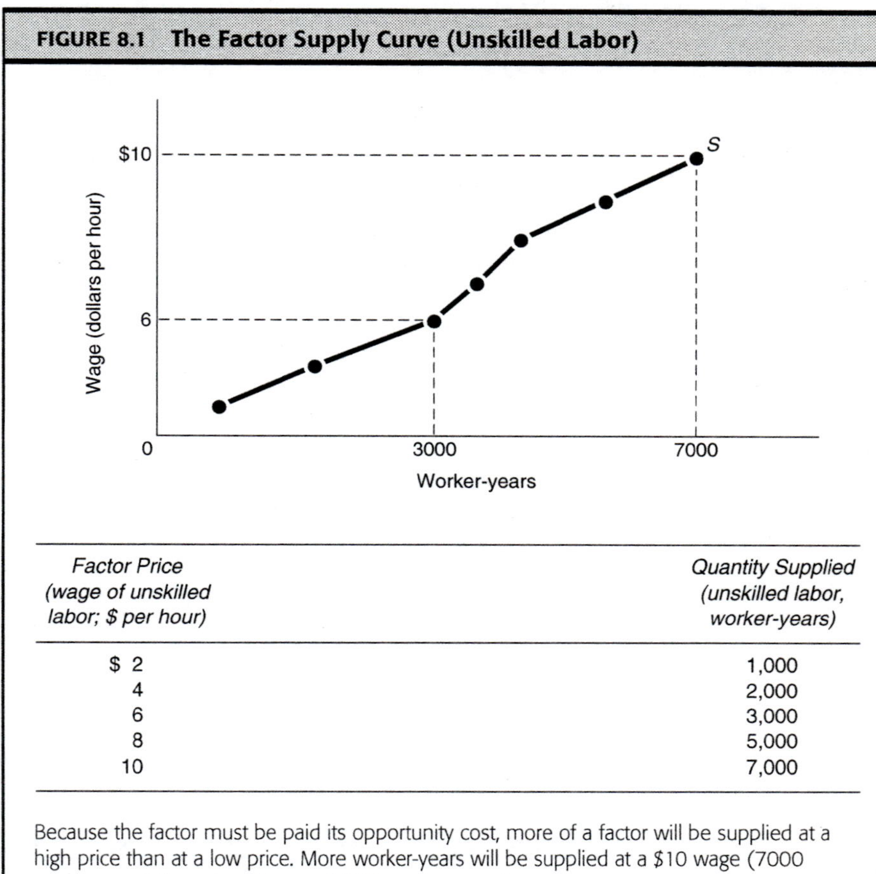

Factor Price (wage of unskilled labor; $ per hour)	*Quantity Supplied (unskilled labor, worker-years)*
$ 2	1,000
4	2,000
6	3,000
8	5,000
10	7,000

Because the factor must be paid its opportunity cost, more of a factor will be supplied at a high price than at a low price. More worker-years will be supplied at a $10 wage (7000 worker-years) than at a $6 wage (3000 worker-years).

EXAMPLE 8.1 LABOR AND DERIVED DEMAND: THE CASE OF THE HANDWRITTEN BIBLE

Newspaper accounts relate the strange story of a handwritten bible that had been passed down from generation to generation of an American family. The bible, done in beautiful miniature handwriting by a teenage girl working steadily for six years, was being offered for sale at an asking price of several million dollars. Experts questioned whether anyone would pay such a large sum of money for the book, primarily because there was no demand for a handwritten bible. Although there was no question about its unique artistry and the time that went into its production, the lack of demand meant that the bible was sold for only a few thousand dollars.

The demand for a factor of production is a **derived demand** because it results (is derived) from the demand for the goods and services the factor of production helps to produce.

The demand for a factor of production is a **derived demand** because it results (is derived) from the demand for the products the factor of production helps to produce. There is a clear linkage between the demand for the product the factor produces and the demand for the factor. If consumers reduce their demand for tomatoes, the demand for workers employed in tomato growing would also fall. When the demand for new houses falls, there is unemployment in the lumber-producing states.

The **marginal product of a factor of production (*MP*)** is the increase in output that results from increasing the factor by one unit.

Marginal Productivity The **marginal product of a factor of production (*MP*)** is the increase in output that results from increasing the factor by one unit, holding all other inputs and the level of technology fixed.

The law of diminishing returns states that as ever larger quantities of a variable factor are combined with a firm's fixed factors, the marginal product of the variable factor will eventually decline. As the firm expands its output, *MP* will fall in the short run.

The marginal product of any factor depends on the quantity and quality of the cooperating factors of production.

The marginal product of any factor of production depends on the quantity and quality of the cooperating factors of production. The farmworker's *MP* will be higher on one acre of fertile Kansas wheat land than on one acre of rocky New England soil. The *MP* of the farmworker will be higher when working with modern farm machinery than with hand implements.

Marginal Revenue Product On the output, side, the firm maximizes profit by producing that output at which marginal revenue and marginal cost are equal. The firm is also guided by profit maximization in its input decisions. The two decisions are basically the same, since deciding on the quantity of inputs determines the level of output.

To understand how firms choose the profit-maximizing levels of factor inputs, consider unskilled labor. Unskilled labor cooperates with other factors that are fixed in supply in the short run. What rule would the firm follow to maximize profits? The firm will continue to hire more unskilled labor as long as the extra revenue produced by those extra units exceeds their additional cost. The addition to revenue of an extra unit of factor input is **marginal revenue product (*MRP*)**.

The **marginal revenue product *(MRP)*** of a factor of production is the extra revenue generated by increasing the factor by one unit.

MRP is the product of marginal product (*MP*) and marginal revenue (*MR*); $MRP = MR \times MP$. *MP* measures by how much output increases when there is a one-unit increase in the factor. *MR* measures by how much revenue increases per unit of increase in output. The product of the two therefore equals *MRP*.

Figure 8.2 illustrates *MRP*. It shows a firm that can sell all it wants at the prevailing $2 product price. The first unit of labor adds five units to output (output rises from zero to five units), which, at a product price of $2, adds $10 to revenue. The *MRP* of the first unit of the factor is therefore $10. The fourth unit of the factor adds two extra units to output (output rises from 12 to 14), and thus adds $4 to revenues.

The marginal revenue product curve is the firm's factor demand curve.

Figure 8.2 illustrates the actions of a profit-maximizing firm. This firm can hire all the unskilled labor it wants at a wage of $6 per hour. The profit-maximizing firm would continue to expand its labor force as long as the *MRP* of an additional unit equals or exceeds the extra cost. Accordingly, this profit-maximizing firm would hire three workers at a $6 wage. The fourth unit of labor would not be hired because it adds more to cost than to revenue. If the wage had been $2 instead of $6, the firm would have hired five units of labor.

FIGURE 8.2 The Factory Demand Curve for Unskilled Later: The Firm and the Market

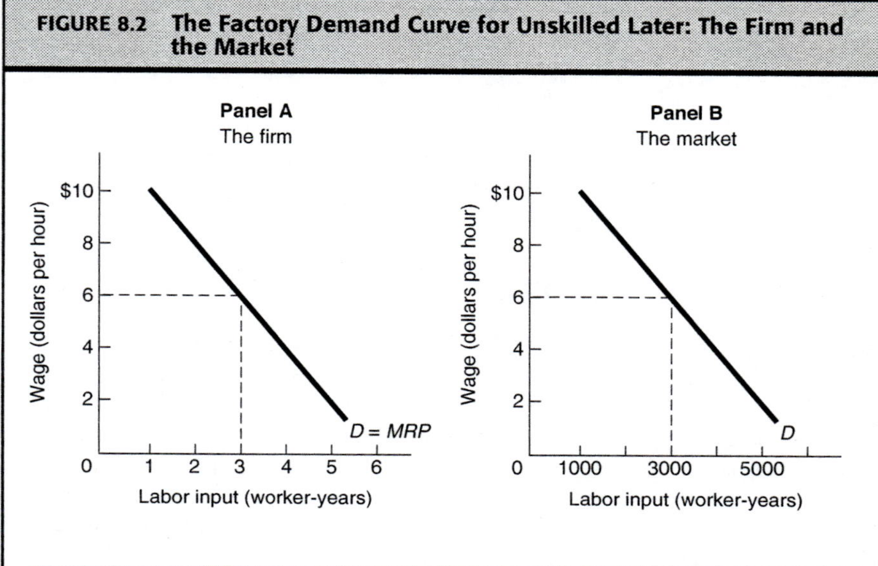

Labor (years) *(1)*	*Output* *(2)*	*Product Price* *(3)*	*Total Revenue* *(4)*	*Marginal Revenue Product* *(5)*
0	0	$2	$ 0	
1	5	2	10	> $ 10
2	9	2	18	> 8
3	12	2	24	> 6
4	14	2	28	> 4
5	15	2	30	> 2

Columns 1 and 2 give the amount of output produced by different amounts of labor input. Column 3 gives the product price. Total revenue is the product of Columns 2 and 3. Marginal revenue product is the increase in revenue in the previous column associated with a one-unit increase in the factor.

Panel A shows the demand curve of the firm for unskilled labor. The demand curve is the marginal revenue product curve of the firm and is negatively sloped because of the law of diminishing returns. Panel B shows the market demand curve. The market consists of 1000 identical firms; therefore the market demand curve is 1000 times the individual firm demand curve. Note that the diagrams for the firm and the market have quite different scales.

Figure 8.2 shows that because firms equate *MRP* with the additional cost of hiring one more unit *the* MRP *curve is the firm's demand curve for that factor.* The firm's demand curve for unskilled labor is graphed in Panel A; it shows that the *MRP* curve is the factor demand curve of the firm.

The *MRP* curve is the firm's demand curve for that factor.

The firm's demand curve for factors of production is negatively sloped because of the law of diminishing returns. As more of the variable factor is employed, its marginal productivity declines. Because *MRP* is the product of marginal revenue and marginal product, *MRP* declines—a lower factor price is required to induce the firm to hire more of the factor.

The market demand curve is the summation of the demand curves of individual firms. Since the individual firm's factor demand curve is negatively sloped, the market demand curve is also negatively sloped. If this market is composed of 1000 identical firms, the market demand curve (Panel B) is the summation of the 1000 individual firms.

Factor Market Equilibrium

The demand for a factor increases whenever *MRP* increases. *MRP* increases when the price of the product rises or when the marginal productivity increases.

Figures 8.1 and 8.2 combine in Figure 8.3 to show the determination of factor prices. Figure 8.1 gave the market supply curve of unskilled labor, Figure 8.2, Panel B, gave the market demand curve for unskilled labor. Like product markets, the factor market achieves equilibrium at the price at which the quantity demanded equals the quantity supplied. In this case, equilibrium is achieved at a price of $6 and a quantity of 3000 units.

Increases in the product's price and in *MP* raise factor prices.

Notice that shifts in the factor supply or demand curves disrupt the equilibrium and cause the factor price to change. Figure 8.4, Panel A, shows the effect of an increase in the product price, and Panel B shows an increase in productivity (*MP* at each level of factor input rises). In Panel A, an increase in the product price raises *MRP;* employers are now willing to hire more of the factor at each factor price. This increase in factor demand raises the factor price. An increase in productivity has the same effect: *MRP* increases and the demand for the factor increases. Again, the factor price rises.

FIGURE 8.3 Factor Market Equilibrium

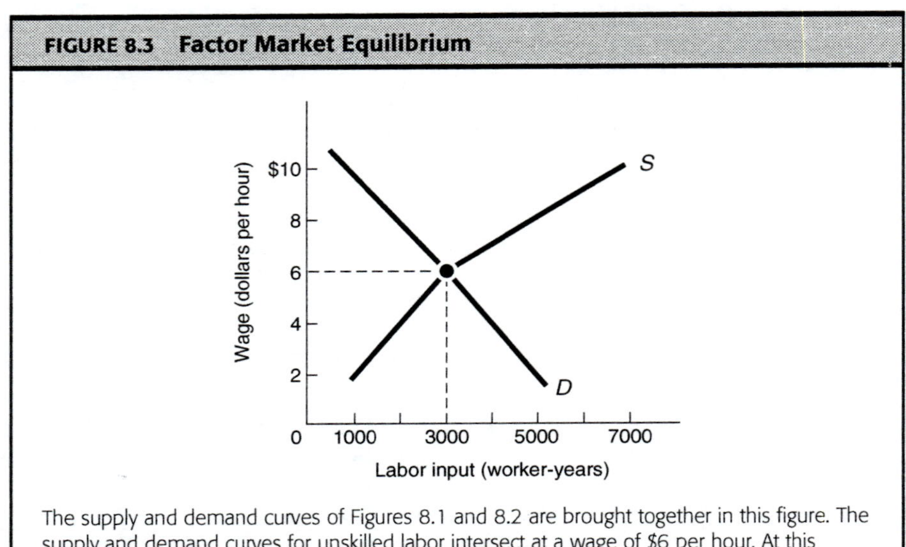

The supply and demand curves of Figures 8.1 and 8.2 are brought together in this figure. The supply and demand curves for unskilled labor intersect at a wage of $6 per hour. At this wage, the quantity demanded equals the quantity supplied.

FIGURE 8.4 Shifts in Factor Demand (Unskilled Labor)

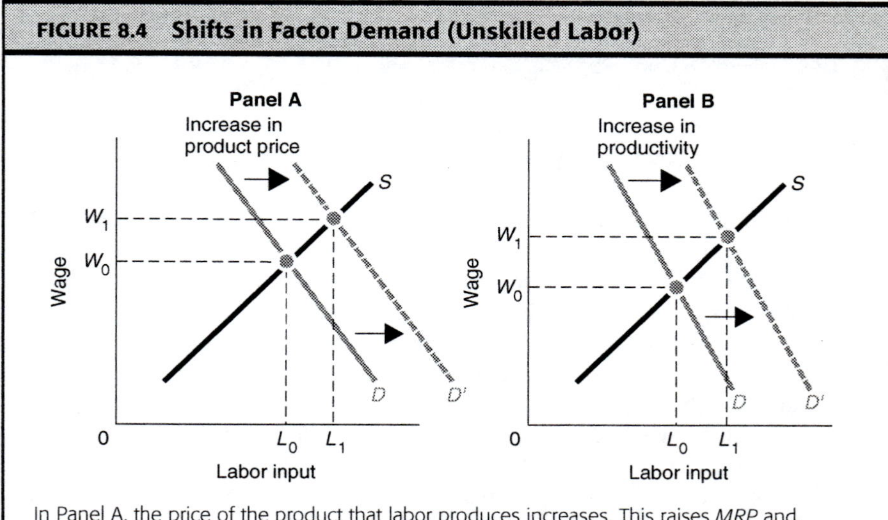

In Panel A, the price of the product that labor produces increases. This raises *MRP* and, hence, causes a rightward shift in the demand curve from *D* to *D'*. The wage rate is bid up, and the equilibrium quantity of labor increases. In Panel B, the productivity of labor increases, and this also raises *MRP*, causing a rightward shift in the demand curve (from *D* to *D'*). The wage rate is bid up, and the equilibrium quantity increases.

Labor Markets

A **labor market** brings buyers and sellers of labor services together to agree on conditions of work and pay.

The prices (wages) of labor of different grades and types are determined in a **labor market,** which is any arrangement that brings buyers and sellers of labor services together to agree on conditions of work and pay. (Figures 8.1 to 8.3 show how a market for unskilled labor might work.) Labor markets can be local, national, or even international. Fast-food chains hire teenage employees in local labor markets but recruit their top executives in the national labor market. Professional soccer players are recruited in an international labor market. Some labor markets operate according to a well-defined set of rules established by government; labor markets with strong unions often follow strict rules on hirings, firings, and work conditions. With the falling cost of the communications, labor markets have become globalized (see Example 8.2).

The labor market differs from other factor markets in four respects. First, people cannot be bought and sold like land or capital; slavery is against the law in modern societies. Second, we have different preferences concerning jobs. Third, we have alternative uses of our time; we can engage in household production or leisure activities if we do not work in the labor market. Fourth, workers can join together into labor unions to affect their conditions of work and pay.

Wage Differentials

Supply and demand explain why some people and some occupations earn more than others: Jobs are different, and people are different.

EXAMPLE 8.2 THE GROWING GLOBAL LABOR MARKET

One of the constants of the labor market over time has been that people were relatively immobile across countries. Although they could emigrate from one country to another, this would be a rather gradual process. If workers wanted higher-paying jobs in higher-income countries, they had to emigrate. If firms wanted to hire workers in low-wage countries, they would have to move their business to these countries. The new age of the computer and low-cost telecommunications is creating a new global workplace. Businesses in high-income countries can now hire low-paid but skilled workers in other countries without either the business or the worker crossing a border. Russia, for example, boasts an abundant supply of skilled computer programmers willing to work at a fraction of wages in the United States. Through modems, they can carry out their computer programming in Russia and instantaneously transmit their work to the United States. Companies like AOL hire skilled workers in India to handle the technical questions of subscribers via online communications. Starwood Hotels (Sheraton and Westin) reservation lines are answered by reservationists in Ireland, and Swiss Airlines uses reservationists in India to answer telephone inquiries.

As this process of globalizing the world labor market continues, there should be a gradual equalization of wages across countries, as the accompanying diagram (Figure 8.5) shows. As telecommuting jobs move, say, from the high-wage United States to the low-wage India, the demand for labor in the United States falls, thereby depressing the U.S. wage, and the demand for Indian labor rises, thereby raising the Indian wage.

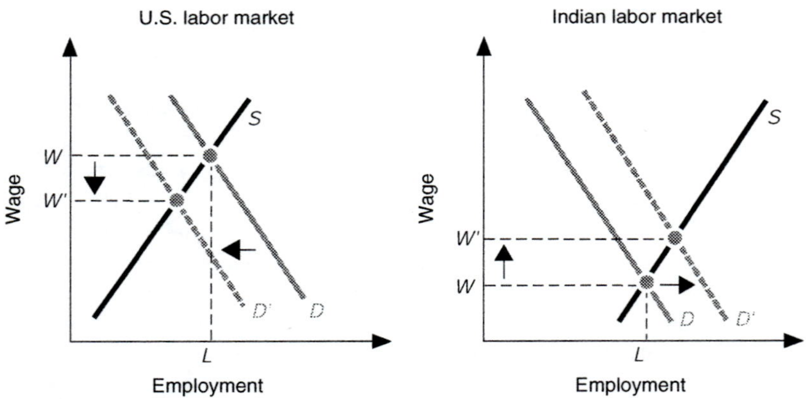

FIGURE 8.5 Telecommuting's Effect on U.S. and Indian Wages

Explanation: As jobs telecommute from the United States to India, the demand for U.S. labor falls and the demand for Indian labor increases. The wage differential between the United States and India is therefore narrowed.

Jobs Are Different The supply curve of labor to a particular occupation is influenced by the general desirability of the job. We dislike dirty, monotonous, and dangerous jobs; we like interesting and rewarding jobs in pleasant surroundings. Figure 8.6 shows the effect of work conditions on wages in two occupations—offshore oil

FIGURE 8.6 Wages in Offshore Oil Drilling and Food Processing

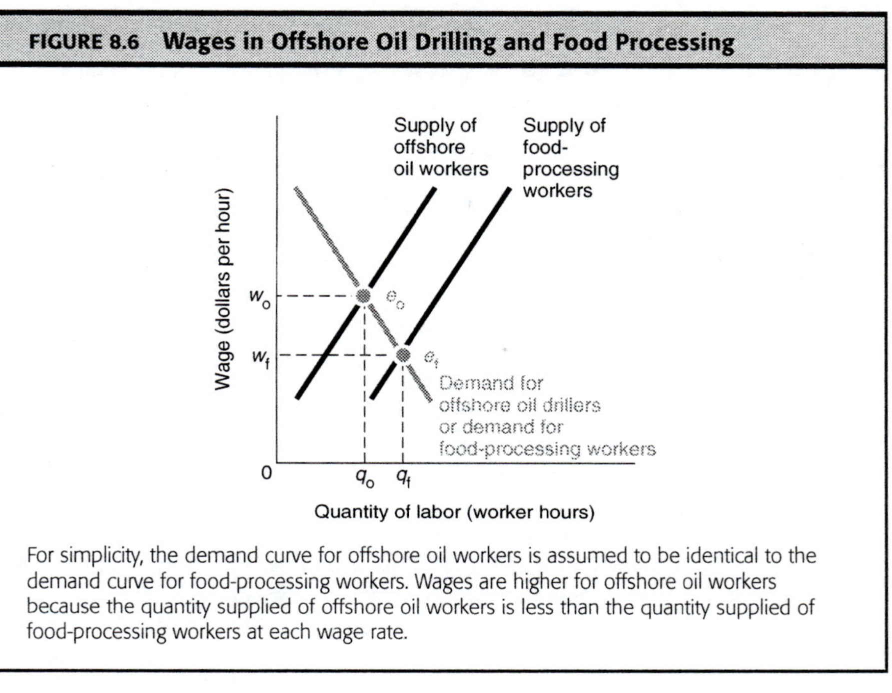

For simplicity, the demand curve for offshore oil workers is assumed to be identical to the demand curve for food-processing workers. Wages are higher for offshore oil workers because the quantity supplied of offshore oil workers is less than the quantity supplied of food-processing workers at each wage rate.

drilling and food processing. For simplicity, the demand for labor in the two occupations is assumed to be the same, but the labor supply curves are different. Because offshore oil drilling—a dirty, monotonous, and dangerous job—is less desirable than work in a food-processing plant, the supply of labor to food processing will be greater than to offshore oil drilling. Accordingly, offshore oil workers receive a higher wage. Wage differentials to reward workers for unfavorable job conditions are called **compensating wage differentials.**

Compensating wage differentials are the higher rewards that must be paid to compensate for undesirable job characteristics.

People Are Different Compensating wage differentials reward people for taking undesirable jobs, yet some quite desirable jobs are well paid relative to less desirable jobs because people are different. Some individuals are qualified for a large number of occupations; others are qualified for only a few. Only a limited number of people have the peculiar abilities to become university presidents, trial lawyers, star athletes, renowned classical musicians, brain surgeons, or Nobel laureate physicists. Surgeons must have extremely sensitive and sure hands; trial lawyers must be articulate and able to think on their feet; professional basketball stars must be tall, agile, and imbued with a strong competitive spirit. The number of individuals qualified to carry out these jobs is fewer than the number qualified to dig ditches, work checkout counters, or perform unskilled factory labor. People are divided into **noncompeting groups** in labor markets—the ditchdigger does not compete with the brain surgeon for available jobs; the brain surgeon does not compete with the seven-foot-tall basketball player.

Noncompeting groups are those groups of people differentiated by natural ability and education, training, and experience to the extent that they do not compete with one another for jobs.

Human Capital, Productivity, and Income Distribution

Human capital is investment in schooling, training, and health that raises productivity.

Any activity that raises the productivity of a resource is an investment.

Just as businesses invest in plant and equipment to increase their earnings, people invest in **human capital** to raise their own productivity and lifetime earnings. They can invest in extra schooling and technical education. They can pay the costs of moving to better jobs and can invest in medical care to improve their health or appearance. Expenditures on human capital are as much an investment as those of a firm building a new plant or acquiring new machinery. *Any activity that raises the productivity of a resource is an investment.*

If human capital investment translates into higher lifetime earnings, why doesn't everyone acquire human capital? While human capital investment yields benefits, it also has its costs. A university optometry degree costs tuition, books, and four years of sacrificed earnings. Moving from a depressed region to a boom town means paying moving costs, along with the emotional costs of pulling up roots.

People evaluate the costs and benefits of human capital investment differently. Some are willing to wait for rewards that are five years away; some place a very high value on having money now. For those with wealthy parents, the costs of a college education may be small; for those who have to work their way through college, the costs are high. Just as rational economic agents participate in activities whose marginal benefits exceed their marginal costs, we acquire additional human capital as long as the marginal benefits exceed the marginal costs. The *optimal* amount of human capital expenditure occurs where marginal costs and marginal benefits are equal.

People acquire additional human capital until marginal costs and marginal benefits are equal.

Human capital theory suggests that inequality is partially the result of the conscious choice between more money now (going straight from high school to work) and more money later (going to college and delaying earning income). As long as people assess costs and benefits differently and as long as the costs and benefits are different to them, different people will acquire different amounts of human capital. (See Example 8.3.)

The Macroeconomic Labor Market

The Employment Act of 1946 commits the federal government to create and maintain "useful employment opportunities . . . for those able, willing, and seeking to work." Concern with employment dates back to the severe unemployment during the Great Depression of the 1930s—a historical event that has left a lasting imprint on the American consciousness. In 1929, less than 3 percent of the labor force was unemployed. By 1933, one in every four workers was unemployed!

The Definition of Unemployment

A person is **unemployed** if he or she did not work at all during the previous week, actively looked for work during the previous four weeks, and is currently available for work.

According to the Bureau of Labor Statistics, a person is **unemployed** if he or she:

1. Did not work at all during the previous week.
2. Actively looked for work during the previous four weeks.
3. Is currently available for work.

EXAMPLE 8.3 EDUCATION IS A GOOD INVESTMENT

Our productivity depends on our human capital; the more productive we are, the more we earn. The chart provides the median annual earnings of men and women in the year 2000 arranged according to level of educational attainment. For both men and women, earnings rise with each higher level of education. High school graduates earn more than high school dropouts. B.A. degree holders earn more than those with an incomplete college education. Ph.D. holders earn more than those with an M.A. Men with high school diplomas earn about $10,000 per year more than those with an incomplete high school education. (Women with a high school diploma earn $5000 more per year.) Men with a college degree earn almost $20,000 more per year than high school graduates. (Women with college degrees earn $15,000 more than those with high school degrees.)

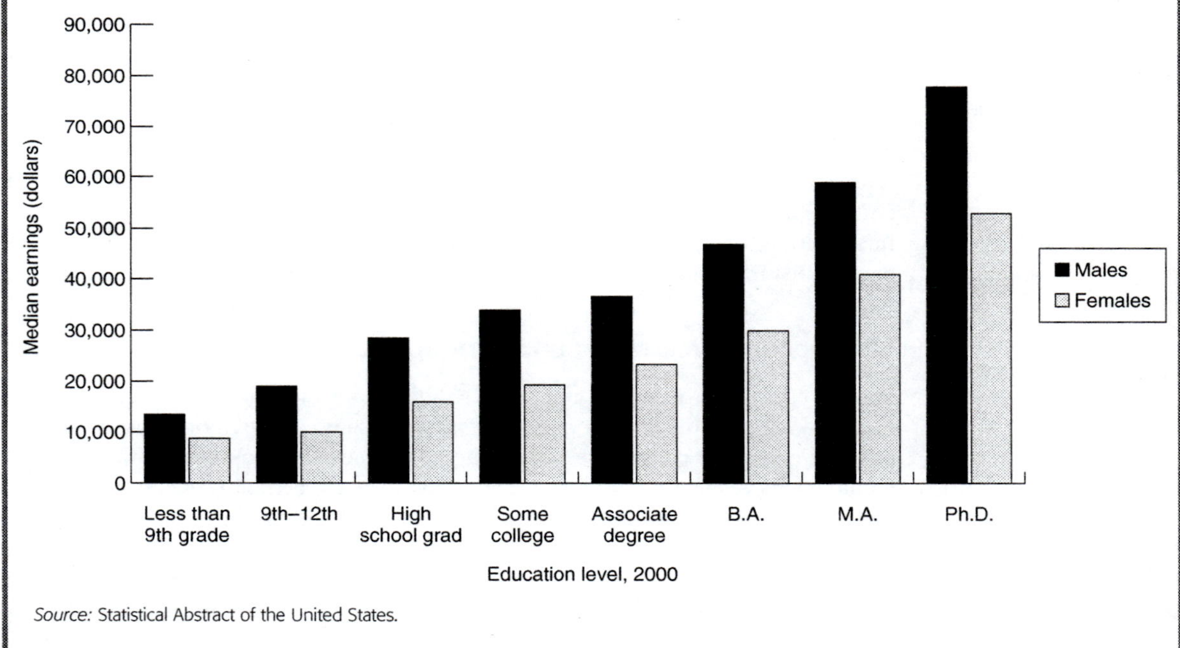

Source: Statistical Abstract of the United States.

The **labor force** equals the number of persons employed plus the number unemployed.

The **unemployment rate** equals the number of unemployed divided by the labor force (the sum of employed and unemployed persons).

Persons who have been laid off and are waiting to be recalled to their old jobs are unemployed even though they are not looking for jobs. Each adult is classified into one of three categories: (1) employed, (2) unemployed, (3) not in the labor force. The **labor force** equals the number of persons employed plus the number unemployed. The third category consists of people such as full-time homemakers, full-time students, and retired persons, who remain out of the labor force.

The **unemployment rate** measures the percentage of people who are, according to the three criteria, unemployed. The unemployment rate equals the number of unemployed divided by the labor force (the sum of employed and unemployed persons).

In macroeconomics, the unemployment rate is the most closely watched indicator of the labor market.

Figure 8.7 shows that during economic downturns (shown as shaded areas), there is a general tendency for the unemployment rate to rise. There is no clear long-term trend in the unemployment rate, although rates near double digits were confined to the mid- and late 1970s and very early 1980s.

Frictional and Cyclical Unemployment

Frictional unemployment is the unemployment associated with the changing of jobs in a dynamic economy.

Cyclical unemployment is unemployment associated with general downturns in the economy.

Both employed and unemployed persons can search for jobs. The unemployed search for new jobs; the employed look for better jobs. Part of this searching is a natural consequence of the changing economy. The unemployment associated with the normal changing of jobs in a dynamic economy is called **frictional unemployment.**

Cyclical unemployment is unemployment associated with general downturns in the economy. During cyclical downturns, fewer goods and services are purchased, employers cut back on jobs, and people find themselves without jobs. Many workers in basic industrial employment (steel, autos, farm equipment) are unemployed and return to their jobs only when the economy improves. Policy makers and average citizens fear cyclical unemployment. As the job market worsens, jobs are more difficult to find, students cannot find work upon graduation, and employees go to work fearing that they might get laid off that day.

Macroeconomic Supply and Demand for Labor

We can apply microeconomic principles to the labor market as a whole. The entire economy's demand for labor depends on its marginal productivity, which will fall as more and more people are hired. The willingness of people to work in market employment depends on the wage rate, in the form of the real wage rate.

In macroeconomics, the cost of hiring labor is not simply the nominal wage (*W*). Employers relate the nominal wage to the price of the product (*P*). If the wage goes up 10 percent but the price of the product also goes up 10 percent, labor doesn't cost the producer more per unit of production. **Real wages** are measured by money wages, *W,* divided by the price level, *P*—that is, *W/P.*

Real wages are measured by money wages, *W,* divided by the price level, *P*—that is, *W/P.*

In Figure 8.8 real wages are on the vertical axis and employment is on the horizontal axis. The demand-for-labor curve, *D,* is downward sloping because business will not hire more workers unless real wages fall. The supply-of-labor curve, *S,* is upward sloping: If you want more workers, they must be offered higher real wages. The intersection of the *S* and *D* curves determines the level of real wages and employment. *L* is the level of employment, where all who want to work have jobs except those in the normal process of job change.

Figure 8.8 shows a labor market in equilibrium. At the prevailing real wage, the quantity of labor supplied equals the quantity of labor demanded, yet even in this case, there will still be frictional unemployment. How much unemployment depends on the frictions involved in matching labor demand with labor supply. The total demand for labor consists of all those working (*L*) plus vacancies (*V*). The total supply of labor consists of all those working (*L*) plus those unemployed (*U*).

FIGURE 8.7 The Unemployment Rate

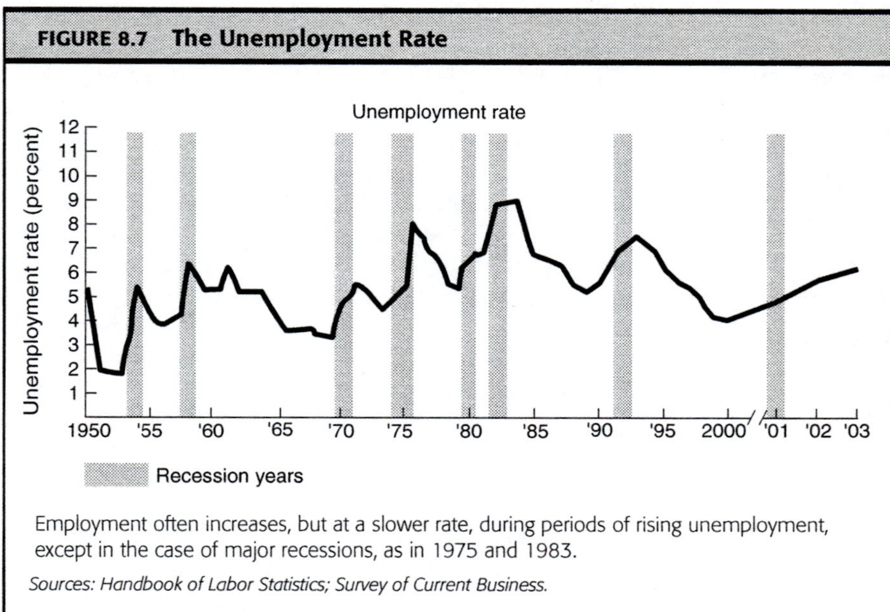

Employment often increases, but at a slower rate, during periods of rising unemployment, except in the case of major recessions, as in 1975 and 1983.

Sources: Handbook of Labor Statistics; Survey of Current Business.

FIGURE 8.8 Macroeconomic Labor Market Equilibrium

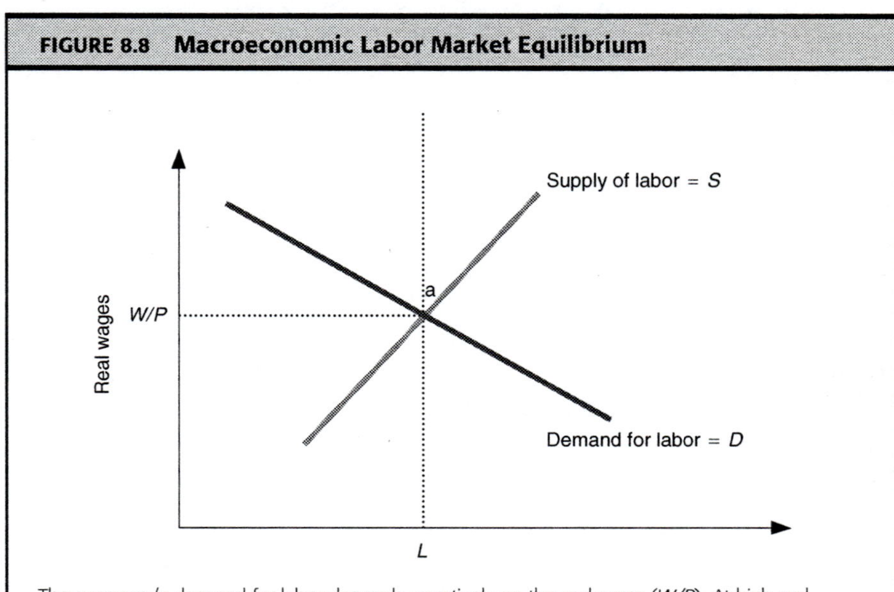

The economy's demand for labor depends negatively on the real wage (*W/P*). At high real wages, labor is "expensive," and few workers will be hired. Workers base their willingness to work in the labor force on the real wage. A higher real wage is required to attract more workers.

The natural rate of unemployment is that rate at which the number of available jobs (V) is equal to the number of qualified unemployed workers (U).

The equilibrium in Figure 8.8 shows a labor market at the natural rate of unemployment. One way of defining the natural rate of unemployment is that rate at which the labor force is in balance—that is, the number of available jobs (V) is equal to the number of unemployed workers qualified to fill those jobs (U).

The **natural rate of unemployment** is when there is an approximate balance between the number of unfilled jobs and the number of qualified job seekers.

Alternatively, the natural rate occurs when the labor market is in balance. In a dynamic economy, jobs are created while other jobs disappear. The labor market is in approximate balance when the number of jobs being created roughly equals the number of qualified applicants available to fill those jobs. As new jobs are created or as people vacate established jobs, workers with the appropriate skills and qualifications are entering the labor force or moving from other jobs to fill these vacancies. There may be imbalances in particular occupations, but on average there can be a balance between jobs and job seekers. The unemployment rate at which this balance is attained is the **natural rate of unemployment**—that rate at which there is an approximate balance between the number of unfilled jobs and the number of qualified job seekers.

Wage Flexibility and Unemployment

Figure 8.8 raises the question of why there should be unemployment above the natural rate. If the labor market is like other markets, the wage should fall whenever there is a gap between the number of people wishing to work and the number of jobs available at the prevailing wage. As it falls, more jobs will be offered but fewer people will wish to work. Just as price changes eliminate surpluses in product markets, so should wage changes eliminate unemployment. If wages, however, do not respond to labor surpluses, unemployment can be created and persist over time.

Much of modern macroeconomics focuses on why wages are less flexible than other prices. One explanation is that labor is often hired under long-term contracts, which specify the wage rate over time, sometimes more than one year. If labor supply or demand conditions change during the contract period, the wage rate cannot change.

If nominal wages are inflexible, and the demand for labor falls, unemployment in excess of the natural rate can be created.

Figure 8.9 shows the possible effects of inflexible wages, whatever their causes, on unemployment. It shows a labor market that is initially at full employment—at the natural rate of unemployment. The real wage is at equilibrium, such that the demand for labor equals the supply. Let us now say that the demand for labor falls for some reason. In order for a new equilibrium to be established, the real wage must fall, but in order for that to happen, the nominal wage must fall. (It is unlikely that prices will increase when demand is falling to drive down the real wage.) If the nominal wage is unable to fall, the real wage cannot drop, and the number of workers who want jobs at the prevailing real wage exceeds the number of available jobs. Figure 8.9 shows that if nominal wages are inflexible and the demand for labor falls, unemployment in excess of the natural rate can be created.

Unemployment in excess of the natural rate caused by downturns in the demand for labor is cyclical unemployment. In Figure 8.9, the amount of unemployment measured by the distance *ba* is cyclical unemployment.

A **labor union** is a collective organization of workers and employees whose goal is to affect conditions of pay and employment.

Unions, Layoffs, and Inflexible Wages

Labor unions are collective organizations of workers and employees. Currently, about one in nine members of the American labor force belongs to a union, down from a

FIGURE 8.9 Unemployment and Inflexible Wages

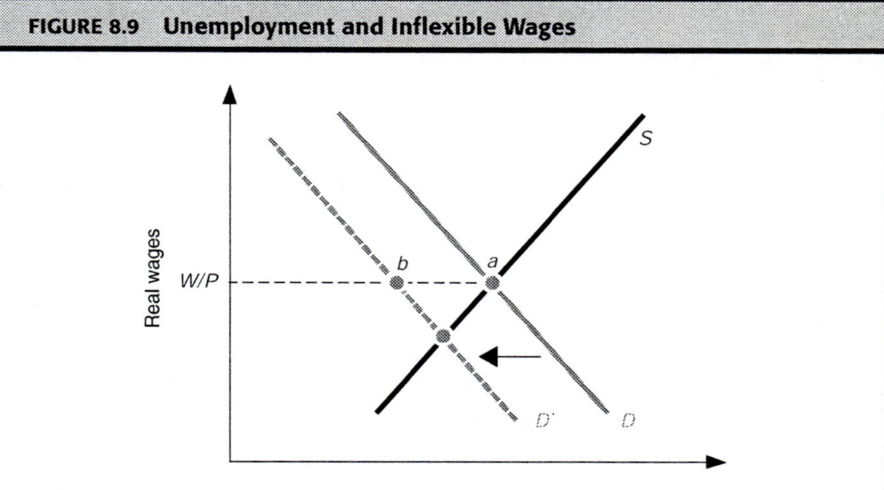

Explanation: We begin with the labor market at the natural rate of unemployment, denoted by *a.* The real wage (*W/P*) is such that the number of workers who want jobs equals the number of jobs available. There is now a reduction in the demand for labor from *D* to *D′*. If *W* is inflexible, the real wage cannot fall. The real wage remains at its original level and the number of desired jobs (*a*) exceeds the number of available jobs (*b*). The distance *ba* measures the amount of unemployment in excess of the natural rate.

peak of one in four in the 1950s. Most American unions are affiliated with the AFL-CIO (American Federation of Labor–Congress of Industrial Organizations).

Collective bargaining is union bargaining with management.

A **strike** occurs when unionized employees cease work until management agrees to specific union demands.

Unions have two main economic objectives—higher pay and job security for their members. The instrument used by unions to achieve these objectives is collective bargaining, reinforced by the threat of strike. **Collective bargaining** is union bargaining with management in the name of all its members. A **strike** occurs when unionized employees cease work until management agrees to specific union demands.

The two union objectives—higher pay and high employment of union members—are not compatible. If the union bargains for a higher wage, fewer union members will be employed. Hence, unions must balance the benefits of higher wages against the costs of less employment. To cushion the effect of higher wages on employment, unions use work rules to protect the most senior union members from unemployment and have also attempted to increase the demand for labor by "Buy American" campaigns, work rules, and protection from foreign imports.

Empirical studies show that union members earn from 10 to 25 percent more. Higher wages also mean that union members who lose their jobs cannot find alternate employment that pays them as much.

Figure 8.10 shows the unionized sector initially at full employment. At the initial real wage, there is a balance between the number wanting jobs (*b*) and the number of jobs offered (*s*). If there is now a decrease in demand (due, let's say, to a reduction in the demand for the product, such as cars or steel), the demand curve shifts to *D′*. The number of union members wanting jobs at the real wage exceeds the number offered, and a number of union members are laid off.

FIGURE 8.10 Layoff Unemployment, Unionized Sector

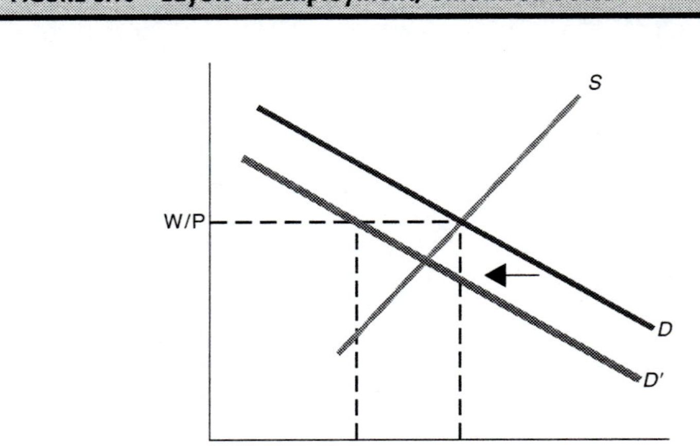

This figure shows the initial supply (*S*) and demand (*D*) for union labor. The labor market is in balance. The number of union members prepared to work equals the number of jobs (L_0). When demand falls (to *D'*), the real wage does not change, and the number of union members wanting jobs (L_0) exceeds the number of jobs, necessitating layoffs. Laid-off union members do not seek lower-paying jobs in nonunionized employment.

When laid-off union workers want to be recalled, their unemployment does not cause wages to fall generally in the economy.

Unlike the non-unionized sector, laid-off union workers do not necessarily search for new jobs in the non-unionized sector. Because they earn more in unionized jobs than in the nonunionized sector, they are inclined to wait to be recalled to their old jobs when economic conditions improve (when the economy again wants more cars and steel). If laid-off workers do not seek employment in the non-unionized sector, the supply of workers in non-unionized employment does not increase. Non-union wages are therefore not bid down. When laid-off union workers wait to be recalled, their unemployment does not cause wages to fall generally in the economy.

The next chapter examines how we spend and save what we earn. It also shows how these decisions depend on the interest rate.

Summary

1. Prices of the factors of production are determined in factor markets—markets in which firms purchase land, labor, and capital inputs.
2. Buyers of factors of production can be price takers or price searchers. Price taking is more common than price searching because firms must compete against all other firms that use the same inputs.
3. The supply of factors depends on their opportunity costs. A factor price that at least equals the value of the next-best alternative use of the factor must be paid to attract the factor. The supply curve is usually positively sloped because high factor prices are more likely to equal or exceed the factor's next-best alternative use.

4. The demand curve is negatively sloped. It is a derived demand that depends on the demand for the final product. The firm's demand curve will be its marginal revenue product curve. Marginal revenue product (*MRP*) is the increase in revenue caused by increasing the employment of the factor by one unit.
5. People are different and jobs are different. Because jobs are different, compensating wage differentials must be offered. Because people are different, the labor force is divided into noncompeting groups. Workers also join together into labor unions to affect conditions of pay and work. People acquire human capital to raise their productivity and lifetime earnings. Also, people must choose between household production, leisure, and labor market work. These choices are based on opportunity costs.
6. The macroeconomic labor market considers the supply and demand for labor to the economy as a whole. Both depend on the real wage, which is the nominal wage rate divided by the price level. The intersection of the labor supply or labor demand curves determines the amount of employment. The natural rate of unemployment is the rate that balances vacancies and unfilled jobs. The number of vacant jobs equals the number of qualified job seekers.
7. Unionized workers earn more than in comparable jobs in the nonunionized sector. If they are laid off due to a decrease in demand for their services, they are likely to wait to be recalled when economic conditions improve rather than actively look for work in the nonunionized sector.
8. If wages are inflexible for some reason, such as long-term contracts, the wage cannot fall to restore equilibrium, and unemployment will result. Much of modern macroeconomics explores wage inflexibility.

Questions and Problems

1. Explain why firms must pay the factors of production their opportunity costs. What happens when the firm pays a factor of production a payment in excess of opportunity costs? What is this type of payment called?
2. What should happen to the wage rate of carpenters if the prices of new homes were to go up? If the productivity of carpenters were to go down? Explain.
3. On the last $1000 spent, a firm obtained 10 units of output per dollar spent on capital and 20 units of output per dollar spent on labor. What should the firm do? Is it maximizing profits?
4. Job X is generally more desirable than Job Y, yet Job X pays more. Explain.
5. Union strategy in collective bargaining is affected by the elasticity of demand for labor. Explain why.
6. What prevents unions from bargaining for the highest possible wage?
7. Explain why laid-off union workers may not seek alternate employment in the nonunionized sector.
8. When our compensation increases, we usually want to work more. Why may this not always be the case? Consider what you would do if your wage quadrupled. Use the analysis of the labor/leisure trade-off to explain the backward-bending labor supply curve.
9. Explain why the real wage determines the supply and demand for labor to the macroeconomy and not the nominal wage.

10. Use supply and demand curves to show why wage rigidities can cause unemployment.

11. If General Motors workers are laid off and do not seek jobs in other industries (they are waiting to be recalled), what effect would this have on wages throughout the economy?

12. Consider a labor market in which workers are hired each day for one day at a time and the pay is decided that day. Would there be a great deal of unemployment in this type of labor market? Explain your answer.

13. Joe and Bill are identical in all respects, but Bill earns twice as much. Using the theory of wages in this chapter explain why this may be so.

14. There are 1 million workers unemployed in the economy, yet there are all kinds of help-wanted ads in the papers for computer programmers and accountants. Do these help-wanted ads prove that the economy has an unemployment rate below the natural rate?

CHAPTER 9

SAVING, INVESTMENT, AND INTEREST RATES

Chapter Preview

How much we consume, save, and invest affects our own lives and, collectively, the entire economy. This chapter continues the study of microfoundations of macroeconomics by examining how households decide how much to consume and save and how businesses decide how much to invest. In both cases, the interest rate affects these decisions.

Consumption and Savings

Household saving is what we have left over from our income after buying goods and services and paying our income taxes.

Households spend their limited income to buy goods and services and to pay taxes. What they do not spend on goods and services or income taxes they save. **Household saving** is what we have left over from our income after buying goods and services and paying our income taxes. We can save only by not consuming. When we save, we accumulate assets: We can buy stocks, mutual funds, or bonds; we can put money aside in CDs, passbook savings accounts, or checking accounts. We can consume in an almost infinite number of ways: We buy food, clothing, entertainment, travel, and long-lasting goods like television sets, automobiles, and washing machines.

Economists have long considered what motivates households to consume and save. Basically, we have concluded that how much of our income we consume depends on two major factors: how much income we earn after taxes and the interest rate. This notion can be summarized in the form of a consumption function, which states that a household's consumption (C) is a function of its income (Y) and the interest rate (r):

$$C = f(Y, r)$$

The **consumption function** shows how much a household wishes to consume (C) at each level of income and interest rate.

The **consumption function** (f) shows how much a household wishes to consume at each level of income and interest rate. The consumption function does not assert that all consumption and saving decisions are determined by our income and by the interest rate. Rather, it says that these are important and significant determinants of how much we spend.

The **saving function** shows how much a household wishes to save (S) at each level of income and interest rate.

Given that saving is what is left over from our income after consumption, saving is also a function of income and the interest rate. The **saving function** (F) shows how much a household wishes to save (S) at each level of income and interest rate:

$$S = F(Y, r)$$

Figure 9.1 plots the consumption function and the saving function in four separate diagrams. The top two diagrams show what happens to C and S when only Y is allowed to change (the interest rate is held constant). The bottom two diagrams show what happens to C and S when only the interest rate is allowed to change (Y is held constant). For obvious reasons, both C and S increase when income rises. As household income increases, we will usually spend more and save more. When interest rates rise, we should save more and hence spend less because, as will be discussed below, the interest rate is the reward for saving.

Life-Cycle Consumption

There are two ways of looking at the relationship between consumption and income. The short-run approach is to say that Y refers to current household income. We base

FIGURE 9.1 Household Consumption and Saving Depend on Income and Interest Rates

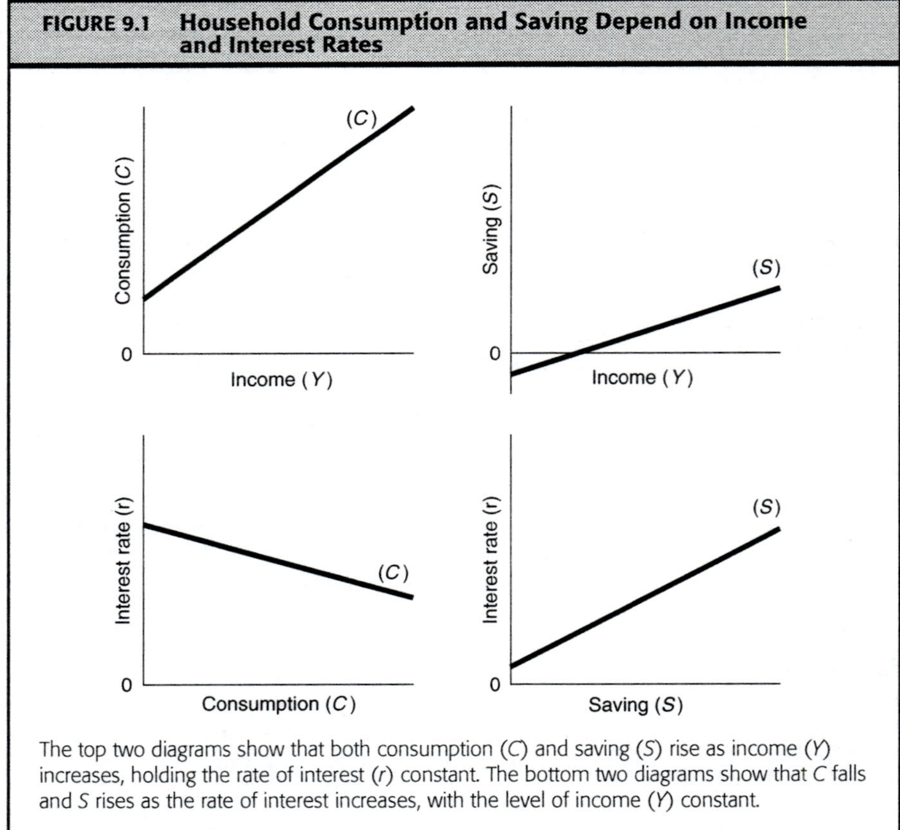

The top two diagrams show that both consumption (C) and saving (S) rise as income (Y) increases, holding the rate of interest (r) constant. The bottom two diagrams show that C falls and S rises as the rate of interest increases, with the level of income (Y) constant.

our consumption and saving decisions on what we are currently earning. If our current earnings increase, we will spend more and save more. A number of economists—Irving Fisher, Milton Friedman, and Franco Modigliani (the latter two won Nobel prizes in economics)—claim that we take a longer-run view when we make our spending and saving decisions. This longer-run view is often called the *life-cycle theory of consumption.*

The **life-cycle theory of consumption** states that households base their consumption and saving decisions on the long-term income they expect to earn over their lifetimes.

The **life-cycle theory of consumption** states that households base their consumption and saving decisions on the long-term income they expect to earn over their lifetimes. Accordingly, they will consume more than their income while young because they anticipate that their income will increase as they mature. As households mature, they will consume less of their income in order to save for their old age. When they are old, they will again consume more than their income as they live off the savings accumulated earlier.

Figure 9.2 illustrates life-cycle consumption. It shows a household comprising two adults (of the same age) starting at 18. This household's income increases up to age 55 and then starts to decline until it reaches a very low level at age 85. If this household based its consumption decisions only on its current income, it would have to consume little when "young" and "old" and would do most of its consuming during its peak earning years. The life-cycle hypothesis, however, states that households are forward-looking and want to avoid these excessive swings. They do so by consuming more than their income (they borrow) when they are young, by consuming less than their income when they are mature (they save), and by again consuming more than their

FIGURE 9.2 Life-Cycle Consumption

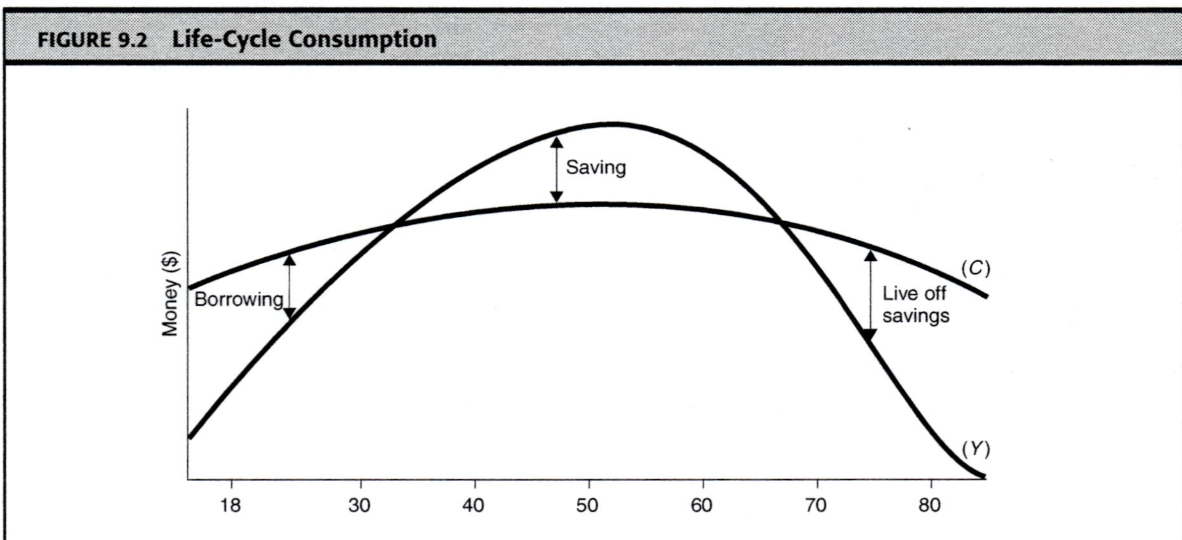

The *Y* line shows the income of the household as it ages. It starts as a "young" household at age 18 with low income; its income rises as it matures (to age 55). As it grows "old," its income falls. The *C* line shows how a forward-looking household adjusts its consumption and saving in response to this pattern of lifetime income. It consumes more than its income while young (its borrowing is the vertical distance between *C* and *Y*). It consumes less than its income as it matures (its saving is the vertical distance between *C* and *Y*), and it consumes more than its income when old by living off savings accumulated earlier.

As a consequence of life-cycle consumption, households are able to smooth out fluctuations in their consumption that would have occurred had they based their consumption and saving decisions only on their current income.

income when they are "old." The vertical distance between the consumption line and the income line shows the amount of borrowing (*C* greater than *Y*) or saving (*Y* greater than *C*) that is taking place in each phase of the life cycle.

As a consequence of life-cycle consumption, households are able to smooth out fluctuations in their consumption that would have occurred had they based their consumption and saving decisions only on their current income. As Figure 9.2 shows, *C* is much smoother than *Y*. (See Example 9.1 for some statistics.)

Real versus Nominal Interest Rates

Figure 9.1 shows that how much households save and consume also depends on the interest rate. If individual households base their decisions on what to save on the interest rate, so must all households combined. We would therefore expect more total household saving at high interest rates than at low interest rates. Let us consider why we save more when interest rates are high.

We can consume our income now; when we do, we get instant gratification. We don't have to wait to enjoy a new TV set or automobile. If we are to be persuaded to postpone consumption, there must be some kind of reward, and the interest rate constitutes that reward. An increase in the rate of interest provides a larger reward for postponing consumption into the future, holding other factors constant.

When you put $100 in the bank this year in return for $105 next year, you are making an exchange of present consumption ($100) for future consumption ($105). If there is no inflation, next year's $105 represents a 5 percent gain in goods and services. If there is inflation, the $105 will not purchase 5 percent more in goods and services in a year. For example, with 2 percent inflation, the $105 will buy only about 3 percent more in goods and services in one year. The trade-off between present and future consumption is summarized by the real rate of interest, which is the nominal or observed interest rate minus anticipated inflation.

The **nominal rate of interest** is the contractual interest rate that is earned in credit markets.

The **real rate of interest** is the nominal rate minus anticipated inflation.

The **nominal rate of interest** is the contractual interest rate that is earned in credit markets. The **real rate of interest** is the nominal rate of interest over some period minus the expected rate of inflation over the same period.

If, for example, Jim lends Jill $1000 for one year, both will need to try to anticipate what the inflation rate will be for a one-year period. If the loan is for five years, then both will have to try to anticipate what inflation will be over a five-year period. The real-interest-rate formula does not claim that we can correctly anticipate inflation. It just says that we try.

The real interest rate is forward-looking. At the beginning of the period, we cannot know the real interest rate that lenders will actually earn. Lenders make their decisions based on the current nominal rate minus the expected inflation rate over the period of the loan. Actual inflation can be different from expected inflation. After the fact, however, we can look back and observe the actual real interest rate by deducting the actual inflation rate from the nominal rate. In the 1980s, for example, the nominal interest rate on 30-year government bonds averaged about 10.5 percent while the rate of inflation averaged about 4 percent. Thus, holders of 30-year government bonds averaged a 6 percent real rate of interest. During the late 1990s, the real rate of interest dropped to about 3 percent. The nominal interest rate on 30-year government bonds ranged from 5.0 to 6.3 percent while the inflation rate averaged about 3 percent. For more, see Example 9.2.

EXAMPLE 9.1 THE LIFE-CYCLE HYPOTHESIS AND NET WORTH

A household's net worth is the value of its assets, such as stocks, bonds, bank accounts, and the value of its home or vehicle minus its debts, such as mortgage debt or credit card debt. At the end of 2002, the net worth of U.S households was almost $40 trillion, an almost $2 trillion decline because of the falling stock market of that year. If we divide $40 trillion by the 105 million U.S. households, we get an average net worth per household of about $350,000.

The life-cycle hypothesis states that young households do not accumulate assets because they can look forward to saving as they grow older. Assets are accumulated primarily during the prime working years and then assets are drawn down during the retirement years. If households plan for the future perfectly, they would draw their assets down to virtually nothing at the time of their death.

The accompanying figure shows median and mean net worths of U.S. households by age groups. The mean figure is simply the combined net worths of all households in that age category divided by the number of households in that age category. The median figure is the net worth that splits the distribution of net worths in the middle. Half of the households in that age category have net worth below the median and the other half have net worth above that figure. The mean figures are well above the medians because the high net worths of the richest households push up the mean.

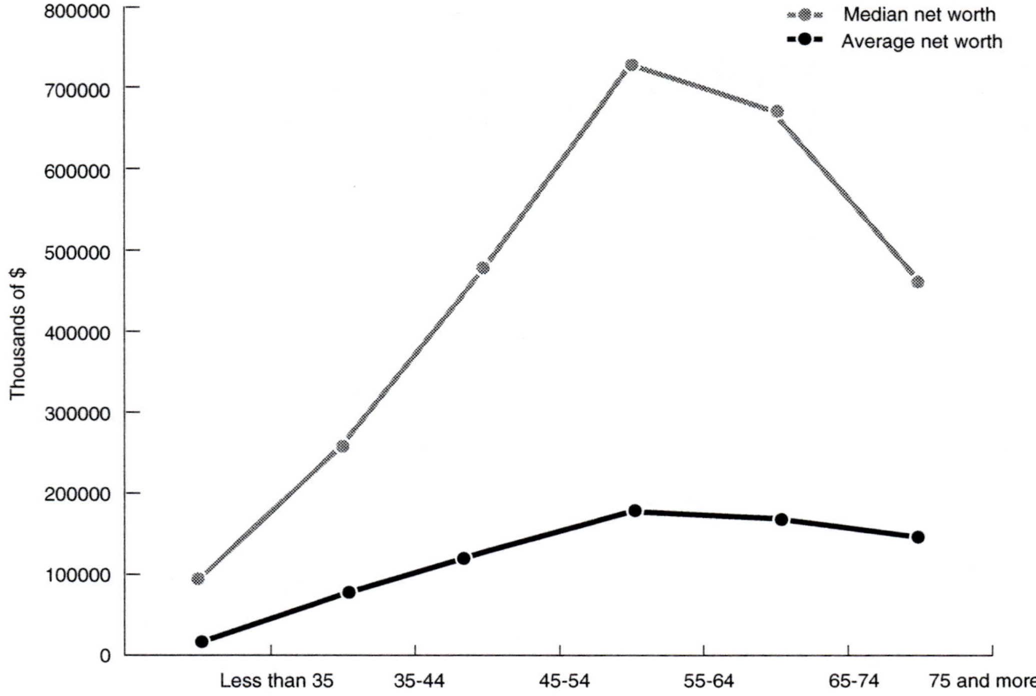

FIGURE 9.3 The Net Worth of U.S. Households, 2001

continued

Both the median and the mean figures provide support for the life-cycle hypothesis. Household net worth peaks in the years before retirement and then starts to decline. What is remarkable about these statistics is the high net worth of the elderly. Households headed by a person age 75 or over have an average net worth of almost a half million dollars and a median net worth of $155,000. These figures suggest a prominent bequest motive—namely, a desire to leave behind an inheritance. These statistics also belie the stereotype of the elderly as poor.

Source: Federal Reserve Board Survey of Consumer Finances

Interest Rates and Saving

To compensate for delaying consumption, a positive real rate of interest is required to encourage people to save. Changes in the real rate of interest affect the terms on which we can exchange current and future consumption. When the real rate of interest rises from 3 percent to, say, 6 percent, the real value of a dollar invested today rises from $1.03 to $1.06 next year. Thus, a higher interest rate translates into cheaper future consumption. If a dollar saved today commands more future consumption, we have an incentive to save more today. Figure 9.4 shows the positive relationship between the real rate of interest and the amount of saving, where other

EXAMPLE 9.2 READING INFLATIONARY EXPECTATIONS FROM INTEREST RATES

The real interest rate equals the nominal interest rate minus the anticipated rate of inflation. This means that the anticipated rate of inflation equals the nominal interest rate minus the real interest rate. If we knew the real interest rate (the rate that savers must receive after adjustment for inflation in order to make loans), we could immediately calculate what people expect inflation to be over the life of the loan.

The accompanying table gives interest rates on U.S. government securities arranged by the maturity of the government bond (from 1 year to 20 years) on 26 August 2003. If we assume, for example, that the current real rate of interest is 2 percent per annum, then we get the following average inflation rates anticipated over the life of the bond. With a 2 percent real rate of interest, people expect prices to fall over the next 12 months, to scarcely rise over the next two years, but to rise at an average rate of 3.43 percent over the next 20 years.

Maturity	*Interest rate*	*Implied Anticipated Inflation*
1 year	1.35	–0.65
2 years	2.02	0.02
3 years	2.59	0.59
5 years	3.52	1.52
10 years	4.53	2.53
20 years	5.43	3.43

FIGURE 9.4 Saving and the Rate of Interest: The Macroeconomy

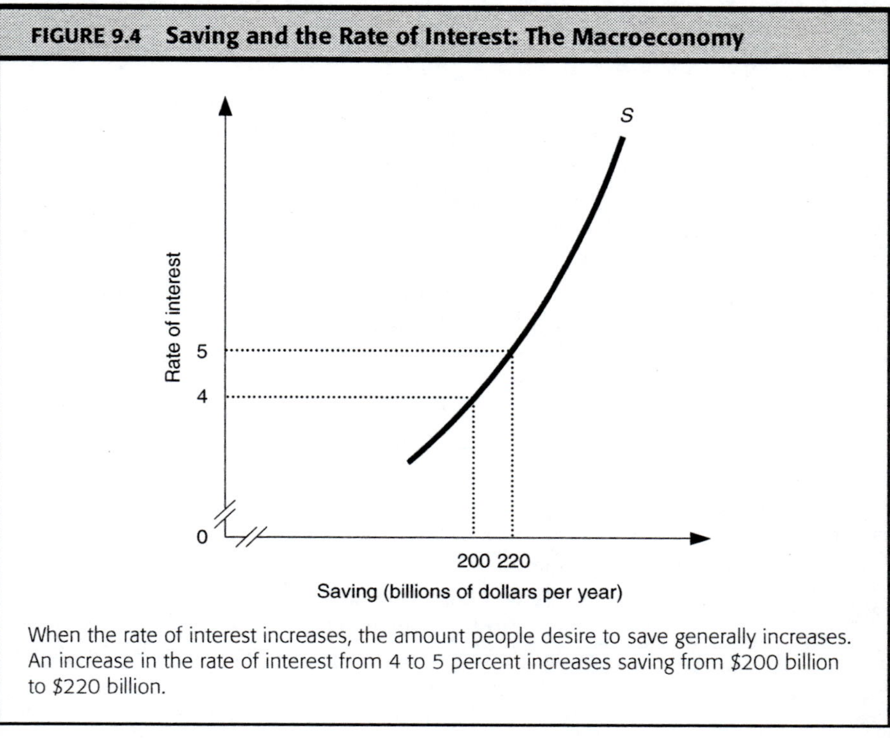

When the rate of interest increases, the amount people desire to save generally increases. An increase in the rate of interest from 4 to 5 percent increases saving from $200 billion to $220 billion.

factors, such as current income, are constant. The amount we save depends on the real rate of interest. If interest rates rise in real terms, we save more.

Interest Rates and Investment

Investment refers to business investment in new plants, equipment, and inventories.

In economics, the term **investment** refers to business investment in new plants, equipment, and inventories. It does not refer to financial investments in stocks, bonds, and savings accounts. Business investments can be costly. A new manufacturing plant may cost several billion dollars. An offshore drilling rig may cost $100 million. Businesses can finance their investments out of their own savings (for example, from the profits they plow back into the company), but more often than not they finance investment by using the savings of others, such as the household saving we just discussed.

In considering how much investment to make, businesses must weigh a number of factors. Investment can be undertaken to lower production costs or increase or maintain sales: The greater the increase in expected sales or the greater the reduction in average costs of production, the more profitable the new investment is. But the firm also incurs immediate costs when it invests—that is, it must purchase new capital goods. The firm's immediate cost of acquiring additional capital is, basically, the prevailing cost of borrowing funds, or the interest rate.

The amount of investment a typical firm will want to make at different interest rates depends on the *rates of return* that the firm believes it can earn on the various investment projects.

Suppose a $10 million investment project promises to add $1 million to profits each year for a very long (almost infinite) period. The rate of return on this $10 million investment, in this example, is 10 percent—the annual addition to profit divided by the cost of the project. The project will be carried out if the interest rate is less than 10 percent because the rate of return exceeds the cost of acquiring capital. Determining rates of return of different investment projects is much more complicated than this example, but the principle is that investment projects are chosen when the rate of return exceeds the rate of interest.

In any given year, a firm chooses among a number of potential investment projects. Some will offer higher rates of return than others. In making investment decisions, a firm will rank investment projects by rate of return. As long as a project promises a rate of return higher than the interest rate, the firm will want to carry out the project. Since additional investments exhaust the opportunities available to the firm, eventually the rate of return will be driven down to the market interest rate. Firms carry out additional investments as long as their rate of return (R) exceeds the market rate of interest (r). Therefore, the last (marginal) investment project should yield a rate of return equal to the market interest rate, such that $R = r$.

Firms carry out additional investments as long as their rate of return (R) exceeds the market rate of interest (r).

The firm's investment demand curve is negatively sloped, like other demand curves. At high rates of interest, fewer projects offer rates of return equal to or greater than the interest rate. The lower the interest rate, the greater the number of investments that the business will wish to undertake. What holds for individual firms also holds for the economy as a whole: At low interest rates, there is a greater quantity demanded of investments than at higher interest rates. The **investment demand curve** of the economy shows the amount of investment desired at different interest rates. In Figure 9.5, an interest rate of 10 percent yields an investment demand of $200 billion. An interest rate of 8 percent yields an investment demand of $220 billion.

The **investment demand curve** of the economy shows the amount of investment desired at different interest rates.

Credit Markets and Interest Rates

Business firms that wish to invest must borrow from those with savings to lend. Although a large portion of the economy's investments are paid for directly by the savings of business firms (out of their profits or depreciation accounts), business firms lacking such internal savings must borrow. Such borrowing takes place in credit markets. **Credit markets** are markets in which borrowers come together with lenders to determine conditions of exchange such as interest rates and the duration of the loan.

Credit markets are markets in which borrowers come together with lenders to determine conditions of exchange such as interest rates and the duration of the loan.

Figure 9.4 showed the supply curve of savings and Figure 9.5 showed the demand for saving (in the form of the demand for investment), both relative to the interest rate. Figure 9.6 brings the two together to show the demand curve for investment funds together with the supply curve of savings. The **market** (or **equilibrium**) **rate of interest** is the rate that equates the quantity of investment with the quantity of saving. At any other interest rate, saving and investment will not be equal. For example, at an interest rate above the equilibrium rate, savers will want to lend more than investing firms wish to borrow, and the interest rate will drop.

The **market** (or **equilibrium**) **rate of interest** is the rate that equates the quantity of investment with the quantity of saving.

FIGURE 9.5 The Investment Demand Curve for the Macroeconomy

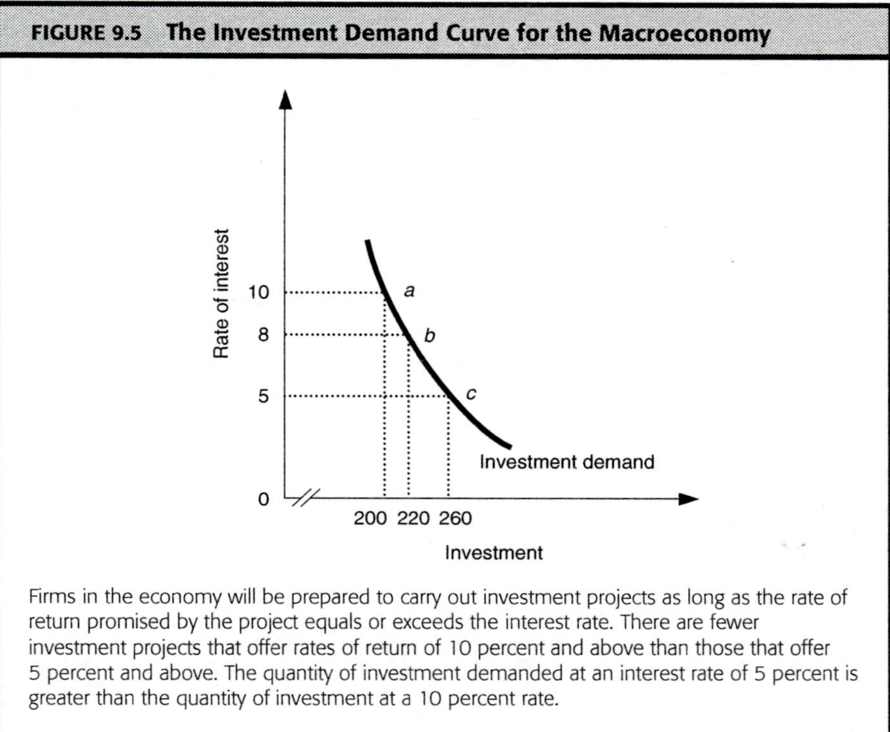

Firms in the economy will be prepared to carry out investment projects as long as the rate of return promised by the project equals or exceeds the interest rate. There are fewer investment projects that offer rates of return of 10 percent and above than those that offer 5 percent and above. The quantity of investment demanded at an interest rate of 5 percent is greater than the quantity of investment at a 10 percent rate.

An increase in thrift lowers interest rates and causes more investment to be undertaken.

Figure 9.7 shows the effect of an increase in the thrift of households, shown by a rightward shift in the economy's saving function. Now households wish to save more at each rate of interest than before. The result of this increase in thrift is a lower interest rate and a greater volume of investment. An increase in thrift lowers interest rates and causes more investment to be undertaken. The increase in investment adds to our stock of capital and makes us a more prosperous and productive nation.

The Structure of Interest Rates

Figures 9.4 through 9.7 represent a simplification. In reality, borrowing occurs in credit markets not simply to finance investment. Households borrow to finance home purchases and new cars. Governments whose budgets are in deficit borrow. Some businesses lend their savings to others and do not plow them back into the business. Nevertheless, the analysis in Figures 9.4 to 9.7 describes the general process of interest rate determination. Our analysis also is a simplification in that it talks about *the* rate of interest. In fact, at any one point in time, there are a number of interest rates.

The interest rate as the price of credit is not the same for all borrowers. Banks may pay as little as 1 percent when they borrow from their depositors, while charging loan customers 9 percent for automobile loans. The U.S. Treasury may pay 3 percent to purchasers of its six-month Treasury bill and 5 percent on a three-year Treasury bond,

FIGURE 9.6 The Credit Market: Saving and Investment Together

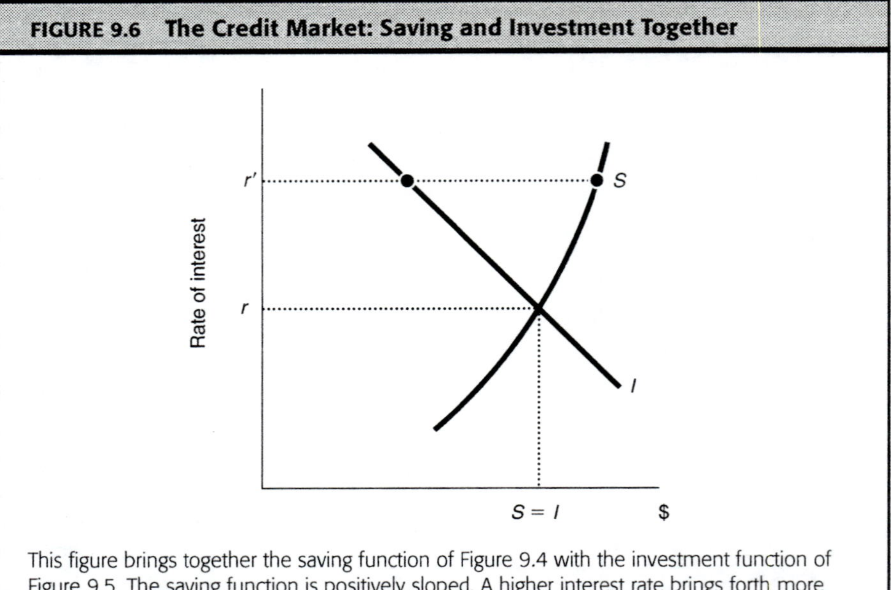

This figure brings together the saving function of Figure 9.4 with the investment function of Figure 9.5. The saving function is positively sloped. A higher interest rate brings forth more saving. The investment demand function is negatively sloped. Higher interest rates discourage investment. The credit market is in equilibrium at interest rate *r*, where the amount of desired saving equals the desired amount of investment. At *r′* the desired amount of saving exceeds the desired amount of investment. In effect, lenders cannot find enough borrowers, and the interest rate drops.

Different interest rates are paid on different financial assets.

whereas a near-bankrupt company may pay 20 percent on a six-month bank loan. Different interest rates are paid on different financial assets. Interest rates vary with the conditions of *risk, liquidity,* and *maturity* associated with a loan.

Risk Borrowers with good credit ratings pay lower interest rates than borrowers with poor credit ratings. To be competitive and earn a normal profit, lenders must be compensated for the extra risk of lending to borrowers with poor credit ratings. If one type of borrower fails to repay bank loans 1 percent of the time, banks will require that borrower to pay an interest rate at least 1 percent above the interest rate charged borrowers with a 0 percent risk of default. The extra 1 percent is called a *risk premium.* Lenders who demand 10 percent interest per month from those with poor credit histories are demanding an enormous risk premium because of the high default rate on such loans.

A financial asset that can be turned into cash quickly or with a small penalty is said to be **liquid.**

Liquidity A financial asset that can be turned into cash quickly or with a small penalty is said to be **liquid.** People may be willing to hold savings accounts paying 3 percent interest when six-month certificates of deposit pay 6 percent simply because the former can be turned into cash quickly and without penalty. Interest rates usually vary inversely with liquidity.

FIGURE 9.7 The Effect of an Increase in Thrift of Households

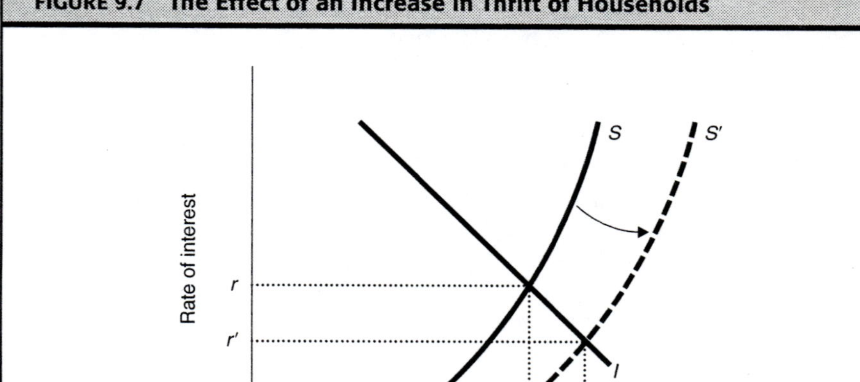

The increase in household thrift is shown by the rightward shift of the saving function from *S* to *S′*. Households want to save more at each interest rate. The result is that the interest rate drops and more investment is undertaken.

Maturity Interest rates also vary with the term of maturity. A corporation borrowing $1000 for one year may pay a lower annual rate of interest than if it borrows the same $1000 for two years. If the credit market expects the interest rate on one-year loans to be 6 percent during one year and 12 percent during the next, the interest rate on a two-year loan covering the same period will be 9 percent—the average of the two interest rates.

Investment Cycles and Bubbles

The theory of investment says that the amount of investment businesses wish to undertake depends upon perceptions of future profits. Because the future is unknown, the moods of investors can change dramatically within a short period. If businesses suddenly become pessimistic about the future, they will cut back on their investment plans. Stock markets are sensitive gauges of investor expectations of the future. A surge in the share prices of high-tech companies (even those that have never made a profit) tells us that stock market investors see them earning substantial profits in the future. Such a surge of optimism began in the mid-1990s as shares of the speculative NASDAQ exchange soared. There was talk of a "new economy" of never-ending rapid growth as businesses took advantage of the new technologies of the computer and information revolution. New businesses attracted speculative investors to pour billions of dollars into fiber-optic cables, virtual marketing ventures, new cellular phone companies, and new gadgets for the computer age. Virtually any small business located in Silicon

Valley with a new concept to sell could find ready investors. Few heeded warnings of "irrational exuberance." The investment bubble of soaring share prices of high-tech companies burst in 1999 as it became evident that the anticipated profits of "new economy" companies would be earned in the very distant future at best. As businesses and stock market investors realized that they had overestimated future profits, the stock market fell. In looking at their investment plans, businesses soberly realized that they had over invested in projects that yielded little or no return and that the prospect of future profits was so bleak that little new investment was warranted.

Figure 9.8 charts the rates of growth of business investment in the 1990s and shows the resulting volatility of business investment, and it shows that the bursting of the investment bubble in 1999 was not a one-time phenomenon. It was, however, one of the most spectacular collapses of investment of the twentieth century.

The investment bubble of the 1990s illustrates a theory of investment cycles. It says that whenever businesses and investors overestimate the future rate of profits (they perceive it to be well above the cost of capital, or the interest rate), they will over invest. As more and more questionable investment projects are undertaken, the actual rate of return on investments will be pushed down well below the interest rate. As businesses realize what has happened, they have no reason to invest, and the amount of investment collapses until the time comes when there are again investments that yield actual returns above the interest rate.

FIGURE 9.8 Percentage Changes in Investment (Adjusted for Inflation)

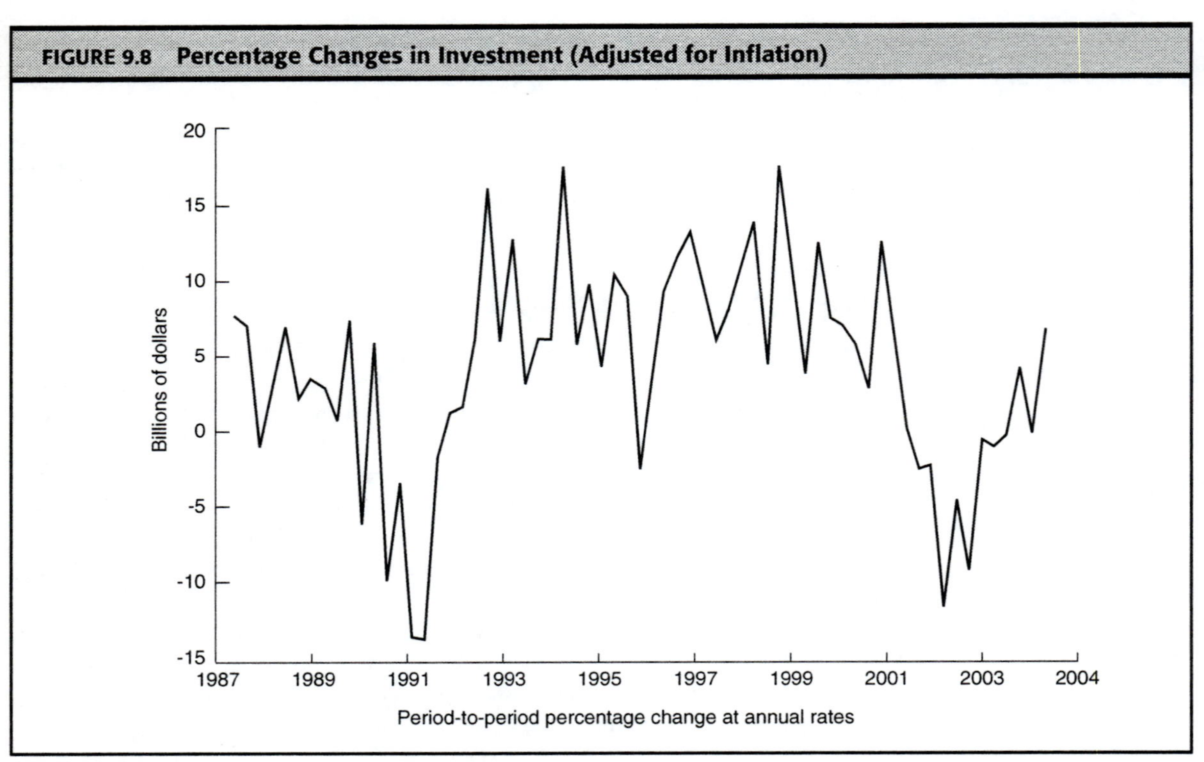

Investment cycles occur when businesses make poor investment decisions and drive actual rates of return below the interest rate.

Investment cycles occur when businesses make poor investment decisions and drive actual rates of return below the interest rate.

The next chapter provides another foundation for the study of macroeconomics. It examines the role of government.

Summary

1. The amount of consumption and saving of households depends on their income and on interest rates. These relationships are called *consumption functions* and *saving functions.* Consumption and saving depend positively on income. Saving varies positively with interest rates. Saving is what is left over from income after consumption and income taxes.
2. The life-cycle theory of consumption says that households take a forward-looking approach to planning their consumption over the life cycle. They borrow during the early life cycle, save during the mature phase, and draw down their savings when they are old.
3. The interest rate constitutes a reward for refraining from consuming now. The nominal interest rate equals the real rate plus the anticipated rate of inflation. People base their saving and investment decisions more on the real rate than on the nominal rate of interest.
4. Businesses wish to undertake the investment projects that yield rates of return in excess of the interest rate. Hence, the investment demand curve is negatively sloped.
5. The credit market brings together savers and business investors. The credit market sets an equilibrium rate of interest that equates the quantity of investment demanded with the quantity of saving.
6. There are many interest rates. The structure of interest rates depends on risk, maturity, and liquidity.
7. Investment bubbles occur when businesses overestimate future profits. Such bubbles create investment cycles.

Questions and Problems

1. Pawnbrokers charge interest rates sometimes as high as 10 percent per week. The U.S. government borrows from the public at 5 percent per year. Explain why the two interest rates are so different.
2. Use supply and demand diagrams to show what will happen if businesses suddenly become more optimistic and raise their estimates of the rates of return they can achieve on their investment projects.
3. According to the life-cycle hypothesis, which of the following two families will save more (each household earns the same amount of income): a family of 25-year-olds or a family of 45-year-olds?
4. If people suddenly expect a higher rate of inflation, what will happen to nominal interest rates? What will happen to real interest rates?

5. The interest rate that the government pays on its 30-year bonds is 6 percent today. Tomorrow it must pay 8 percent. What could have happened?
6. Assume that stock market investors overestimate the future profits of the economy. They invest billions of dollars in companies that undertake new investments. When they realize that the expected profits will not come in, what will happen to stock prices and to the amount of investment?
7. Consider a two-person household. One person is 25 years old; the other is 50 years old. The younger person has a much higher income. Which person would be expected to save more?
8. Which would be more volatile—the amount of investment spending or the amount of consumption spending? Explain your answer.
9. If the real rate of interest is 3 percent and the interest rate on 10-year bonds is 5 percent, what does this tell us about anticipated inflation?

CHAPTER 10

GOVERNMENT SPENDING, TAXATION, AND DEFICITS

Chapter Preview

Like households and firms, governments make expenditures and take in revenues. The major differences are that government expenditure decisions are made ultimately by voters in a democratic society, operating through elected officials, and that government revenues are collected primarily in the form of taxes. This chapter examines the impact of government on the macroeconomy.

No Market Test for Government Spending

Private economic decisions are regulated by a simple rule: Any economic activity will be carried out as long as its marginal benefits exceed its marginal costs. Public decisions should strive for this same type of rationality. At a minimum, government spending should be undertaken only if it yields benefits equal to or greater than its costs. Taxes should not be imposed unless they yield benefits equal to or greater than costs.

In the private sector, firms do not carry out any activity whose marginal revenues do not cover marginal costs. If a private firm tried to produce a product whose benefit to society, as reflected in its price, was less than its cost, the firm would incur losses and eventually go out of business. A **market test** ensures that private goods and services yield benefits equal to or greater than their costs.

A **market test** ensures that private goods and services yield benefits equal to or greater than their costs.

Government spending is carried out by the 87,000 federal, state, and local governments in the United States. The federal government focuses on national and international matters such as defense, international diplomacy, and a national highway system. State governments spend their funds on state universities, state highways, and the state court system. Local governments spend their funds on local schools, roads, and police protection.

Exhaustive expenditures are government purchases that divert resources from the private sector, making them no longer available for private use.

Transfer payments transfer income from one individual or organization to another.

Government expenditures are either exhaustive expenditures or transfer payments. **Exhaustive expenditures** are government purchases that divert resources from the private sector, making them no longer available for private use. **Transfer payments** transfer income from one individual or organization to another. When a local government hires a police officer or repairs a road, this is an exhaustive expenditure.

Payments to families with dependent children transfer income from taxpayers to poor families and constitute a transfer payment.

In 2002, the government purchased 35 percent of all goods and services. In an economy that produced $11 trillion worth of goods and services, government purchases totaled almost $3.4 trillion. Exhaustive expenditures accounted for 66 percent of total government spending (see Figure 10.1). The remaining 34 percent of government expenditures were transfer payments. Most transfers are made by the federal government; state and local governments make a greater amount of exhaustive expenditures on goods and services than the federal government does.

Transfer payments affect the distribution of income among families but do not change the amount of goods and services that are exhausted (consumed) by government. The Social Security transfer program transfers income from currently employed workers to retired or disabled workers.

FIGURE 10.1 Government Expenditures for Goods and Services (Exhaustive) and Transfer Payments, 2002

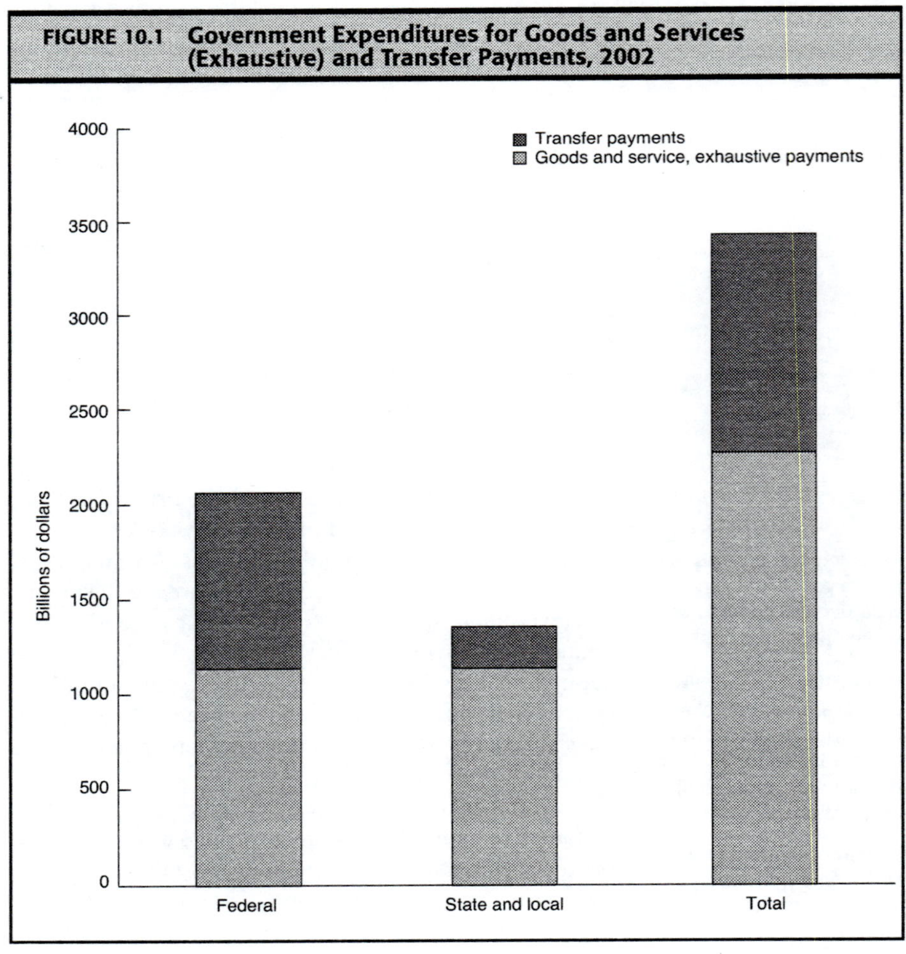

Taxation

Unlike private firms, government rarely sells its goods and services. If government attempted to sell national defense or a legal system, for example, it could not hope to cover costs. Therefore, except in rare cases, government programs must be financed through taxes. Throughout history there has been intense discussion about the principles of fairness and efficiency in relation to taxation.

Principles of Taxation

The **benefit principle of taxation** argues that those who benefit from a public expenditure program should pay for the program.

The **benefit principle of taxation** states that those who benefit from a public expenditure program should pay for it. Examples are a tax on gasoline to pay for highways or a flood control tax on homes that fall in a flood control district.

Benefit taxes offer two basic advantages. First, people who do not benefit do not pay. If non-drivers were taxed to build roads, they would be subsidizing drivers. Second, benefit taxes are more likely to ensure that benefits equal or outweigh the costs. If community members who benefit from a public expenditure are unwilling to vote for the program, they are revealing that they do not think the benefits of the program outweigh the costs.

A problem with benefit taxes is that it is often difficult to determine who benefits. Exactly who benefits from police protection, public education, interstate highways, environmental protection, national defense, or a new sports stadium? Even where it appears easy to assign benefits, such as in the case of public education, it may not be. Not only the person receiving public education but society as a whole is made better off by having an educated labor force and a more enlightened voting public.

The **ability-to-pay principle of taxation** states that those better able to pay should bear the greater burden of taxation, whether or not they benefit.

The alternative approach to benefit taxation is taxation according to ability to pay. The **ability-to-pay principle of taxation** states that those better able to pay should bear the greater burden of taxation, whether or not they benefit.

According to the ability-to-pay principle, the rich should bear a heavier responsibility for public schools, national defense, flood control, public hospitals, and poverty programs simply because they are better able to pay than the poor. In fact, the rich may benefit less, because they tend to use private schools and private hospitals and do not benefit from welfare programs.

An ability-to-pay tax system has its problems. If the beneficiaries of government programs do not pay for them, voters may approve programs that yield benefits below costs. If the majority of voters are poor and do not have to pay for government programs, why shouldn't they vote in favor of all programs that yield them positive benefits regardless of the cost? An ability-to-pay tax system could discourage work effort. Those who work harder and earn more are penalized by having to pay more for government programs that benefit others.

Taxes and Private Decision Making

Taxes affect economic decision making. Whether spouses work is affected by the tax rates that married couples pay; business investment decision are affected by tax treatment; high sales taxes on tobacco products raise prices and discourage consumption; deductions of mortgage interest from taxable income encourage home ownership.

Experts and politicians have long debated whether taxes should be *neutral*—affect private decision making as little as possible—or whether taxes should be used to promote social goals. Most governments use taxes designed to affect private behavior.

With a **proportional tax,** taxpayers earning different incomes pay the same percentage of their income as taxes. With a **progressive tax,** higher-income taxpayers pay a higher percentage of their income as taxes. With a **regressive tax,** high-income taxpayers pay a smaller percentage of their income as taxes.

The **marginal tax rate** is the ratio of the increase in taxes to the increase in income.

Progressive and Regressive Taxes The higher the income, typically the higher the income tax, but tax systems can be either proportional, progressive, or regressive. With a **proportional tax,** taxpayers earning different incomes pay the same percentage of their income as taxes. With a **progressive tax,** higher-income taxpayers pay a higher percentage of their income as taxes. With a **regressive tax,** high-income taxpayers pay a smaller percentage of their income as taxes.

A progressive tax system redistributes income from the rich to the poor. The burden of the tax is heavier on the rich, and income is shifted from the rich to the government. If government programs benefit the poor proportionally more than the rich, then the income is redistributed.

Marginal Tax Rates Private decision making is affected by the **marginal tax rate,** which is the ratio of the increase in taxes to the increase in income. A taxpayer who earns $50,000 in one year pays an income tax of $10,000. In the next year, with tax rates unchanged, the individual earns $60,000 and pays an income tax of $15,000. His or her income has risen by $10,000, and the income tax has risen by $5000. Therefore, the marginal tax rate is 50 percent ($5000/$10,000). A marginal tax rate of 50 percent means that for every *extra* dollar earned, 50 cents goes to taxes and the remaining 50 cents stays with the taxpayer as after-tax income.

The marginal tax rate can have an effect on work effort. Consider two people, both contemplating working to earn an extra $1000. The first has a marginal tax rate of 80 percent, the second a marginal tax rate of 5 percent. The first would keep only $200 of the extra $1000 after taxes; the second would keep $950 after taxes. Because effort and time must be expended to earn extra income, the first person is likely to conclude that earning an additional $1000 would not be worth the trouble; the second person would be more likely to expend the extra effort to earn the extra money.

Government Revenues

Figure 10.2 shows how government collects revenues. The federal government raises $1.6 trillion of its $1.9 trillion in revenues from personal income taxes and payroll (Social Security) taxes. Over time, the payroll tax has risen from a minor share of federal government revenue to about one-third of the total. The federal income tax is progressive, while the payroll tax falls on all employed persons and is regressive. The federal government collects the relatively small remainder of its revenues in the form of corporate profit taxes and sales taxes. State and local governments collect most of their revenues through sales taxes, which tend to be regressive. Because our tax system is a combination of progressive and regressive taxes, it is extremely difficult to determine whether it is progressive or regressive overall.

The Size of Government

The most common measure of the size of government is government's share of total spending of the entire economy. In the year 2002, the spending of federal, state, and

FIGURE 10.2 Revenues of Federal and State and Local Government, 2002

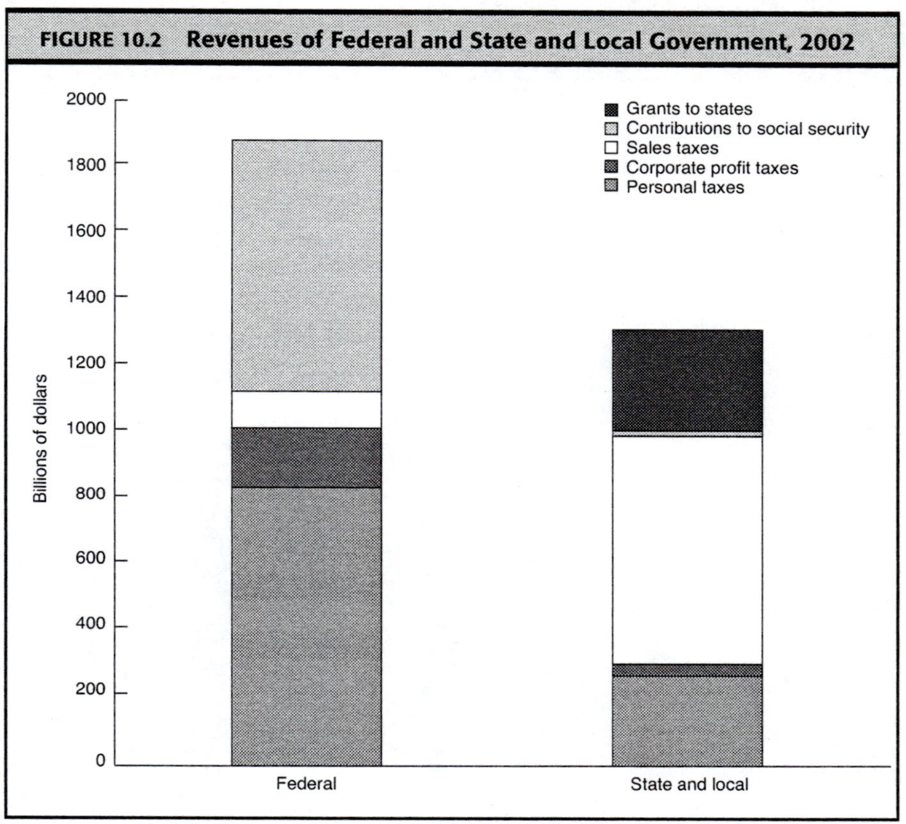

local governments combined was about $3.4 trillion in an economy where total spending was around $11 trillion. Thus, government in the United States accounts for more than 30 percent of all spending. (See Figure 10.1.)

Figure 10.3 shows that taxes as a percentage of total economic spending have a smaller share in the United States than in most other affluent countries. The distribution of taxes shows that other countries have higher tax burdens, largely because they have to collect enormous amounts for social security.

Taxes collected and resources spent by government capture only part of the burden of government.

The Federal Budget

The budget of the federal government deserves special attention. Because the spending and taxation actions of state and local governments are diffused and uncoordinated, they are beyond the direct control of national policymakers. The expenditure and taxation decisions of the federal government, on the other hand, are subject to control by the federal executive and legislative branches. They can be used to regulate the pace of economic activity.

FIGURE 10.3 Government Revenues by Type of Taxation as a Percent of Total Economy

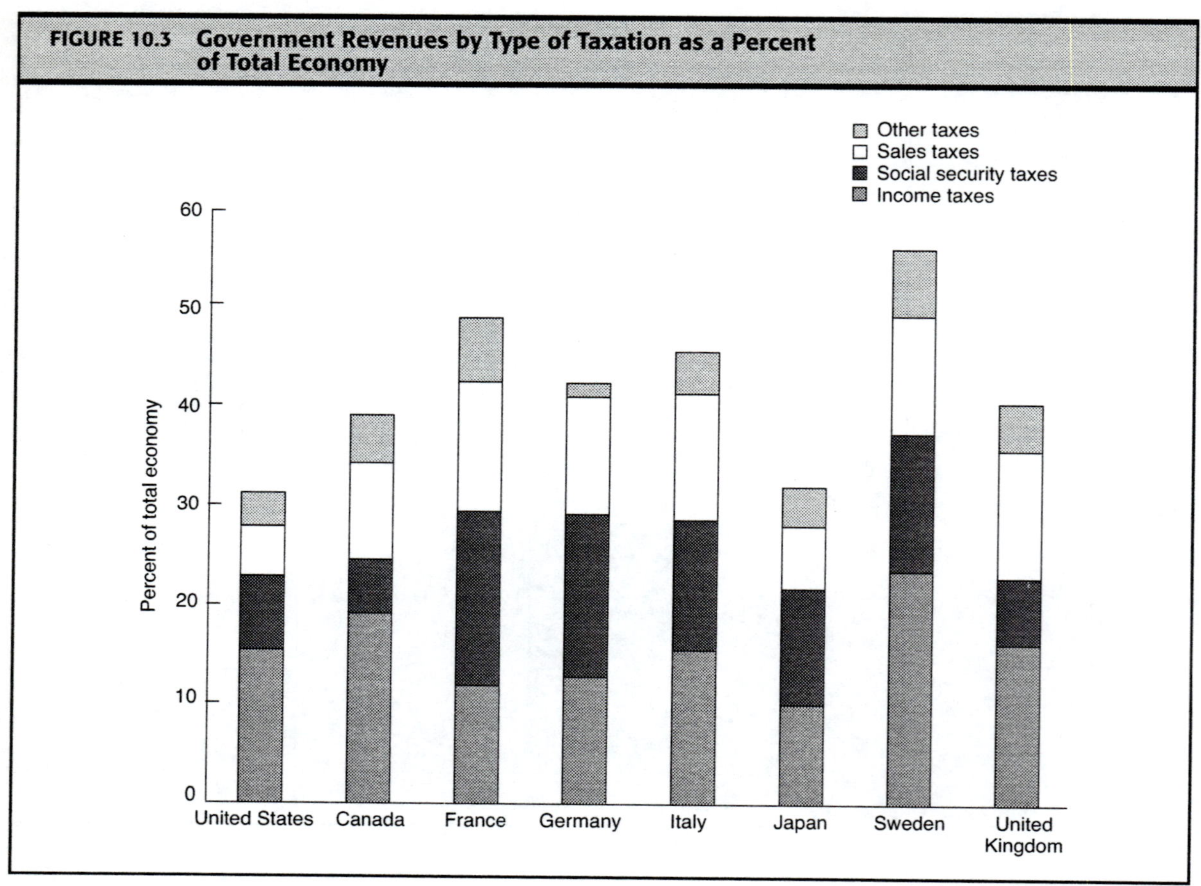

Deficits and Debt

The federal budget runs a **deficit** if federal expenditures exceed federal tax collections and other revenues.

Like any economic unit, the federal government can take in more than it spends or spend more than it takes in. The federal budget runs a **deficit** if federal expenditures (G) exceed federal tax collections and other revenues (T)—that is, if $G > T$. The federal budget is in surplus if $G < T$. If the federal budget is in deficit, the federal government is spending more than it is taking in. Households that spend more than they take in add to their debt. The same is true for the government. If $G > T$, the federal government is adding to its debt.

The **national debt** is the total of outstanding federal government IOUs (outstanding government bonds).

The **national debt** is the accumulated debt of the federal government. It is the total of outstanding federal government IOUs (outstanding government bonds) on which the federal government must pay interest until the bonds are paid off at their maturity. (See Figure 10.4.)

Most of the national debt is owed to the public. A small proportion is held by government agencies, but most of it is owned by American citizens. Currently, about 20 percent of the national debt is owed to foreigners.

FIGURE 10.4 National Debt

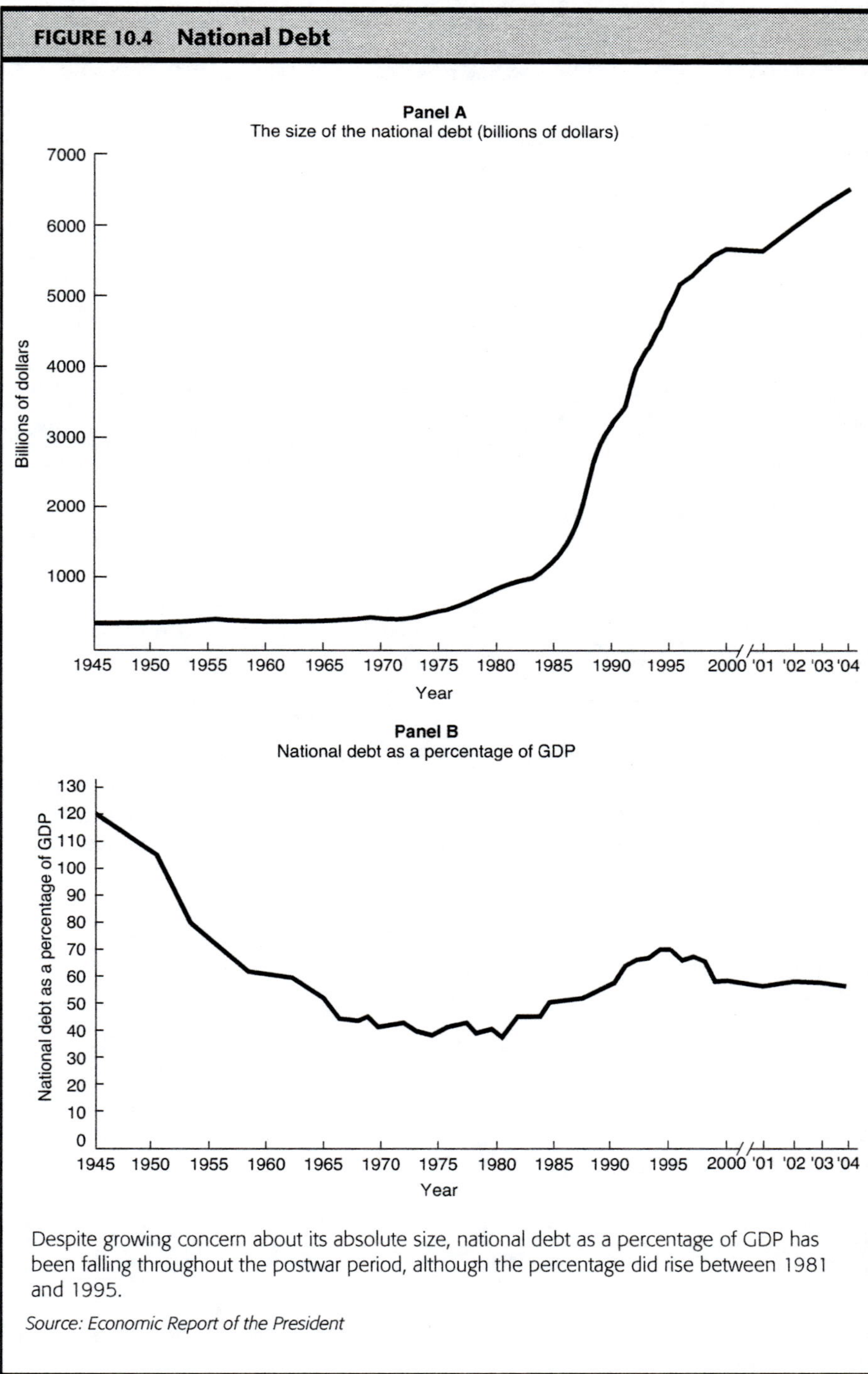

Despite growing concern about its absolute size, national debt as a percentage of GDP has been falling throughout the postwar period, although the percentage did rise between 1981 and 1995.

Source: Economic Report of the President

National debt is **internal** if it is owed to the citizens of the country. It is **external** if it is owed to citizens of other countries.

National debt is **internal** if it is owed to the citizens of the country. It is **external** if it is owed to citizens of other countries. In the case of an internal debt, when interest payments are made, or the principal is paid, income is transferred from one citizen to another. Tax dollars are used to pay the interest and principal to the owner of the federal government's IOU. The recipient of interest and principal payments is typically a taxpayer, so the net transfer of income from taxpayers to owners of debt may be small. In the case of an internal debt, interest and principal payments do not alter the amount of income in the country; they affect only the distribution of income among its citizens. Interest and principal payments on an external debt *do* cause a transfer of income from taxpayers to the foreign owners of the debt and lower the amount of income in a country. Example 10.1 shows how the burden of the debt is distributed among generations.

EXAMPLE 10.1 THE BURDEN OF THE DEBT ON DIFFERENT GENERATIONS

The Congressional Budget Office publishes generational accounts, which compute the net payment burden on different generations if current tax and transfer payment programs continue into the future.

The accompanying table depicts these amounts for selected generations. Older generations are expected to be net recipients, since they have paid low taxes but receive substantial Social Security and Medicare benefits. Younger generations will pay more than they receive because of their greater income, payroll, and sales taxes. Men aged 30 could expect to pay out almost $270,000 more in taxes than they receive in benefits. Women aged 30 pay out less than half of men their age ($111,000) because of their greater longevity.

For newborns, these numbers represent net payment burdens to be paid over their entire lifetimes. Note that these generational accounts show the burden on younger generations assuming that they receive the same benefits as current retirees. The picture would be much worse if benefits for future generations are cut.

Net Tax Payment (present value)

Age in 1998	Male	Female
0	$122,100	$61,100
10	169,400	82,000
20	238,200	109,400
30	268,100	111,400
40	236,900	77,800
50	152,900	10,500
60	10,800	– 95,600
70	– 92,400	– 135,900
80	– 83,600	– 112,300
90	– 61,500	– 74,300

Source: Congressional Budget Office, *Generational Accounts for the United States: An Update,* Technical Paper Series 2000–1, February 2000.

Problems of Deficit Reduction

Over the last decade, the impact of deficits on the economy has been hotly debated. Politicians, economists, and the general public favor deficit reductions. Although U.S. presidents have made strong deficit-reduction pledges in their campaigns, no president had been able to produce a balanced federal budget until President Clinton (with the strong support of a Republican Congress) in 1998. Why was it so difficult to achieve a balanced budget in the last quarter-century?

First, approximately 75 percent of all federal government spending is for relatively uncontrollable outlays—government expenditures whose level is determined by existing statutes, by contracts, or by other obligations. Federal government outlays for nondefense discretionary programs accounted for less than 20 percent of the total. To cut the size of the federal deficit, federal revenues must be increased, federal outlays must be reduced, or a combination of the two must take place. In any particular year, budgetary authorities have little leeway for reductions. In addition to relatively uncontrollable outlays, tax revenues are also largely out of the control of budgetary authorities, insofar as they depend on the state of the economy.

There is no popular way to reduce the deficit. Spending cuts are vigorously opposed by those who benefit from the spending program; tax changes that raise government revenues are just as vigorously opposed by those who would pay higher taxes. Affected parties are able to lobby their elected officials, who then find it difficult to vote in favor of unpopular spending cuts or tax increases. Tax increase proposals are further complicated by the desire to raise only those tax items that will not reduce work effort or capital formation. If work effort and capital formation drop, income drops and there is less income to tax. Although everyone favors deficit reduction, few are willing to pay the personal price of a lower deficit, particularly when it comes to giving up spending and tax programs that are of benefit to themselves. This fact, more than any other, explains why it is difficult to reduce the deficit substantially.

The 1990s was a decade of unprecedented prosperity. During periods of prosperity, government tax collections rise and transfer payments to support the unemployed and the poor decline. As a consequence, the federal budget achieved surpluses in the period 1998 through 2001, and government projections incorrectly predicted large surpluses for the first decade of the twenty-first century. As Example 10.2 shows, these projected surpluses depend on the degree of future prosperity.

Majority Rule: The Power of the Median Voter

The most common method of making public-choice decisions in democratic societies is majority rule. Let us consider a simple example, a community that consists of only three voters. In this community, a proposal for flood control would require two votes for passage. The community would have to decide how much flood control, if any, to authorize.

If each incremental unit of flood control represented an additional foot of height to a proposed dam, let us suppose that the marginal cost of supplying flood control is $12 per unit for each successive foot. The tax would be spread equally among the three voters at $4 per person per unit of flood control. The voters would

EXAMPLE 10.2 WHERE DID THE $4 TRILLION SURPLUS GO?

One of the most heated issues of the 2000 presidential election was what to do with the projected $4 trillion surplus expected to accumulate by the year 2010. Two years later, the discussion turned to trillion-dollar deficits! If one carefully examines the official projections, what happened to the 2010 "surplus" becomes clear.

First, more than half of the "surplus" was due to surpluses in Social Security ($2.3 trillion), which should not be used for general revenues anyway.

Second, of the remaining non–Social Security "surplus" of $1.5 trillion, $960 billion was scheduled to be spent for health initiatives (to prop up Medicare, prescription drugs, and additional spending), leaving a cumulated surplus of only $500 billion.

Third, the $4 trillion surplus projection was based on the assumption that we would have no recession for a decade. The relatively mild recession from March to November 2001 caused an unexpected loss of revenues of almost $30 billion.

Fourth, and most importantly, the projections assumed that the limits of the Balanced Budget Act would be observed for the next decade. These agreements limited the growth of federal government spending to 3.2 percent per year—only slightly above the projected rate of inflation. Between 1959 and 1999, federal government spending rose by 7.6 percent per year. This means that these budget projections assumed that Congress and the President would be satisfied with spending increases equal to 40 percent of the historical average. If spending actually increased by 4.5 percent per year (only 1 percent over the target), about $2.5 trillion of the projected $4 trillion "surplus" would disappear. In fact, federal governments spending rose an average of more than 6 percent annually after 1999.

Fifth, the budget "surpluses" of 1998–2000 were primarily the result of the "peace dividend" that allowed defense spending to be reduced from 5 percent of GDP in 1990 to 3 percent of GDP in 2000. Were it not for this "peace dividend," there would have been no surplus in these years. Defense spending could not be reduced further, especially in light of the wars in Afghanistan and Iraq. Cuts in the future must come from other sources—and political resistance to such cuts will be intense.

Source: Budget of the United States Government, Mid-Session Review, Fiscal Year 2001; http://w3.access.gpo.gov/usbudget/fy2001/pdf.

benefit differently from flood control, but each person's tax would equal $4 times the quantity of flood control authorized. At a price of $4 per unit of flood control, Adam (*A*) wants a 40-foot dam; Barbara (*B*) wants a 120-foot dam, and Carl (*C*) wants a 140-foot dam. *B* is the **median voter,** the voter whose preferences are such that 50 percent of the voting population desires less of the public good and 50 percent desires more of it.

The **median voter** is the voter whose preferences are such that 50 percent of the voting population desires less of the public good and 50 percent desires more of it.

If the community were to propose a 40-foot dam or less, each member of the community would vote for flood control; support would be unanimous. For each person, the dam would bring in more benefits than costs. Yet *B* and *C* would not be happy with such a low dam. At 40 feet, both *B* and *C* would be receiving marginal benefits well in excess of marginal costs (the $4 per-unit tax). They both prefer a higher dam. If the community proposed a 120-foot dam (the dam height favored by the median voter, *B*), both *B* and *C* would vote in favor. Individual *A* would vote against a 120-foot dam. As this example shows, majority rule results in the selection of the public programs favored by the median voter. The median voter's preferences determine the outcome.

Under **majority rule,** the median voter determines the outcome.

The decisive role of the median voter in voting under **majority rule** raises three important problems:

1. *Social choices need not respond to individual wants.* Many people are not satisfied with government because they are almost always in the minority. Others, who are at times in the majority and at other times in the minority, are more satisfied with majority rule because they do not know in advance whether they will be in the majority or in the minority.
2. *Majority voting rules may not reflect the intensity of preferences.* Since the median voter determines the outcome, a change in the intensity of any one preference has no impact. In the example, if *A* is not willing to vote for *any* flood control at a $4 per-month tax, the outcome is not changed one iota. If *C* now wants a 400-foot dam, the outcome is also unchanged.
3. *Majority voting need not be efficient.* The efficient allocation of public goods occurs when marginal social costs and marginal social benefits are equal. The intensity of voter preferences determines the marginal social benefits, yet the actual voting outcome is determined only by the median voter. If preferences of nonmedian voters change in favor of flood control, the efficient quantity of flood control would increase but the actual outcome would remain the same.

Logrolling

Logrolling permits the approval of projects by vote-trading coalitions that would be opposed by a majority if considered in isolation.

When public choices involve multiple decisions, there is no assurance that majority rule will prevail. **Logrolling,** or pork-barrel politics, can result in policies that are actually opposed by the majority.

In simple majority rule involving single-issue choices, intensities of preference do not matter. The vote of a person passionately against a measure is offset by the vote of a person marginally in favor. However, real-world politics involves complex decisions. Multiple political decision making opens up the possibility of strategic voting such as logrolling or vote trading. If *A* strongly favors a new interstate highway and is mildly opposed to building a new ship channel, and *B* strongly favors a new ship channel but is mildly opposed to the interstate highway, *A* and *B* form a coalition in which each agrees to support the other's pet project, and each project is approved by majority vote. Therefore, logrolling permits the approval of projects by vote-trading coalitions that would be opposed by a majority if considered in isolation. (See Example 10.3.)

Rational Ignorance

Rational public-choice decisions require that voters be aware of the costs and benefits of their voting decisions. Information is costly, and economic agents gather information

EXAMPLE 10.3 DAIRY SUBSIDIES: RATIONAL IGNORANCE AND LOGROLLING

The U.S. government spends several billions of dollars per year to support the U.S. dairy-farming industry, a classic example of special-interest legislation. Why did Congress pass this dairy-subsidy program? The benefits to specific dairy farmers are very large. Big dairy operators stand to be the big winners. The losers are the consumers of milk, who must pay for the program with higher milk prices. Farm experts estimate that the government dairy program raises retail milk prices by 4 percent, but a 4 percent price increase costs the average household only 2 cents per day. In addition to higher milk prices, the dairy-subsidy program also costs the average taxpayer an extra $18 per year on his or her federal income taxes.

The dairy-support program is complicated. The average taxpayer may be better off paying the costs of the program (being rationally ignorant) than going through the trouble of gaining information.

The large dairy cooperatives are generous givers to the major political parties. A recent dairy bill was supported by key politicians from tobacco-producing states because it was combined with a tobacco support bill. Logrolling and vote trading ensured the passage of this dairy-support bill even though it was opposed by consumer coalitions, the American Farm Bureau, and the National Cattlemen's Association.

only as long as marginal benefits from additional information outweigh marginal costs. Because of costly information, it may be in the voter's interest to not be fully informed as to the consequences of voting decisions. **Rational ignorance** is a decision not to acquire additional information because the marginal costs of acquiring it exceed the marginal benefits. Rational ignorance often applies to the gathering of information by voters because the marginal costs of acquiring information about public choices may be greater than for private choices. In making private choices, individuals must inform themselves about the prices and qualities of cars, television sets, and food products. In making public choices, individuals must gather information about complex and confusing public issues. Should a new flood control project be built? To whom should a cable franchise be awarded? Is enough being spent on national defense? To which countries should foreign aid be granted?

Rational ignorance is a decision not to acquire additional information because the marginal costs exceed the marginal benefits.

The combination of multiple-issue voting and rational ignorance works to the advantage of **special-interest groups,** minority voting groups with intense preferences about specific government policies.

Special-interest groups are minority voting groups with intense preferences about specific government policies.

Special-interest groups, such as dairy farmers and domestic steel manufacturers, are very well informed about public policies (dairy price supports or tariffs and quotas on foreign steel) that affect their economic well-being. Profits, and even survival, often depend on the passage of favorable legislation. The benefits to special-interest groups of being informed about specific government programs are substantial. But the cost for the average voter of finding out about special-interest legislation is large relative to the benefits. Most citizens believe that protection in the steel and dairy industries creates domestic jobs, and the costs to them are either small or hidden. Special-interest legislation may raise milk prices only a few cents and steel prices by a dollar or two per ton. Therefore, the result of this information imbalance is special-interest legislation that hurts the majority a little bit at a time but helps special-interest groups significantly. Thus, a central problem of public choice is that benefits of government policies are highly concentrated while the costs are highly diffused. The result is government programs whose costs exceed their benefits.

A central problem of public choice is that benefits of government policies are highly concentrated while the costs are highly diffused.

Summary

1. In the public sector, there is no automatic market test to ensure that benefits equal or exceed costs. Government spending is either exhaustive expenditures or transfer payments.
2. The two principles of taxation are the benefit principle and the ability-to-pay principle.
3. Taxes can affect private decision making unless the tax system is neutral.
4. Taxes can be progressive, regressive, or proportional. Progressive taxes lead to marginal tax rates that rise with income. The higher the marginal tax rate, the greater the effect on incentives.
5. The federal budget is in deficit when tax collections are less than outlays, meaning that the national debt has been increased. The national debt has increased substantially in the 1980s, but over the long run, it has declined as a percentage of economic activity. National debt is either external or internal. Deficit reduction is difficult because most federal spending is relatively uncontrollable in the short run. In the long run, deficit reduction requires unpopular spending cuts and unpopular tax increases.
6. Rational public choice is hampered by national ignorance, special interest groups, and the median voter rule.

Questions and Problems

1. Explain why a tax system that is "fair" may not be efficient. What is meant by an efficient tax system?
2. Explain why educated people with a large number of school-aged children tend to be located in communities with good schools. How good would you expect public schools to be in retirement communities?
3. Reilly pays an income tax of $2000; Smith pays an income tax of $10,000. If Smith has a taxable income of $100,000, how much taxable income would Reilly have to earn for the tax system to be proportional? For the system to be regressive?
4. Last year Jones earned $5000 more income and paid $4000 more in taxes. What is Jones's marginal tax rate?
5. If the tax system is proportional, what happens to the marginal tax rate as income rises?

6. Explain the principle of a market test and why public spending differs from private spending.
7. If I want a tax reduction to increase work effort and risk taking, would I grant everyone a $500 tax reduction or would I lower marginal tax rates?
8. There are only three people in a community. They must vote on how much to spend on road improvement. The first voter wants to spend $1000, the second $2000, the third $3000. If a vote were taken, which sum would pass? Would the outcome change if the third voter wanted to spend $100,000?
9. From what you have learned in this chapter, will governments be more inclined to run surpluses or deficits?
10. A family earns a gross income of $50,000. It pays $10,000 in income taxes. What else do we need to know to determine how much it saves?

PART FOUR

ESSENTIALS OF MACROECONOMICS

The previous three chapters provided the microeconomic foundations of macroeconomics by examining employment and unemployment, consumption, saving, investment, interest rates, and the role of government. The next five chapters examine the macroeconomic topics of economic growth and the business cycle.

Macroeconomics deals with two major issues: What causes an economy to grow over long periods of time and what causes economies to grow unevenly over time—sometimes growing rapidly, other times shrinking into recession. The first issue is studied under the format of economic growth; the second under the format of the business cycle. We study the business cycle because it affects employment, unemployment, government deficits, interest rates, and inflation. The business cycle also plays a prominent political role. If the economy is good, incumbents, including the president, are usually reelected.

CHAPTER 11

MACROECONOMIC ISSUES: ECONOMIC GROWTH AND THE BUSINESS CYCLE

Chapter Preview

Macroeconomics is the study of economic growth and the business cycle. Macroeconomics focuses on inflation and unemployment, seeking to explain their causes, consequences, and cures. This chapter defines and describes trends in growth, inflation, and unemployment and sets forth the major issues of macroeconomics.

The Ideal Macroeconomic World

In an ideal world, all who wanted to work would have satisfactory jobs; prices would be stable; living standards would be rising steadily; the economy would not have booms and busts, energy crises, or harvest failures. This ideal world, however, does not exist. Some people who want to be gainfully employed aren't; at times, a large percentage of those wanting to work are without jobs. Sometimes prices are stable; at other times they rise at an alarming pace. During one period, jobs are easy to find and wages and incomes are rising. In another period, jobs are hard to find and incomes are stagnant or falling.

Macroeconomists study employment, inflation, booms and busts, and economic growth. They look at the trade-offs among macroeconomic goals. Are stable prices consistent with ample jobs? Can rapidly rising living standards be combined with stable prices? Do we require the government to control the macroeconomy?

Economic growth is the expansion of output over the long run.

The description of the ideal macroeconomic world shows that macroeconomics focuses on two main topics—economic growth and the business cycle. **Economic growth** is the expansion of the economy's output over the long run. The business cycle measures the short-run fluctuations around the economy's expansion of output.

Figure 11.1 plots the output of the United States economy over more than a century. It shows that in some periods, output expands; in other periods, output contracts. These ups and downs are the business cycle. The black line shows the general process of economic growth—namely, the tendency of the economy to grow over time. It is this economic growth that determines our standard of living over a long period.

FIGURE 11.1 U.S. Output (1891–2000)

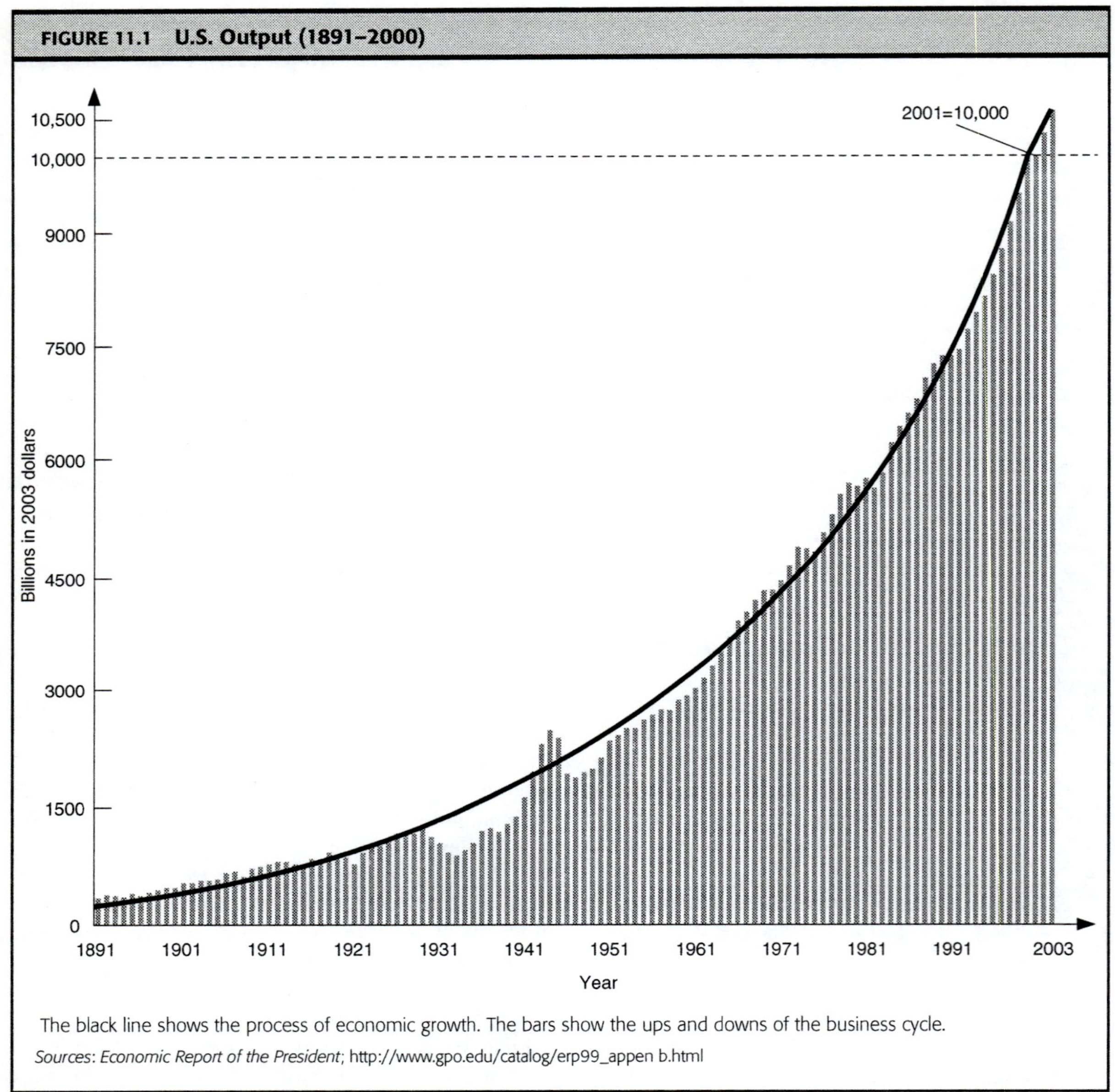

The black line shows the process of economic growth. The bars show the ups and downs of the business cycle.

Sources: *Economic Report of the President*; http://www.gpo.edu/catalog/erp99_appen b.html

Economic Growth

Economic growth occurs when the production possibilities frontier (PPF) expands outward and to the right. In Figure 11.2, economic growth is depicted as a shift from *xx* to *yy* and then from *yy* to *zz*.

FIGURE 11.2 The Effect of Increasing the Stock of Capital on the PPF

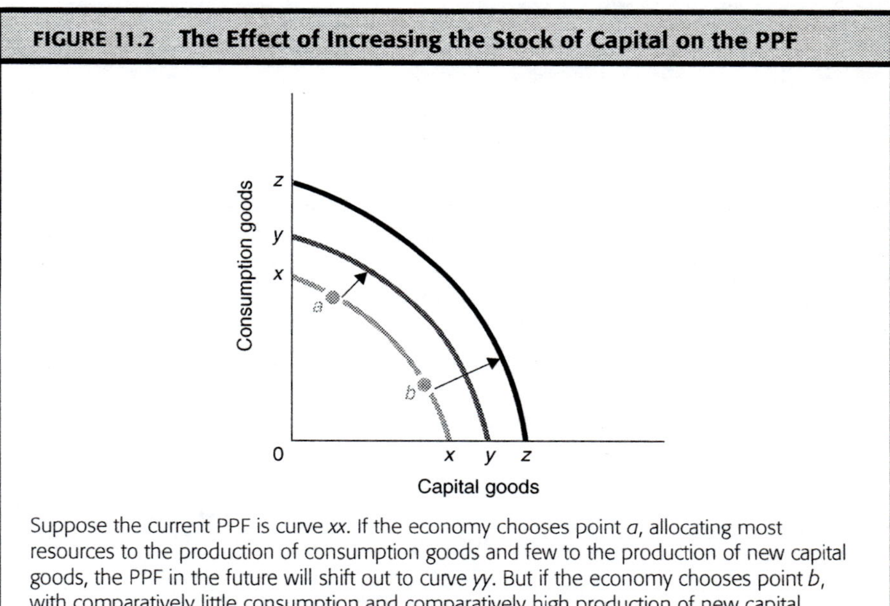

Suppose the current PPF is curve *xx*. If the economy chooses point *a*, allocating most resources to the production of consumption goods and few to the production of new capital goods, the PPF in the future will shift out to curve *yy*. But if the economy chooses point *b*, with comparatively little consumption and comparatively high production of new capital goods, the future PPF will shift out further–to *zz*.

There are two basic sources of economic growth—that is, of outward shifts in the economy's PPF. The sources are increases in productive resources and technological progress.

Capital Accumulation

Because land and natural resources are essentially fixed by nature, productive resources are expanded by increasing the quantity and quality of labor and by increasing the stock of capital. The quantity of labor expands as young people enter the labor force and as the percentage of adults who actually work in the labor force rises. The quality of labor increases as the labor force acquires more skills and training.

Investment is addition to the stock of capital. The rate at which society expands its capital depends on the amount of investment.

It is important to distinguish between the stock of capital itself and additions to the stock of capital, called **investment**. The rate at which society expands its capital depends on the amount of investment.

Among its many other choices, society must choose between capital goods and consumer goods. Capital goods are the plants, equipment, and inventories that add to the capital stock. Consumer goods satisfy consumer wants in the present. The capital goods/consumer goods trade-off is shown in Figure 11.2.

Take an economy whose current PPF is *xx*. It has a choice of trading off more consumption today for less capital tomorrow (point *a*) or less consumption today for more capital tomorrow (point *b*). Whether *a* or *b* is chosen affects economic growth. If *a* is chosen, the capital stock expands moderately and the economy moves to a higher PPF, labeled *yy*. If *b* is chosen, there is a greater expansion of the capital stock and the economy moves to an even higher PPF, labeled *zz*. The society that selects *a* will satisfy more wants today but will experience less economic growth and will be less able to satisfy future wants, ceteris paribus.

Technological Progress

Technological progress causes the PPF to shift out. More output is produced from the same inputs.

Technological progress occurs when the economy is able to produce more output from the same amount of productive resources. Technological progress is also shown as an outward and upward shift in society's PPF. The sources of technological progress range from advances in science (new drought-resistant wheat, the transistor) to new applications of technology (the application of computer technology to word processing and hotel and airline reservation systems) to improvements in management methods (the development of more streamlined management structures).

Economic growth determines standards of living. When output expands more rapidly than population, material living standards rise. The high living standards enjoyed in the United States, Europe, and Japan are the products of more than a century of economic growth. Whether the have-not nations enjoy more satisfactory standards of living in the future depends on their economic growth.

Extensive and Intensive Growth: Production Functions

Economies grow when total inputs expand and when available inputs are used more effectively. The more effective use of inputs shows up as increases in output per unit of input—that is, as increases in factor productivity.

Production functions show the relationship between inputs and output. They show how much output can be produced from different amounts of labor and capital with a given state of technology.

The sources of economic growth can be explained by production functions. **Production functions** show the relationship between inputs and output. They show how much output can be produced from different amounts of labor and capital with a given state of technology.

The total output of the economy (Y) depends on the amount of labor and capital inputs used by the economy and on the state of technology. This relationship can be expressed as:

$$Y = F(K, L, T)$$

where K stands for capital inputs, L for labor inputs, and T for technology. If K or L increases, or if technology improves, the economy produces more output.

Extensive growth results from the expansion of factor inputs.

Intensive growth results from increases in output per unit of factor input.

Extensive growth is economic growth that results from the expansion of factor inputs (K and L). **Intensive growth** is growth that results from increases in output per unit of factor input. To expand labor inputs (L), we must sacrifice leisure or household production to produce more market output. To expand capital inputs (K), we must sacrifice current consumption for future consumption.

Factor inputs (L and K) grow quantitatively and qualitatively. Inputs grow quantitatively when more hours are worked, more machines are placed in service, or more factories are built. As workers acquire additional skills and become healthier, the labor input grows qualitatively. As the quality of the labor force increases, one hour's work produces more output than before.

Intensive growth occurs when the same volume of factor inputs produces more output. The major source of productivity improvements is technological change (*T*). Scientists and engineers discover new and improved technologies for combining industrial inputs. Agronomists develop new drought-resistant grains. New modes of communication—fax, e-mail, networks—allow manufacturers to deliver their products at lower costs. Such efficiency improvements can be attributed to advances in technological knowledge.

Improvements in the way resources are combined create efficiency improvements. The assembly line replaces handicraft production. New management techniques make possible the efficient management of enterprises.

We can also express the production function in terms of annual growth rates as:

$$\dot{Y} = 0.67\dot{L} + 0.33\dot{K} + \dot{T}$$

where the dots stand for annual rates of growth ($\dot{Y} = \Delta Y/Y$) for example. This equation says, quite logically, that the growth rate of output depends on the growth rate of inputs and the growth rate of technology. Because there are two inputs, labor and capital, usually growing at different rates, we must calculate their impact on growth as a weighted average. If, for example, $\dot{L} = 1\%$ and $\dot{K} = 3\%$, we must combine them according to their relative importance. This is typically done by using labor and capital's respective shares of total earnings as weights. For example, 0.67 is labor's usual share of the economy (as measured by how much of total income labor earns), and 0.33 is capital's usual share of total income. (See the chapter appendix for further explanation of functions and growth rates.)

The sources of growth explain the relative contributions of labor, capital, and technology to growth.

With this equation, we can calculate the **sources of economic growth**. The sources of growth explain the relative contributions of labor, capital, and technology to growth. If *Y* grows at 3 percent per annum, *L* at 1 percent, and *K* at 3 percent, then 0.67 (0.67×1) of 1 percent of the 3 percent growth is "explained" by the growth of labor, 1 percent (0.33×3) is explained by the growth of capital, and the remainder (1.33 percent) is explained by the advance of technology. These growth figures are roughly representative of the growth experience of the United States over the past 50 years. Table 11.1 summarizes this calculation.

Diminishing Returns Versus Technological Improvements

Insofar as total output per worker (*Y/L*) is a good measure of average living standards, we can also express the production function as:

$$Y/L = f(K/L, T)$$

which states that output per worker increases when there is more capital per worker and when technology improves. Economies that have accumulated considerable capital per worker, such as the United States, produce more output than those that have little capital per worker, such as India.

Panel A of Figure 11.3 shows a typical output-per-worker production function: Output per worker increases as capital per worker increases, but eventually additional increases in capital per worker yield ever smaller increases in output per worker,

TABLE 11.1 Sources of Economic Growth

(a) Growth Rate of		*(b)* Growth Explained by	*(c)* Percentage of Growth Explained by
Output	3%	—	—
Labor	1%	0.67%	22.0%
Capital	3%	1.00%	33.0%
Technology		1.33%	45.0%
Total		3.00%	100.0%

The first two figures in column *b* are the products of the growth rates of labor and capital times their income shares. The third figure equals 3 − 0.67 − 1.00. The figures in column *c* are the figures in column *b* divided by the total growth rate (3).

The **law of diminishing returns** states that as more and more capital is combined with the same amount of labor, eventually its returns will diminish in the form of smaller and smaller increases in output per worker.

due to the law of diminishing returns. The **law of diminishing returns** (first encountered in Chapter 5), as applied to this case, states that as more and more capital is combined with the same amount of labor, eventually its returns will diminish in the form of smaller and smaller increases in output per worker.

Why? As workers begin to work with capital, their productivity will increase substantially, but at some point they will reach an optimal combination of labor and capital. Once they go beyond this optimal point, increases in capital per worker have relatively small effects on output per worker.

FIGURE 11.3 The Output-per-Worker Production Function, Diminishing Returns, and Technological Change

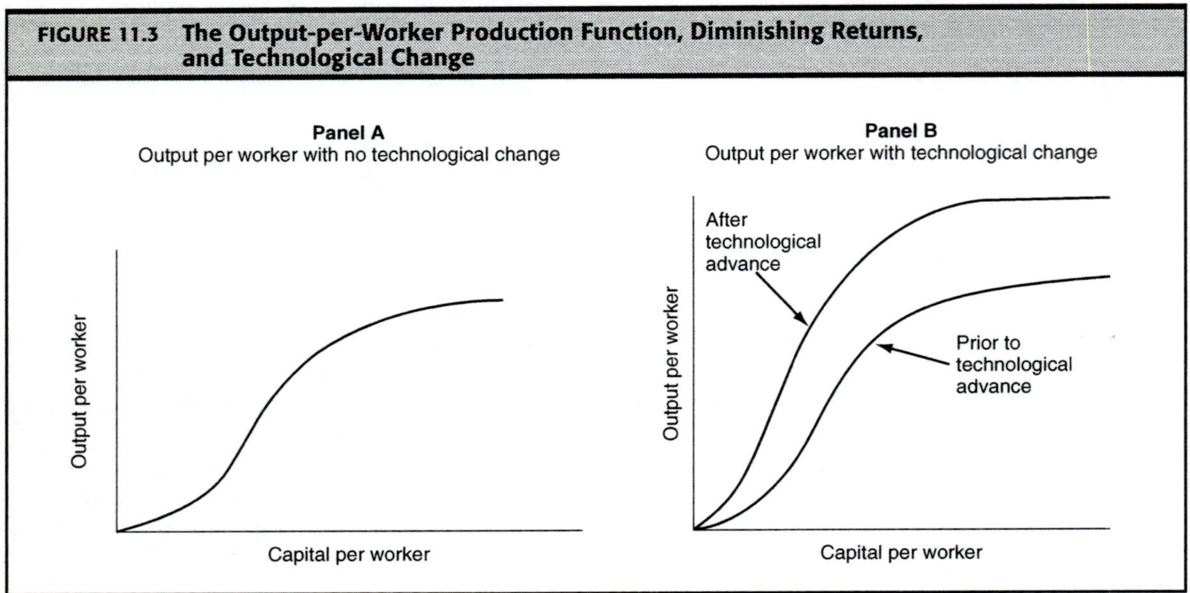

Panel B of Figure 11.3 shows the effect of technological advances (the *T*) on the output-per-worker production function. As technology improves, the whole curve shifts up, and diminishing returns are delayed to a higher level of output per worker.

Hence, the process of economic growth can be viewed as a battle between technological progress and diminishing returns. As long as technology continues to improve, diminishing returns can be avoided. Worker productivity and living standards can continue to rise indefinitely with technological progress.

Growth Policy

For the advanced industrialized economies, the major source of economic growth has been intensive rather than extensive growth. They grew principally because they use their available resources more efficiently, not because they are expanding their resources. (See Example 11.1.)

Economies are in a position to affect their growth through increases either in efficiency or in inputs. As Figure 11.2 showed, an economy that chooses to invest more now and consume less now builds its stock of capital faster and should grow more rapidly. Countries that invest in education and training improve the quality of their existing labor resources. Governments that favor free-market institutions and free international trade create an environment favoring growth.

Productivity-enhancing policies, like human capital investments and increased spending on research and development, serve to improve economic efficiency and to promote economic growth. Whereas economists earlier may have thought that productivity improvements were exogenous (determined by outside forces), they now conclude that countries can indeed adopt policies that raise factor productivity.

The experiences of the four Asian "Tiger" economies show that countries can pursue policies that create rapid economic growth. The economies of Hong Kong, Singapore, Taiwan, and South Korea, starting in the early 1970s, recorded high rates of investment, spent significant resources on human capital, and pursued growth of export markets. The high growth rates they achieved between 1970 and the present changed them from low-income economies to affluent economies. The "Asian crisis" that began in 1997 slowed their growth, but it appears that this "Asian miracle" will continue.

Business Cycles

Over the long run, economies expand the volume of goods and services they produce. The labor force grows, the capital stock expands, and scientific and technological advances raise productivity. The American economy today produces a volume of output more than 20 times greater than a century ago. The growth of economic output, however, is not smooth. During some periods, growth is well above the long-run trend; in other periods, growth is below the long-run trend. In extreme cases, output even shrinks. Employment and unemployment are connected to the pace of business activity. When output is expanding, employment opportunities are expanding, and the unemployment rate falls. When output contracts, the unemployment rate rises because there are fewer employment opportunities.

EXAMPLE 11.1 TECHNOLOGICAL PROGRESS: MOORE'S LAW

Technological progress causes economic growth by allowing economies to produce more output from the same inputs. Because outputs can now be produced with fewer inputs, technological progress lowers the cost of production and allows consumers to buy better products at lower prices. The most phenomenal example of technological progress is described by Moore's Law. For the past three decades, Moore's Law, named after Intel's chairman Gordon Moore, has held that the number of transistors on a chip of a given size doubles every 18 months. For example, in 1972, Intel Corporation's newest microprocessor had 3500 transistors. In 2000, Intel's latest Pentium 4 processor microprocessor (a fraction of the size of the 1972 version) had more than 40 million transistors. Moore's Law means that every year, consumer electronics are getting cheaper, faster, and better. Advanced video game players and digital cameras now have all their capabilities on one silicon chip. Personal computers have all their functions except memory on a single chip.

The enormous increase in computational power and the lowering of the cost of electronic products are an example of how technological progress can generate economic growth independently of increases in labor and capital inputs.

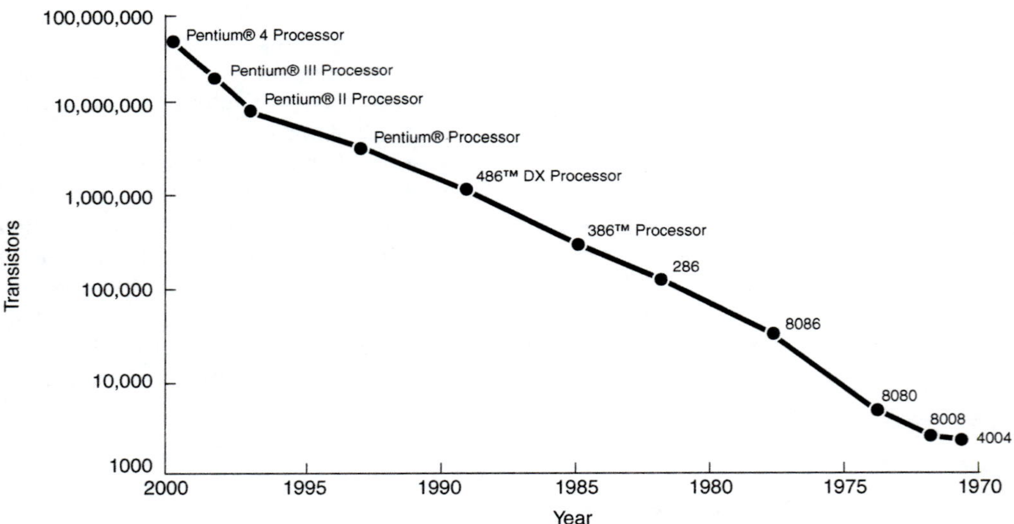

Figure 11.4 Moore's Law

Source: www.intel.com/research/silicon/mooreslaw.htm

A **business cycle** is the pattern of upward and downward movement in the general level of real business activity.

A **business cycle** is the pattern of upward and downward movement in the general level of real business activity. Business cycles deal with fluctuations in economic activity.

Phases of the Business Cycle

Business cycles are divided into four phases, shown in Figure 11.5.

The four phases of the business cycle are **recession, trough, recovery** (or **expansion**), and **peak**.

1. During **recession**, or downturn, output declines for six months or more. The unemployment rate rises, corporate profits fall, and economic activity declines. If the decline is prolonged and severe, this phase is called a *depression*.
2. The **trough** occurs when output stops falling. The economy has reached a low point from which recovery begins.
3. The **recovery**, or **expansion**, phase of the business cycle is characterized by rising output, falling unemployment, rising profits, and increasing economic activity.
4. The **peak** is the final stage of the business cycle and precedes recession. Output growth ceases after the peak is reached.

The duration of a business cycle is the length of time it takes to move through one complete cycle—from peak to peak or from trough to trough. No two business cycles are alike. Some are brief and involve only small downturns in economic activity; others, such as the Great Depression, are prolonged and severe, with enormous declines in output and employment. The average duration of the American business cycle since 1924 has been five years; the recession phase has averaged one year in length, and the recovery phase four years. Because the American economy has grown substantially since 1924, the recovery phase should be much longer than the recession phase. (See Example 11.2.)

FIGURE 11.5 Phases of the Business Cycle

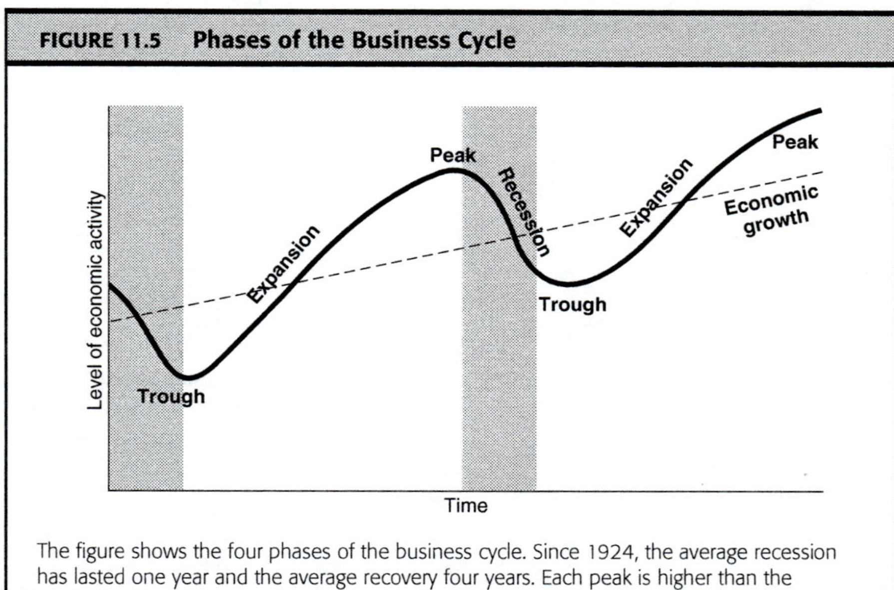

The figure shows the four phases of the business cycle. Since 1924, the average recession has lasted one year and the average recovery four years. Each peak is higher than the previous one because of long-term growth of output. The dotted line shows the long-term growth of the economy.

EXAMPLE 11.2 U.S. BUSINESS CYCLES

The length of the business cycle can be measured either as the amount of time (number of months) between one peak of the cycle and the next or as the time it takes to move from trough to trough. The Great Depression began in August 1929 and was actually two business cycles (a second downturn began in May 1937). The business expansion that began in February 1961 was the second longest recorded expansion on record (lasting until December 1969). The expansion that began in March 1991 was the start of the longest expansion on record, which ended in March of 2001. The current expansion began in November.

American Business Cycles, 1924–Present

Trough	*Peak*	*Length of Cycle, Peak to Peak (months)*
July 1924	October 1926	41
November 1927	August 1929	34
March 1933	May 1937	93
June 1938	February 1945	93
October 1945	November 1948	45
October 1949	July 1953	56
May 1954	August 1957	49
April 1958	April 1960	32
February 1961	December 1969	116
November 1970	November 1973	47
March 1975	January 1980	62
July 1980	July 1981	12
November 1982	July 1990	108
March 1991	March 2001	120
November 2001	Still in progress	—

Source: *Statistical Abstract of the United States* (1994), Table 866, p. 557.

The Impact of the Business Cycle

The business cycle affects both society and private lives. Recessions and depressions mean more unemployment, lower incomes, and less output; cyclical upturns mean rising income, more employment, and greater prosperity. The Great Depression of the 1930s still haunts the memories of older Americans, while the deep recessions of the mid-1970s and early 1980s reminded Americans that "hard times" are not a phenomenon of the past. Presidential elections tend to be won or lost on the basis of the business cycle—voters are asked by the presidential challenger whether they were better off before the incumbent president entered office. Presidents tend to be regarded as successful in their domestic policies if output and employment expand during their term.

Macroeconomic theory must explain the causes of the business cycle and explain the policy options available to deal with the business cycle.

Since 1924, the American economy has gone through 14 complete business cycles. The longest uninterrupted period of prosperity was the decade of the 1990s. The recession that began in mid-1990 and ended in mid-1991 played a major role in the presidential election of 1992, electing a Democratic president for the first time since 1976. The economic growth and prosperity that followed the 1991 trough were major factors in the reelection of Bill Clinton in 1996. The election of George W. Bush in 2000 was surprising in view of the apparent prosperity that reigned at the time. In such circumstances, the incumbent party usually keeps the White House.

If the business cycle captures only the transitory ups and downs of the economy (and the downs are of relatively brief duration), why does it command so much attention? Why can business cycles determine presidential elections? As the great English economist John Maynard Keynes noted in his famous *General Theory*, published in 1936, we live in the short run. Whether we have a job today matters a great deal to us. Whether interest rates are high right now determines whether we can buy a home now. Whether the stock market is rising or falling is important to us today. The long-run forces, such as technology and capital formation, that determine economic growth have a more profound effect on our lifestyles over the duration of our lifetimes, but they are less perceptible and occur more slowly than changes in the business cycle.

Macroeconomic Variables: Output, Prices, and Employment

Like microeconomics, macroeconomics deals with outputs, prices, employment, and wages. However, instead of looking at specific products and industries, macroeconomics looks at the economy as a whole. Macroeconomics is particularly interested in the total output of the economy, called *gross domestic product (GDP)*. Rather than looking at individual prices, macroeconomics studies the price level of the economy as a whole and its rate of change, called *inflation*. Rather than looking at employment in a particular industry, macroeconomics examines *employment* and *unemployment* for the economy as a whole. Macroeconomics requires aggregate measures of output, inflation, and unemployment that can be used for the whole economy.

Measuring Real Output: GDP

Gross domestic product (GDP) is the market value of all final goods and services produced by the factors of production located in the country in one year's time.

The most general measure of the level of business activity is the total volume of goods and services produced by the economy over a specified period of time. This total output is measured by **gross domestic product**, or **GDP**, which is the market value of all final goods and services produced by the factors of production located in the country in one year's time. GDP includes only final goods. The circular-flow diagram in Chapter 2 shows that the final goods and services flow from the business sector to households. Intermediate goods, which remain entirely within the business sector, are not an end in themselves. Moreover, the value of intermediate goods (the steel used to produce cars or the raw cotton used to produce cotton shirts) is already included in the value of final goods. The price of the family car includes the cost of the steel and other materials that went into making it. The price of the cotton shirt includes the cost of the raw cotton that went into it.

GDP is the value of all final goods and services produced by the economy. The final expenditures of the economy are divided into four categories:

Personal Consumption Expenditures (*C*) These are the goods and services purchased by households for consumption purposes. They are consumed either immediately (for example, food or electricity) or gradually over time (autos and washing machines).

Government Expenditures for Goods and Services (*G*) Government produces goods and services by hiring civil servants and schoolteachers, constructing public buildings and submarines, and employing law enforcement officers and judges. As government services are typically not sold, there are no established market prices. Government services are, therefore, typically valued at the cost of supplying them.

Transfer payments are payments to recipients who have not supplied goods or services in return. They are simply transfers of income from one person or organization to another.

Transfer payments are payments to recipients who have not supplied goods or services in return. They transfer income from one person to another. Transfer payments are not counted in *G* because they are not a payment for services rendered. When the recipient of a transfer payment uses these funds to buy goods and services, the purchased goods and services are counted under consumption expenditures.

Depreciation is the value of the existing capital stock that has been consumed or used up in the process of producing output.

Investment (*I*) Investment is defined as expenditures that add to the economy's stock of capital (plants, equipment, structures, and inventories). Unlike intermediate goods, which are immediately used up in production, capital is partially used up in making other goods. A steel mill may have a useful life of 40 years. In producing steel in any one year, only a small portion (one-fortieth) of the mill is consumed; the ore and coking coal, on the other hand, are entirely consumed. The using up of capital is called **depreciation**.

Net Exports of Goods and Services (*X* − *M*) If all final expenditures by households, businesses, and government were added together, their sum would not equal the total output of the economy. Some items, produced by other countries (imports designated by *M*), must be subtracted from total purchases to obtain domestic production figures. Some of the domestic economy's output is exported to other countries (exports denoted by *X*) and does not show up in domestic consumption figures. These goods and services must be added back in. Net exports add exports and subtract imports from total output.

Thus, GDP can be expressed as:

$$\text{GDP} = C + I + G + X - M$$

Real GDP measures the volume of real goods and services produced by the economy by removing the effects of rising prices on nominal GDP.

Nominal GDP is the value of final goods and services for a given year expressed in that year's prices.

Real GDP Since GDP is measured in dollars, it can rise either because prices are rising or because more goods and services are being produced. Macroeconomics focuses its attention on the volume of "real" goods and services produced because that determines economic welfare and employment opportunities. Movements in the output of goods and services are captured by movements in real GDP.

Real GDP measures the volume of real goods and services produced by the economy by removing the effects of rising prices on nominal GDP. **Nominal GDP** is the value of final goods and services for a given year expressed in that year's prices. Real GDP measures the changing volume of output in terms of constant prices of a specific year.

The Equality of Output and Income The circular-flow diagram shows that firms pay income to the factors of production to produce output. For every dollar of final output produced, the economy produces a dollar's worth of factor income in the form of wages, rent, interest, and profit. If the economy produces $10 trillion worth of GDP, $10 trillion worth of factor income is created. Thus, GDP can be calculated either by adding up the value of all final goods and services the economy produces or by adding up the sum of all incomes earned in the economy.

Income earned by households can be used for three purposes: These are saving(S), consumption(C), or income and payroll taxes(T). Hence, GDP also equals the sum of C, S, and T:

$$\text{GDP} = C + S + T$$

From Gross National Product (GNP) to Personal Income

Gross national product (GNP) measures the production of the factors of production supplied by residents of the country, whether that production took place at home or abroad.

Because GDP includes items such as sales taxes (indirect business taxes) and depreciation, which do not accrue to owners of factors of production, we use other income concepts to measure the amount of income earned by the factors of production. These income concepts are national income, personal income, and personal disposable income.

To move from GDP to GNP, one must add factor income receipts from foreigners, which represent the goods and services produced abroad using the labor and property supplied by U.S. residents, and subtract factor income payments to foreigners, which represent the goods and services produced in the United States using the labor and property supplied by foreigners. GDP measures the production taking place in the country, not the production produced by the factors of production owned by the country's citizens. Hence, GDP is regarded as a better measure of total production within a country.

National income equals GNP minus depreciation and indirect business (sales) taxes. National income equals the sum of factor payments made to the factors of production in the economy.

National income equals GNP minus depreciation and indirect business (sales) taxes. National income equals the sum of factor payments made to the factors of production in the economy.

Personal income equals the sum of all income received by persons—national income *minus* retained corporate profits, corporate income taxes, and social security contributions *plus* transfer payments received by individuals.

Personal income equals the sum of all income received by persons. Personal income equals national income *minus* retained corporate profits, corporate income taxes, and social security contributions plus transfer payments received by indiiduals.

Not all of national income accrues to individuals as personal income. Corporations retain a portion of their profits to reinvest; the corporate income taxes paid to government do not enter into personal income; social security contributions are deducted from income.

Personal disposable income measures the amount of personal income left over after personal income taxes.

The Equality of Investment and Saving By definition, GDP equals the sum of consumption, investment, government purchases of goods and services, and net exports. GDP also equals the amount of income generated that can be spent on consumption, saving, or taxes. In Chapter 17, we show the effects of net exports, but for now, we consider an economy with net exports equal to zero. Thus $(X - M)$ drops out of the picture. Because GDP equals the uses of total income, we have:

$$C + I + G = C + S + T$$

which reduces to:

$$I = S + G - T$$

The **natural level of real GDP** is that level of output the economy produces when it is at the natural rate of unemployment.

Chapter 10, on government, showed that $G - T$ is the government surplus (if positive) or deficit (if negative). A surplus shows that government as a whole is saving, and a deficit shows that government is dissaving (which means to save a negative amount by borrowing or dipping into savings). The above equation therefore shows that the amount of investment in an economy is limited by the amount of private saving (S) and of public saving (or dissaving), $G - T$.

The Natural Level of Output

Chapter 8 showed that, at the natural rate of unemployment, the number of qualified job seekers and the number of available jobs are equal. It is easy to see that there will be a relationship between the unemployment rate and real GDP. At high rates of unemployment, more workers are unemployed and, hence, less output is produced. As the unemployment rate falls, real GDP rises. Accordingly, there will be a level of real output associated with the natural rate of unemployment called **the natural level of real GDP**, that level of output the economy produces when it is at the natural rate of unemployment. (See Figure 11.6.)

FIGURE 11.6 The Natural Rate of Unemployment and the Natural Level of Real GDP

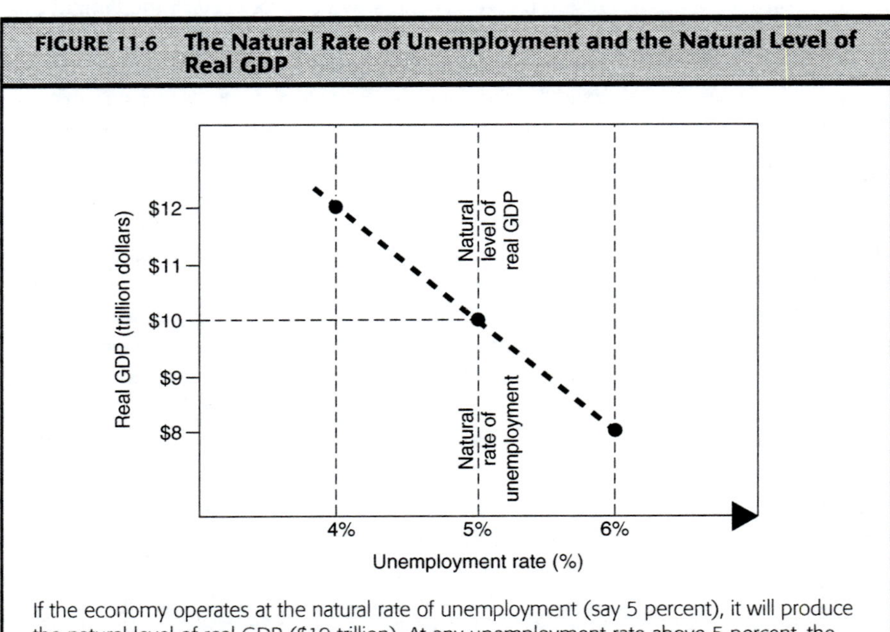

If the economy operates at the natural rate of unemployment (say 5 percent), it will produce the natural level of real GDP ($10 trillion). At any unemployment rate above 5 percent, the economy will produce less than the natural level of real GDP. At any rate below 5 percent, it will produce more than the natural level of real GDP.

There is an association as well between the natural rate of unemployment and wages. If the labor market were not in balance (say there were too few people and too many jobs), employers would compete among themselves for workers, and wages would be bid up. This bidding would result in an increase in inflationary pressures. If there were too many people and too few jobs, workers would bid wages down, and there would be a reduction in inflationary pressures. Only at the natural level of real GDP would the pressure on wages be constant.

Figure 11.6 shows the relationship between output (real GDP) and the unemployment rate. In this case, the natural rate of unemployment is 5 percent, and the real GDP that the economy produces at 5 percent unemployment is $10 trillion. Thus, $10 trillion is the natural level of real GDP. Figure 11.6 shows that if the economy were to produce less than the natural level of real GDP, it would (by definition) have an unemployment rate above the natural rate. When the labor market is in balance at the natural rate, inflationary pressures should be constant. If the current rate of inflation were 3 percent per year and the economy is at the natural rate, we would expect the inflation rate to continue at 3 percent. At the natural rate of unemployment, the rate of inflation will remain constant.

Summary

1. Macroeconomics is the study of economic growth and the business cycle.
2. Economic growth occurs when the production possibilities frontier shifts upwards and to the right.
3. Production functions show the relationship between economic output and inputs, given the state of technology. The output-per-worker production function shows the relationship between labor productivity and capital per worker, given the state of technology. Production functions are subject to the law of diminishing returns.
4. Economic growth can be explained by the increase in productive resources and by technological progress. Growth due to labor or capital increases is extensive growth. Growth due to technological advances is intensive growth. Technological progress is the most important source of growth. Societies that choose capital accumulation over current consumption will grow more rapidly, ceteris paribus. Economic growth can be either extensive or intensive, the latter caused by increases in productivity.
5. Business cycles are the patterns of upward and downward movements in the level of economic activity. A business cycle is divided into four phases: recession, trough, recovery (or expansion), and peak. Real GDP is the most common measure of the level of business activity. GDP is the sum of personal consumption, government expenditures on goods and services, investment, and net exports.
6. The value of output and the value of income are equal. National income, personal income, and personal disposable income are alternate measures of the total income of the economy.
7. The natural rate of unemployment is full employment. It is reached when the labor market is in balance. The natural level of output is that real GDP produced when the unemployment rate is at the natural rate.

Questions and Problems

1. Explain why unemployment and the duration of unemployment can have both voluntary and involuntary elements. Give examples where the voluntary element dominates; where the involuntary element dominates.
2. Why isn't the definition of the unemployment rate *the ratio of unemployed to the number employed?* What is the difference between the number employed and the labor force?
3. Evaluate the statement "A rising unemployment rate means that the number of jobs is contracting."
4. Nominal GDP rises 15 percent, and prices rise 10 percent. What is the rate of increase of real GDP? What is the relationship between unemployment and nominal GDP? Between unemployment and real GDP?
5. In an economy that is growing in the long run, would you expect the recovery phase to be longer or shorter, on average, than the recession phase?
6. Show what would happen to the PPF if (a) there were a significant technological breakthrough or (b) if the number of able-bodied people willing to work declined.
7. Real GDP is growing at 4 percent per year. Labor is growing at 2 percent and capital at 5 percent. What percentage of growth is explained by improvements in technology?
8. What would happen to output per worker as capital per worker expanded if there were no technological progress?
9. If the government has a balanced budget and zero net exports, and private saving equals $400 billion, how much investment is there?
10. The natural rate of unemployment is 5 percent and the current unemployment rate is also 5 percent. The economy is producing a real GDP of $800 billion. What is the natural level of real GDP?
11. The annual growth rate of output is 3 percent. The annual growth rate of labor is 1 percent and the growth rate of capital is 3 percent. What is the growth rate of technological progress?
12. In question 12, what percentage of the growth of output is explained by technological progress?
13. What happens to the Production Possibilities Frontier if the capital stock grows? Show your answer with a diagram.

APPENDIX CHAPTER 11

FUNCTIONS AND GROWTH RATES

This chapter uses mathematical notation to describe the relationship between output (Y) and labor (L) and capital (K) inputs:

$$Y = F(K, L, T) \qquad (1)$$

All this says is that the amount of output the economy produces (Y) depends on how much capital (K) and labor (L) the economy has at its disposal and on the state of its technology (T). All three factors positively affect output. If we have more L and K, we expect more output. If technology improves, output will increase.

The chapter uses dots above variables to denote annual rates of growth. A growth rate measures the rate at which something is changing. Take the following figures:

	Y
2004	120
2005	130

We calculate $\dot{Y}$ by dividing the 2005 figure by the 2004 figure and subtracting 1, or 130/120 − 1 = 1.083 − 1 = .083. The .083 tells us that Y grew by 8.3 percent.

We can express the production function $Y = F(K, L, T)$ in terms of rates of growth, where $\dot{Y} = f(\dot{K}, \dot{L}, \dot{T})$. It is this equation we use in the chapter to calculate the sources of economic growth. We can measure $\dot{K}$ and $\dot{L}$ but we can't directly measure $\dot{T}$. We can only calculate it as a residual—as what is left over. Economists normally use the share of L and K of income (how much of total income is earned in the form of wages and salaries versus interest, profits, and dividends) to add together labor and capital growth. We use L's share of income as 67 percent and K's share of income as 33 percent. This allows us to express the growth rate equation as:

$$\dot{Y} = 0.67\,\dot{L} + 0.33\,\dot{K} + \dot{T} \qquad (2)$$

From this we can calculate how much output growth has been created by labor and capital growth. The growth created by improvements in technology we have to calculate as a residual.

Another growth calculation we wish to make is the growth of per capita output, where per capita output is Y/P, where P stands for population. In the long run, P

and L grow at about the same rate, so we can also calculate it as the growth of Y/L. The growth rate of Y/L equals the growth rate of $Y(\dot{Y})$ minus the growth rate of $L(\dot{L})$. Consider that if Y and L grow at the same rate, then Y/L will not change. Only if Y grows faster than L will Y/L grow. We can therefore calculate the growth rate of Y/L by subtracting L from each side of (2) above:

$$\dot{Y} - \dot{L} = 0.67\dot{L} + 0.33\,\dot{K} + \dot{T} - \dot{L} = 0.33(\dot{K} - \dot{L}) + \dot{T} \qquad (3)$$

which is the equation for calculating the sources of per capita GDP growth.

CHAPTER 12

AGGREGATE SUPPLY AND AGGREGATE DEMAND

Chapter Preview

This chapter brings together aggregate demand and aggregate supply to explain output, employment and unemployment, and the price level. Economists have different views of aggregate supply. This chapter contrasts the Keynesian view with the classical and monetarist views. The basic question of aggregate supply—why the economy supplies more at a higher price level—is examined in both the short- and the long-run context.

Supply and Demand in Micro and Macro

The chapters on microeconomics showed the key importance of supply and demand curves in explaining enterprise outputs, product prices, wages, and interest rates. The foundations of microeconomic supply and demand curves were shown to be strong. The law of demand provides the foundation for the demand curve, and the law of diminishing returns provides the foundation for the supply curve.

Aggregate supply and demand play a similar role in macroeconomics to that of supply and demand in microeconomics, but the shapes of aggregate supply and demand curves are based on entirely different principles. On the vertical axis, we have the *aggregate price level,* not individual prices, as in microeconomics. On the horizontal axis, we have the total output of the economy, *real GDP,* not the output of an individual enterprise or a particular industry. We cannot apply the law of demand to aggregate demand because it applies only to cases where, when the price of one good rises, people can substitute now-cheaper goods. When the aggregate price level rises, people cannot substitute cheaper goods because all prices, on average, have risen. Similarly, it is difficult to generalize about how all enterprises in the economy will respond to an increase in the general price level because when prices rise generally in the economy, so do costs of production. As we show below, how enterprises at large respond to increasing prices depends on what is happening to their costs, most notably their labor costs.

In modern macroeconomics, there is more agreement about aggregate demand than about aggregate supply.

Classical and Keynesian Economics

There are two different views of how the macroeconomy functions: One view—originated by the classical economists, who wrote in the nineteenth century—is that the macroeconomy has strong self-stabilizing forces that keep it at or near full employment. The macroeconomy, according to the classical economists, achieves this stability on its own and does not require government intervention. The other view, originated by John Maynard Keynes in the late 1930s, is that the macroeconomy is inherently unstable. If left to its own devices, it can get stuck at high levels of unemployment, producing a real GDP well below its potential. The danger is that people can lower their consumption and investment spending, leaving the economy with less aggregate spending than is required for full employment.

The classical model taught that real GDP was determined by the supply of resources and their productivity. David Ricardo, David Hume, and Jean Baptiste Say believed that economies would operate at or near full employment.

Chapter 11 showed that when an economy produces $10 trillion worth of final goods and services ($C + I + G + X - M$), it also produces the income with which these goods can be purchased. It is always and everywhere true that aggregate income equals aggregate output, but the classical economists went one step further. They argued that aggregate supply created its own demand. This assertion is called **Say's law.**

Say's law states that whatever aggregate output is produced will be demanded.

There is enough income to purchase what has been produced, but what if income recipients save their income? According to Say's law, the interest rate will adjust to ensure the equality of desired saving and desired investment; what desired saving withdraws from the spending stream will automatically be reinjected by the same amount of desired investment. If desired saving exceeds desired investment at the prevailing interest rate, some people who want to loan funds will not find borrowers—the interest rate will be too high. The interest rate, therefore, will fall, cutting the amount of desired saving and raising the amount of desired investment, until the two are equal.

Because the interest rate adjusts so that desired saving equals desired investment, desired *aggregate expenditures* equal actual output.

To the classical economists, unemployment was caused by wages that were too high; unemployment would eliminate itself as wages fell. Because high unemployment was seen as an excess supply of labor caused by above-equilibrium wage rates, the unemployed would need only to accept lower wages to obtain jobs.

The policy prescription of the classical model was **laissez-faire,** a hands-off, minimal role for government in economic affairs. The classical proponents of laissez-faire believed the economy was capable of healing itself.

Laissez-faire means a hands-off, minimal role for government in economic affairs.

The Great Depression of the 1930s shook the belief in the classical model. Between 1929 and 1933, real GDP in the United States declined by 30 percent. Unemployment rose from 3.2 percent of the labor force in 1929 to 24.9 percent in 1933 and was still 17.2 percent in 1939. Between 1929 and 1933, real investment dropped by 75 percent while real consumption fell by 20 percent. Such a substantial downturn did not appear to be the temporary disequilibrium described by the classical model.

The Great Depression caused Keynes to formulate a new theory of macroeconomics.

The Great Depression set the stage for the "Keynesian revolution." John Maynard Keynes, the noted English economist, argued that economies can reach a fairly stable equilibrium from which they will budge only slowly, at much less than full employment. In the very long run, economies operate at full employment, but, as Keynes remarked. "In the long run, we are all dead." Keynes rejected the laissez-faire approach as being too slow and costly. He felt that government must intervene to ensure full employment.

This chapter uses the tools of aggregate supply and demand to illustrate these different views of macroeconomics.

Aggregate Supply and Demand

Aggregate supply and demand are the most powerful tools of macroeconomics.

Aggregate supply and aggregate demand are the most powerful analytical tools in macroeconomics. Macroeconomics must explain inflation, unemployment, and the business cycle. In a single market, the equilibrium price and equilibrium quantity are the results of the interaction of supply and demand. The same is true of the macroeconomy—only at the macro level, it is the price level and the economy's total output that are determined by the interaction of aggregate supply and aggregate demand. Changes in aggregate supply and demand cause changes in the price level (inflation) and in total output. Because total output determines the amount of employment and unemployment, movements in employment and unemployment are also explained by aggregate supply and demand.

Aggregate Supply and Demand Defined

The **aggregate demand curve** shows the quantities of total output agents are prepared to demand (buy) at different price levels.

The **aggregate supply curve** shows the quantities of total output all firms in the economy are willing to supply at different price levels.

The **aggregate demand curve** shows the quantities of total output economic agents in the economy are prepared to demand (buy) at different price levels. This chapter explains why the aggregate demand curve is negatively sloped—that is, why economic agents wish to purchase less real output at higher price levels. A representative aggregate demand curve is given in Figure 12.1 and labeled *AD.*

The **aggregate supply curve** shows the quantities of total output all firms in the economy are willing to supply at different price levels. There is controversy about the shape of the aggregate supply curve. For now, let us assume that it is positively sloped to simplify the discussion. A positively sloped aggregate supply curve is given in Figure 12.1 and labeled *AS.* The positive slope says that a higher price level is required to get the economy to produce more output.

Macroeconomic Equilibrium

Macroeconomic equilibrium occurs at the price level at which the aggregate quantity demanded equals the aggregate quantity supplied. Figure 12.1 shows that equilibrium occurs at that output (Y) and price level (P) at which the aggregate supply curve intersects the aggregate demand curve. If the economy attempted to settle at a macroeconomic equilibrium at a price level below P, where the aggregate quantity demanded exceeded aggregate quantity supplied, the price level would rise, the

FIGURE 12.1 Macroeconomic Equilibrium: Equality of Aggregate Demand and Aggregate Supply

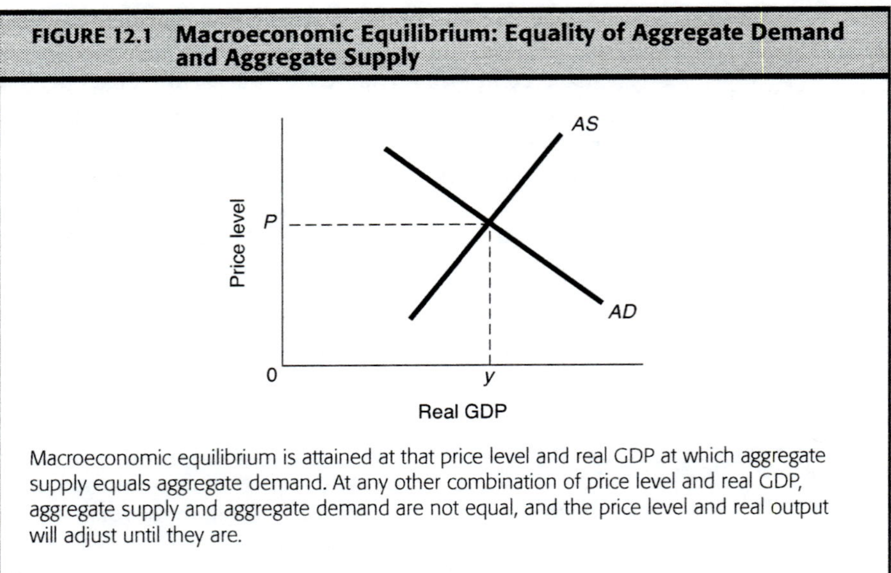

Macroeconomic equilibrium is attained at that price level and real GDP at which aggregate supply equals aggregate demand. At any other combination of price level and real GDP, aggregate supply and aggregate demand are not equal, and the price level and real output will adjust until they are.

quantity demanded would fall, and the quantity supplied would increase. Such adjustments would take place until the economy settled at the equilibrium where the aggregate supply and aggregate demand curves intersected.

Shifts in Aggregate Supply and Aggregate Demand

The macroeconomic equilibrium of aggregate supply and aggregate demand determines the price level and how much output, and, at the same time, how much employment and unemployment the economy produces. Shifts in aggregate demand and supply curves determine whether output and employment are increasing or decreasing and whether the price level is rising or falling. In order to understand the determinants of inflation and unemployment, we must understand the determinants of aggregate supply and aggregate demand.

Aggregate Demand

Students of economics are accustomed to downward-sloping demand curves. The quantity demanded of a product is less at higher prices than at lower prices, but the law of demand is based on relative prices. An increase in the price of good *X* raises its price relative to substitute goods, and consumers will switch their purchases from *X* to other goods. Aggregate demand schedules, however, reveal how *aggregate demand* responds to changes in the *general* price level. While the law of demand applies to individual commodities, it does not apply to aggregate demand. As the general price level rises, prices and wages are generally rising. Substitutions will be made for those things whose prices are rising more rapidly than those for other things, but, on balance, the law of demand does not predict a decrease in aggregate demand when prices rise generally.

For a higher price level to elicit a smaller aggregate quantity demanded, higher prices must cause economic agents to reduce their expenditures.

The aggregate demand curve shows what quantities of real goods and services agents in the economy are prepared to buy at different price levels. Remember that the economy buys four types of final goods and services: personal consumption expenditures (C), investment expenditures (I), government purchases of goods and services (G), and net exports ($X - M$).

Aggregate demand (AD) therefore equals the real amounts of $C + I + G + (X - M)$ that economic agents wish to purchase at different price levels (Figure 12.2). If an increase in the price level (P) causes economic agents throughout the economy to reduce their real spending on any of the above expenditure categories, then the AD curve will have a negative slope (as drawn in Figure 12.2). Three reasons can be given for why $C + I + G + (X - M)$ falls as P rises.

The Real Balance Effect

As the price level rises, the purchasing power of wealth falls. For example, a family has accumulated net assets worth $50,000. As prices rise, the purchasing power of

FIGURE 12.2 The Aggregate Demand Curve

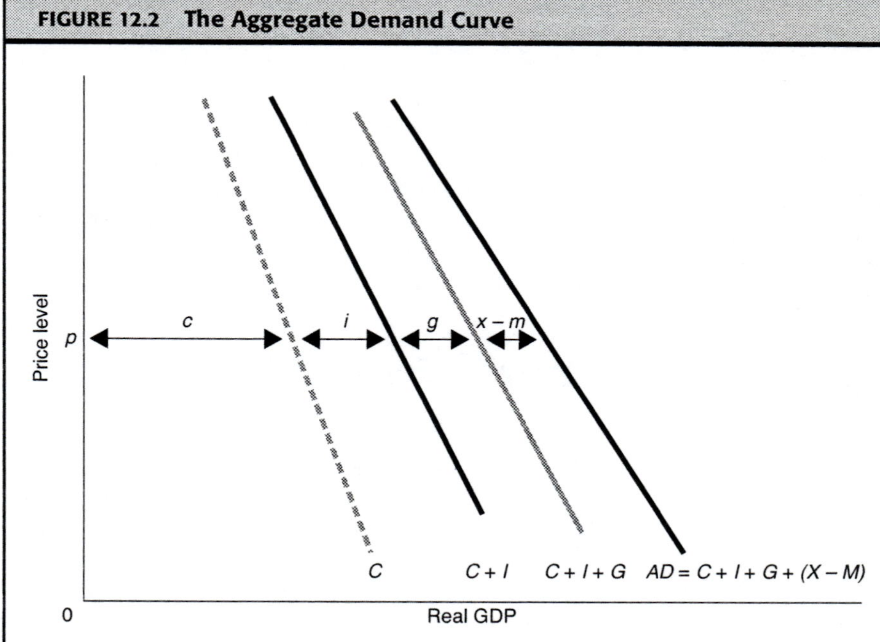

The aggregate demand curve $AD = C + I + G + (X - M)$ shows that people are willing to purchase larger aggregate quantities of goods at lower prices. At the particular price level p, people buy the quantities c, i, g, and $(x - m)$ of consumption, investment, government goods, and net exports respectively. The AD curve shows a larger response to a price change than any of the components because it reflects the real balance, interest rate, and foreign trade effects of a lower price level.

that $50,000 falls, and the family feels poorer. As a consequence, it cuts back on its purchases of real goods and services—that is, *C* falls. This effect of rising prices on consumption is called the **real balance effect.**

The **real balance effect** states that at higher price levels households will purchase less real consumption because their wealth will purchase less.

As the price level rises, consumers desire to spend less on real consumption at each level of real GDP. The increase in the price level has caused a smaller quantity of real GDP to be demanded.

The Interest Rate Effect

The **interest rate effect** is higher prices raising interest rates and thereby discouraging investment.

As the price level rises, the demand for credit increases. The goods and services whose purchase is often financed by credit—cars, plants, equipment, and inventories—cost more, and businesses and households must borrow more. The increased demand for credit causes interest rates to rise, and business investment is discouraged. Thus, as prices rise from a lower to a higher level, interest rates rise and real investment (*I*) declines, and a smaller quantity of real GDP is demanded at a higher price level.

The Foreign Trade Effect

The **foreign trade effect** occurs when a rise in the domestic price level (holding foreign prices and the exchange rate constant) lowers the aggregate quantity demanded by pushing down net exports (*X* – *M*).

As the domestic price level rises relative to foreign price levels, holding constant the exchange rate (the value of the dollar in terms of foreign currencies), domestic goods become more expensive relative to foreign goods. Exporters will face stiffer competition and imports will appear cheaper. As a consequence, exports (*X*) will fall and imports (*M*) will rise. Thus, net exports (*X* – *M*) will fall. For example, if the U.S. price level rises, ceteris paribus, American farmers can export less of their wheat and American consumers will buy more Japanese cars and Swiss watches. As a consequence of this **foreign trade effect,** an increase in the domestic price level will cause net exports to fall. If the price level falls, the aggregate quantity demanded will increase because net exports will increase.

The real balance, interest rate, and foreign trade effects cause the aggregate demand curve to have a negative slope.

Aggregate Supply

Economists have different views about the shape of the aggregate supply curve. In this chapter, three views of aggregate supply—the Keynesian depression model, the classical model, and the short-run model—are presented. The short-run model is the aggregate supply concept that is used in subsequent chapters.

The aggregate supply curve shows the quantities of real output all firms in the economy are prepared to supply at different price levels. The aggregate supply curve considers why economic agents in the economy might supply more goods and services at a higher price level.

The Classical Aggregate Supply Curve

The classical economists felt that the price level would have no effect on real output; economic agents would supply the same total quantities of goods and services at a high price level as at a low price level. In effect, classical economists were con-

Money illusion could cause economic agents to think that a change in the price level is actually a change in real wages or relative prices and so change their production and employment decisions.

fident that economic agents were not subject to **money illusion,** a change in production and employment decisions in response to proportionate changes in money prices and money wages. The money illusion of rising money prices and wages could cause economic agents to think that real wages or relative prices have changed and hence result in changes in production and employment.

In the short run, with a constant supply of resources and a constant technology, prices and wages tend to rise or fall at the same rate. Some prices rise relative to others; some wages rise relative to others, but, on average, wages and prices are moving together. Under such circumstances, a rising price level would not change employment or output decisions. Workers would base their employment decisions on real wages—what real goods and services money wages would buy; as long as they realize that money wages and prices are rising at the same rate, they know that higher money wages have not made them any better off. There would be no reason for them to work more or to work harder. As long as firms recognize that their selling prices and costs are rising at the same rate, there would be no reason for them to supply more output at a higher price level because the higher prices have not made the firm any better off.

The classical aggregate supply curve is vertical because it assumes no money illusion.

The classical aggregate supply curve in Figure 12.3, Panel A, is vertical. It assumes that the price level has no real effect on the economy. Economic agents will not be subject to money illusion. Individually, they may respond to changes in real wages and relative prices, but for the economy as a whole, they will recognize that inflation does not cause real wages and relative prices to change. Therefore, the supply of goods and services is not affected by inflation.

In fact, the classical economists felt that economies tend to operate at full employment. If people are unemployed, the wage rate will drop as unemployed workers compete among themselves for jobs. This competition for jobs will keep the economy at full employment.

The Keynesian Aggregate Supply Curve

In the Keynesian model, the aggregate supply curve has a backward *L*-shape, as shown in Figure 12.3, Panel B. The flat ("Keynesian") part of the aggregate supply curve characterizes an economy with substantial unemployment that cannot be removed by lower wages because wages are not falling. Workers are willing to work at prevailing wages; firms need only offer them employment. For this reason, the aggregate supply of goods and services can be expanded without any increase in wages and prices. As long as this condition prevails, the aggregate supply curve is horizontal. However, when full employment is reached, the supply curve becomes vertical. All those willing to work at the going wage are already employed. The economy cannot produce more real output. Any effort to increase employment and output will only drive up money wages and prices without any increase in real output (thus the vertical aggregate supply curve at full employment).

Short-Run Aggregate Supply

Modern economists use a blend of Keynesian and classical economics to describe the behavior of aggregate supply (see Figure 12.3, Panel C). They recognize that

FIGURE 12.3 Equilibrium of Aggregate Supply and Aggregate Demand

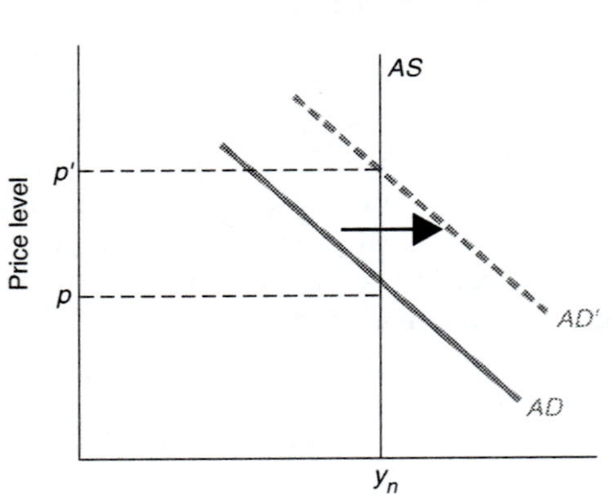

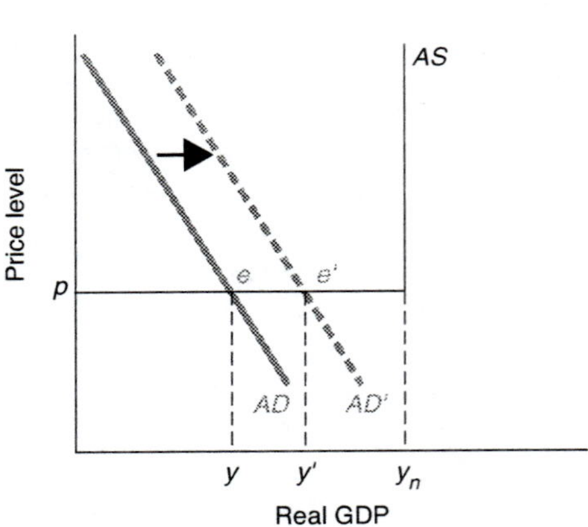

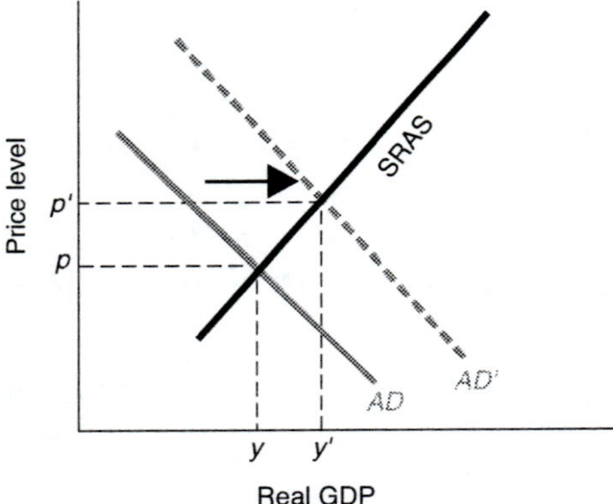

In the classical quantity theory (Panel A), the economy operates at full employment. Real GDP is fixed. When aggregate demand increases (from *AD* to *AD'*), there is no increase in real output. The only effect is an increase in the price level from *p* to *p'*.

This graph brings together the aggregate demand curve and the *L*-shaped Keynesian aggregate supply curve in the upper right graph. In Panel B, equilibrium occurs at point e, which represents an equilibrium at less than full employment and illustrates the Keynesian case of an economy in a depression. If aggregate demand increases (shifts from *AD* to *AD'*), real GDP and employment can be increased without an increase in prices.

The modern short-run aggregate supply curve (*SRAS*) in Panel C shows that an increase in aggregate demand raises both prices and real GDP.

in the short run, an increase in the price level could cause firms to supply more real output. Modern economists agree that people are, indeed, subject to money illusion and that rigidities in the system (such as labor contracts that fix money wages for a period of years) cause temporary changes in real wages and relative prices. In the short run, prices and wages are not perfectly flexible because some are fixed by multiyear contracts. The wages of auto workers may be fixed by a two- or three-year contract. Suppliers of natural gas may have agreed to a selling price for an 18-month period. In the long run, prices and wages are perfectly flexible upwards or downwards.

Multiyear wage contracts reduce the flexibility of the economy to adjust wages and prices to changes in business conditions.

The major reason for short-run wage inflexibility is that major union wage contracts typically cover a two- to three-year period. Such multiyear contracts set nominal wages over the life of the contract. A three-year wage contract negotiated during a period of optimism concerning future business conditions will call for wage increases over the life of the contract. If business conditions decline and there is a weak demand for labor, employers must still pay the agreed-upon wage increases in the second and third years of the contract.

Employers agree to pay unionized workers a higher wage than they could earn elsewhere. In return, workers implicitly agree to wait to be recalled when laid off during bad times, and the employer agrees that laid-off workers will be the first to be recalled when conditions improve. The employer will not necessarily reduce the wages of those employed during business downturns. Rather, wages tend to be held steady throughout the cycle. Improvements in business conditions—not lower wages—cause jobs to reappear. These types of arrangements also cause wages and prices to be inflexible.

Short-run aggregate supply (*SRAS*) is the schedule of the real GDPs that firms are prepared to supply at different price levels, holding the expected price level constant.

Short-run aggregate supply (*SRAS*) is the schedule of the real GDPs that firms are prepared to supply at different price levels, holding the expected price level constant. Why does it show that higher prices raise output? The inflation that firms and workers expect determines the outcome of wage bargains. If inflation is expected to be 10 percent over the next 12 months, workers may be satisfied with a 10 percent wage increase. If the same workers expected no inflation, they might agree to a 0 percent wage increase. The higher the expected prices, the higher the wages that business firms will agree to pay their workers.

Short-run aggregate supply shows what happens to output when the price level changes unexpectedly.

In the short run, a great many wages are tied to expected prices, but actual prices need not be the same as expected prices. If prices rise faster than expected, businesses find themselves in a favorable position. Their selling prices are rising faster than their contract wages, and profits increase. This causes firms to expand output.

In Figure 12.4, the expected price level is 100. This will determine the wage rates for a significant fraction of the work force for the short run. If the actual price level turns out to be the one expected, firms will supply Y_n worth of output. If the actual price level exceeds that expected, however, firms will find themselves in a profitable position. With input costs (including labor costs) fixed, selling prices rise faster than costs during an unanticipated inflation, and production is raised as business profitability improves.

The short-run aggregate supply curve is positively sloped because unanticipated increases in the price level lower real wages and raise selling prices relative to costs.

If the price level unexpectedly falls—say, from 100 to 95 in Figure 12.4 —profitability will fall. Workers are on contracts calling for steady wages; firms may have negotiated the purchase of materials at fixed prices. Their selling prices are falling more rapidly than their costs, and they respond by producing less. Firms become more willing to fire unsatisfactory workers and to lay off workers not currently needed. Unanticipated deflation reduces real output.

FIGURE 12.4 The Short-Run Aggregate Supply Curve *(SRAS)*

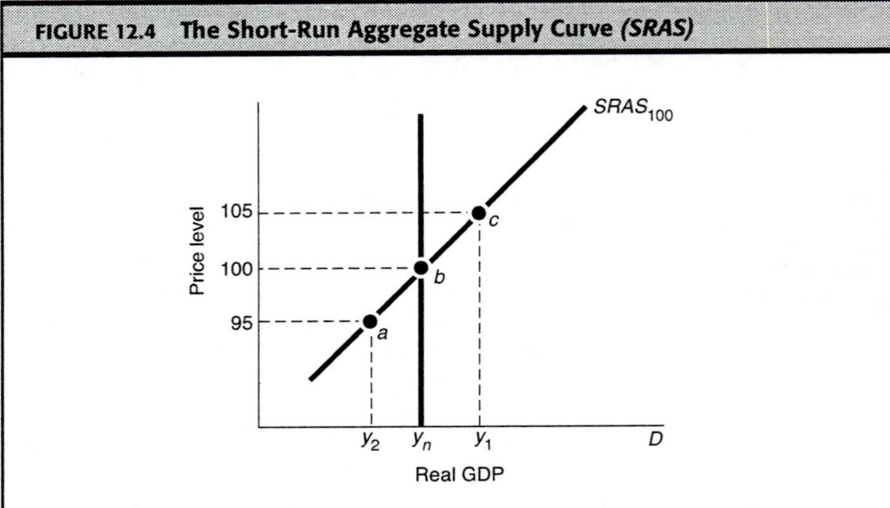

The aggregate supply curve $SRAS_{100}$ is based on the expected price level of 100. If prices rise to a level higher than anticipated—say, to a price level of 105—output rises to y_1. Unanticipated inflation stimulates output because prices of products rise faster than producing firms' costs. When prices fall more than anticipated—from 100 to 95—output falls to y_2. Unanticipated deflation discourages output because prices of products fall more than producing firms' costs.

Shifts in Aggregate Supply and Demand Curves

Movements in the price level, output, and unemployment are explained by shifts in aggregate supply and aggregate demand curves. These shifts disrupt the established macroequilibrium.

Demand Shocks

Increases in aggregate demand have markedly different effects on output and prices in the Keynesian supply model, the classical supply curve, and the modern short-run aggregate supply curve. Any factor that causes $C, I, G,$ or $X - M$ to increase independently of the price level will shift the aggregate demand curve to the right (an increase in *AD*). Any factor that causes $C, I, G,$ or $X - M$ to decrease independently of the price level will shift the aggregate demand curve to the left (a decrease in *AD*).

The Classical Model (Figure 12.3, Panel A) In the classical model with a vertical supply curve, increases in aggregate demand do not raise output; they only raise prices. In an economy with flexible wages and prices, the economy operates at full employment (y_n); therefore, increases in aggregate demand translate into higher prices, not into more output.

The Keynesian Model (Figure 12.3, Panel B) Because the Keynesian supply curve is horizontal below full-employment output (y_n), if the initial equilibrium is below full employment, increases in aggregate demand cause more output and employment without driving up prices. In the Keynesian high-unemployment model, demand increases do only good! They increase output and do not raise prices. Once full employment is reached (the vertical section of the aggregate supply curve), further increases in aggregate demand only cause higher prices.

The Short-Run Aggregate Supply Model When inflation is unanticipated, an increase in aggregate demand raises both prices and output in the short run (see Figure 12.4) because *SRAS* is upward sloping. The new equilibrium is established at a higher price level and a higher real GDP.

Supply Shocks

A **supply shock** is a shift in aggregate supply caused by some external factor that causes costs of production to change.

Supply shocks, such as OPEC's acquisition of control over crude-oil exports in the early 1970s, poor worldwide harvests, or natural disasters, reduce aggregate supply. When supply shocks raise the input costs of businesses, they raise the price level at which businesses are willing to supply a given volume of real output. At higher energy prices or higher raw material prices, business firms are less willing to supply output at the same price level as before, and the short-run aggregate supply curve shifts to the left.

Such a supply shock occurred when OPEC raised the price of oil in 1973–1974 and when Iran and Iraq went to war in 1979. The substantial rise in oil prices raised costs of production, resulting in a reduction in aggregate supply. When oil prices fell sharply in the mid-1980s, the resulting decline in production costs caused short-run aggregate supply to increase.

Supply shocks can be either *adverse* or *beneficial.* An adverse supply shock raises costs, so the short-run aggregate supply curve shifts to the left. A beneficial supply shock occurs when costs fall so that the short-run aggregate supply curve shifts to the right.

Figure 12.5 shows the effect of an adverse supply shock on prices and real output in the short run. Initially, the economy is operating at the natural level of output y_n. People expect this situation to continue, but bad harvests occur on a worldwide basis. The prices of foods, fibers, and foodstuffs rise. These price increases represent cost increases to producers, so aggregate supply falls (the short-run aggregate supply curve shifts to the left). With the reduction in aggregate supply, the price level p rises. As p rises, the economy moves up the aggregate demand curve. The end result of the adverse supply shock is that the price level has risen; inflation has been created. The economy ends up producing less real output (actual output is less than the natural real output), and unemployment has increased.

Adverse supply shocks create inflation and unemployment.

Note that higher price levels (inflation) can be caused either by increases in aggregate demand or by decreases in aggregate supply. In the first case, inflation is accompanied by increasing output. In the second case (falling aggregate supply), inflation is accompanied by falling output.

The Long-Run, Self-Correcting Mechanism

Economists have long debated whether the economy will automatically return to full employment if, for some reason, it is operating above or below full employment. Can

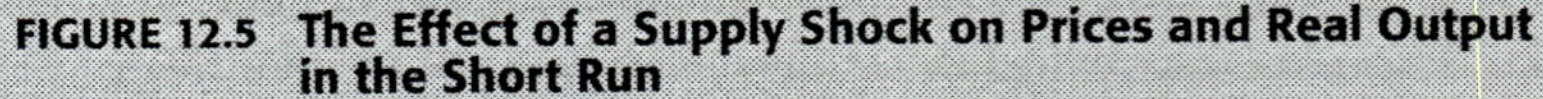

FIGURE 12.5 The Effect of a Supply Shock on Prices and Real Output in the Short Run

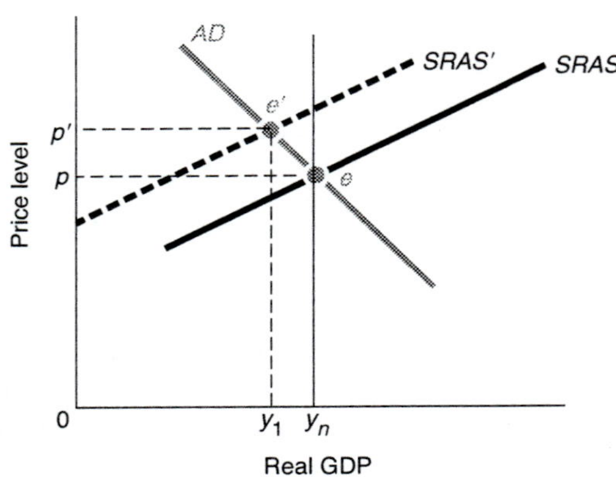

The economy is initially operating at point *e*. This equilibrium has persisted long enough so that households and business firms expect it to continue into the future. Aggregate supply is reduced (from *SRAS* to *SRAS'*) by disastrous harvests. At the original price level, *p*, aggregate demand exceeds aggregate supply and prices begin to rise. The economy moves along *AD* (from *e* to *e'*) until a new equilibrium is established at *e'*. Supply shocks can cause the economy to operate below y_n (can create unemployment and less real output) and can raise prices in the short run.

an economy in a depression or deep recession cure itself? Or is some kind of government intervention required? Consider an unexpected increase in aggregate demand that raises both prices and output in the short run. Figure 12.6 shows an unexpected increase in aggregate demand due to an unanticipated increase in investment or government spending. Initially, the economy is producing at natural real GDP. At the original price level, the aggregate quantity demanded exceeds aggregate quantity supplied after the demand increase, and the price level begins to rise. As the price level rises, there is a movement up the short-run supply curve from *a* to *b*. The new equilibrium is established at a higher price level, and the economy has moved above y_n.

The net effect of the increase in aggregate demand is that real output has risen above the natural level, unemployment has fallen below the natural rate, and prices have risen.

The movement from *a* to *b* in Figure 12.6 shows what happens initially when economic agents are caught off guard by an unanticipated increase in the price level. In the short run, unanticipated inflation causes economic agents to supply more output. In the long run, however, they can adjust their expectations to higher prices. They can demand higher wage increases and renegotiate supply contracts at higher prices. These adjustments raise the costs for firms and cause aggregate supply to fall. This causes the economy to supply less total output at the same price level as before (*SRAS* moves to the left).

FIGURE 12.6 The Self-Correcting Mechanism

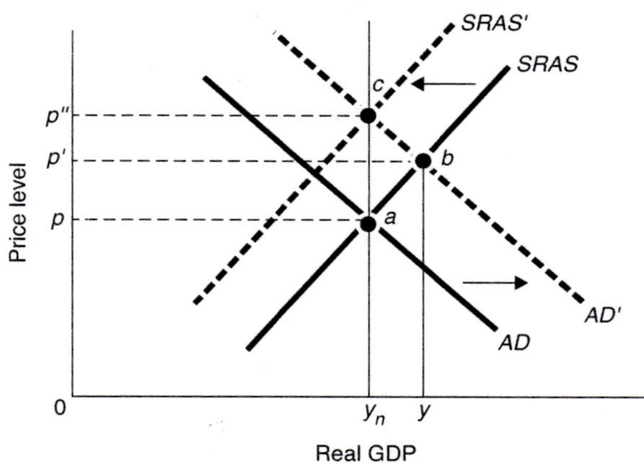

Initially, the economy's aggregate supply curve (*SRAS*) intersects the aggregate demand curve (*AD*) at natural real GDP, y_n. There is a positive demand shock (aggregate demand shifts from *AD* to *AD'*). Cost increases lag behind price increases; the economy now produces at point *b* with an output *y* above natural real GDP, and the price level rises from *p* to *p'*. In the long run, economic agents adjust to the higher price level by reducing aggregate supply, as long-term contracts are adjusted to higher prices. Aggregate supply shifts from *SRAS* to *SRAS'*, and the economy is restored to producing at point *c* with natural real GDP but at an even higher price level (*p''*).

As economic agents adjust to higher inflation, aggregate supply falls (the short-run aggregate supply curve shifts to the left) until the economy is restored to natural real GDP. The demand increase has pushed the economy above natural real GDP only temporarily. As people adjust, the economy returns to producing the natural level of real GDP.

Demand changes cause the economy to produce more or less than natural real GDP *only* in the short run; in the long run, the economy returns to producing the natural level of real GDP as it adjusts in the long run to price changes. The self-correcting mechanism that causes the economy to return to the natural rate is price and wage flexibility. If the economy is operating above natural real GDP, prices and wages will naturally rise; short-run aggregate supply falls, and the economy returns to natural real GDP. If the economy is operating below natural real GDP, prices and wages will naturally fall; aggregate supply increases, and the economy again produces natural real GDP.

In the long run, the economy produces at the natural level of GDP because of the self-correcting mechanism.

Policy Implications of the Self-Correcting Mechanism

The tendency of the economy to return to y_n means that the economy's long-run output and employment cannot be controlled. At best, increases in aggregate demand can temporarily push the economy above y_n. If the economy happens to be below natural real GDP, policies can push it back to y_n by increasing aggregate demand.

EXAMPLE 12.1 EVIDENCE OF A SELF-CORRECTING MECHANISM

The late nineteenth and early twentieth century was a period of numerous supply and demand shocks—wars, investment booms and busts, shifts of employment from agriculture to industry and services, stock market binges, major technological changes, and new resource discoveries. It was also a period of laissez-faire macroeconomic policy. The available evidence suggests no long-term trend in unemployment rates from the 1880s to the Great Depression. Unemployment rates fluctuated, but they returned to a fairly "normal" unemployment rate. In France during this period, the unemployment rate ranged from a low of 4.7 percent to a high of 10.2 percent, yet returned after such fluctuations to 6.5 percent. The German unemployment rate ranged from 0.2 to 7.2 percent, yet returned to around 2 percent. The English unemployment rate ranged from 0.4 to 7.8 percent but returned to 3 percent. From 1890 to 1929 there was no discernible trend in the U.S. unemployment rate, which ranged from a low of 1.4 percent to a high of 18.4 percent and returned to an unemployment rate in the range of 4 to 5 percent.

The data from the nineteenth and early twentieth centuries is consistent with the theory of the long-run self-correcting mechanism. At this time, there were no deliberate government efforts to regulate aggregate demand, yet the unemployment rate kept returning to the natural rate.

However, the self-correcting mechanism can accomplish the same thing as wages and prices adjust over time. Yet, as Keynes remarked, "In the long run, we are all dead." How long must the economy wait for self-correcting actions to restore the economy to the natural rate? (See Example 12.1.)

Summary

1. The classical model taught that supply creates its own demand and that flexible wages and prices move the economy naturally toward full employment. Laissez-faire was viewed as the best macro policy. The Great Depression raised doubt about the classical model and prepared the way for the Keynesian revolution. The Keynesian model analyzes economies in deep depression; Keynesian economics deals with economies with unemployed resources. If aggregate demand increased in such an economy, increases in real GDP would be forthcoming.
2. The aggregate without rising prices demand curve is downward sloping because of real balance, foreign trade, and interest rate effects.
3. The aggregate supply curve shows the quantities of real GDP the economy is prepared to supply at different price levels. The classical supply curve is vertical. The Keynesian aggregate supply curve is horizontal at less than full employment. At full employment, the Keynesian supply curve becomes vertical.
4. Modern economists use the natural rate of unemployment for full employment.
5. The short-run aggregate supply curve is upward sloping. Fixed contracts and other rigidities explain its upward slope.

6. Macroeconomic equilibrium occurs at that real GDP and price level at which aggregate supply and aggregate demand are equal.
7. If there is an unanticipated increase in aggregate demand, the unemployment rate can fall below the natural rate.
8. Supply shocks cause the aggregate supply curve to shift. An adverse supply shock causes the unemployment rate and the price level to rise.
9. In the long run, a self-correcting mechanism causes the economy to return to the natural level of real GDP.

Questions and Problems

1. During the Great Depression, stock prices fell, as did the Consumer Price Index. What effect would these two events have had on aggregate demand?
2. What role do fixed contracts play in explaining short-run aggregate supply?
3. Both workers and businesses anticipate a 2 percent inflation rate. The actual inflation rate turns out to be 5 percent. How would this "surprise" affect their productive behavior?
4. Explain how the self-correcting mechanism uses changing prices and wage rates to return the economy to its natural rate. Would the self-correcting mechanism work if wages were permanently fixed?
5. Explain why aggregate demand is so important in the Keynesian model and less important in the classical model.
6. If all wages and prices in the economy were free to adjust instantaneously to increases in aggregate demand, how would the self-correcting mechanism work differently?
7. The classical economists felt that economies would tend to operate at full employment. Why did they believe so?
8. Explain why we cannot use the law of demand to explain the slope of the aggregate demand curve.
9. Why would the self-correcting mechanism be supportive of the policy of laissez-faire?
10. Explain what happens to the price level and to real GDP when the following ceteris paribus changes occur:

    a. Aggregate demand increases; aggregate supply increases.
    b. Aggregate supply increases; aggregate demand does not change.
    c. Aggregate demand falls; aggregate supply does not change.

11. If the aggregate supply curve is vertical, what will be the effects on output and the price level when aggregate demand increases? when aggregate demand decreases?
12. What should be the effect on real GDP if there were a significant increase in the price of crude oil? Explain your answer in terms of aggregate supply and demand curves.

CHAPTER 13

MONEY AND BANKING

Chapter Preview

Macroeconomics is the study of inflation, unemployment, and the business cycle. Money plays a key role in explaining inflation and the business cycle. This chapter defines *money* and its functions. It discusses fractional reserve banking and shows how the Federal Reserve System controls the money supply.

What Is Money?

Throughout history, many things—gold or silver coins, paper money, cattle, and even beads, stones, and red parrot feathers—have served as money. Money is the medium of exchange used in transactions that transfer ownership of goods and services and assets from one person to another. The money supply is controlled by the country's central bank and its currency is issued by the government. (See Example 13.1 for an exception.)

The Three Functions of Money

Money is a medium of exchange, a unit of value, and a store of value.

Money is used to buy things, to measure values, and as a means of savings.

Money Is a Medium of Exchange For money to serve its most important function as a medium of exchange, it must be generally accepted as a means of paying for things and settling debts. Money serves as a common object acceptable to all parties in a transaction and eliminates the need for barter. If there were no generally acceptable medium of exchange, the shoemaker who wanted to buy a bushel of wheat would have to find a wheat farmer who wanted to buy shoes, and the two would have to strike an agreement on the terms of exchange. It is difficult to conceive of a modern economy functioning efficiently on this **double coincidence of wants**. With money as a medium of exchange, the shoemaker who wants to buy wheat can buy from any seller of wheat, not just one who wants shoes; the buyer of shoes can buy from any seller of shoes, not just one who wants to buy wheat.

A **double coincidence of wants** occurs where the buyer and seller both want to obtain goods produced by the other.

EXAMPLE 13.1 PRINTING YOUR OWN MONEY: THE SIMEC

A retired law professor, Giacinto Auriti, who detests the Italian government's monopoly on printing money, has printed at his own expense his own currency, which he calls the *simec*. Auriti has distributed simecs among the populace of his native village of 10,000 people and stands ready to redeem any simecs presented to him at the rate of two lire for one simec. Currently, around two billion simecs, worth around $1.9 million, are in circulation. Merchants in particular clothing stores, as well as jewelers, accept simecs. Some merchants come to Auriti to convert simecs into lire. Others use them for their own purchases, keeping the currency in circulation. When the currency's rapid spread worried local officials, the police were ordered to impound the simecs. A court ruled, however, that while it is illegal to counterfeit, it is not illegal to print your own currency. The major threat to the simec is that Auriti may issue too many of them. He believes that cash should be distributed freely and plans to dole out regular payments to villagers. He also detests taxes and wishes to compensate taxpayers with simecs.

Source: "A Legal Tender of One's Own," *New York Times*, 30 January 2001, p. W1.

Money prices serve as the common denominator in which the values of all goods and services are expressed.

Relative prices are determined by dividing one money price by another.

Money Is a Unit of Value The value of a good is what it can be exchanged for. In a barter economy, a pair of shoes might be worth, for example, two cotton shirts, 1 percent of a milk cow, or ten loaves of bread. It is, obviously, inconvenient to keep track of values by remembering each commodity's terms of exchange with every other commodity, and it becomes very complicated with fractions of commodities—such as 1 percent of a cow. Money prices serve as the common denominator in which values are expressed. Relative prices are determined by dividing one money price by another. If a pair of shoes costs $40, a loaf of bread $1, and a cow $1000, the price of shoes relative to all these commodities is immediately evident.

Money Is a Store of Value People accumulate wealth by not spending all their disposable income. They accumulate assets—stocks, bonds, gold, works of art—which can be held over a period of time and can be converted eventually into money. But wealth can also be stored in the form of money. The medium of exchange can act as a store of value. Inflation reduces the usefulness of money as a store of value because the amount of goods and services that each stored dollar can purchase falls as prices rise.

The Supply of Money

There are several concepts of money because a number of assets perform many of the functions of money. Some perform these functions more closely than others.

Monies

In the United States, a number of things obviously qualify as money. Coin, issued by the U.S. Treasury, and paper currency, issued by the Federal Reserve Banks, are accepted as media of exchange, units of account, and stores of value. Persons can buy goods with dollar bills; the prices of goods and services are expressed in dollars, and dollars serve as a store of value.

Demand deposits are deposits in checking accounts.

Checking account deposits, called **demand deposits** by bankers and economists, are also money. Goods can be purchased by check: We can use checking account money as a store of value and as a unit of account.

Near Monies and Liquidity

Other assets, such as certificates of deposit from commercial banks, bank saving deposits, and government bonds or shares of corporate stock, perform some of the functions of money, but none of them serve as an immediate medium of exchange. One cannot go into a store and buy goods with a bank certificate of deposit, a government bond, or a share of Microsoft stock. However, bank time deposits, government bonds, and corporate stock all can substitute, to a greater or lesser extent, for money because they can be converted into currency or checking account money. A government bond can be sold, and payment can be received in cash or by check; the bank certificate of deposit can be converted into checking account money.

Being able to convert an asset into money does not mean that it can be converted immediately or at no risk of loss of value. Assets differ according to their liquidity.

Liquidity refers to how quickly and with what risks an asset can be converted into money.

The more **liquid** the asset, the more closely it substitutes for money. Money is perfectly liquid.

Liquidity refers to how quickly and with what risks an asset can be converted into money. A low-interest, bank savings account (a passbook account) can be converted into cash any day the bank is open. Although many people are unaware of this restriction, banks can insist on a 30-day notification before the depositor can withdraw funds from a time-deposit savings account. A share of Microsoft stock also can be converted into money any day the stock market is open, but the stock may have to be sold at a considerable loss if the seller needs the money quickly.

If one were to rank various assets according to their liquidity, at the top would be currency, coin, and checking account money—all perfectly liquid. Then would come passbook savings accounts; certificates of deposit, ranked according to their length of maturity; government bonds; stocks; and finally, homes, boats, and stamp collections. Assets that are very close to being money are called *near monies*.

M1 is the sum of currency and coins, checking account deposits held by the public (excluding the banks' own checking accounts), travelers' checks, and other deposits (such as NOW and ATS accounts) upon which checks can be written.

M2 equals M1 plus savings deposits and small time deposits plus money-market, mutual-fund shares plus other highly liquid assets.

Definitions of Narrow and Broad Money Supply

Because there are both monies and near monies, there are alternate definitions of the nation's money supply. Financial authorities currently use two main definitions, called *M1* and *M2*. M1 is the narrow money supply; M2 is the broader money supply that includes both money and some near monies.

M1 is the sum of currency and coins, checking account deposits held by the public (excluding the banks' own checking accounts), travelers' checks, and other deposits (such as NOW and ATS accounts) upon which checks can be written.

The broad money supply, M2, includes monies and some near monies. M2 includes assets that can be readily converted into M1 with no risk of loss yet are not accepted as a medium of exchange. **M2** equals M1 plus savings deposits and small time deposits plus money-market, mutual-fund shares plus other highly liquid assets.

Table 13.1 shows the breakdown of the money supply between M1 and M2. The broad money supply is almost five times as great as the narrowly defined money supply. Currency and coin account for 50 percent of M1 and 10 percent of M2. Checking account money is half of M1. Because deposits in the banking system account for most of the U.S. money supply, either narrowly or broadly defined, it is necessary to learn about the business of banking.

Banks

In the United States, the banking system consists of commercial banks and thrift institutions, such as mutual savings banks, credit unions, and savings and loan associations. Commercial banks account for about 60 percent of all the banking system's assets.

Financial Intermediation

Financial intermediaries link lenders and borrowers.

Commercial banks and thrift institutions serve as financial intermediaries. **Financial intermediaries** link lenders and borrowers. They intervene between the ultimate lenders and the ultimate borrowers. When people deposit money in their savings accounts, they do not have to seek out borrowers prepared to pay them interest. They

TABLE 13.1 The U.S. Money Supply, M1 and M2

Component	*Amount (billions of dollars)*
Currency and coin *plus*	649
Demand deposits* *plus*	323
Travelers' checks *plus*	8
Other checkable deposits† *equals*	306
M1 *plus*	1286
Savings deposits at all depository institutions *plus*	3146
Small time deposits at all depository institutions‡ *plus*	830
Money-market, mutual-fund shares and other deposits *equals*	870
M2	6132

Note: The data are for 2 August 2003

*Demand deposits at all commercial banks other than those due to other banks, the U.S. government, and foreign official institutions.

†Other checkable deposits include NOW and ATS accounts, credit union share draft balances, and demand deposits at mutual savings banks. NOW (negotiated order of withdrawal) accounts pay interest and are otherwise like demand deposits. ATS (automatic transfer services) accounts transfer funds from savings accounts to checking accounts automatically when a check is written.

‡A small time deposit is one issued in a denomination less than $100,000.

Source: www.federalreserve.gov

are making funds available to the bank to loan out to borrowers. The bank, with its staff of loan officers and credit investigators, determines which borrowers receive loans for car purchases, home mortgages, or business loans.

Banks make a profit by paying their depositors a lower rate of interest than the interest rates they charge on loans. Depositors and borrowers are willing to accept this arrangement because they are saved the task of finding each other and assuming the risk of bad loans. Moreover, financial intermediaries are willing to borrow short and lend long—something individual lenders would be reluctant to do. The commercial bank, for example, borrows money from a depositor who may have purchased a six-month certificate of deposit and then loans this money to a borrower for 25 years on a home mortgage.

The Business of Banking

The **balance sheet** of the bank summarizes its current financial condition by comparing its assets and liabilities.

The balance sheet of a bank (or any other business) is called a *T-account* because assets are recorded on the left side of the *T* and liabilities on the right side. The **balance sheet** of the bank summarizes its current financial condition by comparing its assets (what it owns) and liabilities (what it owes others).

The Balance Sheet of Commercial Banks The combined assets of all commercial banks are shown in Table 13.2. Assets must equal liabilities plus net worth—all assets must be claimed by someone, either by the owners of the bank or by nonowners. The net worth of the owners of commercial banks equals total assets minus liabilities to nonowners—the sum of deposit liabilities and other borrowings.

The consolidated balance sheet shows that bank assets are made up primarily of loans (63 percent), securities (23 percent), and other assets. Commercial bank reserves, consisting of reserves held by the Federal Reserve System and vault cash, make up less than 1 percent of commercial bank assets.

The Main Business of Banking Bank liabilities are its deposits, which are primarily in the form of checking account deposits, savings deposits, and time deposits.

TABLE 13.2 Consolidated Balance Sheet of Commercial Banks

Assets (billions)		*Liabilities (billions)*	
Reserves	327	Demand deposits	655
Loans	4439	Time deposits	4150
Commercial	919		
Real Estate	2239		
Consumer	593		
Securities	1856	Other borrowings	2095
Other assets	761	Net worth	483
Total	7383	Total	7383

Source: www.federalreserve.gov. Data are for August 2003.

The main business of **banking** is the making of loans.

The **interest rate spread** is the difference between the interest rates that banks pay their depositors and the interest rates they receive on their loans and investments.

Basically, commercial **banks** do business by accepting deposits and either investing these funds in interest-bearing securities or loaning them out to borrowers. Banks earn profits through the **interest rate spread**, which is the difference between the interest rates that banks pay their depositors and the interest rates they receive on their loans and investments. The major business of banking is the making of loans.

A **fractional-reserve banking system** exists when bank reserves are less than bank deposit liabilities. In modern banking, reserves are only a small fraction of deposit liabilities.

Fractional-Reserve Banking The consolidated balance sheet reveals the most striking feature of the business of banking. For every dollar of deposit liabilities, the average bank has only 1 cent of reserves!

A **fractional-reserve banking system** exists when the ratio of bank reserves to deposit liabilities is less than 1. In other words, bank reserves are less than bank deposit liabilities. In modern commercial banking, reserves are only a small fraction of deposit liabilities. Banks can operate on a fractional-reserve system because there is a constant inflow of deposits and outflow of withdrawals. As long as deposits come in at about the same rate as withdrawals, banks need only keep a small percentage of deposit liabilities in the form of ready reserves. When a customer cashes a check, the outflow is likely to be balanced by a cash deposit from another customer.

The irony of banking is that fractional-reserve banking works as long as people are confident that they will be able to withdraw their deposits. Therefore, they leave their funds in the bank. The minute they lose this confidence, depositors rush to withdraw their deposits, and reserves are never sufficient to cover all deposits. Runs on banks caused by loss of confidence have historically caused banks to fail.

The Federal Reserve

Most modern countries have a central bank—a banker's bank. In the United States, the central bank is the Federal Reserve System—the Fed, for short. The Federal Reserve System became a reality in 1913 when Woodrow Wilson signed the Federal Reserve Act.

The Structure of the Fed

The Fed is a decentralized central banking system divided into 12 Federal Reserve Districts. Regional Federal Reserve banks are located in Boston, New York, Philadelphia, Cleveland, Richmond, Atlanta, Chicago, St. Louis, Minneapolis, Kansas City, Dallas, and San Francisco. (See Figure 13.1.)

The Fed is coordinated by a seven-member Board of Governors, located in Washington, D.C. Each member of the board is appointed by the president of the United States, subject to Senate approval, and serves a 14-year term. Terms are staggered so that the appointees of a single president cannot dominate the board. The chairman, appointed by the president with the approval of the Senate, is the most powerful member and serves for four years. The current chairman is Alan Greenspan.

The Federal Open Market Committee (FOMC) consists of seven members of the Board of Governors and the presidents of five regional Federal Reserve banks. The official function of the FOMC is to direct the buying and selling of government securities on the Fed's account. Since government securities are IOUs of the federal

FIGURE 13.1 The 12 Federal Reserve Districts

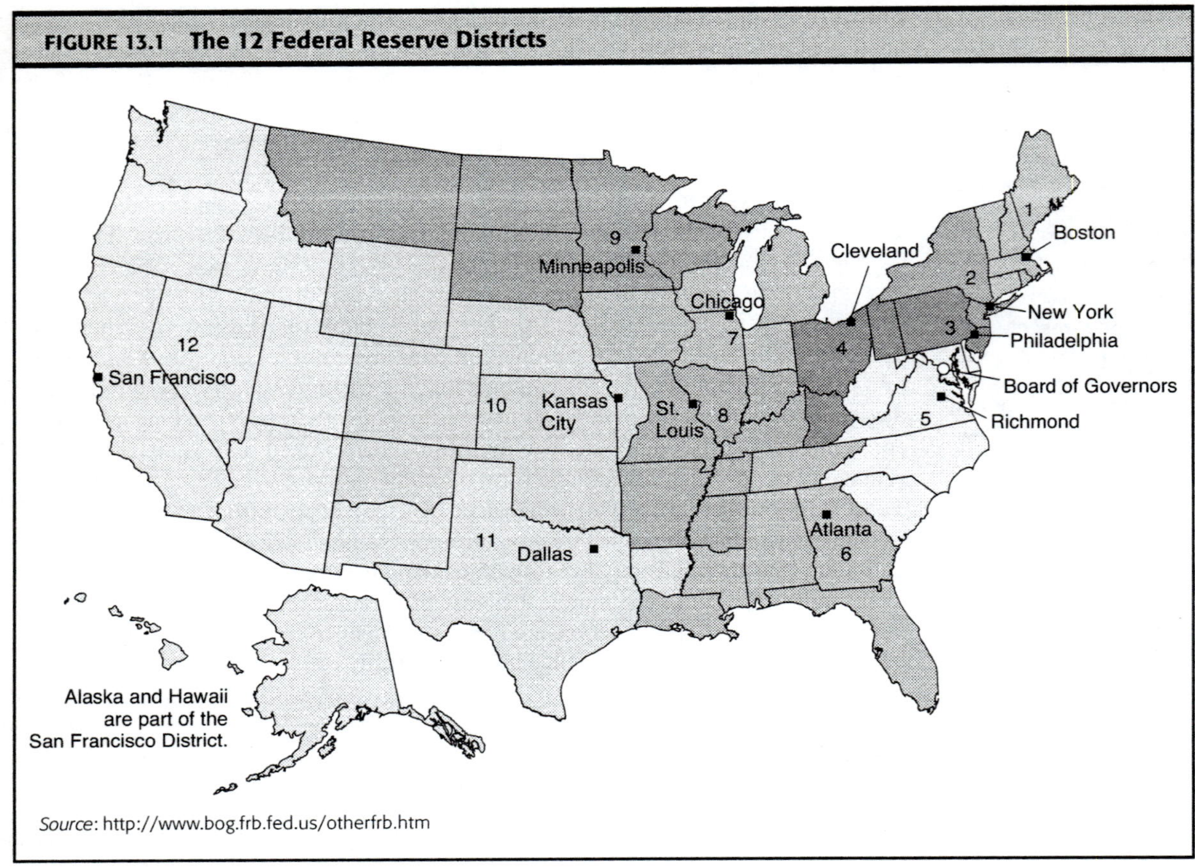

Source: http://www.bog.frb.fed.us/otherfrb.htm

Open-market operations are purchases and sales of federal government securities (bonds and bills) on the Fed's account as directed by the Federal Open Market Committee.

government and are continuously traded on the open market, FOMC purchases and sales of government securities are called **open-market operations**.

The Federal Reserve System has more independence than other governmental agencies because of the long terms of the board members and because it does not depend on Congress for funding. The Fed earns a healthy profit. In a legal sense, the Fed is responsible to Congress, but Fed actions are taken without congressional approval. However, it is not free from political pressures. There have been conflicts between the president and the Fed and between Congress and the Fed. There is always the threat that the independence of the Fed could be reduced by congressional action.

Not all banks are members of the Federal Reserve System. All national banks must be members, but state-chartered banks may join if they choose. Currently, less than 40 percent of all commercial banks are member banks, yet member banks account for about 75 percent of commercial-bank assets. Nevertheless, the Fed has had considerable authority over nonmember banks since 1980.

Functions of the Fed

The Fed supervises the banking system and controls the money supply.

The Fed has two basic functions. The first is to ensure the orderly operation of the nation's banking system, which it does by bank supervision, check clearing, meeting currency needs, and lending funds to banks. The second is to control the nation's money supply. The rest of this chapter is devoted to explaining how the Fed controls the money supply—by setting the rules of the game for banks and by buying and selling government securities.

The Fed is a banker's bank. It provides the same services to banks that banks provide their own customers. All member banks maintain deposit accounts, their "checking account," at the Fed. These accounts form the bulk of reserves and can be converted into currency at the bank's request. Thus, the Fed can meet the cash needs of banks.

The Fed meets the credit or borrowing needs of banks as well. Any depository institution holding reserves at the Fed is entitled to borrow funds. In the technical language of banking, a bank that borrows from the Fed is said to have "access to the discount window." There are limits, however. The Fed's discount window is available only for temporary and immediate credit needs of the bank.

A **reserve requirement** is a rule stating the amount of reserves that must be on hand to back bank deposits. A **required reserve ratio** is the amount of reserves required for each dollar of deposits.

Excess reserves are reserves in excess of required reserves.

The Fed sets **reserve requirements.** American banks are required, by law, to hold reserve levels that meet a designated **required reserve ratio**—an amount of reserves that must be on hand to back bank deposits. A required reserve ratio is the amount of reserves required for each dollar of deposits.

A required reserve ratio of 5 percent means that banks must hold 5 cents for every dollar of deposits. The combined balance sheet of a commercial bank illustrates the notion of a fractional-reserve banking system, where reserves are only a small fraction of outstanding deposit liabilities. Currently, the Fed requires that commercial banks maintain reserve ratios of 3 to 12 percent on checking accounts, and ratios of 0 to 3 percent on time and savings accounts. Reserves held in excess of required reserves are called **excess reserves**.

The Monetary Base

The Fed can do something that other economic agents cannot do: It can inject money into the economy or withdraw it from circulation. Most of the cash in the U.S. economy consists of Federal Reserve notes, which only the Fed can issue.

The Fed puts money into the economy every time it buys something; whenever the Fed sells something, it takes money out of the economy. Imagine, for a moment, that you, like the Fed, could print money. Each time you bought something with the money you printed, everyone else (taken together) would have more money. Each time you sold something, you would get some of your money back and everyone else (taken together) would have less money. In just this way, Fed purchases inject money into the economy; Fed sales withdraw money from the economy. The principal assets bought or sold by the Fed are the government securities it holds. It is for this reason that the Fed injects or withdraws money by buying or selling government securities.

Banks keep most of their reserves on deposit at the Fed. When your bank is short of vault cash, it makes a withdrawal from the Fed, just as you make a withdrawal from your bank when you are short of pocket cash. Because the Fed gets its currency needs from itself—it has the power to print as much money as it needs—it can inject its printed money into the economy through these reserve withdrawals of member banks.

The **monetary base** equals reserves on deposit at the Fed plus vault cash plus currency in circulation. It increases when the Fed buys something and decreases when the Fed sells something.

The quantity of bank reserves plus currency in circulation is called the **monetary base**. Whenever your bank draws cash from the Fed, the reserves on deposit with the Fed fall by the same amount that the bank's vault cash rises. Nothing happens to the monetary base. Whenever you draw a dollar out of the bank, bank reserves fall by a dollar and currency in circulation rises by a dollar. Again, this does not change the base. Only when the Fed buys or sells something does the monetary base change. If it buys something, the monetary base rises; if it sells something, the monetary base falls.

For example, suppose the Fed buys a computer for $2500 from IBM. The Fed pays for it by writing a check on itself. When IBM deposits the $2500 check at First City Bank of New York, three things can happen: (1) If First City simply deposits the check at the Fed, First City's reserves on deposit at the Fed will rise by $2500; (2) if First City simply cashes the check (that is, deposits the check at the Fed and then requests vault cash), its vault cash will rise by $2500; or (3) if IBM cashes the check, instead of depositing it as in the previous two examples, IBM's pocket cash (currency in circulation) will rise by $2500. A combination of these three things could also happen, but the combined rise in reserves on deposit, vault cash, and currency in circulation would have to equal $2500. Thus, the monetary base must rise by $2500.

In exactly the opposite manner, if the Fed sold a used computer for $100, the monetary base would fall by $100 through a combination of a fall in reserves on deposit at the Fed, vault cash, and currency in circulation.

A good way to think about the monetary base is to consider it the Fed's currency debt. Each Federal Reserve note is a "liability," a somewhat antiquated term, since nothing backs the currency. (See Example 13.2.) Because the reserves banks have deposited at the Fed may be converted into currency at their option, bank reserves plus vault cash plus currency in circulation equal the Fed's total currency liability.

How Banks Create Money

The nation's money supply consists of currency in circulation plus the checkable deposits in banks. When the Fed increases the monetary base by $1, the money supply immediately rises by $1. In the previous example, when the Fed bought a computer from IBM for $2500, the money supply initially went up by exactly $2500. Either currency in circulation or IBM's checking account, or some combination, rose by $2500. The monetary base is far less than the money supply. For example, in Figure 13.2, the money supply in 2003 was $1286 billion, and the monetary base was only $745 billion. Each dollar of monetary base eventually goes to support almost two dollars of actual money. To understand how banks create money, let us consider bank transactions in more detail.

EXAMPLE 13.2 THE DOLLAR AND "IN GOD WE TRUST"

The Federal Reserve issues the paper currency of the United States, called *Federal Reserve notes*. These notes state: "This note is legal tender for all debts public and private." Along the top of the note, the words are "In God We Trust." Forty years ago, the legal declaration read: "This note is legal tender for debts public and private and is redeemable in lawful money at any Federal Reserve Bank." This statement was empty because the Federal Reserve notes themselves were the lawful money of the United States! In the 1950s, a Cleveland man tested this promise by requesting that a $20 bill be converted into lawful money. The Federal Reserve Bank sent him two $10 bills! The man persisted, sending in one of the $10 bills, and ended up with two $5 bills and a letter explaining that "lawful money" was not defined. Soon after this incident, the promise of redemption was dropped and the words "In God We Trust" were added!

Bank Transactions and the Money Supply

We make six types of bank transactions:

1. Cash deposits
2. Cash withdrawals
3. Deposits of other people's checks
4. Payments of bills by check

FIGURE 13.2 The Monetary Base and the Money Supply

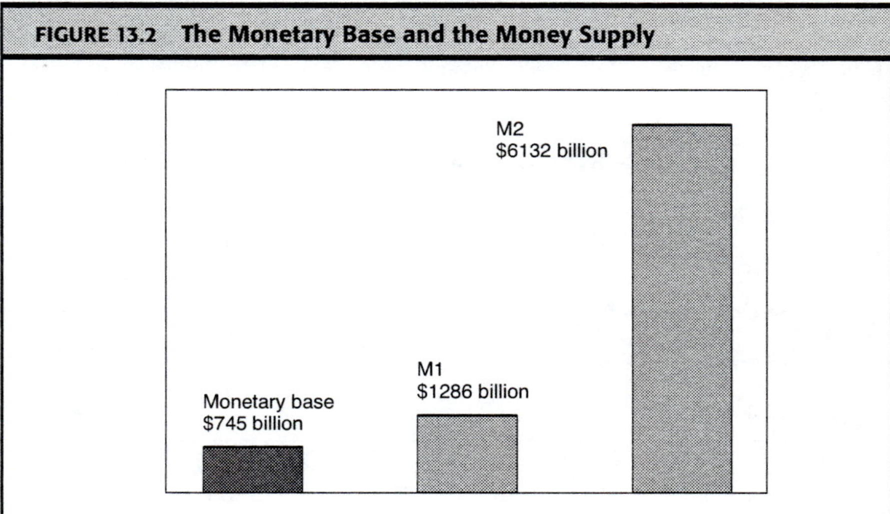

This diagram illustrates the relative size of the monetary base in relation to M1 and M2 as of August 2003.

Sources: www.federalreserve.gov and http://research.stlouisfed.org

5. Borrowing of money from the bank

6. Repayments of bank loans

Transactions 1 through 4 have no immediate effect on the supply of money, but Transactions 5 and 6 immediately affect the country's money supply.

Table 13.3 shows why nothing immediately happens to the money supply when $100 is withdrawn, deposited, received, or paid by check. Consider Transaction 1, where $100 cash is deposited in Bank A. The immediate effect is that currency in circulation falls by $100, and deposits at Bank A rise by $100. The act of depositing cash changes the composition of the money supply but not its total quantity. Likewise, withdrawing cash does not affect the total money supply. In Transaction 2, currency in circulation rises and deposits at Bank A fall, but the money supply still remains the same as before. In Transaction 3, a person deposits a $100 paycheck in Bank A, and the bank on which the check is drawn, Bank B, suffers a $100 reduction in its deposits; again, nothing happens to the money supply as a whole. In Transaction 4, a $100 telephone bill is paid by a check drawn on Bank A. Bank A's deposits fall by $100, and the telephone company's bank, Bank B, finds its deposits rising by $100. The money supply still does not change.

But, in Transaction 5, Bank A loans $100 to a customer. It does so by setting up a $100 bank deposit for its loan customer in exchange for the customer's IOU. At this instant, nothing happens to currency in circulation or deposits in other banks. Thus, the money supply rises by exactly $100—the increase in the customer's deposit at the bank—at the moment the loan is made. In Transaction 6, a customer of Bank A repays a loan to Bank A. The check of $100 is written against the customer's account. The bank reduces the account by $100 and reduces the amount the customer owes by exactly $100. At that moment, the money supply falls by $100.

When banks make loans or investments, money is created. When loans are repaid or investments are sold by banks, money is destroyed.

When banks make loans or investments, money is created. When loans are repaid or investments are sold by banks, money is destroyed.

Excess Reserves and Money Creation

Banks create money whenever they make loans or investments with their customers' deposits. Banks don't intend to create money; their only goal is to make a profit

TABLE 13.3 How Bank Transactions Affect the Money Supply

Transaction	*Currency in Circulation*	*Deposits at Bank A*	*Deposits at Bank B*	*Money Supply*
$100:				
1. Cash deposited in Bank A	–$100	+$100	0	0
2. Cash withdrawn from Bank A	+100	–100	0	0
3. Paycheck deposited in Bank A	0	+100	–$100	0
4. Bill paid by check drawn on Bank A	0	–100	+$100	0
5. Loan by Bank A put in checking account	0	+100	0	+$100
6. Car payment to Bank A by check drawn on A		–100	0	–$100

from their business of furnishing checkable deposits and making loans and investments. How much money can each bank create? A bank can create money equal to its excess reserves. One bank alone lending its excess reserves would have little effect on the money supply. However, one bank's lending can start a chain of bank lending. The entire system of banks can engage in the multiple creation of bank deposits out of a given amount of excess reserves!

Individual Banks and Money Creation Almost everyone has borrowed money from the bank to buy a car. Imagine that Lucy Smith decides to buy a new sports car. The price is $22,000. Lucy puts down $2000 and borrows $20,000 from her bank. What happens? The bank increases Lucy's account by $20,000, assuming she has credit approval, in return for her $20,000 IOU. She may agree to repay the loan by making monthly payments. The instant Lucy's account is increased by $20,000, two debts are created: the bank's debt to her and her debt to the bank. Why is money created? All that has happened is that one person's debt (Lucy's IOU) has been exchanged for another person's debt (the bank deposit). The exchange of debts between ordinary people does not create money, but banks are not ordinary people. The nation's money supply after the loan is made will be higher by exactly $20,000, since the quantity of checkable deposits has risen by that amount and nothing has happened to the amount of currency in circulation. Lucy's debt has been monetized. The **monetization of debt** is the creation of demand-deposit liabilities in the process of making bank loans.

The **monetization of debt** is the creation of demand-deposit liabilities in the process of making bank loans.

A single bank can create money equal to its excess reserves. Suppose Lucy's bank had $300,000 in deposits and held $50,000 in reserves before the loan to Lucy. With a reserve requirement of 10 percent, or $30,000, the bank has $20,000 in excess reserves. Thus, Lucy's bank has the following assets and liabilities:

Lucy's Bank: Before Loan

Assets		Liabilities	
Reserves	$50,000	Deposits	$300,000
(Excess reserves:	$20,000)		
Loans and investments	250,000		

When $20,000 is lent to Lucy, the bank's assets and liabilities will be:

Lucy's Bank: Immediately After Loan

Assets		Liabilities	
Reserves	$50,000	Deposits	$320,000
(Excess reserves:	$18,000)		
Loans and investments	270,000		

The new loan immediately increases the bank's deposits by the $20,000 added to Lucy's bank account.

So far, the money supply has risen by exactly $20,000, but the process does not stop here. When Lucy writes a $20,000 check to the car dealer, her checking account falls by $20,000 and the car dealer's checking account goes up by $20,000. The bank that made the loan to Lucy loses $20,000 in reserves to the bank holding the $20,000 deposit of the car dealer. The odds are that the borrower of money and the recipient of the money use different banks, so a bank cannot afford to lend out more than its excess reserves. (The amount lent is the approximate amount of reserves that will be lost to other banks.) As soon as the car dealer deposits Lucy's check, Lucy's bank has the following balance sheet:

Lucy's Bank: After Loan Funds Spent

Assets		Liabilities	
Reserves	$30,000	Deposits	$300,000
(Excess reserves:	$ 0)		
Loans and investments	270,000		

The Money-Creating Powers of a System of Banks Many banks can do what one bank cannot do. Assume that the car dealer's bank had $400,000 in deposits and $360,000 in loans and investments with no excess reserves prior to Lucy's car purchase. Thus:

Car Dealer's Bank: Before Car Sold

Assets		Liabilities	
Reserves	$40,000	Deposits	$400,000
(Excess reserves:	$ 0)		
Loans and investments	360,000		

When Lucy buys the car, the car dealer's bank has a fresh deposit of $20,000. The car dealer's bank now has the following balance sheet:

Car Dealer's Bank: Immediately After Car Sold

Assets		Liabilities	
Reserves	$60,000	Deposits	$420,000
(Excess reserves:	$18,000)		
Loans and investments	360,000		

The bank now has $60,000 in reserves and $420,000 in deposits. The new deposit creates excess reserves of $18,000, since the bank has a 10 percent reserve requirement and must hold $42,000 in reserves against its deposits. The car dealer's bank is now in a position to create $18,000 simply by making a loan to somebody else for that amount. When this occurs, the money supply will increase again, but by $18,000—a fraction of the original $20,000. If there is no cash leakage into currency in circulation, the new loan will end up as a fresh deposit in yet some third bank. A **cash leakage** is a withdrawal of currency from a bank. The third bank will find

A **cash leakage** is a withdrawal of currency from a bank.

its excess reserves increasing by \$16,200 [= \$18,000 − (0.1) × 18,000]. When those excess reserves are lent out, the money supply will increase again, but by that smaller amount. The process will continue, again and again, until the original excess reserves are totally exhausted into either new loans or, possibly, leakages of cash out of the banking system.

The ratio of the change in deposits to excess reserves is called the **deposit multiplier**.

A system of banks can create deposits equal to a multiple of its excess reserves. The ratio of the change in deposits to excess reserves is called the **deposit multiplier**, which is equal to the reciprocal of the reserve requirement ratio. If reserve requirements were 10 percent, \$1 reserves would support \$10 in deposits; if reserve requirements were 20 percent, one dollar in reserves would support \$5 in deposits.

Cash Leakages or Injections

A multiple expansion of bank deposits follows when the monetary base is increased; similarly, a multiple contraction occurs when the monetary base is decreased. The money supply can also increase if banks decide to hold a smaller amount of excess reserves. Thus, both the Fed and the banks can act to increase or decrease the money supply.

Does the public have any role in determining the money supply? Whenever individuals deposit cash in a bank, excess reserves are created and the multiple expansion of bank deposits is initiated. When individuals withdraw cash, a multiple contraction of deposits occurs. From 1929 to 1933, the money supply fell by 25 percent, from \$26.6 billion to \$19.9 billion, while the amount of currency held by the public actually increased. The monetary base stayed relatively constant. What happened? The stock market crash of 1929 frightened the public into drawing its cash out of the banks, which were not insured at the time. These cash withdrawals initiated a multiple contraction of bank deposits and the precipitous 25 percent reduction in the nation's money supply.

The Federal Reserve System in 1929 did nothing to offset the massive currency drain from the banks. As we shall see, the money supply affects economic activity. Thus, the Fed and the public were both partly responsible for the magnitude and length of the Great Depression. The modern Fed never would have allowed the dramatic withdrawals or injections of cash to affect the money supply so significantly. It stands ready to offset cash withdrawals by increasing the monetary base. The Fed made the mistake in 1929 because it was inexperienced; at that time, it was only 16 years old. Moreover, massive bank scares are a thing of the past because the Federal Deposit Insurance Corporation now insures each deposit up to \$100,000. (See Example 13.3.)

How the Fed Controls the Money Supply

The most important function of the Fed is to control the supply of money in the economy. As we shall see later, by expanding the money supply, the Fed can speed the pace of economic activity. Conversely, by contracting the money supply (or by slowing down its growth), the Fed can slow the pace of economic activity.

EXAMPLE 13.3 MORAL HAZARD AND BANK LENDING: TWO EXAMPLES

Moral hazard occurs when economic agents have an opportunity to change their behavior for opportunistic gain after a contract is concluded. In the case of bank lending, the existence of deposit insurance or knowledge that troubled banks will be bailed out creates moral hazard problems, as is illustrated by the two cases described here.

In the early 1980s, Congress deregulated banking by removing many restrictions on commercial banks and thrifts. The combination of deregulation and deposit insurance provided by the Federal Deposit Insurance Corporation (FDIC) proved lethal, and unintended consequences followed. Basically, the FDIC method of insuring deposits creates an incentive problem. Even though there is a $100,000 limit on insured deposits, any amount can be insured by spreading deposits over many banks and using intermediaries. There is no incentive for banks to provide, or for consumers to demand, information on how well the bank is doing. Deposits are as safe in a poorly run bank as in the best-run bank. The incentive to monitor the performance of banks falls on the shoulders of regulators.

Banks lent money to real estate developers and corporations without examining the credit worthiness of their business plans. They even lent money to themselves. When these investments failed, so did banks and thrifts. Bank failure rates in the late 1980s and early 1990s increased ten fold over the bank failure rates in the 30 years from 1950 to 1980.

The ultimate cost to U.S. taxpayers of bailing out all these failed banks was in excess of $300 billion.

The Asian crisis of 1997 and 1998 provides a second example of moral hazard. In the early 1990s, international banks loaned hundreds of billions of dollars to governments and businesses in high-risk economies such as Thailand, Malaysia, and Indonesia. They made these loans, often indiscriminately, perhaps because they felt that if these loans could not be repaid, the International Monetary Fund (IMF) and various governments would provide emergency bail-out funds as they had for Mexico three years earlier. Without this expectation, banks would have been more careful in their lending.

Instruments of Monetary Control

The Fed has three instruments to control the supply of money: open-market operations, reserve requirements, and discount rates.

Open-Market Operations The Fed can inject reserves into the economy by buying something; it can withdraw reserves from the economy by selling something. The "something" that the Fed buys and sells to control reserves is federal government securities. The Open Market Committee of the Fed directs the buying and selling of government bonds, bills, and notes on the Fed's account. For example, the Fed buys $100,000 worth of government securities from John Doe. When Doe deposits the Fed's $100,000 check in his bank account, his bank finds that its demand deposits have risen by $100,000 and its reserves with the Fed have also risen by $100,000. But with a 10 percent required reserve ratio, the bank needs only $10,000 in reserves to cover the $100,000 deposit, so it has $90,000 of excess reserves. When it loans out excess reserves, the money supply expands. If the Fed had sold $100,000 of its government securities, the reverse would have happened. Doe's bank would have found itself with insufficient reserves, and the money supply would contract.

Open-market operations are the Fed's major instrument to control the money supply. By buying government securities, the Fed expands the monetary base. By selling government securities, the Fed contracts the monetary base.

Open-market operations give the Fed considerable flexibility. The Fed can inject or withdraw large or small amounts of reserves by making large or small purchases or sales of government securities. If the public decides to convert its checking accounts into cash, the Fed can inject new reserves to offset the drain from the monetary base. The Fed makes use of this flexibility by regularly engaging in open-market operations.

Reserve Requirements A second instrument of monetary control is the Fed's power to set reserve requirements. If the Fed raises required reserve ratios, banks do not have sufficient reserves to back outstanding deposits, and they must contract the money supply. If the Fed lowers the required reserve ratio, banks find that they have excess reserves to loan out, and the money supply expands. Changes in reserve requirements are seldom used to control the money supply because they tend to shock the banking system by the sudden loss or gain of excess reserves. The Fed finds it easier and more convenient to manipulate bank reserves through open-market operations than through reserve requirements.

The **discount rate** is the interest rate the Fed charges banks that wish to borrow reserves.

Discount Rates The Fed can affect the supply of money and credit conditions by changing the **discount rate**, the interest rate the Fed charges banks that wish to borrow reserves from it. Unanticipated withdrawals can leave banks with deficient reserves; banks can make up these deficiencies by borrowing from the Fed at the discount window. Banks are not encouraged to borrow from the Fed to make up long-term deficiencies in their reserves; rather, the discount window is for temporary reserve needs. The discount rate affects the money supply by affecting banks' willingness to borrow reserves. When the discount rate is high relative to the interest the banks can earn on loans, it is relatively expensive for banks to keep reserves. When the discount rate is low, banks are more willing to borrow reserves. Lowering the discount rate encourages banks to follow a more lenient credit policy; raising the discount rate causes banks to think twice about making loans.

Generally speaking, the Fed sets the discount rate to keep it in line with other interest rates in the economy. If interest rates are generally rising, the Fed raises the discount rate. Otherwise, banks would be too tempted to borrow reserves to make profitable loans. The Fed also uses the discount rate to send signals to the banking community. An increasing rate says that credit should be tighter; a decrease is seen as a move to looser credit.

Summary

1. Banks are financial intermediaries that borrow money from ultimate lenders and lend this money to ultimate borrowers. Most lending is done by financial intermediaries. Commercial banks are chartered by state banking authorities (state banks) and by the U.S. Treasury (national banks). Commercial banks offer their customers checking account services and savings accounts. They

earn money by loaning out funds they have borrowed or investing these funds in government securities. Banks make money by borrowing at a lower interest rate than the rates they receive on their loans or investments.

2. Bank balance sheets summarize the claims on the assets of the bank. The assets claimed by the owners of the bank are the net worth of the bank; the assets claimed by nonowners are the liabilities of the bank. The major liabilities of commercial banks are demand (checking) deposits and time deposits. Banks must maintain reserves to meet the cash needs of their depositors. Reserves are held as cash in the vault and as reserve balances at the Fed. Reserves are much less than the demand-deposit liabilities of the bank.
3. The Federal Reserve System, established in 1913, is the bankers' bank. It is the central bank of the United States. The Fed consists of 12 district banks, a Board of Governors, and a Federal Open Market Committee in charge of buying and selling government securities. The Fed imposes reserve requirements on banks. A reserve requirement is a rule that a bank must hold a prescribed portion of its outstanding deposits as reserves. Banks can borrow from the Fed at the discount window to meet their temporary cash needs by paying the discount rate. By buying and selling things, the Fed injects money into the banking system and takes money out of the banking system. When the Fed buys anything, the sum of reserves on deposit with the Fed, vault cash in banks, and currency in circulation increases by the amount of the purchase.
4. The monetary base equals reserves with the Fed, vault cash, and currency in circulation. It is smaller than the money supply. The Fed controls the monetary base by buying and selling government securities through open-market operations.
5. Banks create money by monetizing debt. They use reserves to make loans, and, in the process, they create money. Demand deposits are money, and banks make loans from their deposits. An increase in reserves leads to a multiple expansion of deposits. Although any one bank can only lend out its excess reserves, the banking system, as a whole, can lend out a multiple of the increase in reserves. The deposit multiplier is the ratio of the change in deposits to the change in reserves.
6. The Fed has an arsenal of weapons to control the money supply: open-market operations, the discount rate, and the required reserve ratio. The most potent instrument of monetary policy is open-market operations, which allow the Fed to inject or withdraw reserves.

Questions and Problems

1. Explain why an injection of $100 of new reserves will have a larger effect on the money supply with a low required reserve ratio.
2. Jones borrows money from Smith. What is the effect of this transaction on the money supply? Why? Jones borrows money from First National Bank. What is the effect on the money supply? Why do the two transactions have a different effect on the money supply?

3. With a reserve ratio of 20 percent, how much money can First National Bank loan out when it receives a deposit of a $10,000 check written on the Fed's account? How much can the banking system as a whole loan out when this happens?

4. Explain why the Fed prefers to use open-market operations rather than changes in reserve ratios when both act to alter bank reserves.

5. Consider the balance sheet of a car dealer's bank immediately after a car is sold.

  a. What would be the balance sheet of the bank immediately after making a loan equal to its excess reserves?

  b. What would be the balance sheet after the borrower writes a check on those funds?

6. Explain why a bank loan changes the monetary base while a cash withdrawal does not.

7. What would happen to deposit expansion if banks decided not to lend out their excess reserves?

8. List the factors that raise the independence of the Fed.

9. Is money in a certificate of deposit at your bank money? Are shares of IBM stock money?

10. Explain why credit cards are not money. (*Hint*: Consider all of the functions of money.)

11. Given the three instruments of monetary policy, explain why monetary policy is primarily carried out through open-market operations.

12. If people decide to hold their assets in the form of cash rather than in their checking accounts, what would happen to the money supply, ceteris paribus?

CHAPTER 14

INFLATION

Chapter Preview

Price stability is one of the goals of macroeconomic policy. We do not want to have prices rising at too rapid a rate, and we don't seem to want prices to fall generally. This chapter studies the rate at which prices increase—called *inflation*. We are interested in why prices increase or fall and in how to control the rate of price change and the consequences of price increases on things that matter, such as employment and living standards.

One could say that the main topic of microeconomics is the price system—how prices of products and the factors of production are determined. But in microeconomics, our primary concern is relative prices. Microeconomics teaches that prices signal relative scarcities in terms of how one price stands relative to another. Money prices are pictured as not very meaningful. Now we turn away from relative prices to money prices as a whole.

Earlier chapters in the macroeconomic sequence indeed refer to money prices as a whole. The aggregate supply and demand curves of Chapter 12 relate aggregate demand and aggregate supply to the price level. Chapter 9 points out that the nominal interest rate is affected by expectations of price changes in the future. Chapter 8 explains that the real wage is the nominal wage divided by the price level. All of these cases relate to the general level of prices and its rate of change, not to the relative prices of microeconomics.

For almost a decade, we have not had rapid increases in prices. We are now accustomed to prices that rise 1 to 3 percent per year, and such increases do not appear alarming. In fact, the concern has moved in the opposite direction. We are now told to worry that prices may generally fall, as they have been doing in Japan, and that this would be harmful to the economy. But memories are short. In 1979, prices rose 13 percent, and in 1980, they rose 12.5 percent. In 1980, banks were charging their best customers 15.3 percent per year. Surveys showed that the number-one concern of the American public was inflation, not unemployment or low economic growth. Just as in the 1990s we thought that we had conquered the business cycle, only to see it return in 2000, so must we worry about an eventual return of high rates of price increases.

Inflation Definitions

Inflation is a general increase in prices. The inflation rate is expressed as an annual rate of increase.

Inflation is a general increase in prices, occurring when prices in the entire economy are rising on average. The inflation rate is usually expressed as an annual percentage increase. During inflations, some prices rise more rapidly than the average; others rise more slowly than the average; some prices even fall during inflations. Whether inflations are perceived as moderate or excessive is a relative matter. In the mid-1950s, the American public was alarmed about an inflation rate of 2 percent per annum. During some years in the 1970s, when prices rose almost 10 percent per year, an inflation rate of 2 percent, or even 5 percent, would have been viewed as modest. In countries like Brazil, Argentina, and Russia, where prices have more than doubled annually in recent years; the high American inflation rates of the 1970s and early 1980s would be viewed as welcome relief.

A **hyperinflation** is a very rapid and constantly growing rate of inflation.

There is a special term for runaway inflations. A **hyperinflation** is a very rapid and constantly growing rate of inflation. At a minimum, prices double every year; at worst, prices can double daily or hourly.

The world has experienced a number of hyperinflations. The best known is the German hyperinflation of the 1920s, which aided Hitler's rise to power. The American South experienced a hyperinflation during the Civil War. The newly independent states of the former Soviet Union underwent hyperinflations in the 1990s. Those who have experienced hyperinflation have witnessed its destructive effects and tend to fear inflation more than others do.

Price Indexes

A **price index** shows the current year's cost of buying a particular basket of goods as a percentage of the cost of the same basket of goods in some earlier year.

If all prices rose at the same rate, say 3 percent per year, the inflation rate would obviously be 3 percent per annum. But some prices rise more rapidly than others; relative prices change. How does one calculate the general rate of increase of prices—the inflation rate—when prices are rising at different rates? Most **price indexes** show the current year's cost of buying a particular basket of goods as a percentage of the cost of the same basket of goods in some earlier year. For example, if only apples and oranges are produced in a hypothetical economy, and ten apples, at $1.00 each, and five oranges, at $2.00 each, are sold in 2004, the cost of buying that market basket in 2004 is $20.00. In 2005, when apples cost $1.50 each and oranges cost $4.00 each, the cost of the same basket of goods is $35.00. The 2005 price index stands at 175 ($35.00/$20.00)—the basket of goods is 75 percent more expensive in 2005 than in 2004.

Price indexes may overstate the effect of price increases on living standards because they measure the increasing cost of buying a fixed bundle of goods. Even if oranges have risen in price more rapidly than apples, the calculated price index assumes that people continue to buy the same relative quantities of apples and oranges. In reality, we blunt the effect of soaring orange prices by substituting apples.

The two price indexes used most commonly to measure the rate of inflation are the **Consumer Price Index (CPI)** and the **GDP** (gross domestic product) **deflator**.

The **Consumer Price Index** measures the change in consumer prices.

The Consumer Price Index (CPI) The CPI measures the change in the cost of buying a 1982–1984 market basket of consumer goods purchased by an average urban family of four. The Consumer Price Index is reported regularly by the news media.

The wages of many union members, government employees, and retirees are tied (indexed) to the CPI; when it goes up, their wages and benefits automatically go up. (See Example 14.1 for a critique of the CPI.)

The **GDP deflator** measures the change in the prices of all goods and services produced by the economy.

The GDP Deflator The CPI measures only changes in the prices of the consumption of goods and services that families purchase. It does not measure the other goods and services that the economy produces for uses other than personal consumption. Currently, 65 percent of the total output of the American economy is devoted to personal consumption. The remaining 35 percent is expended on business investment, government services, and exports. The CPI, therefore, is not the most comprehensive measure of the rate of inflation.

The GDP deflator measures the change in the prices of all final goods and services produced by the economy. Over the past 35 years, the GDP deflator has not behaved much differently than the CPI.

Trends in Inflation

The **annual rate of inflation** is calculated by taking the annual rate of change in the Consumer Price Index or the GDP deflator.

The **annual rate of inflation** is calculated by taking the annual rate of change in the Consumer Price Index or the GDP deflator. The pattern of inflation since 1955 is shown in Figure 14.1, Panel A. This chart shows why people have come to think of rising prices as one of the constants of life, along with death and taxes: The CPI

EXAMPLE 14.1 ARE WE OVERESTIMATING INFLATION? THE BOSKIN COMMISSION

The most widely cited measure of inflation is the Consumer Price Index (CPI), measured monthly by the Bureau of Labor Statistics. Over the past five years, average annual inflation, as measured by the CPI, has been around 3 percent. A government commission, headed by economist Michael Boskin, was appointed to study whether the CPI was providing accurate measures of inflation. In its final report, the Boskin Commission concluded that we may be overstating inflation, perhaps more than 1 percent per annum! This means that U.S. inflation may have been one-third or more lower than we thought. Why did the Boskin Commission conclude that the CPI overstates inflation? First, the CPI does not adjust for the modifications in consumer spending that households make automatically when relative prices change. When fish becomes cheap and beef expensive, we shift our spending to fish without a great loss of consumer satisfaction. The CPI, however, has households making the same purchases every year no matter what happens to relative prices. Second, the CPI does not make adequate adjustments for quality improvements in products, such as automobiles or consumer electronics. We may be paying more for these products, but their quality has risen so that we may be getting them at actually cheaper prices when we adjust for the higher quality.

How we measure inflation is extremely important. Most of the Social Security trust fund deficit would disappear if we used the Boskin measure of inflation, insofar as Social Security payments would be indexed to a CPI that is rising more slowly. Projected government deficits would be smaller in that payments to government workers and the military, which are also indexed to the CPI, would rise at a slower pace.

has shown a price decrease in only one of the last 48 years (1955). Inflation rates greater than 10 percent per annum were recorded in the mid-1970s, the late 1970s, and the early 1980s. From 1982 to the present, the inflation rate has been low relative to that in the 1970s.

Long-run historical patterns in inflation can also be seen in Figure 14.1, Panel B, which shows annual inflation rates over a long period. This figure reveals a surprising conclusion: Sustained increases in prices are a fairly new phenomenon. Prior to 1930, prices were as likely to fall as to rise. Deflations (downward movements in prices) were just as common as inflations (upward movements). The unusual feature of the last half-century has been the notable absence of periods of deflation. Unlike earlier periods, when inflation tended to be weakened by a following deflation, the postwar era has been one of continuing increases in prices, albeit at different rates.

Macroeconomic theory must explain why inflation has been persistent in recent years after almost 150 years of no discernible trend. It must explain why the inflation rate rose so substantially in the 1970s and why inflation slowed in the 1980s and 1990s.

The Effects of Inflation

Many people mistakenly think that rising prices automatically lower living standards. If income is rising faster than prices, living standards are rising; if income is rising

FIGURE 14.1A Two Views of Inflation: Annual Percentage Change

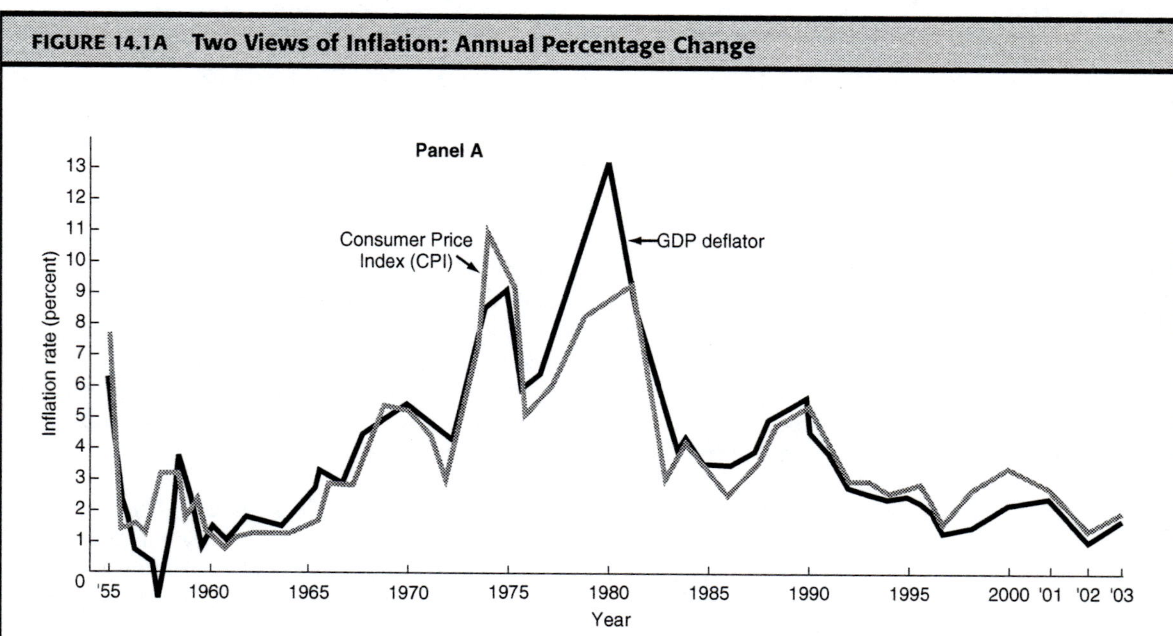

The rate of inflation as measured by the CPI and GDP deflator accelerated sharply from the early 1960s to 1981. After 1981, the inflation rate slowed. This figure shows why most Americans regard inflation as inevitable; there have been no episodes of deflation for almost a half-century.

Sources: Statistical Abstract of the United States; Economic Report of the President

FIGURE 14.1B Inflation Rate (1892–2003)

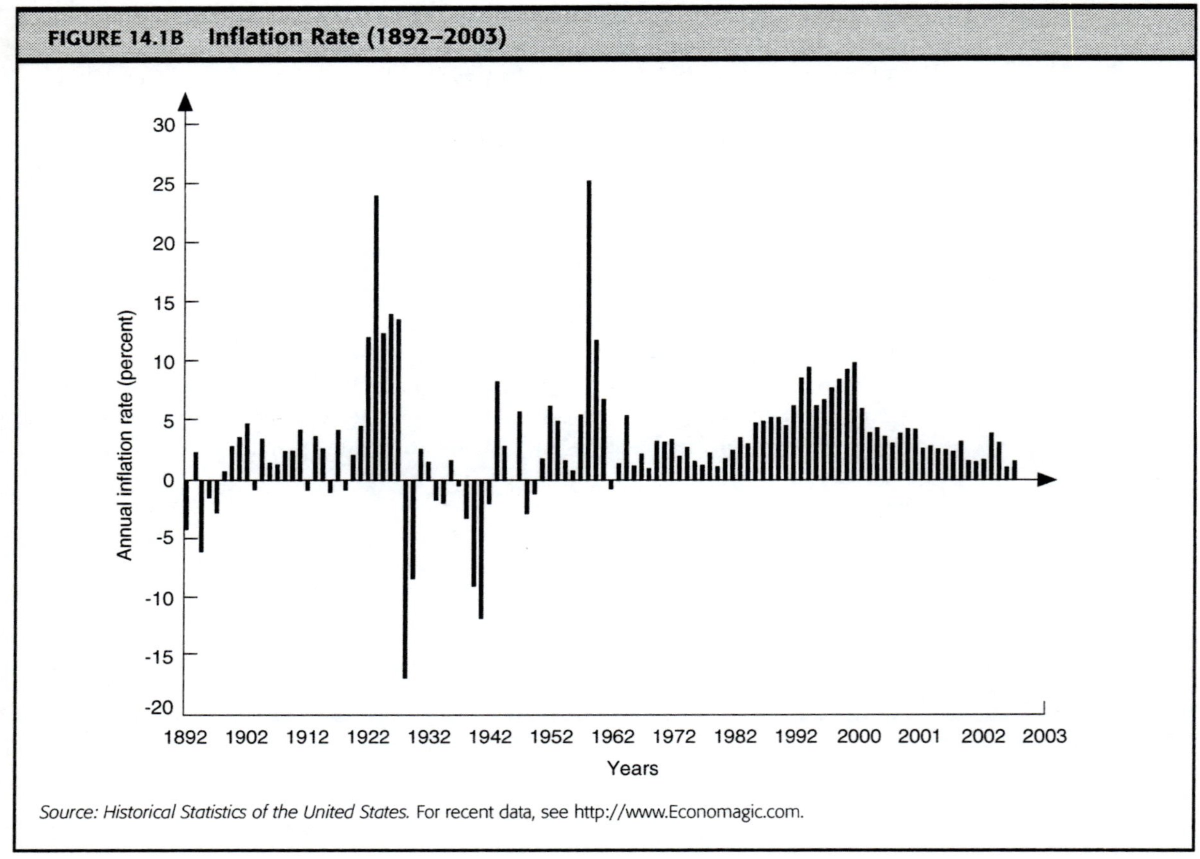

Source: Historical Statistics of the United States. For recent data, see http://www.Economagic.com.

Inflation has accelerated in recent years after virtually 150 years of no discernible trend.

more slowly than prices, living standards are falling. It is the relationship between changes in income and prices that determines the direction of change of economic well-being. During the early 1930s, prices were falling, but incomes were falling faster than prices. During the inflationary 1970s, prices almost doubled, but income more than doubled. During the rapid growth of the 1990s, inflation was moderate. There is no simple relationship between inflation and living standards. However, inflation is a potential problem for the three reasons explained in the paragraphs that follow.

Inflation and Income Redistribution Not everyone is against inflation! Because income may be redistributed during an inflation, those who fear they will experience a drop in their living standard fear inflation. The losers from inflation are those on fixed incomes; people working in professions where wages rise more slowly than inflation; union members with wage contracts that increase more slowly than inflation; people who have loaned out funds at low interest rates; and persons who have invested in fixed-income assets, like bonds, that fall in value as inflation rises.

Inflation acts like a tax on fixed money receipts, or assets, and like a subsidy on fixed money payments, or liabilities. For example, Smith borrows $1000 from Jones in 2004 and agrees to repay Jones $1100 in 2006. Because inflation reduces the purchasing power of the $1100, the value of the $1100 is eroded. If the goods and services Smith can buy in 2004 with the $1000 exceed the value of the goods and services Jones can buy in 2006 with $1100, income has clearly been redistributed from Jones to Smith.

The amount of income redistribution depends on whether economic agents anticipate inflation. If Jones correctly anticipates inflation between 2004 and 2006, Jones can charge a higher interest rate so that he or she will be able to buy more goods and services in 2006 with the repaid money than Jones would have been able to buy in 2004 with the original sum. Lenders will not loan out money at interest rates that are not high enough to compensate them for the declining value of money. If the union leadership correctly anticipates the rate of inflation, it will not accept contracts that raise wages more slowly than inflation. Income redistribution occurs only when people are surprised by inflation.

Income redistribution occurs only when people are surprised by inflation.

Inflation and Efficiency Hyperinflations have disastrous effects on economic efficiency. During the worst hyperinflations, virtually all economic activities are devoted to avoiding the inflation tax. Workers must be paid twice daily so that they can run to stores with wheelbarrows full of money to buy goods before prices rise even further. People refuse to accept money payments, and barter transactions become the order of the day. Investment activities turn from the productive activities of building plants and buying equipment to speculative activities such as buying jewelry, gold, and foreign currencies whose values might keep up with inflation.

The negative effects of inflation are much less extreme during moderate inflations. Nevertheless, anticipated inflation channels economic activity into the search for ways to beat the inflation tax and diverts talent away from productive economic activity.

Inflation, Output, and Employment Economic agents base their economic decisions on relative prices. Because inflation, on average, does not make firms better off (costs tend to rise as fast as selling prices) or make workers better off (rising prices tend to offset rises in money wages), there appears to be no reason why inflation should cause more output to be produced or more employment to be available.

Modern macroeconomic theory teaches that unanticipated inflation can, indeed, affect the output decisions of firms and the employment decisions of individuals. Workers who incorrectly anticipate a low rate of inflation sign employment contracts that call for small wage increases. When inflation accelerates, their employers are able to raise their selling prices while their labor costs remain low. Accordingly, firms increase output and employment.

Rapid inflation diverts resources from productive to nonproductive investments and reduces the economy's productive capacity.

Demand- and Supply-Side Inflation

Chapter 12 introduced aggregate supply and aggregate demand. Surprisingly, aggregate supply and demand analysis can explain inflation as well as they can explain output.

Panel A of Figure 14.2 illustrates **demand-side inflation** caused by an increase in aggregate demand. The increase in aggregate demand causes the price level to rise and more output to be produced. Increasing prices are associated with more output and, hence, more employment (less unemployment). In the case of demand-side inflation, there is a trade-off between higher prices and unemployment. Higher prices mean less unemployment.

Demand-side Inflation occurs when aggregate demand increases and pulls prices up.

Supply-side Inflation occurs when aggregate supply drops and pushes the price level up.

Supply-side inflation occurs when an exogenous increase in costs (which reduces aggregate supply) pushes up prices. Panel B shows a reduction in aggregate supply (an adverse supply shock). Aggregate supply falls when there is an exogenous increase in the costs of firms—that is, an increase caused by something outside the system. Costs could rise exogenously for a number of reasons: price increases in international oil markets, particularly bad harvests, international disorders, or drops in productivity. With a drop in aggregate supply, the price level is pushed up and less output is produced. An adverse supply shock pushes up the price level while reducing output and employment. The adverse supply shock has raised prices and unemployment simultaneously. (See Example 14.2.)

When inflation is moderate, supply-side and demand-side inflation look the same. It is difficult for the individual economic agent to know whether inflation originates on the demand side or supply side. Take a demand-side inflation: As aggregate demand rises, the demand for goods and services and labor generally increases. As individual markets respond to these demand increases, prices and wages rise. Firms see their labor and material costs rising. They also see that the market is prepared to pay a higher price for their product, and they pass their higher costs along to their buyers in the form of higher selling prices. In the firm's view (and in the view of the firm's customers), prices have risen because labor and material costs have risen. Even though the real cause of inflation, in this example, was an increase in aggregate demand, to the individual participants in the economy it appeared as a supply-side inflation.

FIGURE 14.2 Demand-Side Versus Supply-Side Inflation

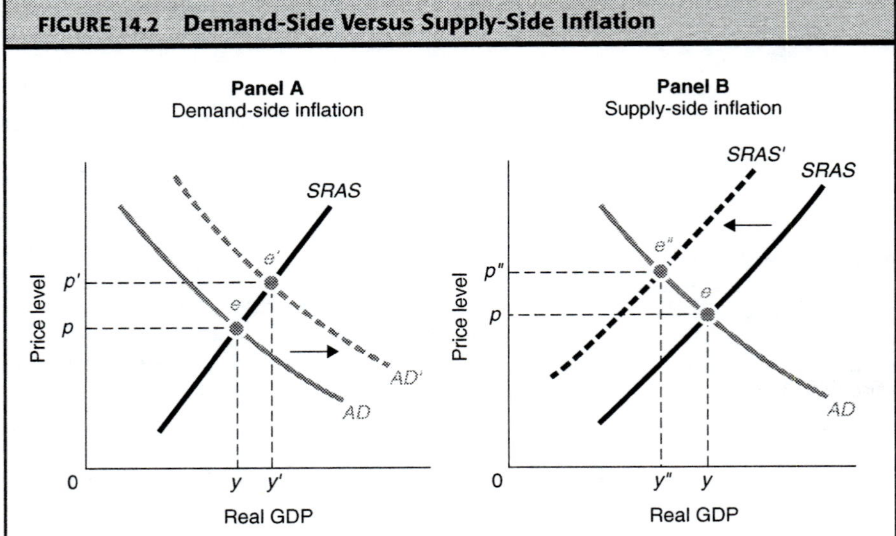

Panel A shows demand-side inflation. The economy is initially in equilibrium at *e*. Aggregate demand increases from *AD* to AD′ and causes the price level to rise from *p* to *p′* as the economy moves up along the short-run aggregate supply curve, *SRAS*, to *e′*. In the short run, output increases from *y* to *y′*. The increase in aggregate demand has pulled prices up. Panel B shows cost-push or supply-side inflation. The economy is initially in equilibrium at *e*. A reduction in aggregate supply from *SRAS* to *SRAS′* causes a movement back along the aggregate demand curve from e to *e″*. Prices rise from *p* to *p″*, output declines from *y* to *y″*; unemployment increases. The reduction in aggregate supply has pushed prices up.

EXAMPLE 14.2 ENERGY SHOCKS AND SUPPLY-SIDE INFLATION

Energy costs represent a significant production cost for industry, transportation, and agriculture. The price of the primary raw material, crude oil, from which we derive energy is determined in world markets beyond the control of oil-consuming nations. If the price of crude oil rises, the cost of production rises, and the aggregate supply curve should shift to the left, creating supply-side inflation. The accompanying chart of the annual rates of increase in the price of crude oil and of CPI inflation shows that when crude oil prices were increasing rapidly, such during the Iran-Iraq war (late 1980s), the First Gulf War, and the build up to the Second Gulf War, the CPI inflation rate was relatively high. When crude oil prices fell as they did during the late 1990s, the rate of CPI inflation also fell. When crude oil price inflation accelerated in the early 1990s, so did the CPI inflation rate. Although energy accounts for only about 15 percent of input costs, this diagram shows that energy prices, through supply-side effects, can have a profound impact on overall inflation.

Sources of Inflation

Figure 14.1 shows that there has been a persistent inflationary trend since the 1930s. What caused this trend? Demand-side inflation or supply-side inflation? If demand-side inflation, what caused aggregate demand to increase steadily?

When aggregate demand increases, the price level will rise unless there is an equivalent increase in aggregate supply. A one-shot increase in aggregate demand would not lead to continuous inflation; rather, the economy eventually would adjust to a new and higher equilibrium price level, at which time inflation would stop. Although adjustments to a new higher price level can be painful, the main concern is persistent or accelerating inflation. Persistent inflation might be caused by continual drops in aggregate supply, but reductions in aggregate supply are caused by random events that are not expected to be persistent. Instead, economists focus on aggregate demand as the cause of persistent or accelerating inflation.

Money and Inflation

Inflation can have two basic causes: decreases in aggregate supply (supply-side inflation) and increases in aggregate demand (demand-side inflation). Although aggregate demand can increase for a number of reasons (reductions in household thrift, increasing government spending, and increasing net exports), economists focus on increases in the money supply as a principal source of increases in aggregate demand. Economic theory supplies a powerful tool, the equation of exchange, that explains the relationship between money and prices.

The **velocity of circulation** is the average number of times money changes hands in the course of a year: $V = \text{GDP}/M$.

Monetary Growth, Velocity, and Inflation

The **velocity of circulation** measures the average number of times money changes hands in the course of a year. Velocity (V) equals nominal GDP divided by the money

FIGURE 14.3 Monetary Growth and Inflation

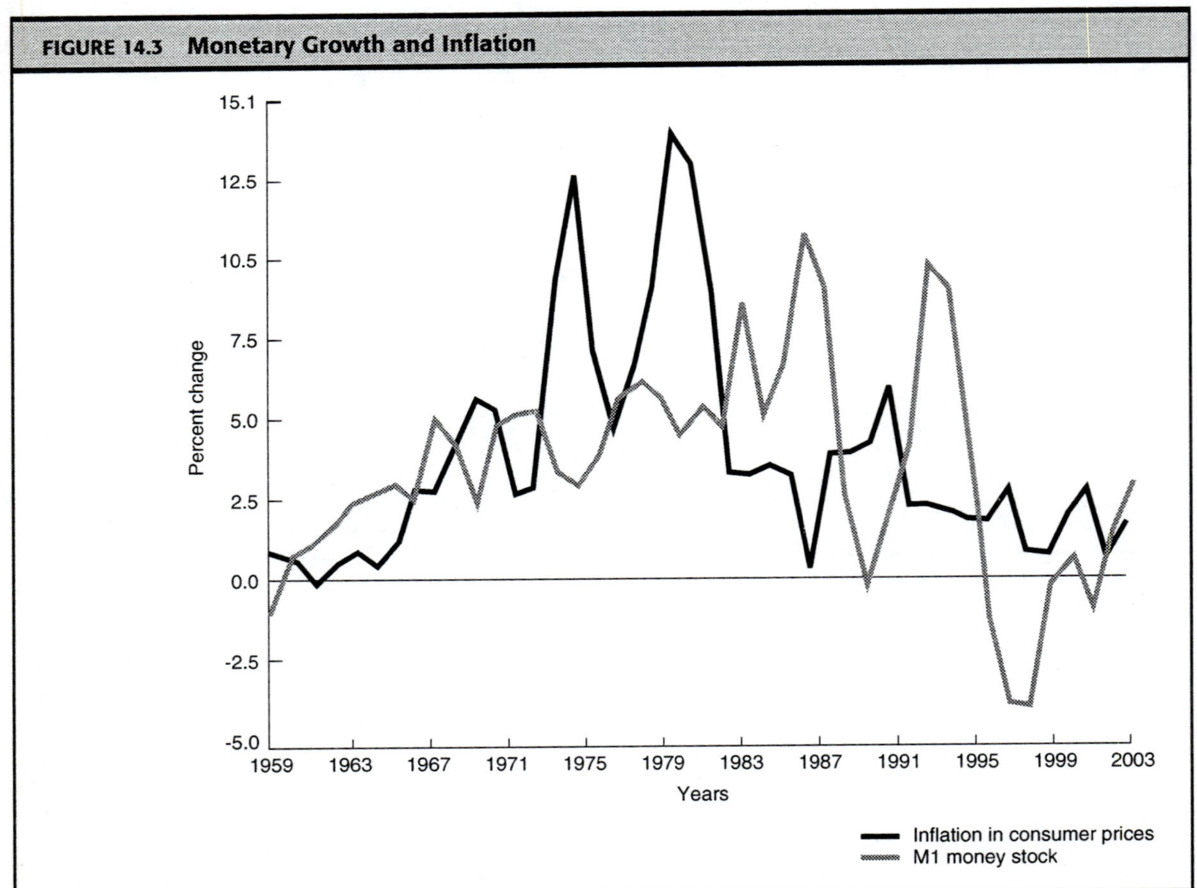

supply (V = GDP/M). Nominal GDP is the value of all final transactions in the economy. Money is the medium of exchange in which transactions are carried out. Nominal GDP in 2003 equaled $10.5 trillion, and the money supply (M1) equaled $1.3 trillion. This means that the average dollar of money supply is used an average almost 9 times in purchasing final goods and services.

Nominal GDP equals real GDP (Y) times the average price level. Hence, velocity can also be expressed as $V = PY/M$. Rearranging this expression, we get:

The **equation of exchange** is $MV = PY$.

$$MV = PY$$

The equation $MV = PY$ is the **equation of exchange**. It explains the relationship between money (M) and prices (P). We can also express the equation of exchange in terms of annual growth rates as:

$$\dot{M} + \dot{V} = \dot{P} + \dot{Y}$$

where the dots refer to annual rates of growth.[1]

The classic explanation of inflation is that inflation is caused by "too many dollars chasing too few goods." The combination of increases in the money supply and velocity determines the rate at which "dollars" are chasing "goods." The growth of real GDP determines the rate of expansion of the supply of goods. With constant velocity, a 5 percent increase in the money supply ($\dot{M}$ = 5%) leads to a 5 percent increase in the total dollars chasing goods (that is, to a 5 percent annual increase in nominal GDP, or $\dot{P}+\dot{Y}$ = 5%); if real GDP expands by 2 percent per annum, there are too many dollars chasing too few goods, and prices are bid up. Prices will be bid up by the difference between the annual growth rate of dollars chasing goods (5 percent) and the annual growth rate of goods (2 percent), or by 3 percent. With velocity constant, $\dot{P} = \dot{M} - \dot{Y}$.

With constant velocity, **excess monetary growth** occurs when the money supply grows more rapidly than real GDP.

With a 2 percent real GDP growth and constant V, the money supply could grow at 2 percent per annum without pulling up prices. If it grew by more than 2 percent, there would be **excess monetary growth.** (Excess monetary growth is the difference between monetary growth and real GDP growth.) With V constant, a 10 percent increase in M would raise prices approximately 8 percent, with a 2 percent growth rate of real GDP.

Table 14.1 provides long-run data for real GDP, M1, and the price level (the GDP deflator) since 1933. It shows that in 2003 GDP was almost 14 times that of 1933 and prices were 13 times those of 1933, but the money supply was 68 times that of 1933. In terms of annual growth rates, real GDP increased at 4 percent per annum, and money at 6.5 percent per annum over the entire period. Using the inflation equation with constant velocity, we would expect an inflation rate of 2.3 (6.3 − 4) percent per annum. In reality, the inflation rate was a much higher 3.9 percent per annum. Excess monetary growth (monetary growth minus GDP growth) "explains" only about 60 percent of inflation since 1933. These figures suggest that velocity has not been constant but has been rising at 1.5 percent (3.9 − 2.3) percent per annum.

---

[1]Let's use a numerical example to show that the growth rate of the product of two variables (PY) equals the sum of the growth rates of each variable:

	P	Y	PY
2001	100	500	50,000
2001	105	550	57,750
Growth rate	5%	10%	15% (= 5% + 10%)

TABLE 14.1 Real GDP (in 1996 dollars), Prices, and Money

Growth factor	*GDP (billions of 1996 prices)*	*GDP Deflator (index)*	*MI (billions)*
1933–73	13.7	13.4	67.7
1933–50	2.4	2.1	5.9
1950–80	2.9	3.3	3.5
1980–2003	2.0	1.9	3.3
Annual growth rate			
1933–73	4.0	3.9	6.5
1933–50	5.3	4.5	11.6
1950–80	3.6	4.0	4.3
1980–2003	3.1	2.9	5.3

Table 14.1 gives data for subperiods of 1933–2003. In each period, money outgrew real GDP, but again inflation was higher than that predicted by a constant velocity. When inflation is faster than predicted by the equation of exchange with constant velocity, this means that velocity is rising.

Increases in velocity magnify the effects of monetary growth on inflation.

Increases in velocity magnify the effects of monetary growth on prices. With a 2 percent growth rate of real GDP, a 2 percent growth of money pushes up prices at a 2 percent rate if velocity grows 2 percent per annum. If velocity had remained constant, a 2 percent growth rate of money would have been consistent with stable prices. With velocity growing, $\dot{P} = \dot{M} - \dot{Y} + \dot{V}$.

In fact, V has increased substantially over the long run. In 1929, V was approximately 3; in 2003 V was approximately equal to 8. The growth of the money supply combined with the rise in velocity provides an explanation for the inflationary trend of the past 70 years.

Velocity, Interest Rates, and Inflationary Expectations

The interest rate is the opportunity cost of money.

Our willingness to hold money depends on its opportunity cost. The opportunity cost of holding assets in the form of money is the interest rate. If you have $10,000 in your checking account, not earning interest, you are losing $1,000 per year at an interest rate of 10 percent. If the interest rate is 2 percent, you are losing only $200 per year. For this reason, velocity is inversely related to the interest rate. When interest rates are high, we do not wish to hold money and we turn over our money as quickly as possible. When interest rates are low, people are more willing to hold money and velocity falls.

Inflationary expectations are the rates of inflation expected to prevail in the future.

The **real interest rate** is the nominal interest rate minus the anticipated rate of inflation.

Interest rates are related to inflationary expectations. **Inflationary expectations** are the rates of inflation that people expect to occur in the future. Recall from Chapter 9 that the **real interest rate** is the nominal interest rate minus the anticipated rate of inflation. For example, if the anticipated inflation rate is 5 percent and the interest rate is 8 percent, the real interest rate is 3 percent (= 8 − 5).

High interest rates accompany high inflationary expectations.

When we anticipate more inflation, the nominal interest rate is higher. When more inflation is anticipated, lenders are less willing to lend at prevailing interest rates because they will be paid back with cheaper dollars. Borrowers want to borrow more because they can pay back their loans with cheaper dollars. Thus, rising inflationary expectations drive up nominal interest rates and, hence, velocity.

There is no way to know for sure how people form inflationary expectations. Economists offer two competing hypotheses of the way expectations are formed.

Adaptive expectations say that it takes time for people to adjust to inflation, thus creating a sustained difference between actual and anticipated inflation.

One view is that people form **adaptive expectations** concerning future inflation exclusively on the basis of what has happened in the past. For example, if the annual inflation rate has been a steady 5 percent yearly for the past ten years, people would likely expect the inflation rate to remain at 5 percent. If the inflation rate jumped to 10 percent, adaptive expectations predict that people would not immediately adjust their anticipated inflation up to 10 percent. In the first year, they might raise anticipated inflation to 7. As inflation continues at 10 percent, people would continue to adjust upward each period until they finally reach a 10 percent anticipated inflation rate. Until they reach 10 percent, actual inflation exceeds anticipated inflation.

With adaptive expectations, when the rate of inflation rises, the anticipated rate of inflation will rise by less than the actual rate. If inflation falls, anticipated inflation will fall by less than the actual decline. Only gradually will people raise or lower anticipated inflation to bring it in line with the actual inflation.

Rational expectations assume that people use not only past experience but also their predictions about the effects of present and future policy actions.

The **rational expectations** hypothesis, on the other hand, concludes that people can change their expectations more quickly. It assumes that people use all available information in forming their expectations—not only past experience but also their predictions about the effects of present and future policy actions.

Using rational expectations, people can change their inflationary expectations instantaneously on the basis of a believable policy pronouncement. If people believe that an announced change in monetary policy will raise the current 3 percent inflation rate to a permanent 6 percent rate, they will immediately raise their inflation projections to 6 percent.

Do people form their expectations by considering the effects of current and future policies? Many people and businesses do indeed study the latest economic projections, money-supply growth statistics, and budget policy changes. Banks, investment firms, labor unions, and even small investors gather information they hope will allow them to anticipate the future, suggesting that they form their expectations on the basis of the rational expectations hypothesis.

Government Spending, Deficits, and Inflation

The **federal deficit** is the excess of federal government expenditures over federal government revenues.

A third potential source of inflation is government deficits. Recall from Chapter 10 that the **federal deficit** is the excess of federal government expenditures over federal government revenues. Deficits can affect inflation through their effect on aggregate demand and on the money supply. Recall also that the federal budget has usually been in deficit.

Direct Effects Deficits caused by increases in government spending or reductions in taxes could raise aggregate demand and, thus, prices. On the other hand, deficits produced by a decline in tax revenues because of a weak economy will likely be associated with a falling rate of inflation. Furthermore, taxpayers may anticipate that larger government expenditures, and a larger deficit, will eventually lead to higher tax obligations. If so, they will be inclined to reduce current spending to save for higher future taxes and thus offset the inflationary effects of the deficit.

Monetary Effects The deficit can contribute to inflation through its effect on monetary growth. If an increase in the deficit causes the monetary authorities to expand the money supply, which happens when the Fed purchases the government debt, inflation can be the result. When the Fed purchases government debt, it injects new reserves into the banking system.

The Fed is not obligated to purchase the government debt. It can be sold entirely to the public, and there is no resulting change in bank reserves. However, a large sale of government debt to the public could raise the demand for credit without any increase in the supply of credit to the banking system, and this could drive up interest rates. Accordingly, the Fed is often tempted, for the sake of holding down interest rates, to buy the government debt.

If the Fed buys government debt, the money supply increases.

Figure 14.4 shows that there is a positive long-run association between the increase in the deficit and inflation.

The Multiple Causes of Inflation

Whereas we can say that persistent, long-term inflation is a monetary phenomenon caused by the money supply growing faster than real GDP, each inflationary period is in reality different. Indeed, the inflation rate rose as the growth rate of the money supply rose, such as generally is the case from 1959 to 1979 and in the late 1990s and early 2000s. There are, however, exceptional periods, such as the oil shocks of the mid- and late 1970s and the late 1980s and early 1990s, where the inflation rate becomes unhinged from monetary growth. In fact, during the oil shocks of the 1970s, inflation rates far exceeded the growth rate of the money supply.

Because inflation has both supply-side and demand-side causes, we cannot explain it simply; rather, the explanation depends on the circumstances.

The next chapter examines macroeconomic policy. It explains how we might use our ability to control the money supply, taxes, and government spending to moderate the business cycle and to attack problems of unemployment and inflation.

FIGURE 14.4 The Relationship Between Deficits and Inflation (Five-Year Changes)

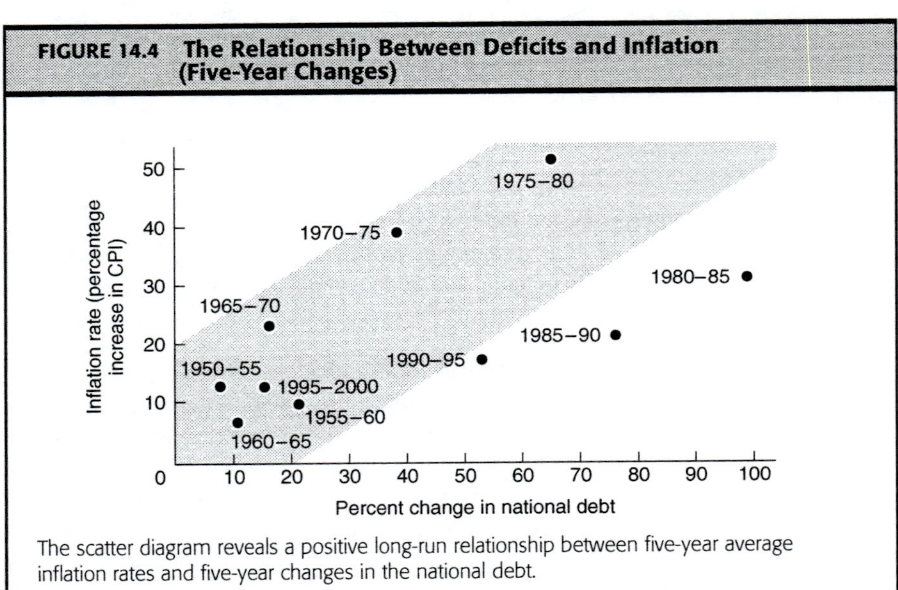

The scatter diagram reveals a positive long-run relationship between five-year average inflation rates and five-year changes in the national debt.

Summary

1. Inflation is a general increase in prices; hyperinflation is a runaway increase in prices. The inflation rate is measured by price indexes—the Consumer Price Index and the GDP deflator.
2. Economic theory must explain why inflation has been present since the early 1930s, reaching double-digit figures in the 1970s and early 1980s.
3. Inflation redistributes income when unanticipated, harms efficiency, and can affect output and employment.
4. The two types of inflation are demand-side inflation and supply-side inflation. In the case of demand-side inflation, both prices and output rise together. In the case of supply-side inflation, prices rise and output and employment fall. In the case of moderate inflation, it is difficult to distinguish demand-side from supply-side inflation.
5. Persistent inflation is a monetary phenomenon. Excess monetary growth occurs when the money supply grows more rapidly than real GDP. If velocity is rising, monetary growth has a larger impact on inflation.
6. Velocity rises with the interest rate because the interest rate is the opportunity cost of holding money. Interest rates rise with anticipated inflation.
7. Inflationary expectations may be formed adaptively or rationally. If expectations are formed adaptively, people are slow to adjust inflationary expectations.
8. The rise in the federal deficit has had a long-run inflationary effect.

Questions and Problems

1. Explain why supply shocks are unlikely to lead to persistent inflation.
2. "All inflation is cost-side inflation. During inflations, costs of production rise and push up prices throughout the economy." Evaluate.
3. How does one determine excess monetary growth? How does this vary with velocity?
4. Explain why only unanticipated inflation redistributes income. Doesn't inflation always redistribute income from creditors to borrowers?
5. Explain why rising prices don't necessarily mean declining living standards.
6. Use hyperinflation to show how inflation reduces economic efficiency.
7. The examples in this chapter explain what happens when there is *unanticipated inflation*. Explain what happens to unemployment in the short and long run when there is *unanticipated deflation*.

CHAPTER 15

MACRO STABILIZATION POLICY

Chapter Preview

The major debate in macroeconomics is over stabilization policy. Should monetary and fiscal authorities actively seek to tame the business cycle, or should the economy be left on its own? Should we follow "rules" or "discretion"? This chapter explains how stabilization policy works and the arguments in favor of activist policy and against. We begin with the two instrument of macroeconomic stabilization: fiscal and monetary policy.

Macroeconomic Stabilization

Fiscal policy refers to changes in government expenditures or tax rates made for the purpose of achieving macroeconomic goals. **Monetary policy** refers to changes in the money supply and credit conditions for the same purpose.

Fiscal policy refers to changes in government expenditures or tax schedules made for the purpose of achieving macroeconomic goals. **Monetary policy** refers to changes in the money supply and credit conditions for the same purpose.

There is no single goal of macroeconomic policy. We would like to have full employment, stable prices, and steady real GDP growth, and to avoid the ups and downs of the business cycle (especially the downs). We want low interest rates. We would like to maintain the international value of the dollar and to achieve growing world trade. The full-employment target was established as a national economic goal by the Employment Act of 1946. Although we do not like high inflation (and the accompanying high interest rates), price stability has not been formally entrenched as a legislative goal.

Policy activism is the deliberate manipulation of fiscal and monetary policy to iron out fluctuations in the business cycle.

Discretionary policy is the setting of monetary and fiscal targets by policymakers, based on their best judgments.

Activism

Policy activism is the use of discretionary fiscal and monetary policy to iron out the business cycle. Its objective is to expand output and employment during the recession phase and to moderate inflation during the expansion, or boom, phase.

Discretionary policy is dictated by human judgment. It sets monetary and fiscal policy by using the best judgments of policymakers. Although the goals of discretionary monetary or fiscal policy are complex, they can be viewed in terms of inflationary and deflationary gaps.

Who exactly are the economic policymakers? On the executive side, the principal policymakers are the Fed, the Treasury, the Office of Management and Budget, the Council of Economic Advisors, and the White House staff. The Treasury is responsible for debt management, the balance of payments, and estimating government revenues. The Office of Management and Budget prepares the annual budget and coordinates government expenditures. The Council of Economic Advisors estimates GDP growth and advises the president on economic affairs. On the congressional side, several committees in the House and Senate, a joint committee, and congressional leaders are responsible for economic policy. The House Ways and Means Committee is responsible for revenue bills and Social Security. The House Appropriations Committee is responsible for government expenditures. The House Banking, Finance, and Urban Affairs Committee is responsible for price control legislation, and the House Education and Labor Committee is responsible for human resource policy. In the Senate, the Finance Committee and the Appropriations Committee are the two most important economic policymaking bodies.

The Fed conducts monetary policy on an ongoing basis through open-market operations and periodic changes in reserve requirements and discount rates. Initiatives for tax reform are prepared by the Department of the Treasury for action by various House and Senate subcommittees.

Inflationary and Deflationary Gaps

Macroeconomic equilibrium occurs where the *SRAS* and *AD* curves intersect. The equilibrium level of output may be larger or smaller than the natural level of output. The equilibrium output, y, in Panel A of Figure 15.1 falls short of the natural level of output, y_n. In Panel B, the equilibrium level of output, y', exceeds y_n. Differences between actual output and y_n indicate a **deflationary gap** or an **inflationary gap.**

A **deflationary gap** exists when the equilibrium level of output falls short of the natural level of output.

An **inflationary gap** exists when the equilibrium level of output exceeds the natural level of output.

A deflationary gap exists when the equilibrium level of output falls short of the natural level of output. An inflationary gap exists when the equilibrium level of output exceeds the natural level of output.

If a deflationary gap exists, as in Panel A, the unemployment rate exceeds the natural rate of unemployment. If an inflationary gap exists, as in Panel B, the unemployment rate falls short of the natural rate of unemployment. Deflationary and inflationary gaps set into motion movements in the price level. When a deflationary gap is present, the unemployment rate exceeds the natural rate; the rate of inflation of wages and prices will begin to drop. When an inflationary gap is present, the unemployment rate is less than the natural rate. Inflationary pressures build up in labor markets, and the rate of increase in wages and prices will accelerate.

An **expansionary monetary policy** increases aggregate demand by increasing the money supply; an **expansionary fiscal policy** increases aggregate demand by raising government spending and/or lowering taxes.

Inflationary and deflationary gaps dictate the choice of discretionary policy. If a deflationary gap is present, discretionary policy should choose an expansionary fiscal or monetary policy—a policy that increases aggregate demand. A contractionary fiscal or monetary policy is called for when an inflationary gap is present. An **expansionary monetary or fiscal policy** increases aggregate demand by increasing

FIGURE 15.1 Inflationary and Deflationary Gaps

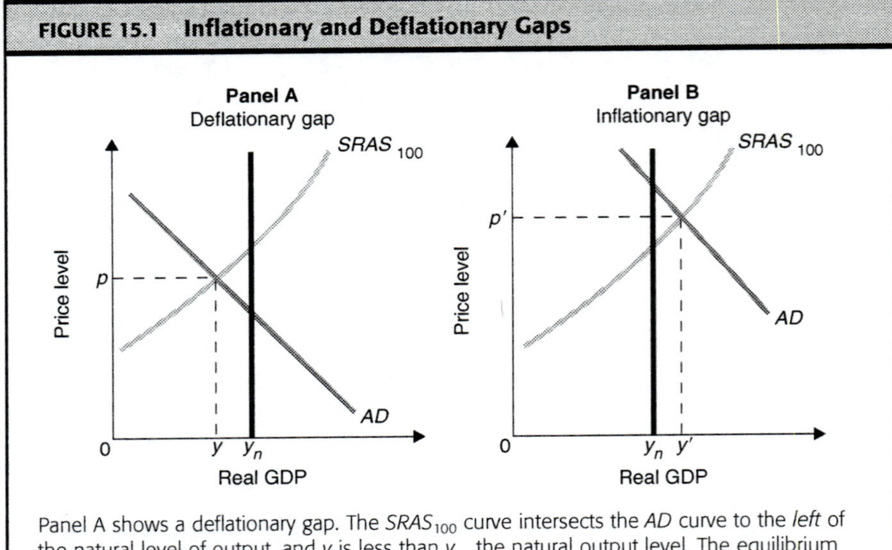

Panel A shows a deflationary gap. The $SRAS_{100}$ curve intersects the *AD* curve to the *left* of the natural level of output, and *y* is less than y_n, the natural output level. The equilibrium price level is *p*.

Panel B shows an inflationary gap. The $SRAS_p$ curve intersects the *AD* curve to the *right* of the natural level of output, and *y′* exceeds y_n. The equilibrium price level is *p′*.

A **contractionary monetary policy** lowers aggregate demand by reducing the money supply; a **contractionary fiscal policy** lowers aggregate demand by lowering government spending and/or raising taxes.

the money supply (monetary policy) or by raising government spending and/or lowering tax rates (fiscal policy). A **contractionary monetary or fiscal policy** lowers aggregate demand by reducing the money supply (monetary policy) or by lowering government spending or raising tax rates (fiscal policy).

Figure 15.2 shows how expansionary policy can be used to close either inflationary or deflationary gaps. Both work by manipulating aggregate demand.

Fiscal Policy

An **entitlement program** requires the federal government to pay benefits to anyone who meets the eligibility requirements of the program.

Payments for entitlement programs and tax collections depend on the general state of the economy.

Governments can affect aggregate demand through government spending and the tax system. Fiscal policy manipulates government spending and taxes to achieve macroeconomic goals. Whether or not intended, government spending and taxation affect aggregate demand.

Many fiscal actions take place automatically and require no policy decisions—as in the case of an **entitlement program,** such as Social Security and unemployment compensation. An entitlement program requires the government to pay benefits to anyone who meet eligibility requirements. Recipients need only demonstrate that they qualify under established rules.

Once the rules are set, the government does not determine the magnitude of entitlement payments. Instead, payments depend on economic conditions. Once income tax rates are set, government tax revenues depend on economic conditions.

FIGURE 15.2 Removing Deflationary and Inflationary Gaps

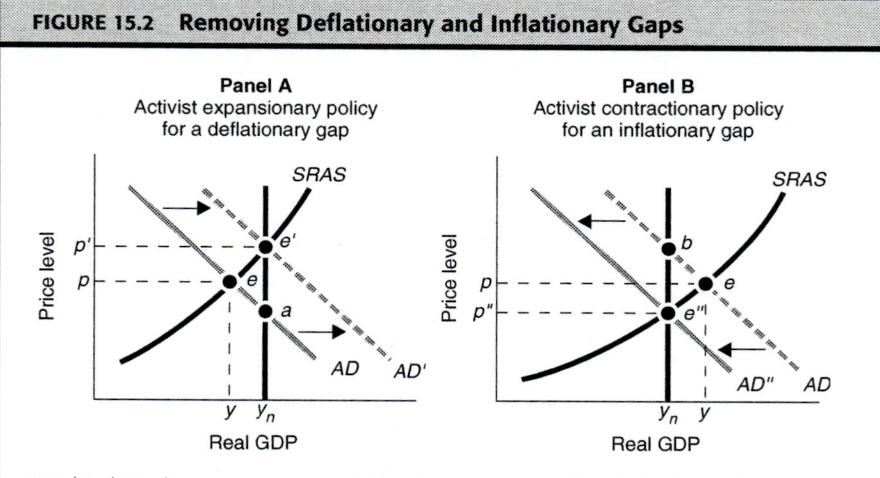

Panel A shows how expansionary activist policy could be used to eliminate a deflationary gap. If the aggregate demand curve could be shifted to the right (from *AD* to *AD′*), the economy could be restored to the natural rate of output, y_n. Panel B shows how contractionary policy could be used to eliminate an inflationary gap. By reducing aggregate demand (from *AD* to *AD″*), the economy could be restored to the natural rate of output.

Other government revenues and expenditures are determined by deliberate, discretionary decisions. Rules concerning eligibility for entitlement programs can be changed; income tax rates can be raised or lowered; major new defense expenditures or public works programs can be started.

Automatic stabilizers are government spending or taxation actions that take place without any deliberate government control and that automatically dampen the business cycle.

Discretionary fiscal policies are government spending and taxation actions that have been taken deliberately to achieve specified macroeconomic goals.

Government spending and taxation can be either **automatic stabilizers** or **discretionary fiscal policies.** Automatic stabilizers are government spending or taxation actions that take place without any deliberate government control and that automatically dampen the business cycle. Discretionary fiscal policies are government spending and taxation actions that have been taken deliberately to achieve specified macroeconomic goals.

Automatic Stabilizers

The tax system and entitlement programs act as automatic stabilizers that moderate business cycles.

The Tax System The amount of income tax revenues government collects is determined by multiplying the average tax rate by the economy's taxable income. If an economy has an average tax rate of 20 percent and if total taxable income is $100 billion, the government will collect $20 billion in income taxes. If total taxable income rises to $150 billion, the government will collect $30 billion. The amount of income tax collected rises and falls with income.

People consume out of disposable income. If the economy goes into a recession with falling income, tax collections fall, thereby moderating the fall in disposable income and thus cushioning the drop in consumption. In an inflationary boom, incomes rise, and tax collections rise to moderate the increase in consumption spending. The tax system cushions fluctuations in consumption by having tax collections fall during bad times and rise during good times.

Unemployment Compensation and Welfare Payments During cyclical downturns, more people are eligible for unemployment benefits. Moreover, families whose incomes decline because of fewer hours of work or unemployment become eligible for welfare assistance. Unemployment compensation and increased welfare payments prevent consumption expenditures from falling as much as they would without these programs.

Automatic stabilizers—the tax system, welfare payments, and unemployment compensation—soften the effects of the business cycle.

Unemployment compensation and welfare programs also moderate the business cycle on the upswing. Welfare recipients leave the welfare and unemployment compensation rolls as they find jobs, and increased deductions from payrolls (to state and local programs and union unemployment funds) reduce the amount of disposable income going to employed workers.

Automatic stabilizers cannot fully neutralize the business cycle. If the economy is operating at full employment and investment falls, the automatic stabilizers will neutralize only a part of the decline in output. Unemployment compensation and other welfare payments restore only a portion of lost disposable income. Falling tax collections restore only a portion of the decline in consumption spending.

Discretionary Fiscal Policy

Automatic stabilizers can only moderate cyclical instability, not eliminate it. Discretionary fiscal policy can be used to attack the business cycle directly. The aim of discretionary fiscal policy is to eliminate inflationary and deflationary gaps.

Autonomous changes in taxes and government spending are changes in tax rates or government spending that do not automatically occur because of changes in income.

Discretionary fiscal policy works through changes in tax rates and autonomous government spending.

Discretionary fiscal policy operates through **autonomous changes** in tax rates and government expenditures. Autonomous changes can be contrasted with automatic stabilizers. Many changes in government spending and taxation are *not autonomous.* They are the automatic stabilizers we have just discussed. An autonomous change in government spending or taxation occurs not because of changes in income but because of changes in policy. *Discretionary fiscal policy works through autonomous changes in taxes and in government spending.*

Expansionary fiscal policy is used to eliminate a deflationary gap. Expansionary fiscal policy consists of raising discretionary government spending, relaxing eligibility requirements for entitlements, and/or lowering tax rates. If tax rates or discretionary spending is changed by the right amounts, the aggregate demand curve could be shifted to the right to intersect the short-run aggregate supply (*SRAS*) curve at e' in Figure 15.2 at the natural level of output.

Contractionary fiscal policy can be used to close an inflationary gap. Contractionary fiscal policy consists of lowering discretionary government spending, tightening eligibility requirements for entitlements, and/or raising tax rates. If tax rates were raised or discretionary government spending reduced by the right amounts, the aggregate demand curve could be shifted to the left to intersect the *SRAS* curve at the natural level of output.

Fiscal policy affects the federal deficit. If it causes expenditures to rise more than revenues, the federal deficit increases. As the previous chapter showed, deficits affect inflation, and the burden of the deficit affects generations differently. Figure 15.4 shows the difficulty of separating the effects of automatic stabilizers from discretionary fiscal policy.

Monetary Policy

Monetary policy is the deliberate control of the money supply for the purpose of achieving macroeconomic goals.

Monetary policy is the deliberate control of the money supply and, in some cases, of credit conditions for the purpose of achieving macroeconomic goals, such as a certain rate of unemployment or inflation.

Chapter 13 introduced the Fed's three instruments of monetary policy—open-market operations, discount-rate changes, and changes in reserve requirements. The Fed controls the money supply through the commercial banking system. When the Fed injects new reserves, banks receive excess reserves that they loan out in credit markets. When the Fed withdraws reserves, banks make fewer loans, and the credit market tightens. As credit eases, market interest rates fall. As credit tightens, interest rates rise. The Fed uses its control of interest rates for discretionary monetary policy.

One of the most complicated relationships in macroeconomics is that between money and interest rates. As was shown in Chapter 9, the interest rate is the opportunity cost of holding assets in money form. As the opportunity cost of money rises (as the interest rate rises), the quantity of money demanded falls. An economywide demand curve for money is shown in Figure 15.3. A larger quantity of money is demanded at a low interest rate. The negatively sloped demand curve for money is also called the *liquidity preference curve* because people are demanding liquidity when they demand money. The supply of money is determined by the Fed. In Figure 15.3, the supply of money set by the Fed is drawn as a vertical line at the amount set by the Fed.

Through its control of bank reserves, the Fed is able to make credit either easier or tighter. In this way, the Fed is able to affect market interest rates.

Panel A of Figure 15.3 shows that when the supply of money is *M* and the demand for money is *LP*, the money market is in equilibrium when the interest rate is *r*. If the supply of money increases from *M* to *M′*, additional credit is being supplied and downward pressure is put on interest rates. The new equilibrium interest rate is *r′* when the supply of money increases to *M′*. In effect, the lower interest rate is required to induce the public to hold the larger stock of money.

Lowering interest rates through an increase in the money supply leads to greater investment (Panel B), as Chapter 9 showed. Business firms have a variety of investment projects that they would like to carry out. Panel C shows the impact of a lower interest rate on the economy. The amount of desired investment increases, shifting the aggregate demand curve out. This, in turn, increases real GDP.

Monetary or Fiscal Policy?

The two major activist policy instruments are monetary policy and fiscal policy. The presence of more than one policy instrument means that policymakers could select

FIGURE 15.3 Expansionary Monetary Policy

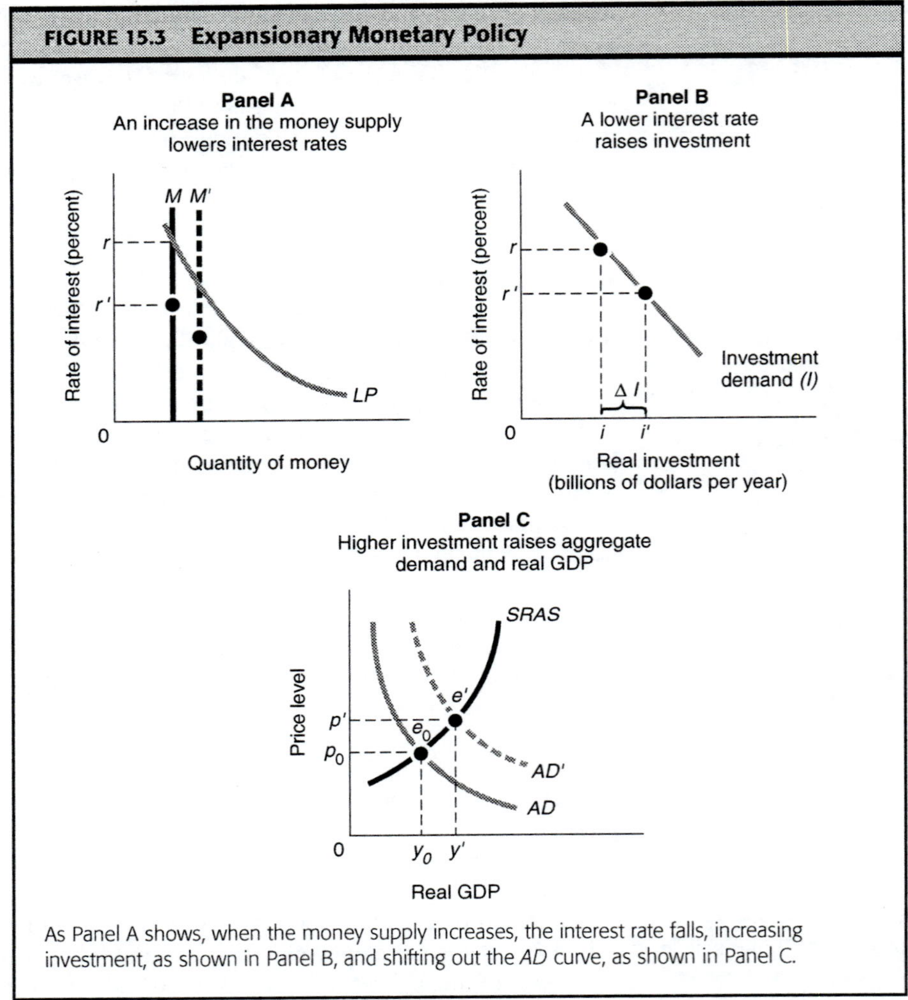

As Panel A shows, when the money supply increases, the interest rate falls, increasing investment, as shown in Panel B, and shifting out the *AD* curve, as shown in Panel C.

the appropriate blend of monetary growth, government spending, and tax rates to achieve their macroeconomic goals.

Monetary policy is conducted by the Fed. The Fed is insulated from current political pressures, but its independence is not complete. Although the Fed must take major political factors into consideration, it is more independent of political pressures than the president, the Treasury, or the Congress. The Fed is in a position to act quickly, quietly buying or selling government securities, to change the money supply. The Fed can buy or sell government securities daily, largely hidden from public view. On a more visible level, the Fed can raise or lower the discount rate, change reserve requirements, and even impose credit controls.

The two instruments of fiscal policy are discretionary government spending and tax policy.

The two instruments of fiscal policy are discretionary government spending and tax policy. The president submits spending budgets to Congress, but only Congress can grant actual spending authorization. Presidents must either sign or veto the spending bills Congress approves. They do not have the authority to cut out only parts of approved spending packages but must accept or reject the entire bill. Although Congress has sometimes sought to gear the total amount of federal spending to specific macroeconomic goals, this approach has not worked well in practice. Given the current appropriation system, it is very difficult to conduct macroeconomic policy by manipulating the amount of federal government spending.

Example 15.1 shows the protracted federal budgeting process.

Congress has the final word on tax policy. Proposals for tax changes can be made by the Treasury or can originate within the Congress. The current tax system is very complex and has been influenced by special-interest groups. Congress has succeeded in passing a number of tax bills that were specifically designed to achieve macroeconomic goals. Taxes were lowered in 1964 and 1981 to stimulate economic activity. The tax reform passed in 1986 was designed to change tax rates and deductions rather than to manipulate aggregate demand. The 1993 tax act of President Clinton raised tax rates for the purpose of reducing the deficit. The tax cuts of 2001 and 2003 were again designed to increase aggregate demand.

Monetary policy is the most flexible policy instrument.

Because of the Fed's independence and the flexibility of open-market operations, the money supply is the most flexible policy instrument. Monetary policy is the

EXAMPLE 15.1 WHY DISCRETIONARY FISCAL POLICY IS DIFFICULT

The federal budgeting process begins with the formulation and submission of the president's budget to Congress according to the following schedule:

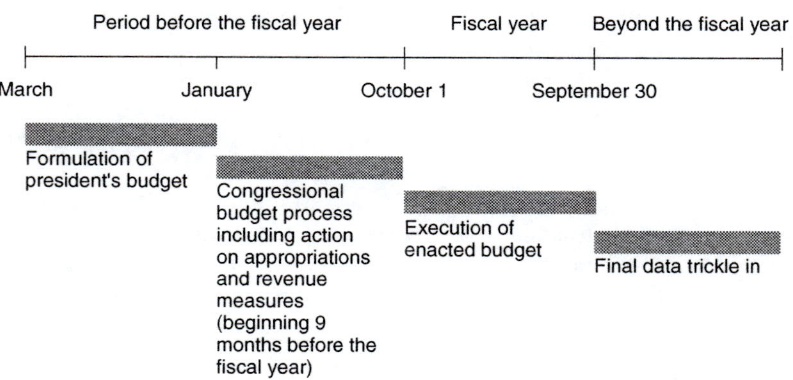

A minimum lead time of 20 months is required between the planning and execution of the federal budget. This lag makes it difficult to conduct discretionary fiscal policy. Final data trickle in throughout the following year; for example, final GDP data are in nine months after the year ends.

With such substantial leads and lags, most economists agree that fiscal policy lacks the necessary flexibility to control the business cycle.

most frequently used instrument of activist policy because of its greater flexibility and independence. Because of the inflexibility and uncontrollability of federal spending, the major instrument of fiscal policy has been tax policy.

There appears to be a consensus that tax policy affects long-term economic growth. If the tax system penalizes innovation and risk taking with exceptionally high income tax rates, long-term economic growth suffers. If the tax system encourages business to acquire modern capital equipment (through various tax incentives), economic growth is promoted.

Recessions, Tax Cuts, and Deficits: The Policymaker's Dilemma

Chapter 10 explained federal government revenues, outlays, and deficits. The federal deficit increases by the amount outlays exceed revenue. If, for example, outlays equal $100 billion and revenues equal $90 billion, the deficit is $10 billion and the federal debt grows by that amount. The rate of increase of the deficit equals the growth rate of outlays minus the growth rate of revenues. If both are growing at the same rate (say 5 percent), there is no change in the deficit. In order for the deficit to be reduced, revenues must grow faster than outlays.

The size of the deficit therefore depends both on the business cycle and upon discretionary fiscal policy. During recessions, automatic stabilizers reduce tax revenues and increase outlays, thereby raising deficits. During periods of prosperity, automatic stabilizers increase tax revenues and reduce outlays.

The size of the deficit therefore depends both on the business cycle and upon discretionary fiscal policy. During recessions, automatic stabilizers reduce tax revenues and increase outlays, thereby raising deficits. During periods of prosperity, automatic stabilizers increase tax revenues and reduce outlays.

The diagram on discretionary policy directs that an expansionary fiscal policy (lower tax rates and more discretionary spending) should be applied during periods of deflationary gaps; that is during recessions. However, the use of expansionary policy during recessions means higher government deficits.

The size of the deficit is obviously affected by discretionary government spending and by autonomous changes in tax rates. If discretionary spending increases and tax rates are lowered, all other things remaining the same, the size of the deficit should increase.

The policymaker's dilemma therefore is that they may increase the size of the deficit substantially when they apply expansionary policy.

The policymaker's dilemma therefore is that they may increase the size of the deficit substantially when they apply expansionary policy.

But if policymakers fail to use expansionary policy during a recession, the deficit will increase on its own due to the effects of automatic stabilizers.

Keynesian Budget Philosophy

The **Keynesian Revolution** argues that policymakers must create rising deficits during recessions.

The **Keynesian Revolution,** which traces its origins to John Maynard Keynes's 1936 publication, *General Theory of Employment, Interest, and Money,* argues that policymakers must accept rising deficits during recessions. By pursuing an expansionary fiscal policy, they can eliminate the deflationary gap and raise employment and output. As employment and output increase, the automatic stabilizers will reduce the size of the deficit.

Keynesian budgetary policy was formally embraced with the passage of the 1964 Johnson tax cut (originally proposed by President Kennedy). Since that time, most governments of the industrialized countries have accepted the Keynesian budget philosophy.

Notice that as the Keynesian budget philosophy suggests tax reductions, preferably before a recession hits; policymakers should try to anticipate and hence prevent recessions. This is a tall order for policymakers. The need for a tax cut may not be evident before the recession hits. Even if it were properly anticipated, the time required for passage of the tax cut would be long. Therefore, it is quite likely that tax cuts must be passed during recessions when the apparent effect on the deficit will be most dramatic.

Supply-Side Economics

Supply-side economics maintains that tax cuts, particularly cuts in marginal tax rates, will substantially increase output and employment by enhancing work effort and risk taking.

Supply-side economics was prominent during the presidency of Ronald Reagan. If the cuts in tax rates are properly devised, it may even be possible to cut tax rates without there being any increase in deficits. The increased income-tax collections due to the stronger economy may offset the tax revenues lost to lower marginal tax rates. The Reagan tax cut of 1981 was, in fact, designed to cut marginal tax rates (which were in excess of 50 percent, in many cases) to promote economic activity.

Supply-side economics is a relative of Keynesian budget philosophy, which also states that tax cuts will increase output and employment and hence eventually increase tax revenues. The difference is that supply-side economists expect very large income and tax revenue increases from tax cuts, while the Keynesian budget philosophy suggests that the revenue losses of tax cuts would not be fully offset by revenue increase from the higher incomes.

Empirical Evidence and Dynamic Scoring

Figure 15.4 shows federal revenues and outlays since 1961. So that the effects of recessions and tax cuts and increases can be clearly seen, only the *growth rates* of revenues and outlays are shown. (Remember, the deficit increases when the growth rate of outlays exceeds the growth rate of revenues.) Years in which recession troughs occurred are shown as solid lines, years of tax cuts are shown as dotted lines, and years of tax increases are also shown. What can we learn from almost a half-century of tax policy and deficits?

First, recessions have a clear negative impact on deficits. During each recession, the rate of growth of federal receipts has dropped, but revenue growth has often remained positive even during recessions. The absolute size of federal revenues has declined (recorded negative growth) with the recession of 1970, the recession of 1982 and the recession of 2001. The size of federal revenues continued to grow during the recessions of 1961, 1975, and 1991. Even during bad economic times, government revenues generally continue to rise.

Second, over the past half-century, there have been no years in which the size of federal outlays has decreased. The question therefore is not whether federal spending will rise or fall but by how much it will rise. Therefore, with federal

FIGURE 15.4 Growth Rates of Federal Receipts and Outlays

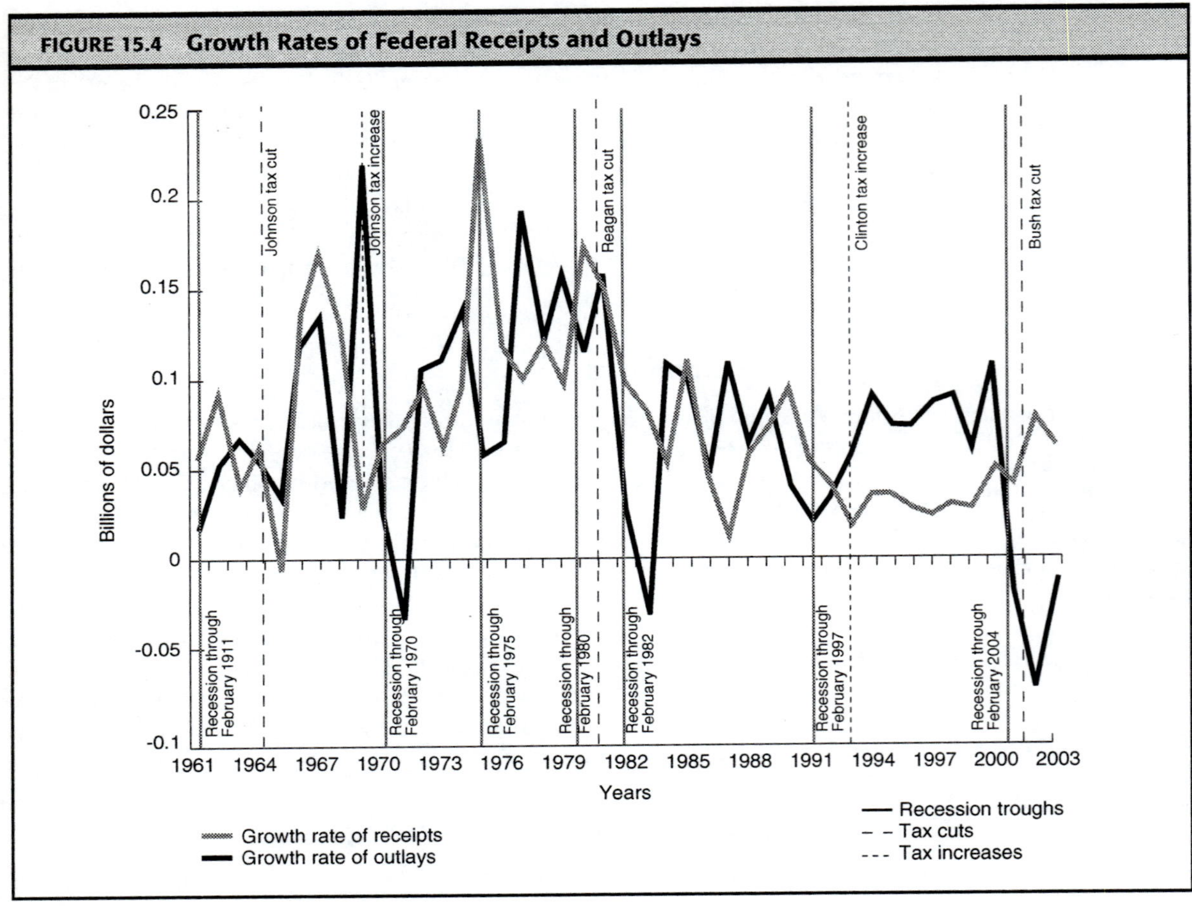

receipts being pushed down even to negative growth during recessions and federal expenditures apparently immune from actual cuts, the deficit tends to grow dramatically during recessions.

Third, there is no apparent tendency to dampen the growth of expenditures during economic upturns. As revenue growth recover from recessionary lows, expenditure rates appear to rise as well. Thus, there is no tendency to run surpluses during prosperity, as Keynes had originally hoped. In fact, Keynes promoted the idea of a cyclically balanced budget.

A **cyclically balanced budget** is one in which the deficits of recession years are offset by surpluses, from expansion years, and there is no long-term increase in the debt insofar as surpluses cancel deficits.

A **cyclically balanced budget** is one in which the deficits of recession years are offset by surpluses from expansion years, and there is no long-term increase in the debt insofar as surpluses cancel deficits.

Fourth, the growth rate of tax revenue tends to fall when taxes are cut, just as they tend to increase when taxes are increased. The growth rate of tax revenues fell after the 1964, 1981, and 1991 tax cuts and rose with the tax increases of 1969 and 1993. Tax cuts need not mean, however, a drop in the level of tax collections. Tax revenues continued to rise after the 1964 and 1982 tax cuts; only their rate of increase fell. The 2001 tax cuts were followed by an actual decline in tax revenues, but this decline was also a consequence of the 1990–1991 recession.

Fifth, a few years after each tax cut, the low growth rate of revenues has reverted to its earlier higher rate. Similarly, the high rate of growth of revenues has reverted to lower rates a few years after tax increases. This suggests that the Keynesian budget and supply-side budget approaches are correct in predicting that tax increases promote economic growth and hence rising tax revenues and that tax increases do the opposite.

Sixth, the period from 1994 to 1998, during which we had a Democratic president and a Republican Congress, was an unusual period of low expenditure growth. During this period, expenditures grew at 5 percent per annum or less before reverting to their more "normal" 5 to 10 percent range. During this same period, economic prosperity and the 1993 tax increase caused revenues to grow at a fast pace. The reduction in the deficit during this period (to an actual surplus in the late 1990s) was therefore caused primarily by low growth rates of federal spending. If federal spending had grown at its more normal rate, there would have been little, if any, deficit reduction.

The fact that tax cuts eventually stimulate economic activity suggests that policy makers must consider the eventual effects of this stimulation on future tax revenues. If tax rates are cut by 10 percent, it would be incorrect to assume that revenues would henceforth be less by 10 percent. If the tax cut causes the economy to grow faster and hence the tax base to increase, the loss of revenue would be less, possibly much less, than the 10 percent.

Dynamic scoring means a projection of future revenues and deficits taking into account the simulative effect of lower tax rates on economic activity.

Policymakers use dynamic scoring to adjust for the simulative effects of tax cuts on future tax revenues. **Dynamic scoring** means a projection of future revenues and deficits taking into account the simulative effect of lower tax rates on economic activity.

Politicians heatedly debate the effect of tax cuts on the deficit and whether the resulting deficit really matters in some way. We cannot foresee the future and therefore cannot do perfect dynamic scoring, but history tells us that tax cuts have been followed by lengthy periods of prosperity. Two extended economic expansions, after 1964 and after 1981, followed significant tax cuts. The 2004 presidential election campaign will involve a heated debate over the wisdom of the Bush tax cuts of 2001 and 2003. Both Keynesian and supply-side budget philosophy, however, dictate tax cuts during periods of recession.

Self-Correction Instead of Activism?

Modern Keynesians believe in the use of activist policy; monetarists believe that activist policy is, at best, ineffective, and, at worst, destabilizes the economy.

The contemporary macroeconomic debate is over the use of activist policy to stabilize the economy. Modern Keynesians believe in the use of activist policy; monetarists believe that activist policy is, at best, ineffective, and, at worst, destabilizes the economy. Rational expectations economists believe that activist monetary policy will, at best, have only a short-run effect.

The self-correcting mechanism teaches that there is a strong tendency for the economy to operate at the natural rate of unemployment in the long run. If the economy happens to be at an unemployment rate above the natural rate, falling wages and prices will eventually return it to the natural rate; if the economy is below the natural rate, rising wages and prices will raise unemployment to the natural rate. The self-correcting mechanism says that the private economy can generate enough steam on its own power, through changing wages and prices, to reach the natural rate of unemployment. No change in monetary or fiscal policy is required.

There is widespread but not complete agreement among economists that the self-correcting mechanism works. Even Keynes felt that, in the very long run, the depression economies of the 1930s would eventually have returned to full employment. If there is agreement that the self-correcting mechanism returns the economy to the natural rate, why do some economists advocate active monetary and fiscal policy to ensure full employment? Figure 15.5 compares the nonactivist and activist approaches. It shows that societies can choose between doing something actively to close inflationary or deflationary gaps, or they can wait for these gaps to close by themselves.

The approach of waiting for self-correction to work is called *nonactivism.*

Nonactivism

Nonactivism calls for fixed monetary and fiscal policy rules.

The policy alternative to activism is nonactivism, or the observance of policy rules. **Nonactivism** rejects activist monetary or fiscal policy. Instead of deliberately altering

FIGURE 15.5 The Policy Options: Self-Correction versus Activism

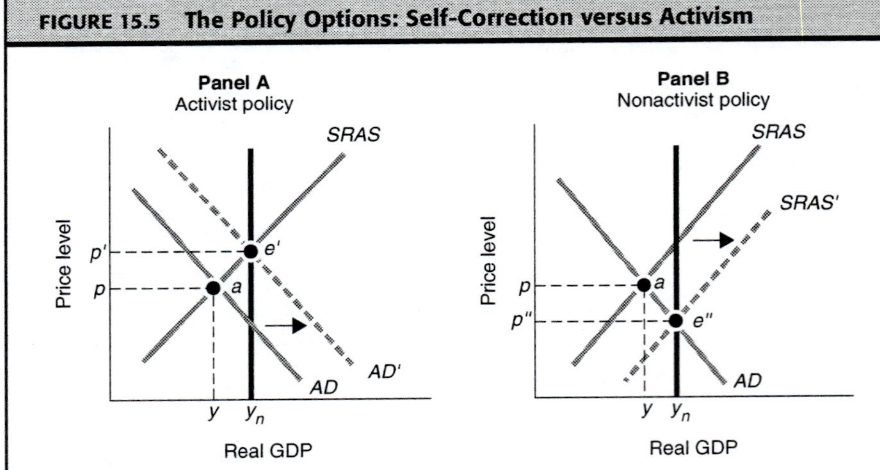

Panel A shows how activist policy can be used to eliminate a deflationary gap. The economy is initially operating at point *a* in a deflationary gap. Expansionary monetary or fiscal policy increases aggregate demand (shifting *AD* to *AD'*), causing the economy to produce a greater output y_n, and the price level to rise from *p* to *p'*.

Panel B shows the nonactivist approach to restoring equilibrium through the self-correcting mechanism. The economy is initially operating at point *a* in a deflationary gap. As a consequence of operating below the natural level of output, the price level falls, and firms supply more output. The short-run aggregate supply curve shifts to the right, from *SRAS* to *SRAS'*. The price level continues to fall until the natural level of output is restored, so the aggregate supply shifts until the economy reaches point *e''*, where it is producing y_n at the new price level *p''*.

monetary and fiscal policy in response to changing economic conditions, fixed rules should be observed.

Nonactivists argue that it is better to do nothing in the face of demand or supply shocks—let the self-correcting mechanism do its work without interference. In arguing for this position, the nonactivists must show that activist policies actually may make the business cycle worse.

Nonactivist Rules

In place of activist monetary and fiscal policies, the nonactivists propose to use fixed rules that monetary and fiscal authorities are obliged to follow.

The two nonactivist rules are fixed monetary growth and a balanced budget over the cycle.

The two most prominent fixed rules suggested by the nonactivists are the following:

1. There should be a fixed monetary growth rule that requires a constant growth of the money supply year after year, regardless of prevailing economic conditions. The money growth rate should be set equal, or nearly equal, to the long-run growth rate of real GDP.
2. The federal budget should be balanced over the business cycle. Surpluses during the recovery phase should wipe out deficits during the recession phase. Government spending should be dictated by the need for public spending, not by the needs of discretionary fiscal policy.

Monetarists argue that such a stable monetary and fiscal framework would provide an ideal setting for economic stability; the self-correcting mechanism would work smoothly and efficiently. A stable monetary and fiscal framework would rule out major destabilizing policy blunders, and cyclical disturbances should be minor and of short duration.

Critique of Activism

Critics of activism contend that monetary and fiscal authorities run the risk of actually destabilizing the economy. They may actually use the wrong medicine.

Nonactivists have made three separate attacks on activism. Monetarists maintain that activist policies fail to improve the business cycle and actually make it worse. Rational expectations economists maintain that activist monetary policies affect only inflation, not unemployment. Real business cycle theorists claim that cycles are caused by technological shocks and hence cannot be controlled by discretionary policy.

The Economy Has Natural Stability Monetarists emphasize the natural stability of the economy. They argue that activist policy has disrupted the natural stability of the economy, and they present historical evidence to support their claim. Monetarists Milton Friedman and Anna Schwartz, in their massive study of the American business cycle over a century's time, concluded that discretionary policy itself has been a major source of instability.[1] According to their analysis, the

[1]Milton Friedman and Anna Schwartz, *A Monetary History of the United States, 1867–1967* (Princeton, N.J.: Princeton University Press, 1963).

Great Depression was a normal business downturn that was transformed into a disaster by government blunders:

1. From 1929 to 1933, monetary authorities allowed the money supply to fall by 25 percent. If the money supply had been held constant in the early 1930s, falling prices would have raised the real money supply and the economy would have expanded.
2. Various government actions taken by Roosevelt's New Deal caused wages and prices to rise after 1933, even though there was mass unemployment. Yet the self-correcting mechanism required falling wages and prices. New Deal policies aimed, however, for higher wages and prices. The power of labor unions was increased; and business firms were given more monopoly power and were encouraged to raise prices and, indirectly, to restrict output.
3. In 1937, the Federal Reserve System doubled reserve requirements; although the money supply should expand when there is massive unemployment. The increase in the reserve requirement brought the needed money growth to a halt and sent the economy into another recession within the Great Depression.
4. Large tax increases were enacted in 1932 and 1937. Enacting tax increases during periods of massive unemployment is not appropriate activist policy.

Monetarists point to the policy blunders of the 1930s as the most spectacular destabilizing effects of activist policies. They cite numerous other instances where activist policies have had destabilizing, rather than the sought-after stabilizing, effects. They concede that the monetary policy of the postwar era has avoided the more disastrous blunders of earlier years. In fact, monetarists argue that the major reason for the dampening of the business cycle after World War II was the more stable monetary growth of this period. By avoiding dramatic swings in monetary growth, they argue, monetary authorities have made the economy more stable.

Monetarists claim that the major cause of greater economic stability after World War II was the more stable growth of the money supply.

Devising Activist Policies Is Difficult Monetarists argue that there are strong reasons to expect destabilizing activist policies. The effect of a change in monetary growth will be felt only after a period of time. To devise appropriate policy, the length of the lag must be known, and policymakers must be able to anticipate future economic conditions. Research shows that the effect on real output and unemployment of an increase in the growth of the money supply will be felt from six months to two years later. Monetary authorities can never be sure when the change in monetary growth will begin to affect the economy. An expansionary monetary policy, designed to cure unemployment, may end up creating inflation. When this occurs, the activist policy is destabilizing.

Monetarists conclude that activism can be destabilizing.

The presence of lags makes it very important to anticipate the business cycle. If policymakers know six months in advance that a recession is coming, it would be much easier to devise countercyclical policy, but recessions have different characteristics in terms of length and predictability. Policymakers do their best to anticipate changes, but they, like everyone else, are uncertain prophets. Accordingly, activist policies must be implemented without knowing what phase the business cycle will be in when the effects of the policy ultimately are felt.

The rational expectations school argues that countercyclical policies, if predictable, will have no impact on output and employment.

Rational Expectations Defeat Policy The rational expectations school argues that countercyclical policies, if predictable, will have no impact on output. Predictable activist policies will be anticipated by economic agents, who will understand that expansionary policies mean more inflation. The aggregate supply curve will shift immediately to the natural rate, albeit at a higher rate of inflation. Output and employment will remain the same; only prices will be higher. Figure 15.6 explains how this can happen.

Real Business Cycles Cause Fluctuations A third critique of activist policy is put forward by theorists of real business cycles, who argue that business cycles are caused by fluctuations in aggregate supply, not by fluctuations in aggregate demand. The major source of fluctuation in aggregate supply is changes in technology, or technology shocks, which cannot be anticipated. If the true source of the business cycle is random technological shocks, it makes little sense to try to control the business cycle by controlling aggregate demand.

The Phillips Curve, the Natural Rate, and Macro Policy

Just as the Great Depression of the 1930s motivated Keynes to develop new theories, economic conditions in the 1970s and early 1980s motivated economists to revise

FIGURE 15.6 How Rational Expectations Defeat Activist Policy

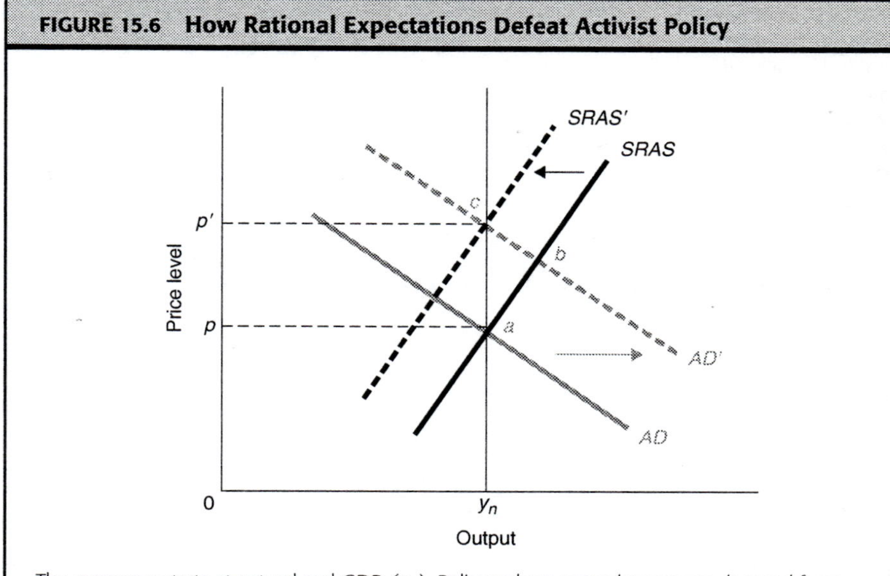

The economy starts at natural real GDP (y_n). Policymakers expand aggregate demand from *AD* to *AD'*. If the demand increase is not anticipated, the economy moves to a higher level of output and prices (point *b*). If the demand increase is anticipated, economic agents adjust immediately to higher inflation. They adjust upward inflationary expectations (the supply curve shifts to *SRAS'*). The economy moves from *a* directly to *c* without any increase in output or employment. Rational expectations have defeated an activist policy.

their views. The 1970s and the early 1980s showed that high unemployment and high inflation could occur simultaneously, and a new term entered the economist's vocabulary: *stagflation.* **Stagflation** is the combination of high unemployment and high inflation. A new macroeconomic measure, the **misery index,** or the sum of the inflation and unemployment rates, began to be used. (See Figure 15.7.)

Stagflation is the combination of high inflation and high unemployment in a stagnant economy.

The **misery index** is the sum of the inflation and unemployment rates.

Data on the relationship between U.S. inflation and unemployment from 1961 to the present (Figure 15.8) show why stagflation surprised economists and politicians in the early 1970s. Prior to the 1970s, high unemployment was usually accompanied by low inflation, and vice versa. The line connecting the 1960s dots traces out a negatively sloped curve called the **Phillips curve,** which graphs the relationship between the unemployment rate and the inflation rate. Its negative slope for the 1960s suggested a difficult policy choice between inflation and unemployment.

The **Phillips curve** graphs the relationship between the unemployment rate and the inflation rate. Its negative slope for the 1960s suggested a difficult policy choice between inflation and unemployment.

The policy implication of the Phillips curve of the 1960s was that inflation could be eliminated only if society were prepared to tolerate an unemployment rate well above the rate of full employment. Inflation was the price of low unemployment!

The dots connecting inflation and unemployment rates for the 1970s, 1980s, 1990s, and early 2000s fail to show a neat trade-off between higher inflation and lower unemployment. The line of the 1970s through the 1990s dissolves into a *swirling pattern.* For the 1970s as a whole, both unemployment and inflation rose together. Commentators of the 1970s proclaimed that the "laws of economics" no longer worked.

The short-run Phillips curve yields a trade-off between inflation and unemployment when inflationary expectations are constant. Stagflation can occur when inflationary expectations rise.

Modern macroeconomics explains why there can be a trade-off between inflation and unemployment in one period and stagflation in another period. *A trade-off will exist when inflationary expectations are constant and stagflation will be present when inflationary expectations are rising.* With stable inflationary expectations, the inflation/unemployment dots will look like the 1960s. With rising inflationary expectations, there will be a rising pattern of both inflation and unemployment.

FIGURE 15.7 The Stagflation of the 1970s and Early 1980s: The Misery Index

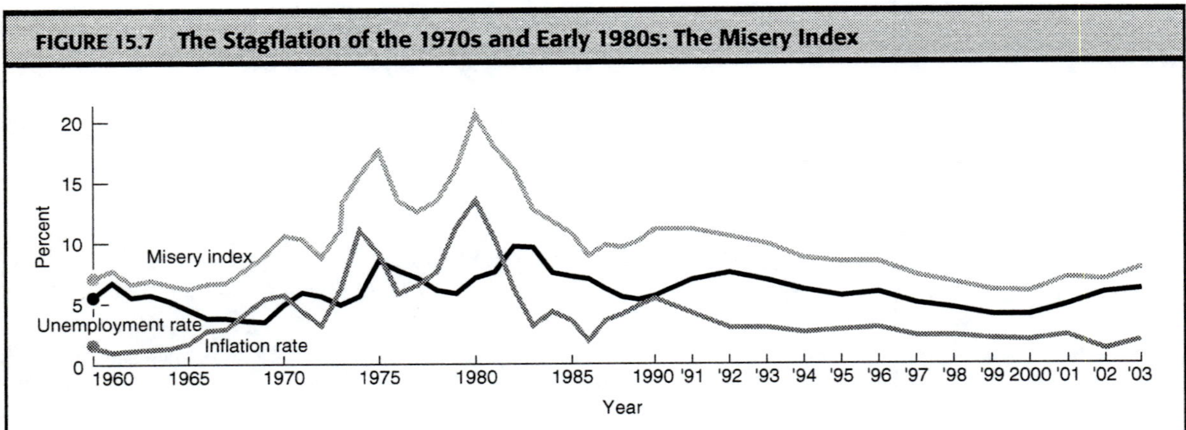

From the mid-1960s to the early 1980s, both inflation and unemployment rose. The combination of rising inflation and unemployment is called *stagflation.* The misery index is the sum of the inflation rate and the unemployment rate.

Source: Economic Report of the President

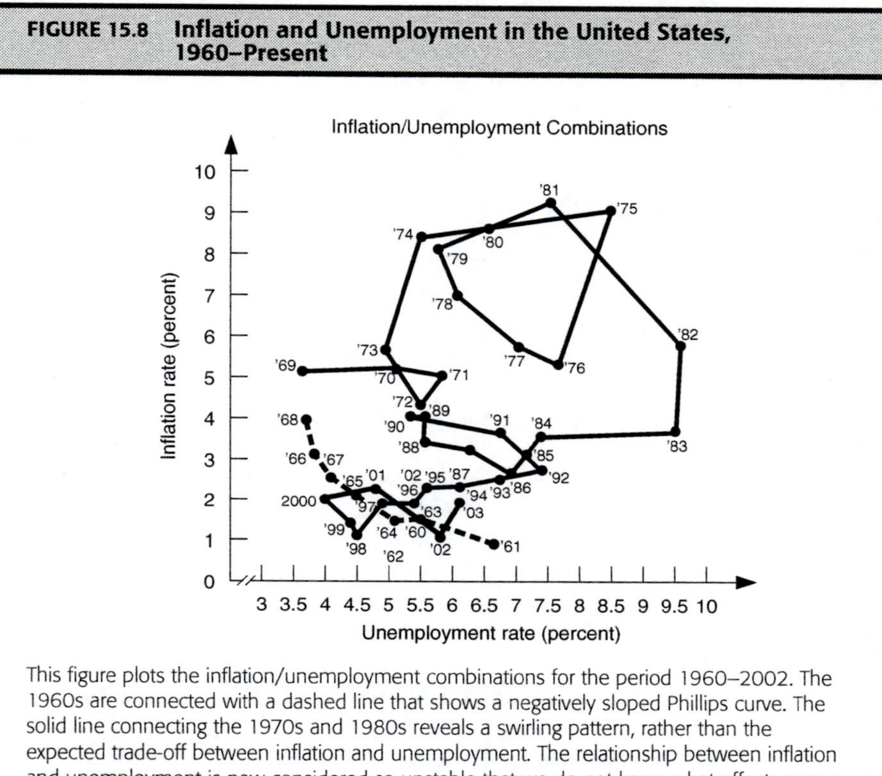

FIGURE 15.8 Inflation and Unemployment in the United States, 1960–Present

This figure plots the inflation/unemployment combinations for the period 1960–2002. The 1960s are connected with a dashed line that shows a negatively sloped Phillips curve. The solid line connecting the 1970s and 1980s reveals a swirling pattern, rather than the expected trade-off between inflation and unemployment. The relationship between inflation and unemployment is now considered so unstable that we do not know what effects macro policy will have on either.

If there are demand changes with stable inflationary expectations, the unemployment rate will fall with rising *AD* and rise with falling *AD*.

When inflation is fully anticipated, changes in *AD* will have no effect on the unemployment rate.

Figure 15.6 (the self-correcting mechanism) explains the breakdown of the stable Phillips curve. It shows, for example, that when an aggregate demand increase is not anticipated, the economy will move from *a* to *b*. It will produce more output and therefore the unemployment rate will fall. If there are demand changes with stable inflationary expectations, the unemployment rate will fall with rising *AD* and rise with falling *AD*. As Figure 15.6 shows, however, if the *AD* changes are fully anticipated, the economy moves directly from *a* to *c*. In this case, there is no change in output and, hence, no change in the unemployment rate. When inflation is fully anticipated, changes in *AD* will have no effect on the unemployment rate.

Policymakers cannot know in advance whether economic agents will anticipate their moves. Therefore, they may not be able to predict the effects of their policies on the unemployment rate.

The most important macroeconomic goal of policy makers is to achieve full employment, which is defined as the natural rate of unemployment—that rate at which the labor market is in balance. With the breakdown of the Phillips curve, it becomes very difficult to know the natural rate of unemployment. In effect, the natural rate of unemployment is that rate that yields constant inflationary pressures. If the labor market is in balance, there is no pressure on wages to increase and then to cause other prices to increase. Thus, in aiming for the natural rate of unemployment with monetary or fiscal policy, policymakers must know in advance the unemployment rate at which inflationary pressures are constant. If they aim for an unemployment rate below the natural rate, they will cause inflation.

Figure 15.7 shows the declining misery index of the 1990s. Both unemployment and inflation fell together, but policymakers had to decide at what unemployment rate inflation would start to rise. Based on past experience, they thought this would occur at 5 to 5.5 percent, and the Fed actually raised interest rates in the late 1990s to prevent the unemployment rate from falling below the natural rate. Yet the unemployment rate continued to drop, as did the inflation rate. A number of economists, therefore, felt that the Fed contributed to the recession of 2000 by aiming for a natural rate of unemployment that was too high.

The Case for Activism

The case for an activist stabilization policy is summed up in one sentence: Waiting for the economy to cure itself by the self-correcting mechanism is too costly. As Keynes famously declared: "In the long run, we are all dead!" Keynes taught that the economy is subject to all sorts of cyclical disturbances. The most important source of instability is private investment spending, which moves erratically in response to change in expectations and credit conditions.

Lost Output and Price Rigidities

When the economy experiences an adverse demand or an adverse supply shock, it will not be operating at full employment. In addition to the private anguish of unemployment, society must bear a social cost—that of lost output. Can society afford to sit back and accept the loss of output while the economy adjusts toward full employment? If the economy had remained at full employment, a larger real GDP would have been produced, and society, at large, would have been better off. Even if the self-correcting mechanism would eventually have returned the economy to full employment after several years, potential output would have been lost in the meantime. This difference between actual output and potential output at full employment is called the **GDP gap**.

The **GDP gap** is the difference between actual output and potential output at full employment.

The GDP gap measures the social cost of unemployed resources.

Keynes thought activist policy could limit the loss of potential GDP. A collapse in private investment spending could be countered by an increase in government spending, a reduction in taxes, or an expansionary monetary policy. If activist policy could engineer an offsetting expenditure increase, there would be no reduction in output and employment.

Activists believe that modern economies are subject to wage and price rigidities that slow down the operation of the self-correcting mechanism.

Activists believe that the self-correcting mechanism works slowly because of wage and price inflexibilities. In the real world, important wages and prices are not free to respond to changes in market conditions. Moreover, laid-off union workers are often inclined to wait to be recalled to former jobs rather than go on the job market. By not searching for new jobs, they do not depress wages generally throughout the economy. Minimum wage laws prevent wages from adjusting.

Prices are also subject to rigidities. For many years oil and natural-gas prices were set by long-term delivery contracts. Prices of many industrial raw materials are fixed in long-term contracts with suppliers. If many wages and input prices are set in long-term contracts, wages and prices become inflexible. When wages and prices are rigid (or slow to adjust) in the downward direction, the self-correcting mechanism of deflation (or disinflation) will be very slow in restoring the economy to full employment.

The Positive Scorecard for Activism

Keynesian activist policies have been pursued since the mid-1960s. The historical record is, therefore, long enough for an evaluation. One fact is clear: Keynesian economics has not conquered the business cycle. The American economy still suffers from inflation, unemployment, and even stagflation—the combination of inflation and unemployment.

FIGURE 15.9 GDP Growth and Unemployment in the United States

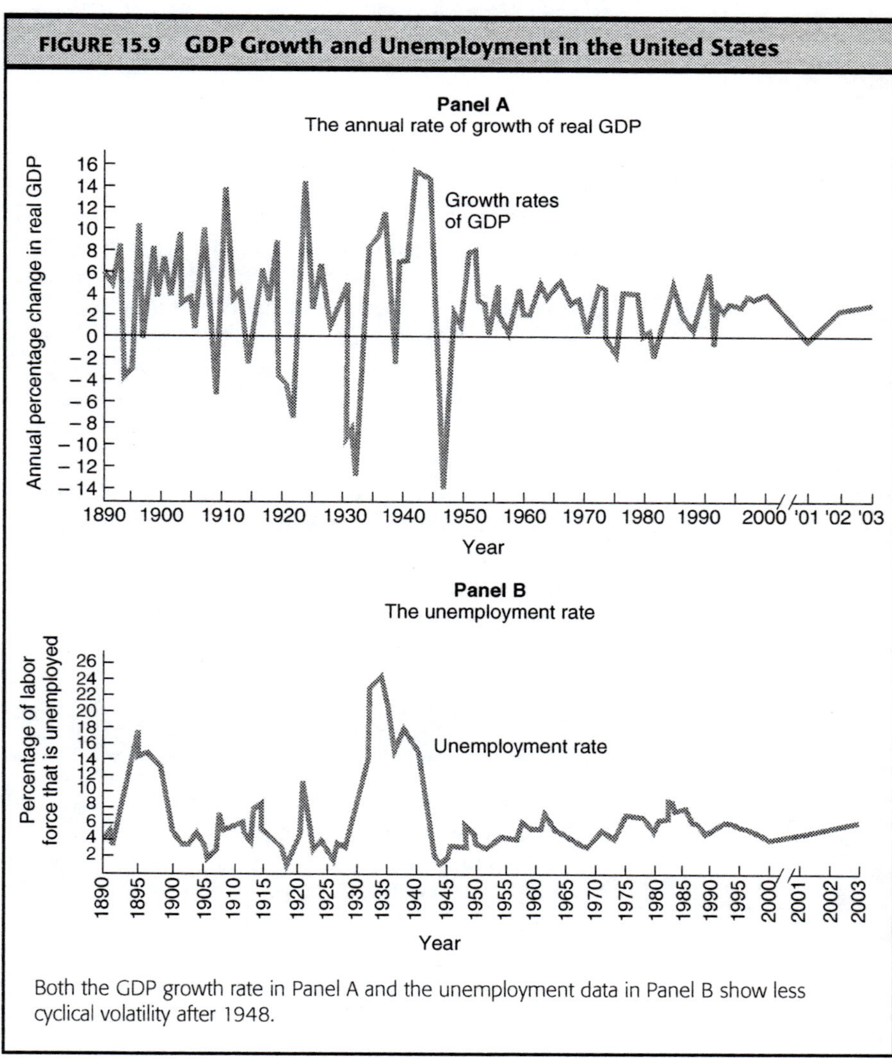

Both the GDP growth rate in Panel A and the unemployment data in Panel B show less cyclical volatility after 1948.

The business cycle has been less volatile in the postwar era.

The continued existence of the business cycle does not prove, by itself, that activism has failed. Advocates of activism can argue that activist policies have prevented the business cycle from being even worse by heading off another Great Depression or a hyperinflation. Figure 15.9 shows that, while the business cycle has not been eliminated, it has become less volatile. Accordingly, modern Keynesians argue that activist policies have spared society substantial volumes of lost output.

U.S. policymakers have consistently chosen the activist policy approach. Rates of monetary growth have fluctuated considerably over the years, although the fluctuations have decreased in recent years. Activist monetary policy has aimed at moderating the business cycle. The Fed has never followed a fixed monetary growth rule.

Summary

1. The stabilization policy alternatives are activist monetary and fiscal policy versus nonactivism. Activist policies aim to stabilize the business cycle. Nonactivist policy uses fixed rules. Because of its greater flexibility and independence, monetary policy is the major instrument of activist policy.
2. The basic debate between Keynesians and monetarists/rational expectations economists is over activism. Keynesians argue that activism is necessary; monetarists and rational expectations economists maintain that activist policies do not work and often make matters worse. The Keynesian case for activism is that the costs of the self-correcting mechanism are too high. The main evidence in favor of activism is the long-term reduction in GDP fluctuations since World War II.
3. The case against activism rests on the following points: The economy is not as unstable as the activists believe; cycles have been caused by policy blunders; and the reduced GDP fluctuations since World War II are because of smaller fluctuations in monetary growth. Activist policy tends to be destabilizing because lags make it difficult to devise discretionary policy.
4. Rational expectations teaches that activist policy will have no effect if policy is anticipated.
5. The nonactivists favor fixed rules. The two rules are a fixed rate of growth of the money supply and a cyclically balanced budget.
6. Activism has been the choice of U.S. policymakers over the years.

Questions and Problems

1. Explain how activist policies would have different effects if they were anticipated than if they were not anticipated.
2. Which type of activist policy would be easier to anticipate—monetary or fiscal policy? According to the rational expectations school, which policy would have a larger effect on output and employment?
3. Would activist monetary policy be easier to conduct if the lag were two months than if the lag were four years? Explain your answer.

4. Why do both monetarists and Keynesians use the declining amplitude of business cycles since the end of World War II as proof of their positions?
5. Explain why monetary policy has been the most widely used instrument of activist policy.
6. The examples in this chapter explain what happens when there is *unanticipated inflation.* Explain what happens to unemployment in the short and long run when there is *unanticipated deflation.*
7. Assume the natural rate of unemployment is 7 percent. If monetary and fiscal authorities adopted policies to aim at a 5 percent unemployment rate, what would happen? Would the short-run experience differ from the long-run experience?
8. Plot the following combinations of inflation rates and unemployment rates:

Year	*Inflation Rate*	*Unemployment Rate*
1	5%	8%
2	10	5
3	10	8
4	12	6
5	12	10
6	14	8

Are these data consistent with the short-run Phillips curve? Explain what is happening to inflationary expectations during this period.

9. Explain the meaning of stagflation. Explain as well why the stagflation of the 1970s was unexpected.
10. Explain the misery index.
11. Use Figure 15.8 to explain the differences in the relationship between the unemployment rate and inflation in the 1960s versus later periods.

PART FIVE

INTERNATIONAL ECONOMICS

The global economy is characterized by ever freer trade among countries. Multinational corporations have replaced national corporations, and a world capital market has replaced national capital markets. These final two chapters are about the global economy. The first explains why trade takes place and discusses the costs of interfering with free trade. The second explains how we arrange international transactions among countries that have different national currencies.

CHAPTER 16

INTERNATIONAL TRADE AND GLOBALIZATION

Chapter Preview

National economics have become integrated into a global economy in which countries trade ever larger quantities of products and capital. International economics studies international trade in goods and services and the monetary consequences of international payments between countries. This chapter explores the reasons for, and consequences of, international trade, and the effects of tariffs and quotas on trade. It shows the advantages of free trade and the economic costs of restricting trade.

Globalization

Human beings have always sought new and exotic products produced by other societies. We have, as Adam Smith remarked, a "propensity to truck, barter, and exchange one thing for another."

Trade depends on the ease of communication and the costs of transporting goods and services over distances. Marco Polo's journey to China, for example, consumed more than half his lifetime; today, the same trip can be made in one day on a commercial jet. Polo's letters from China to Venice took years to deliver; now, such messages can be delivered in seconds by fax or e-mail.

Globalization refers to the degree to which national economic markets and international businesses are integrated and interrelated into a world economy.

The growth of global markets does not take place swiftly and continuously; it is a long-term process with stops and starts. **Globalization** refers to the degree to which national economic markets and international businesses are integrated and interrelated into a world economy. Globalization itself was a response to a powerful economic insight—that trade benefits both parties irrespective of their strengths and weaknesses. The great English economist David Ricardo (1772–1823) demonstrated that both weak and powerful nations benefit from trade by doing those things they do relatively more efficiently than others. His insight persuaded the English Parliament to adopt a free-trade policy in the first half of the nineteenth century. The remarkable success of the English experiment with free trade prompted other countries to reduce barriers to trade imposed by special-interest groups.

The Industrial Revolution brought forth the first strong and sustained wave of globalization. Coal-powered boats and railroads linked markets; the telegraph and later the telephone made long-distance communication possible. Two world wars and the Great Depression halted globalization. However, in the past 50 years we have experienced a renewed explosion of international commerce and trade. We are now truly a "world economy," made possible by the revolutionary developments in transportation and communication and the conscious decisions of countries to lower barriers to trade. This world economy benefits our lives in a variety of ways. We now have a wealth of choices among cars, foodstuffs, computers—almost every product that we consider. Companies are no longer national: A Japanese company located in Germany can be headed by an American president. Stocks of U.S. companies are traded in Japan as we sleep, continue to be traded in London as we begin our day, and complete their trading in New York as we finish lunch. The car you drive might be made in Korea, your neighbor might work for BP Amoco, and your business loan could be from a Canadian bank.

The Haves and Have-Nots

Prosperity is the consequence of sustained growth of per capita real GDP over a long period. The affluent countries located in North America and Europe began to grow long ago, and this cumulated growth has made them rich in material goods.

Although there is no single indicator of the level of economic development, per capita GDP is its most comprehensive measure. Some countries (such as those exceptionally rich in resources) can have a high GDP per capita and yet lack the other characteristics of economic development, such as a highly educated population or an industrial structure geared to industry and services.

The industrialized countries in North America, Europe, Australia, and Japan have attained a high level of economic development. These are the *have* countries. The *have-nots*—the developing countries (DCs)—have not achieved a high level of development. A **developing country** (**DC**) is a country with a per capita income well below that of a typical advanced country.

A **developing country** (**DC**) is a country with a per capita income well below that of a typical advanced country.

The have-not countries are concentrated in Africa, Asia, and Latin America. It is difficult to classify the former communist countries that are currently attempting the transition from socialism to capitalism; they are located somewhere between the have and have-not countries.

Figure 16.1 shows that approximately three out of every four persons worldwide live in a DC. Only 15 percent of the world's population lives in the highly developed countries of the United States and Western Europe and in Canada, Australia, and Japan, and 10 percent of the world's population lives in the former communist countries of the former Soviet Union and eastern Europe. The DCs' share of world population has been rising since 1900 and is projected to rise throughout the twenty-first century.

A comparison of the distribution of world population with the distribution of world income dramatizes how unequally income is distributed. As Figure 16.1 shows, the developed countries, which account for only 15 percent of the world's population, account for 80 percent of the world's GDP. The DCs account for 84 percent of the world population but only 20 percent of world GDP. World output is concentrated in the United States, Western Europe, and Japan. The unequal distribution of income among countries also leads to an unequal consumption of natural resources between

FIGURE 16.1 The Share of Developing and Developed Countries in Population and Production—1800, 1900, 2004

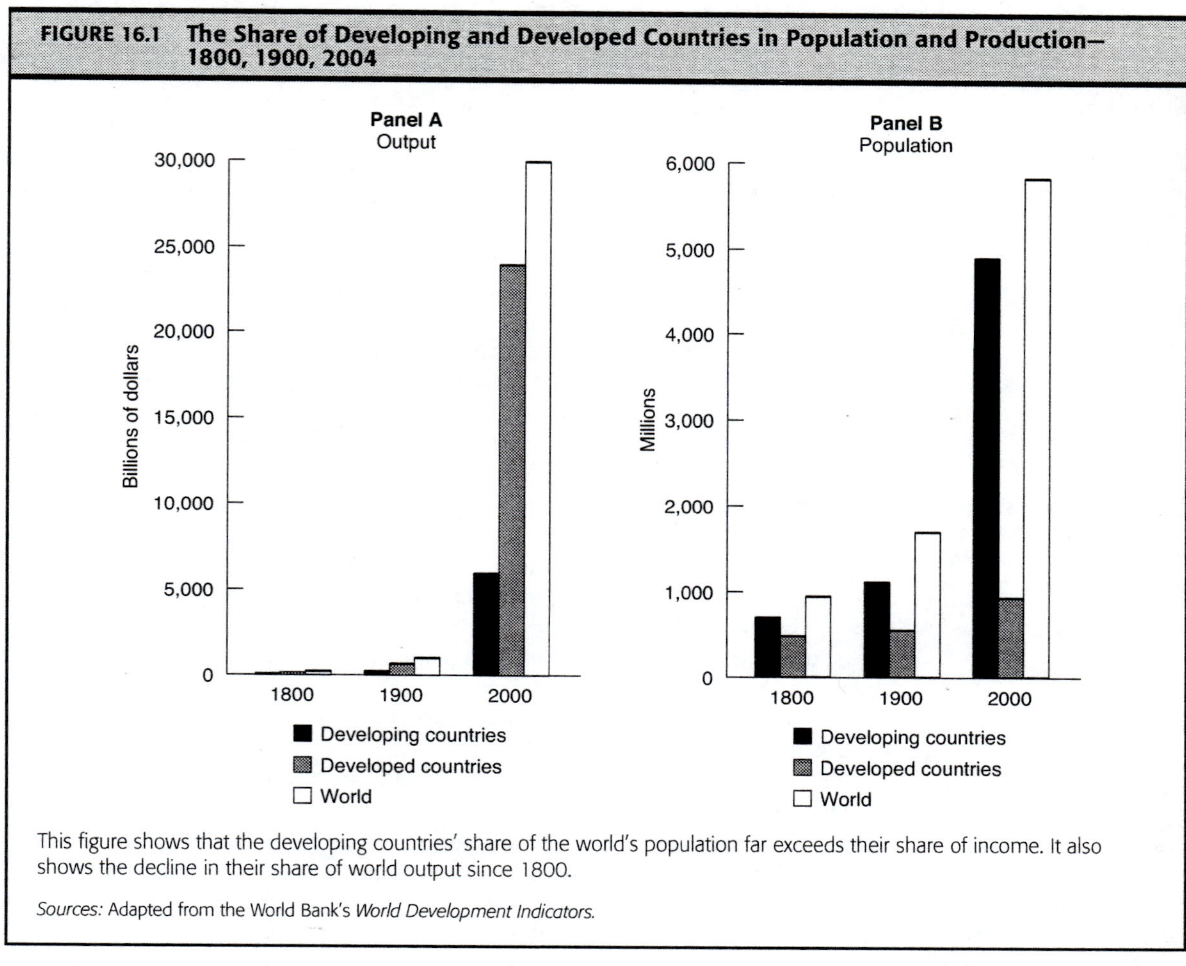

This figure shows that the developing countries' share of the world's population far exceeds their share of income. It also shows the decline in their share of world output since 1800.

Sources: Adapted from the World Bank's *World Development Indicators.*

the rich and poor countries. The industrialized countries consume 71 percent of the world's oil production. Only 9 percent of the world's oil is consumed by the DCs.

Life in a low-income DC is very different from the life we know. Only 1 of 5 people in a low-income DC lives in an urban area (as opposed to 78 percent in the industrial market economies). One of every 7 children dies before the age of 4, compared with 1 out of every 200 in the industrial market economies. In a community of 6000 people there is 1 physician, compared with 11 in the industrial market economies. Life expectancy is 58 years in a typical DC versus more than 75 years in a typical industrialized economy. In a DC, only 1 out of every 2 adults can read or write, and only 1 out of 4 school-age children attends secondary school. Only 2 out of every 100 persons own their own radios, and a private automobile is usually an unheard-of luxury. Residents of DCs come from large families and plan on having a large number of children, many of whom will not survive infancy.

The Law of Comparative Advantage

Ricardo's great insight, which underlies the theory of international trade, shows that both rich and poor countries benefit from international trade via specialization.

Ricardo's great insight, which underlies the theory of international trade, shows that both rich and poor countries benefit from international trade via specialization.

Suppose a shipwrecked sailor were stranded alone on a deserted island—a modern Robinson Crusoe. While the sailor would have to make basic economic decisions whether to make fishnets or fishhooks, sleep, or gather fruits—his deserted island would lack other features of a normal economy. The sailor could not *specialize,* but would have to be a jack-of-all-trades. He would produce only what he needed. There would be no need for money. There would be no concern over who owned what or what their prices were.

In a modern economy, people are specialized. One household buys hundreds of different articles, while the principal breadwinner is highly specialized, such as teaching school or aligning suspension components on an automobile production line. Specialization makes us dependent on the efforts of others. Each person produces only one or two things but consumes many.

Specialization means people will produce more of a particular good than they consume.

Specialization means that people will produce more of a particular good than they consume and that this "surplus" will be exchanged for the goods that they want.

The main reason for specialization is that people, land, and capital all come in different varieties. Some people are agile seven-footers, others are small and slow; some are fast talkers, others scarcely utter a word. Some take easily to math and computers; others are frightened by numbers and technology. Some land is moist; other land is dry. Some land is hilly; other land is flat. Some machines can move large quantities of earth; others can lift heavy loads; others can perform precision metalwork; others can heat metals to high temperatures.

The **comparative advantage** of a resource is its best use.

Because the factors of production have different characteristics and qualities, specialization offers opportunities for productivity advances, when resources are employed to their **comparative advantage.**

The **law of comparative advantage** states that it is better for people or countries to specialize in those activities at which they have the greatest advantage over other people or countries.

Ricardo's **law of comparative advantage** states that it is better for people or countries to specialize in those activities in which their advantage over other people or countries is greatest or in which their disadvantages are the smallest. Consider two extreme cases. Suppose that you can do any, and every, job better than anyone else. Despite you superiority you would not be a jack-of-all-trades because your *margin* of superiority will be greater in one occupation than in another. The job in which your margin of superiority over others is the *greatest* is the job you will do.

Consider the other extreme. Suppose you are less productive in every occupation than every other person. The job in which your disadvantage, compared to that of others, is the *smallest* would be the job that maximizes your income.

The clerks in a local supermarket may not be able to stock shelves or work a cash register as well as a mediocre computer programmer, but they have a *comparative advantage* in that occupation over the computer programmer, even if the programmer could possibly be the best clerk in the supermarket. An attorney may be the fastest word processor in town, yet the attorney is better off preparing deeds than keying them on a word processor. An engineering major may have better verbal skills than an English major, but his or her comparative advantage is in engineering.

International trade is like trade between individuals. Each country is endowed with a particular climate, so much fertile farm land, so much desert, so many lakes and rivers, and certain kinds of people. Some countries have accumulated a great deal of physical and human capital. Each country has endowments of productive factors (land, labor, and capital) inside its borders that cannot be transferred readily to another country. The country's labor force is not easily moved. Even if people want to leave, immigration laws may prevent them from doing so. Thus, each country will have different proportions of land, labor, and capital. Australia has very little labor compared to land and, hence, devotes itself to land-intensive products like sheep farming and wheat production. A country like Great Britain produces goods that use comparatively little land but more labor and capital.

International trade rests on the fact that goods and services are much more mobile internationally than the resources used in their production. Each country will tend to export those goods and services for which its resource base is most suited.

The United States has an abundance of highly skilled technical labor and thus tends to export goods that use highly skilled labor. Because the United States has a comparative advantage in manufactured goods that require intensive investment in research and development (R&D), high-tech industries contribute most to American export sales, such as chemicals, aircrafts, and nonelectrical or electrical machinery. When these new products become standardized, the United States then moves on to the next new product, generated with its research establishment and abundant supply of engineers, scientists, and skilled labor.

Gains from Trade

That trade makes people better off can be illustrated in terms of a simple example. Table 16.1 shows two hypothetical countries, Highland and Lowland. There is only one type of labor in each country, and workers are indifferent to working at one job or another as long as their wages are the same. In Highland, a day's work yields one yard of cloth and one bushel of food; in Lowland, a day's work yields three yards of cloth and six bushels of food. Workers in Lowland are clearly more efficient in both activities than Highland workers—six times more efficient in food production and three times more efficient in cloth production.

Figure 16.2 plots the simple Production Possibilities Frontiers for both countries in the case that each country has 100 days of labor. Figure 16.2 shows that Highland is a much poorer country than Lowland. If households in both countries, for example, wanted to purchase equal quantities of food and clothing, Highland families would have 50*F* and 50*C*, and Lowland families would have 200*F* and 200*C* (as shown by point *a* on each diagram).

The Production Possibilities Frontiers also show what the relative prices of *F* and *C* would be in each country.

TABLE 16.1 Output from a Day's Work: Highland and Lowland

Country	*Food Output from Day's Work (bushels)*	*Cloth Output from Day's Work (yards)*
Highland	1	1
Lowland	6	3

FIGURE 16.2

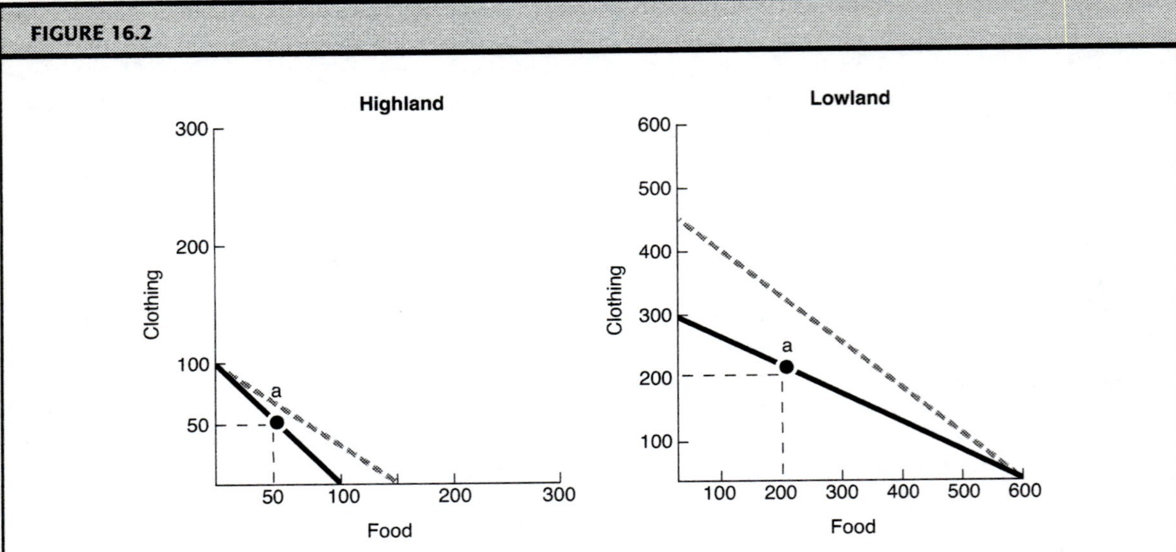

Explanation: The bold lines show the Production Possibilities Frontiers of the two countries. Without trade, they dictate the consumption possibilities of each country and their slopes show the relative domestic prices. The dotted lines show the enhanced consumption possibilities (the gains from trade) when each country specializes and trades.

Lowland workers can produce six bushels of food or three yards of cloth with a day's work—or, equivalently, they can produce two bushels of food or one yard of cloth by working one-third of a day. Lowland workers must therefore pay two bushels of food per yard of cloth; so the food price of cloth in Lowland is:

$$2F = 1C$$

In Highland, workers can produce either one bushel of food or one yard of cloth with a day's work. Thus, Highland workers can buy one bushel of food per yard of cloth—that is, the food price of cloth is:

$$1F = 1C$$

Because production conditions are different in the two countries, the prices are quite different.

Enterprising traders now see profit opportunities. They can buy $2F$ for $1C$ in Lowland; sell $2F$ for $2C$ in Highland; and then resell the $2C$ for $4F$ in Lowland! In so doing, they double their money.

As traders buy Lowland's "cheap" food, its price will be bid up. As traders sell this food in Highland, its "expensive" food prices will be bid down.

Thus, in international markets, the "world" price will settle between the two domestic prices. In our example, let us say that the price settles at $1.5F = 1C$. In both countries, households can buy 1.5 units of food for one unit of cloth.

Figure 16.2 shows that each country should specialize. If Lowland produces only food (600 units), it can sell each unit for 1.5 units of clothing. If it were to sell all its

Gains from trade occur when countries specialize and are able to purchase more by trading in goods than they were able to without trade.

production in international markets, it could buy 450 units of clothing. Similarly, if Highland produced only clothing, it could buy 1.5 units of food for each unit of production. If it sold all its clothing in international markets, it could buy 150 units of food.

The dotted lines show that with international trade, both countries can potentially buy more of each good if they specialize and trade. Thus, they receive **gains from trade.**

Competition Through Wages

No one need tell workers in either country to specialize. With the international price of cloth equal to 1.5*F* (say cloth is $3 and food $2), a worker in Lowland can earn $9 a day in cloth (= $3 × 3) and $12 a day in food (= $2 × 6). Thus, workers in Lowland will choose food production to maximize their daily wages. On the other hand, workers in Highland can earn $3 a day in clothing (= $3 × 1) and only $2 in food ($2 × 1). Thus, workers in Highland will work in clothing to maximize their daily wages.

Lowland workers have a comparative advantage in food production; Highland workers have a comparative advantage in clothing production. While Lowland workers are more efficient than Highland workers in everything, their *greatest* advantage is in food; they are six times as efficient. In clothing production, Lowland workers are only three times as efficient as Highland workers. Hence, workers in Highland find that their *least* disadvantage is in clothing production.

The price system encourages the factors of production to use their special characteristics and skills. The lawyer will make more money in law; the programmer will make more in computer science. All that owners of labor, land, and capital resources have to do is to use their resources to make the most money possible; and specialization will follow naturally.

Daily wages in Lowland are $12 working in food, and those in Highland are $3 working in clothing. The higher Lowland wages reflect superior productivity, but Highland workers can compete with Lowland workers by earning lower wages. (Wages in Highland are one-fourth those of Lowland.) Daily wages in Highland are low enough to allow competition with Lowland in clothing production; Lowland workers are three times as efficient but earn wages four times as high. In the marketplace, in making cloth Lowland's high wages offset its absolute advantage in cloth production.

Workers in low-efficiency ecomonies compete by working at lower wages. The wage differential reflects the productivity differential.

Lowland is six times as efficient in food production and three times as efficient in clothing production as Highland. These efficiency rates mark the limits by which Lowland wages can exceed Highland wages. If Lowland wages were seven times higher than Highland wages, Lowland money costs would be too high to compete; if Lowland wages were only two times higher, it could undercut Highland in everything. Demand and supply for Highland and Lowland workers will ensure that wages in Lowland will be somewhere between six and three times as high as in Highland.

This example shows how workers in high-wage countries (like the United States) can compete with workers in lower wage countries (such as Mexico) and vice versa. Workers in low-efficiency economies compete by working at lower wages. The wage differential reflects the productivity differential.

Trade Barriers

In the real world, not everyone gains from international trade, but the law of comparative advantage demonstrates that the average person gains. To say that the average person gains from trade is to say that the people who gain from international trade benefit by a greater dollar amount than the dollar costs imposed on those who lose. Prohibiting international trade in automobiles imposes costs on Americans. First, consumers would pay higher prices for American cars because they could not purchase German and Japanese substitutes. Second, the reduced volume of imports would lead to fewer exports, so American farmers and other export-oriented businesses would lose. The costs imposed on these invisible Americans would be greater than the benefits to the American automobile industry since, according to the law of comparative advantage, restricting international trade reduces the overall efficiency of the economy.

The theory of comparative advantage provides the optimistic message that trade makes people better off. The gainers gain more than the losers lose. Rich countries can compete with poor countries (and vice versa) because wages adjust to efficiency differences. American workers' wages are higher than in most other countries for this reason.

Trade barriers are tariffs, quotas, and other forms of protection of domestic producers that restrain trade.

Despite the fact that international trade makes people in both trading countries better off, there is pressure to protect domestic producers from foreign competition by imposing **trade barriers,** such a tariffs, quotas, and other forms of protection.

Tariffs

A **tariff** is a tax levied on imports.

An import **tariff** is a tax levied on imports. It raises the price paid by domestic consumers. A tariff on clothing from Taiwan raises the prices paid by American consumers for clothing imports and the prices charged by American clothing producers.

Suppose a country levies a $1 tariff on imported shoes that cost $10 in the foreign market. If domestic and foreign shoes are the same, both imported and domestically produced shoes will sell for $11 in the home market. Because consumers will pay more for shoes than otherwise, the tariff discourages shoe consumption. Because the domestic producer of shoes will be able to charge more for shoes, the tariff encourages domestic production. The $1 tariff discourages shoe imports and foreign shoe production.

Tariffs also protect inefficient firms or industries from competition. Thus, resources are not allocated to their best and most efficient uses. Companies and entire industries that can no longer compete are kept in business, only—eventually—to die a slow death.

Import Quotas

An **import quota** is a limitation on the amount of a specific product that can be imported during a given period.

An **import quota** sets the number of units of a particular product that can be brought into the country. American quotas on imported steel, for example, specify the number of tons of steel of a specified grade that can come into the United States in a particular year. Importers of products that fall under quota restrictions must obtain a license to import the good. The quantity of imports cannot exceed the maximum quota limit. Import licenses can be distributed in a variety of ways. The government can auction them off in a free and fair market, and they would sell for a price that

The scarcity value of import licenses accrues to the government if the licenses are auctioned in a free market but accrues to importers if licenses are allocated by a nonprice scheme.

reflects their scarcity. In such a case, an import license is similar to a tariff: It restricts imports and raises revenue for the government. Import licenses may also be handed out on a first-come, first-served basis, on the basis of favoritism, or according to the amount of past imports by the importer. In such cases, the potential revenue that the government could collect from selling them goes to the lucky few importers who get them. For this reason, importers who are likely to obtain licenses prefer import quotas to tariffs because they can profit from the scarcity value of the licenses. They can then buy a product cheaply in the world market and sell it, at a handsome profit, in the home market.

Strict import quotas have kept domestic sugar prices at morethan double the world price. The importers collect the difference! American consumers pay higher prices, and the government gains no revenues. (See Example 16.1.)

A **voluntary export quota** is an agreement between two governments in which the exporting country "voluntarily" limits the export of a certain product.

Voluntary Export Quotas

A **voluntary export quota** is the result of the bargaining between a home government and a foreign government to impose export quotas to limit the exports to the home country.

EXAMPLE 16.1 SUGAR SUBSIDIES: COSTS, BENEFITS, POLITICS, AND CORRUPTION

U.S. taxpayers pay about $1 billion per year on subsidies to U.S. sugar producers located primarily in Florida. Almost half of these subsidies go to the largest 1 percent of sugar producers. Although the subsidy consists of several elements, some very complicated such as loan guarantees, the key subsidy is the government guarantee to maintain the price of sugar at around 20 cents per pound. If the price falls below that price, the sugar farmer receives a payment for the difference. Insofar as the world market price of sugar is well below 20 cents per pound (it often trades at around 5 cents per pound), the government must limit sugar imports into the United States by issuing import licenses. The import license allows a foreign producer to sell a specified quantity of sugar in the United States. The existence of such import licenses creates opportunities for corruption. An import license to sell 500,000 pounds of sugar in the U.S. at 20 cents per pound would be worth almost $75,000 (500,000 times 15 cents) to a foreign producer whose alternative is to sell to the world market at 5 cents per pound. Foreign producers would compete to obtain these valuable licenses from corrupt officials by offering them bribes.

The actual cost of sugar subsidies is well above the $1 billion cost to taxpayers. Consumers pay some $2 billion in higher costs for sugar.

In most cases, the beneficiaries of protection are visible and the victims are invisible. In the case of sugar, the victims are quite visible. Major food manufacturers and processors would prefer to pay the low world price of sugar, and they lobby against sugar subsidies. A number of anti-sugar-subsidy organizations maintain Web sites to inform voters. Despite their opposition, sugar subsidies have been in effect since the early 1980s, and they remain as strong as ever.

At various times, the American government has negotiated voluntary export quotas with foreign governments that limit their exports to the American market. Unlike tariffs or import quotas, voluntary export quotas do not generate revenue for the importing country or its government. Instead, foreign exporters or the foreign government collect the scarcity value of the right to export to the American market.

Over the last two decades, animal feed, brooms, color TV sets, cattle, cotton, crude petroleum, dairy products, fish, meat, peanuts, potatoes, sugar, candy, textiles, stainless-steel flatware, steel, wheat and wheat flour, and automobiles have been subjected to import quotas or voluntary export quotas. Quotas and "voluntary" export restraints can have an even greater effect an trade than tariffs.

Nontariff barriers are import and export quotas that raise the domestic price of foreign goods.

Like import tariffs, import quotas and voluntary export quotas limit the quantity of foreign goods available in the domestic market. Such **nontariff barriers** raise the prices paid by domestic consumers and charged by domestic producers. Domestic producers benefit from quotas by being able to charge higher prices. The importer who receives a license to buy cheap imports gains, or, if licenses are auctioned, the government gains some revenues. The big loser from quotas is the consumer, who must pay higher prices.

The Costs of Trade Barriers

Exports subtract from domestic consumption; imports add to domestic consumption. The gains from trade consist of imported goods and services that can be obtained more cheaply by importing them than by producing them at home.

In the long run, exports must pay for imports. In the Highland-Lowland example, food exports from Lowland pay for clothing imports from Highland. The more Lowland exports food, the more clothing imports are brought in, and vice versa. The reason exports of goods and services must pay for imports of goods and services is that, in the long run, countries want each other's goods, not each other's money.

If the United States or any country restricts im ports, it necessarily restricts exports.

If the United States or any country restricts imports, it necessarily restricts exports. Tariff or nontariff barriers penalize a host of unseen, and more efficient, export industries.

Why would a representative democracy, which is supposed to act on behalf of consumer interests, establish trade barriers that impose greater costs than benefits? The explanation is that the costs imposed on the community are large in total but so small per person that it is not worth the trouble for any one person to join a committee to fight tariffs on each and every imported good. The benefits to protected sectors are well worth the costs of lobbying. For example, assume people devote about 0.5 percent of all consumption to sugar. A trade barrier that raises the price of sugar by 50 percent helps domestic sugar producers enormously, but it raises the cost of living to consumers by only 0.25 percent (50 percent of 0.5 percent). To the consumer this cost is just too small to worry about. The costs of fighting against each request for protection are prohibitive. The people who would have an incentive to lobby Congress heavily would be the foreign competitors of the domestic import industry that is seeking protection, but these foreign competitors have comparatively little political clout in the United States.

Protectionist Arguments

The economy gains from foreign trade because it can obtain imports more cheaply from abroad than by making them at home. The domestic producers of goods that are close or perfect substitutes for these imports try to convince their governments, and others, that such competition is unfair. The most common argument for protection is that it is unfair to compete against low-wage countries. How can the American worker compete against low-wage workers in Latin America or Asia? Trade union and manufacturing organizations protest the sweatshop conditions that foreign producers operate and organize boycotts against such products.

According to the theory of comparative advantage, high-wage countries can compete effectively against low-wage countries in those industries in which their productivity advantage more than offsets their wage disadvantage. Likewise, low-wage countries can compete effectively against high-productivity countries in those industries in which their wage advantage more than offsets their productivity disadvantage. Every country will have industries in which it has a comparative advantage and industries in which it has a comparative disadvantage. If one country can undercut every other country in every good, its wages, relative to the rest of the world, will be bid up until some industries are unable to compete and the country begins to import. (See Example 16.2.)

The industries in high-wage countries that cannot compete complain that they are subjected to unfair competition because of the low wages in other countries. To some business managers and politicians, it seems unfair to be more efficient on a productivity basis and yet be unable to compete because of high wages. If this view were sound, it would be necessary to erect trade barriers so that all of the industries in which the United States has a comparative disadvantage could supply the home market. The

EXAMPLE 16.2 WHERE WAS THE GIANT SUCKING SOUND?

The North American Free Trade Agreement (NAFTA) was signed in 1993. It allowed for increased freedom of trade between the United States and its neighbors to the north (Canada) and south (Mexico). NAFTA's critics, including organized labor and one presidential candidate (H. Ross Perot in 1992), predicted a "giant sucking sound" of U.S. businesses relocating to Mexico to take advantage of Mexico's cheap labor. After more than a decade of NAFTA, U.S. businesses have not moved to Mexico in large numbers as predicted. International trade theory explains why: Currently, the productivity of the average U.S. worker is almost $75,000 per year. The productivity of the average Mexican worker is $15,000 (http://www.nwpc.dole.gov.ph/apecwages/apecpage.html). The U.S. worker is five times as productive as the Mexican worker, which means that employers can pay U.S. workers five times as much as Mexican workers without any difference in cost per unit of output. U.S. companies have the added advantage of operating in the United States where the legal system and other rules of the game are well established and the political system is stable. Hence, the lower wages of Mexican workers have not served to attract a large amount of business relocation to Mexico.

erection of such barriers, however, destroys American export trade and severely lowers the real income of the American people. It is unfair to erect trade barriers that would raise the incomes of those hurt by import competition but would lower the incomes of everyone else. (See Example 16.3.)

U.S. Trade Policies

Figure 16.3 shows the tariff history of the United States, revealing that tariffs have fluctuated up and down with the ebb and flow of protectionism in the U.S. Congress. In modern times, tariffs hit their highest level with the infamous Hawley-Smoot Tariff Act of 1930. Economists were so appalled by the prospect of this tariff bill that in a rare show of agreement, 1028 of them signed a petition asking President Hoover to veto the bill. Because politics tends to override economics in tariff legislation, the bill was signed. The post–World War II era, however, has seen a steady decline in tariffs.

The Hawley-Smoot Tariff Act, like most of the preceding 18 tariff acts stretching back to 1779, was the result of political *logrolling* in the U.S. Congress. Logrolling occurs when some politicians trade their own votes on issues of minor concern to their

EXAMPLE 16.3 BOYCOTTING SWEATSHOP LABOR

College student activists and labor unions organize boycotts of products produced by sweatshop labor in Third World countries. Such boycotts have particularly targeted sportswear, such a jogging shoes, with lurid descriptions of unsafe working conditions, the use of child labor, and the incredibly low wages and long hours of sweatshop workers. They demand that U.S. consumers not buy such products until workers are paid a living wage and are offered reasonable working conditions. Countries like Indonesia and the Philippines are cited as prime examples of sweatshop labor.

Let us consider the basic economics of sweatshop labor, using Indonesia as an example. The average annual productivity of an Indonesian worker is currently $1706 (http://www.nwpc.dole.gov.ph/apecwages/apecpage.html), which means that such a worker (with a ten-hour day, 360 days per year) produces less than 50 cents of output per hour. The average American worker (8 hour per day and 300 days) produces $31 worth of goods per hour. If the boycotter's demand to pay Indonesian workers a fair wage, say the U.S. minimum wage of $5.15 per hour, were met, the sweatshop would go out of business immediately. No employer can pay a worker $5.15 per hour to produce less than 50 cents worth of goods. Moreover, it should be noted that workers work in sweatshops because they happen to offer the best pay and work conditions available. When the sweatshop goes out of business, they must work for even lower wages.

These simple facts show that the boycotter's protest is really an unwitting protest against the low level of economic development of poor countries, which can only be resolved by steady economic growth over a long period of time. The sweatshops began disappearing from Hong Kong, Taiwan, Singapore, and South Korea after they experienced decades of economic growth driven by their exports to affluent countries. To deny countries like the Philippines and Indonesia such markets on the grounds that they are unfair to their workers means dooming them to a permanent life of poverty.

FIGURE 16.3 Average U.S. Import Duties, 1820–Present

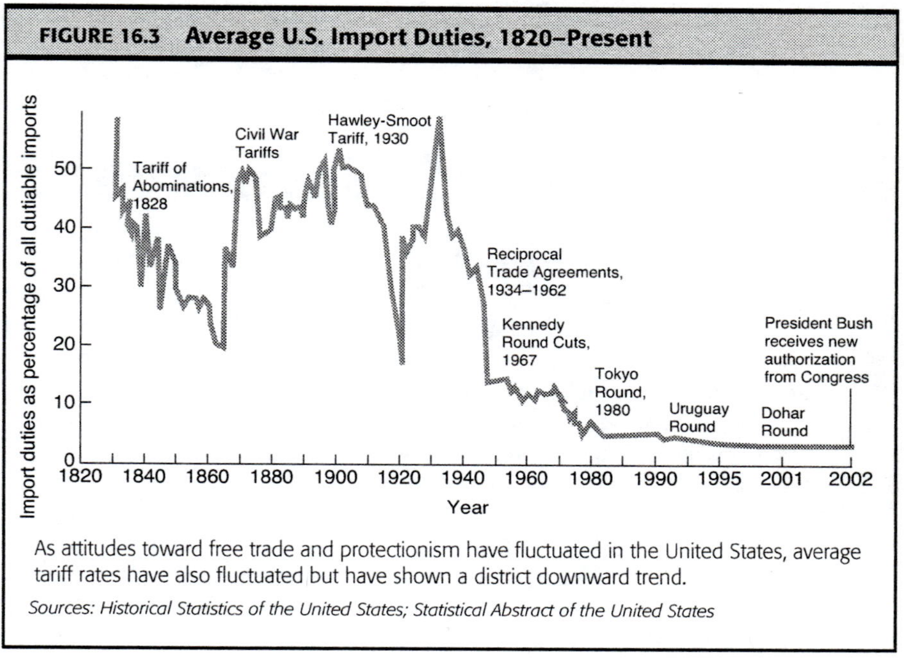

As attitudes toward free trade and protectionism have fluctuated in the United States, average tariff rates have also fluctuated but have shown a district downward trend.

Sources: Historical Statistics of the United States; Statistical Abstract of the United States

constituents in return for other politicians' votes on issues of greater concern to their constituents. Tariffs, historically, are a prime example of the sacrifice of general interests for special interests.

Having established the highest tariff rates in U.S. history, the Hawley-Smoot Act triggered angry reactions overseas. As one nation after another erected trade barriers, the volume of world trade declined. The export markets of the United States shrank at the time of a very deep domestic depression.

In order to secure a larger market for U.S. exports, Congress amended the Tariff Act of 1930 with the Reciprocal Trade Agreements Act of 1934. The president was authorized to negotiate reciprocal agreements that promised to lower U.S. trade barriers or tariffs in return for similar concessions abroad. The fact that Congress did not have to approve the tariff cuts marked a significant change in the power of special interests to influence U.S. tariff policy.

The trade-agreements program broadened under successive extensions and modifications. The Trade Expansion Act of 1962 gave the president the power to reduce tariffs and duties. Under the authority of this act, the United States engaged in multilateral negotiations, known as the Kennedy Round, which resulted in an average reduction of 35 percent. The Trade Reform Act of 1974 resulted in the Tokyo Round (1980) of multilateral reductions, in which tariffs were cut further. The Trade and Tariff Act of 1984 authorized the president to enter into a new round of multilateral reductions in trade barriers (called the Uruguay Round), which was completed in 1995. President Clinton was denied authority by Congress to negotiate reciprocal agreements in 1997. President Bush received renewed authority in 2002.

The trade-agreements program has been an enormous success. In 1932, the average tariff rate was about 59 percent; today the average tariff rate is about 5 percent. These trade agreements are carried out under the General Agreement on Tariffs and Trade (GATT), established in 1948. All of the major countries belong to GATT, and mem-

EXAMPLE 16.4 GLOBALIZATION: SENSELESS IN SEATTLE

The antiglobalization movement came into its own when its violent protests shut down the meeting of the World Trade Organization (WTO) in Seattle in 1999. Thereafter, subsequent meetings of the WTO (in Montreal, Cancun, and numerous other locations) have been marred by protestors who rail against sweatshop labor in poor countries, against genetically modified foods, and for protecting the traditional way of life of have-not countries. The antiglobalization movement comprises ideology-driven leftists and environmentalists, labor unionists, and (behind the scenes) manufacturers who stand to lose from globalization. Supposedly, the antiglobalists claim to be protesting for "global justice" in the name of the poor. However, the only cases of poor countries that have made significant progress over the past half-century are those that have fully engaged in the global economy, such as the Asian Tigers, China, and, more recently, India. To deny the poor countries access to the global market would doom them to lives of poverty, high infant and adult mortality, and malnutrition. The major obstacle to the poor countries benefiting from globalization is the barriers that the rich countries keep in place against agricultural and raw material exports of the developing countries. It is the purpose of WTO negotiations to eliminate these barriers against poor countries. In protesting globalization and the WTO's efforts to reduce trade barriers, the protestors are clearly working against the interests of the poor people of the world.

As the WTO met in Cancun in September 2003 the gap between the rich and poor countries remained great. The rich countries could point to the continued high tariffs of the poor countries, while the poor countries could point to the rich countries' protection of the agriculture (see accompanying chart) .

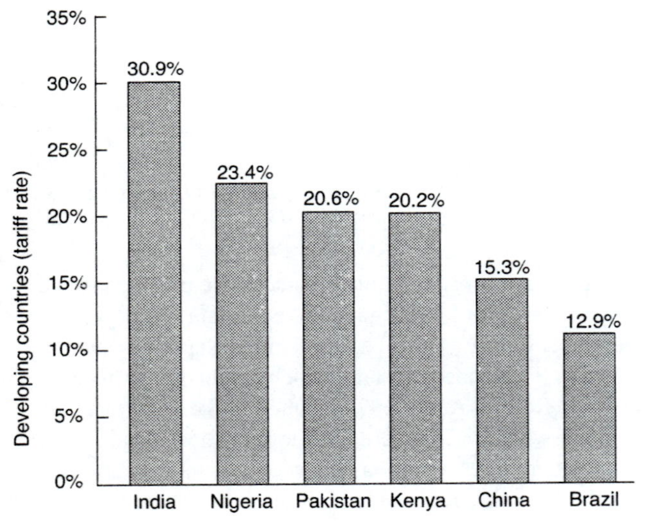

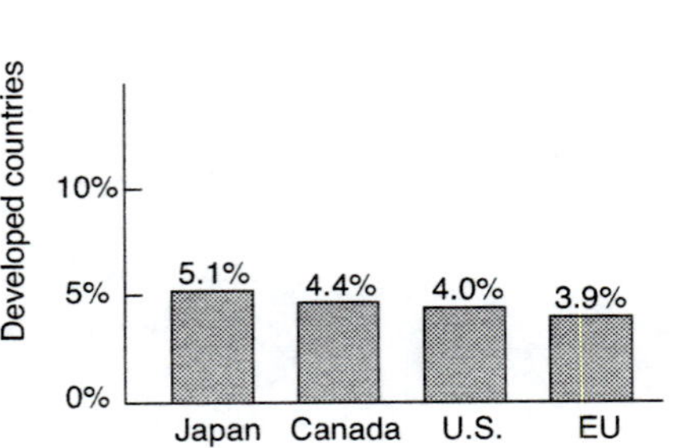

Sources: World Trade Organization; World Bank. Diagram from *Wall Street Journal,* 10 September 2003, p. A22.

bers account for about 85 percent of world trade. GATT is the forum in which international tariff negotiations take place and are supervised. GATT was replaced on 1 January 1995 by the World Trade Organization, or WTO. The WTO is the international body charged with negotiating reduced barriers to trade. Such barriers remain significant primarily with respect to the poorer countries of the globe, whose agricultural products and raw materials are excluded by high protection. (See Example 16.4.)

Summary

1. The world is a global economy. It is divided into affluent (the haves) and developing economies (the have-nots). Only about 15 percent of the world's population lives in affluent countries.
2. Just as trade and specialization can increase the economic well-being of individuals, so specialization and trade between countries can increase the economic well-being of the residents of the trading countries. The basic reason for trade is that countries cannot readily transfer their productive factors to other countries. Countries specialize in those goods for which their factor proportions are best suited. In 1817, David Ricardo formulated the law of comparative advantage, which demonstrates that countries export according to comparative advantage. Countries export those goods in which they are most efficient, or least inefficient, compared to the rest of the world. The United States has an abundance of highly skilled, technical labor. America's exports of high-technology R&D products are determined by the relative abundance of this factor.
3. Even if one country has an absolute advantage over another in the goods they both produce, both countries can still gain by specialization and trade. Countries will specialize in those products whose domestic opportunity costs are low relative to their opportunity costs in the other countries. If countries were denied the opportunity to trade, they would have to use domestic production to meet domestic consumption. Through trade, countries are able to exchange goods at more favorable terms than those dictated by domestic opportunity costs.
4. Money wages reflect the average productivity of labor in each country. Higher average labor productivity will be reflected in higher wages.
5. The major trade barriers are tariffs, import quotas, voluntary export quotas, and other nontariff barriers. A tariff is a tax levied on imports. It raises the price paid by the domestic consumer and the price received by the domestic producer of the import-competing product. Import quotas limit the amount of imports of specified products. They raise the prices paid by domestic consumers and the prices received by domestic producers of import-competing products. Quotas are normally regulated by import licenses. If import licenses are sold to importers, the government receives their scarcity value. If they are not sold, private importers benefit from their scarcity value. Voluntary export quotas direct governments to restrict their exports to another country. Voluntary export quotas create scarcity values for the right to export to the American market, but these scarcity values do not accrue to the United States.
6. The basic argument against protection is that its costs outweigh its benefits. The loss to consumers from a tariff is greater than the gain to the protected industry.
7. The politics of tariffs explains why tariffs are enacted. Although the costs of tariffs are large in total, these costs are small per person.

8. Special-interest groups, therefore, lobby and spend funds to obtain tariff protection.
9. American trade policies have changed over the years. The Hawley-Smoot Tariff Act of 1930 caused a further restriction of trade during the Great Depression by setting very high tariff rates. Since then, legislation has been passed that allows the president to negotiate tariff reductions. As a consequence of this legislation, the average tariff rate declined from 59 percent in 1932 to 5 percent in the early 2000s.

Questions and Problems

1. What are the differences and similarities between an import duty and an import quota?
2. What is the difference between an import quota and a voluntary export quota?
3. Economists agree that tariffs hurt the countries that impose them. Yet nearly all countries impose tariffs. Is something wrong with the economists' argument?
4. Frederic Bastiat, a nineteenth-century French economist/journalist, called tariffs "negative railroads." Explain.
5. A country imports shoes. The world price of shoes is $20 a pair. Show that a tariff of $5 per pair will impose larger costs on shoe consumers than the sum of the benefits to domestic shoe producers and the total tariff revenue from shoe imports.
6. In country A, one day of work produces 10 shoes and 5 loaves of bread. In country B, one day of work produces 2 shoes and 4 loaves of bread. In both countries, the number of days worked equals 1000.

   a. Draw Production Possibilities Frontiers for both countries.
   b. Calculate the standard of living in both countries without trade assuming in both countries that people want to consume equal numbers of shows and loaves of bread.
   c. What would the price of bread be in both countries without trade?
   d. If there were trade between Countries A and B, what would be the range of prices under which shoes and bread would trade in international markets?
   e. With trade, which countries would produce which goods?
   f. Demonstrate that the standard of living in both countries would be higher with trade than without.

7. I can mow 10 lawns and wash 5 cars per day, My neighbor can mow 2 lawns and wash 4 cars per day. In which activity do I have an absolute advantage? In which activity does my neighbor have a comparative advantage?
8. In the Highland-Lowland example, explain how enterprising traders could make large profits when the two countries are opened up for trade.
9. What kind of policy advice does the theory of comparative advantage and the diagram on gains from trade give to poor countries that wish to raise their standard of living?
10. If jogging shoes sell for $50 in the United States and for $20 in other countries, and only 1000 pairs of jogging shoes are allowed to be imported into the United States each year through import quotas, how much would one import quota be worth to enterprising traders?

CHAPTER 17

THE INTERNATIONAL MONETARY SYSTEM

Chapter Preview

This chapter examines the monetary side of the international exchange of goods and services. If focuses on exchange rates among different currencies and on the international monetary system.

This chapter discusses the American balance of payments, international capital movements, fixed versus floating exchange rates, the gold standard, the International Monetary Fund (IMF), and the other institutions that constitute the international monetary system.

Foreign Exchange and Exchange Rates

The Foreign-Exchange Market

Money is the medium of exchange for transactions because it is accepted by sellers in exchange for their goods and services. Sellers generally want the national currency of their own country; thus, Americans want dollars, the English want pounds sterling, the Japanese want yen, the Germans and French want Euros.

When buyers and sellers are in different countries, the buyer needs the currency of the seller's country. A U.S. farmer who sells wheat to a British miller wants to be paid in dollars; a British firm that sells a bicycle to a U.S. cyclist wants pounds sterling. The currency of another country needed for international transactions is called **foreign exchange**. Foreign exchange consists of bank deposits denominated in foreign currency and of foreign paper money.

Foreign exchange is the national currency of another country that is needed to carry out international transactions.

The buyers of international goods and services obtain foreign currency from the foreign-exchange market. This market is dispersed among many large banks and brokers throughout the world. A U.S. importer of a British bicycle pays by depositing pounds in a British bank. The money is transferred by a check, draft, or cable purchased with dollars from the importer's U.S. bank, which holds a pound deposit in a British bank. The U.S. bank gets its pound deposits from British importers of U.S. goods who buy dollars with pounds.

Foreign-exchange rates are the prices of one currency in terms of other currencies.

The price of one currency in terms of another is the **foreign-exchange rate**. Most exchange rates change from day to day and from hour to hour. In on January 2, 2004, the British pound cost $1.75, the Euro $1.26, and one U.S. dollar was worth 107 Japanese yen.

Exchange rates are used to convert prices of one currency into prices of another currency. When the exchange rate is expressed in terms of dollars per unit of foreign currency, the rate can be multiplied by the foreign price to obtain the U.S. price. For example, if a British bicycle costs 60 pounds (£60), the U.S. importer pays $86.40 if the pound is worth $1.44 ($86.40 = $1.44 × 60). When the exchange rate is expressed in terms of foreign currency per dollar, the foreign price can be divided by the rate to obtain the U.S. price. A Japanese car costing 1,410,000 yen costs $11,463 if 123 yen equal $1.

Floating or Flexible Exchange Rates

A **floating** or **flexible exchange rate** is freely determined by the interaction of supply and demand.

A **fixed exchange rate** is set by government decree or intervention.

U.S. demand for foreign exchange comes from its demand for the things that residents of the United States buy abroad; U.S. supply of foreign exchange comes from the demand by foreign residents for the things that they buy in the United States.

Exchange rates can be either fixed or floating. A **floating** or **flexible exchange rate** is freely determined by the interaction of supply and demand. A **fixed exchange rate** is an exchange rate that is set by government decree or intervention.

The U.S. dollar exchange rate is basically a floating exchange rate relative to other major currencies, such as the English pound or Euro. Some currencies have fixed exchange rates among themselves but float against the U.S. dollar or the Japanese yen. Floating exchange rates are determined in foreign-exchange markets in the following manner.

U.S. residents demand foreign exchange to buy imported commodities; to use foreign transportation services and insurance; to travel abroad; to make payments to U.S. troops stationed abroad; to remit dividends, interest, and profits to the foreign owners of U.S. stocks, bonds, and business firms; to grant foreign aid; and to make short-term and long-term investments in foreign assets.

The U.S. supply of foreign exchange is generated by foreigners' demand for U.S. dollars to buy U.S. exports; to travel in the United States; to pay U.S. owners of stock, bonds, and businesses; and to invest in U.S. assets.

To simplify the explanation of the foreign-exchange market, imagine that the world consists of two countries: the United States and the United Kingdom. The U.S. demand for foreign exchange is, thus, its demand for British pounds. Also assume that exports and imports of goods and services are the only things traded.

Figure 17.1 shows the demand curve for foreign exchange by U.S. residents. On the vertical axis is the dollar price of pounds; on the horizontal axis is the number of pounds traded. The demand curve is downward sloping because the higher the price of pounds in dollars, ceteris paribus, the higher the cost of British goods to U.S. buyers. For example, if a British bicycle costs £60 and the pound price rises from $1.30 to $1.50, the bike's price to the U.S. importer will rise from $72.00 to $90.00. This price increase will cause U.S. consumers to buy fewer English bikes and switch to U.S. brands. Thus, the higher the price of the pound, the lower the quantity of foreign exchange demanded by U.S. consumers.

The U.S. supply curve of foreign exchange depends on British importers of U.S. goods. When the English buy U.S. wheat, they supply pounds to the foreign-exchange

FIGURE 17.1 The Foreign Exchange Market

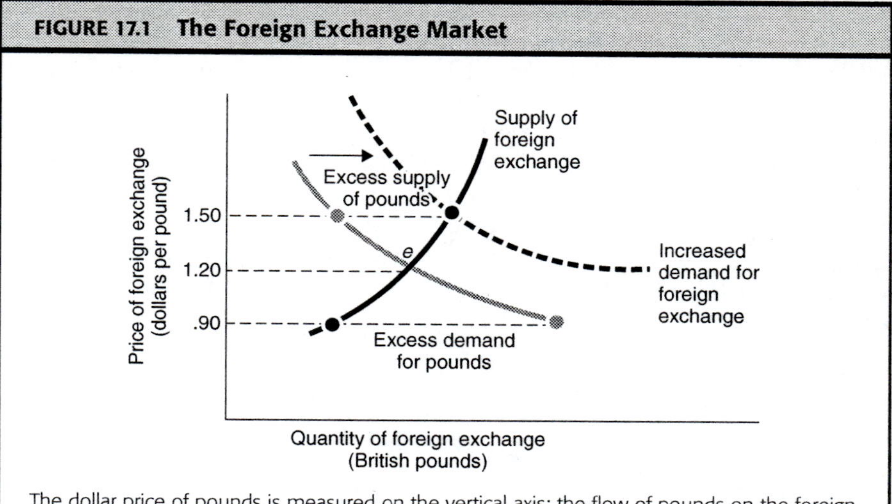

The dollar price of pounds is measured on the vertical axis; the flow of pounds on the foreign exchange market per unit of time is measured on the horizontal axis. The equilibrium exchange rate is \$1.20 = £1. If the exchange rate were \$1.50 = £1, the excess supply of pounds on the market would drive down the price. At \$0.90, there would be an excess demand for pounds on the market, bidding the price up.

If the demand increases (the dotted line), the pound appreciates (rises in value relative to the dollar) and the dollar depreciates.

market by exchanging pounds for dollars. The supply curve is upward sloping because when the dollar price of pounds rises—so that the dollar *falls* in value—U.S. goods are cheaper to foreigners. As a result, foreigners buy more U.S. goods, thereby increasing the supply of pounds available in the foreign-exchange market. For example, if a bushel of American wheat costs \$5.40, a fall in the value of the dollar from £1 = \$1.20 to £1 = \$1.50 lowers the cost of a bushel of wheat from £4.50 to £3.60. The British shift their demand from British to U.S. wheat and increase U.S. wheat consumption, stimulating U.S. exports.

When the price of pounds is \$1.50, Figure 17.1 shows that there is an excess supply of pounds on the foreign-exchange market with the initial demand curve. This excess supply bids the price of pounds down, as in any competitive market. Similarly, at a price of \$0.90, there would be an excess demand for pounds and the price of pounds would be bid up. The market-clearing price of \$1.20 not only equates the supply and demand for foreign exchange but also maintains an equilibrium between U.S. exports and imports. When the pound cheapens, the United States imports more and exports less. When the pound becomes more costly, U.S. exports increase and imports fall.

Exports and imports will not be equalized by exchange rates if there are factors besides exports or imports—such as tourism, dividend payments to foreigners, or foreign investments. Suppose that in addition to exporting and importing, some U.S. residents wish to invest in foreign securities. The solid demand curve in Figure 17.1 shows the U.S. demand for pounds to cover imports of goods. The desire to make new foreign investments shifts the demand curve outward, as shown by the dotted line. The dollar price of pounds rises, or the dollar gets cheaper. This depreciation in the dollar, or appreciation in the pound, makes U.S. goods cheaper and creates an excess of exports over imports equal to the new investment of U.S. residents in England.

A currency **depreciates** if it falls in value on the foreign-exchange market (if it buys less foreign exchange) and **appreciates** if it rises in value on the foreign-exchange market (if it buys more foreign exchange).

The terms **depreciation** and **appreciation** are used in a floating exchange-rate system. If the dollar/pound exchange rate changes from $1.80 to $1.90, the dollar **depreciates** and the pound **appreciates**. If, in Figure 17.1, the demand for British pounds increases, the pound will appreciate (it buys more dollars than before). The dollar depreciates (buys fewer pounds than before).

Purchasing Power Parity

National inflation rates play important roles in determining exchange rates. Countries that have higher rates of inflation can still trade with other the countries because the exchange rate adjusts with the relative purchasing power of the two currencies in their respective countries.

Suppose the United Kingdom and the United States have an exchange rate of $1.20 = £1. British prices now increase 10 percent, while U.S. prices are steady. At the initial exchange rate, British goods become more expensive in the United States; the demand for British goods falls; and the pound depreciates. If the pound depreciates 10 percent (to around $1.08), U.K. prices remain exactly the same to U.S. consumers. The British bike that used to cost £60 now costs £66, but since the pound fell from $1.20 to $1.08, the bike still costs $72 in the United States. The exchange rate has maintained its **purchasing power parity**. A dollar still buys the same goods in the United Kingdom as before the inflation.

Purchasing power parity holds when the exchange rate reflects the relative purchasing power of those two currencies.

The purchase power parity theory was popularized by Sweden's Gustav Cassel in 1917. The theory states that exchange rates will adjust with inflation to maintain purchasing power parity. It works well when the inflation rates between two countries are quite different. When inflation rate differentials are small, exchange rate movements will be dominated by other developments, such as fluctuations in the business cycle, capital movements, and changes in comparative advantage.

Although exchange rates at any particular time are determined by supply and demand in foreign-exchange markets, it is felt that over the long run they will be determined by purchasing power parity. If a currency is undervalued, its goods appear to foreigners to be bargains, the demand for the currency should increase, and the exchange rate will appreciate.

Fixed Exchange Rates

The alternative to floating exchange rates is fixed exchange rates. Exchange rates can be fixed either by having the currency exchange at a fixed rate relative to a precious metal, such as gold, or by having it fixed by government intervention. During the period 1870 to 1914, the world's major economies operated on a **gold standard** in which currency exchange rates had a fixed gold content and hence were rigidly fixed.

In a **gold standard** exchange rates are fixed by the relative gold content.

The **Bretton Woods system** of fixed exchange rate was in effect from 1944 to 1971.

After World War II, the major industrialized countries agreed to have fixed exchange rates, where the exchange rates would be fixed by government intervention. Each participating country would accumulate reserves of foreign exchange, which it could use to stabilize its exchange rate. This system of fixed exchange rates was agreed to at the Bretton Woods Conference in 1944. This system, which remained in place until 1971, was called the **Bretton Woods system**.

Figure 17.2 shows how a country can fix its exchange rate through intervention with its foreign exchange reserves. In this example, the United Kingdom has agreed to maintain its exchange rate at 1 pound equals $2.00. Initially, the supply and demand for pounds intersect at this exchange rate. For a number of reasons (perhaps British prices rise more rapidly than U.S. prices, or maybe British firms wish to invest in the United States), the supply of pounds increases, and there is a tendency for the pound to fall toward the new supply—demand equilibrium of 1 pound equals $1.30. In other words, the pound threatens to *devalue*. **Devaluation** occurs when a currency's official value is lowered from one fixed exchange rate to another.

Devaluation occurs when a currency's official value is lowered from one fixed exchange rate to another.

To prevent the pound's exchange rate from falling, the British government must buy the difference between the quantity of pounds supplied and the quantity of pounds demanded in the foreign-exchange market. The British Treasury can use its reserves of dollars to buy pounds any time the pound's exchange rate threatens to fall below the agreed-upon fixed rate of exchange. In Figure 17.2, the British Treasury would need to buy *ac* worth of pounds.

FIGURE 17.2 Fixed Exchange Rates through Intervention

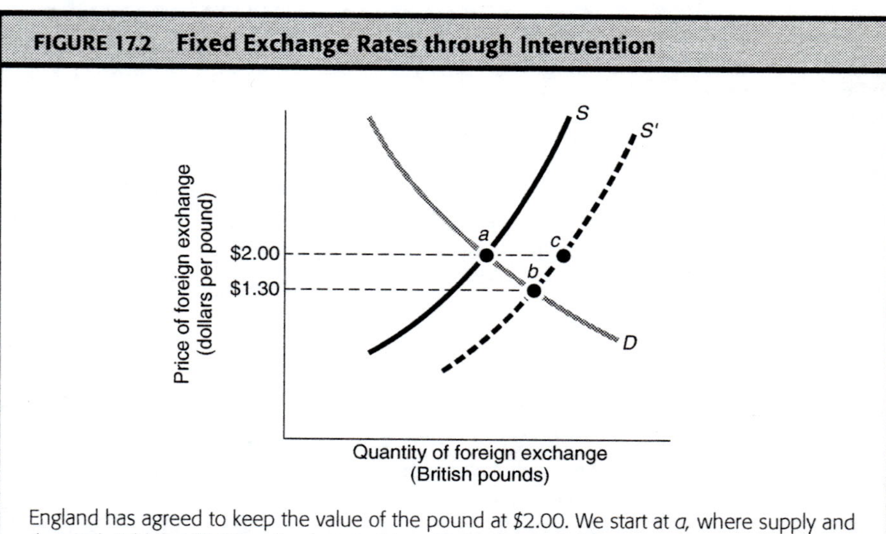

England has agreed to keep the value of the pound at $2.00. We start at *a*, where supply and demand yield the $2.00 exchange rate. The supply of pounds increases, threatening to lower the pound exchange rate to $1.30 (point *b*). In order to keep the exchange rate at $2.00, the British Treasury would have to buy *ac* British pounds in foreign-exchange markets using its reserves of dollars.

As Figure 17.2 suggests, there are limits to which a country can stabilize its exchange rate. If a country experiences continuous increases in the supply of its currency or reductions in the demand for its currency, it may exhaust its supply of foreign exchange. It no longer has reserves to buy its own currency. Moreover, speculators may decide that the country cannot keep buying its own currency and may start to sell the currency for speculative reasons, thereby further increasing its supply and hence the amount necessary to purchase.

If the country sees that it cannot maintain its exchange rate at the fixed exchange rate, it can lower its official value—that is, it can devalue the currency.

International Capital Movements

The balance of payments account says that a country's international capital account equals it current account balance, only with the opposite sign.

Capital movements enable capital-importing nations to raise their physical capital—dams, buildings, roads—above what it would be in the absence of international capital flows. When a country exports capital, it is furnishing residents of another country with funds for financing investments. Thus, capital exports transfer one country's saving into investments in another country.

Recall from Chapter 11 that GDP equals consumption (*C*) plus government spending (*G*) plus investment (*I*) plus exports (*X*) minus imports (*M*). Because GDP also equals total income, GDP equals consumption (*C*) plus saving (*S*). If government spending and taxes are assumed to be zero (for simplicity), we obtain:

The countries that save more than they invest export capital abroad.

$$C + S = C + I + X - M$$

or

$$I = S + M - X$$

This equation states that a country's investment (*I*) equals its own Saving (*S*) **plus** foreign saving ($M - X$), e.g., the amount of saving from other countries in the form of their purchases of the domestic country's stocks, bonds, real estate, and other assets. The export of capital occurs through the surplus of exports over imports. The import of capital is translated through the surplus of imports over exports.

The capital account of any country's balance of payments contains both capital inflows and outflows because investors are seeking to diversify their portfolios of investments and securities. A fundamental principle of sound investment strategy is not to put all one's eggs in one basket. By holding a portfolio of international securities—for example, investments in German companies, Japanese companies, and U.S. companies—an investor can reduce risks.

Net capital movement is influenced by the desire for higher interest rates. For the same kind of risk, investors would place their capital in the country that paid the highest interest rate. Capital exports would raise interest rates in low-interest-rate regions and lower interest rates in high-interest-rate regions. This allocation of capital gives rise to greater production everywhere in the world and, thus, a more efficient utilization of the world's scarce stock of capital.

The U.S. balance of payments account in Table 17.1 illustrates these principles of foreign savings flows. It shows that in the year 2002, the United States had a balance on current account deficit of $480 billion. We bought almost $500 billion more in current transactions with other countries than we sold. The net capital account is + $528 billion, which shows that foreigners invested $528 billion more in U.S. assets than we invested in foreign assets. The foreign savings equation above says that the two figures are equal, but some exports and imports escape the attention of statistical authorities, as do some capital transactions, such as purchases of illegal drugs and the transfer of cash to foreign drug dealers. Hence, we have a statistical discrepancy of $48 billion, which reflects the international transactions in goods and money for which we cannot account.

Chapter 11 also taught that the amount of investment an economy can undertake is limited by the amount of savings, either in the form of domestic or foreign saving. In 2002, the U.S. economy invested approximately $1.5 trillion. Almost one-third of this investment—which contributes to our long-term standard of living—was financed by foreign saving. If foreign saving had been less, then we would have had less investment.

A deficit in a nation's balance of payments, therefore, can be viewed either in the negative light as an inability to "compete" in world markets or as an ability to attract savings from other countries, perhaps due to the fact that foreigners view the country as a better investment opportunity than their own.

The International Monetary System

The world's economies have operated under different arrangements over the past century. Some have used fixed exchange rates, others flexible exchange rates.

The International Monetary Fund (IMF) was established in 1947, three years after the conference in Bretton Woods, New Hampshire. Each member of the IMF was assigned a quota determined by its trade and national income. Each country contributed 25 percent of its quota in gold or U.S. dollars and 75 percent in its own currency. Thus, the IMF accumulated a pool of gold, dollars, and major currencies that could be used to assist member countries having difficulties maintaining the value of their currency.

Under the Bretton Woods system, each country pledged to maintain a par value for its currency in terms of dollars and to maintain its exchange rate within 1 percent of this value by using its international reserves as shown in Figure 17.2. The U.S. dollar served as the anchor of the system by agreeing to convert dollars held by foreign governments into gold at $35 per ounce.

If a country faced a "fundamental disequilibrium," it was allowed to adjust its exchange rate. Countries that had to buy their own currency year after year (due, say, to higher inflation) could devalue their currency.

Speculation proved the weak link in the Bretton Woods system. If a country needed to devalue its currency, speculators would know this fact better than anyone else. The chances of the country raising the value of its currency would be virtually zero. The speculators would be in a no-lose situation—they would sell weak currencies with a vengeance and buy strong ones. For example, the British pound was often weak in the 1960s, and the German mark (DM) was often strong. Accordingly, speculators would sell pounds and buy DMs, forcing the pound to devalue.

The Bretton Woods system collapsed in 1971, when speculators began to speculate against the U.S. dollar. President Nixon, in August 1971, severed the dollar's link with gold. No longer could countries convert dollars into gold at \$35 an ounce; the dollar was set free to fluctuate. After a few attempts to fix the system, the major currencies of the world were floating and the Bretton Woods system was shattered.

The Euro

After the collapse of the Bretton Woods system, the major currencies of the world floated against one another. The daily newspaper would list that day's exchange rate of the dollar to the pound, yen, or Swiss franc. Although the major currencies floated against each other, the notion of fixed exchange rates remained attractive in some countries and regions. The countries of Europe, closely bound together in history, geography, and politics, remained determined to have fixed rates of exchange within Europe. Other countries, particularly in Asia and in Latin America, concluded that they could attract more trade and capital investment if their currencies were fixed to the dollar or to some other major currency.

EXAMPLE 17.1 THE DOLLAR, THE U.S. TRADE DEFICIT, AND ASIAN DEVELOPMENT

The theory in this chapter teaches that the currencies of countries with balance of payments deficits will depreciate. As the currency falls in value, the country will buy less from other countries and sell more, and its balance of payments deficit will disappear. The relative stability of the U.S. dollar relative to Asian currencies, therefore, is a puzzle. Even though the United States economy is running a large balance of payment deficits, both in general and relative to Asian economies in particular, the dollar has not fallen versus Asian currencies.

A likely explanation is that Asian countries require a "cheap" dollar in order to employ their vast amounts of labor reserves, such as the 200 million underemployed Chinese workers. A cheap dollar means that China can continue to sell its products to the huge American market and can bring more and more underemployed workers, particularly from agriculture, into the productive labor force.

How do the Asian economies keep the dollar cheap? With large trade deficits, the dollar should fall relative to the Japanese yen or the Chinese yuan unless Japan and China buy dollars with their own currencies. Indeed, the Asian economies have continued to buy dollars despite its recent decline relative to the Euro. If they did not, their economies would grow more slowly and they could not take advantage of their surplus labor. Note that this arrangement again makes the dollar a "reserve currency" and allows U.S. residents to buy foreign goods and pay for them in paper dollars rather than by selling goods and services abroad.

Source: Michael Dooley, David Folkerts, and Peter Garber, *An Essay on the Revived Bretton Woods System*, NBER Working Paper No. w9971m September 2003.

After the collapse of Bretton Woods, Europe created a European monetary system of fixed exchange rates, but it collapsed in 1992 when Italy, the United Kingdom, and Scandinavia left the system after suffering speculative attacks. Undeterred, Europe embarked on an even more ambitious approach to stable exchange rates within Europe—namely, the creation of a single currency for Europe.

The Treaty of Rome, signed in 1957, established the **European Economic Community**, now referred to as the European Union. It decreed that Europe was to become one common market by eliminating import duties and quotas. The momentous **Maastricht Treaty**, signed in February 1992, concluded that Europe should have a common currency and one central bank and should move toward a political union. The Treaty of Amsterdam, signed on 2 October 1997, abolished border patrols and passport requirements between member states, calling for the removal of immigration barriers among EU member countries by 2004. On 1 January 1999, the European Central Bank was established, and a common currency, the *euro*, was adopted for all bank transactions, although member countries temporarily continued to use their own national currencies. Member countries withdrew their national currencies from circulation on 1 January 2002, and the euro became the sole currency for the EU. Three countries—England, Sweden, and Denmark—opted out of the common currency. They will hold referenda at some point to determine whether to adopt the euro in place of their own national currency.

The EU, as of 2002, consisted of 15 countries (12 of which are members of the euro zone (as we have noted England, Sweden, and Denmark chose not to adopt the euro). The EU's population is 376 million, which exceeds that of the United States (at 277 million) by almost 100 million persons. At roughly $8 trillion, however, the GDP of the EU is less than the $10 trillion GDP of the United States. Hence, the per capita GDP of the EU is some 60 percent of that of the United States. The formation of the EU has therefore created a market that is roughly equal in size to that of the United States, and it has created a currency, the euro, that could ultimately challenge the world dominance of the dollar.

Fixed Exchange Rates and Currency Crises

While the European Union embarked on the course of a single currency for Europe, a number of countries and regions decided to tie their currencies to the dollar. Examples were the then-rapidly growing countries of Southeast Asia (such as the "Baby Dragons"—Thailand, Indonesia, Malaysia, and the Philippines) and Latin American countries such as Argentina. In each case, the hope was that the tying of the national currency to the dollar would encourage foreign investment. If foreign investors knew that domestic profits could be converted back into dollars at a fixed rate, they would be more willing to invest in faraway and exotic markets. Indeed, the growth prospects of the Baby Dragons and Argentina attracted considerable foreign investment, a great deal of which (as in the case of Argentina) was even denominated in dollars. This "dollarization" meant that domestic borrowers had to earn enough profits to pay the interest and principal on their foreign loans in dollars. If their currencies were to depreciate, this would make it difficult to repay outstanding debt.

Although these countries chose to tie their currencies to the dollar, most of their trade was with other countries. For example, the Baby Dragons traded primarily with other Asian countries, such as Japan, whose currency was then falling relative to the dollar. Argentina traded with other Latin American countries whose currencies were also falling relative to the dollar. Their own currencies, fixed as they were to the dollar, therefore became increasingly expensive to their trading partners, and their exports fell and their imports rose. As it became increasingly clear that their competitive trading positions were deteriorating, currency traders and speculators began to doubt that these "dollarized" countries could maintain a fixed exchange rate to the dollar. Foreign investors were also alarmed and reduced their investments and loans, making it even more difficult to maintain a fixed rate of exchange relative to the dollar.

As concern and speculation mounted, these countries experienced currency crises. A **currency crisis** occurs when a country on a fixed exchange rate system is forced to abandon its fixed rate. The Asian Crisis of the summer of 1997 began with Thailand's devaluation of its currency, quickly followed by devaluations of the other Baby Dragon economies. Almost exactly one year later, Russia was forced to dramatically devalue its ruble. In December 2002 and January 2003, Argentina dramatically devalued its peso.

A **currency crisis** occurs when a country on a fixed exchange rate system is forced to abandon its fixed rate.

Currency crises have a number of effects. First, the country no longer earns enough through its exports or its domestic profits to pay its foreign public and private debt, and it must default. Once it defaults, foreign lenders are reluctant to again invest in that country. Second, the collapse of the domestic currency means a substantial decline in the domestic standard of living. A devalued currency means that households can buy fewer imports than before because (with the less valuable currency) imported goods have become quite expensive.

The International Monetary Fund (IMF) was established in 1947 to regulate the Bretton Woods system of fixed exchange rates. After the collapse of Bretton Woods, the IMF had to seek a new role for itself. One such role has been the management of currency crises. When a country is faced with a currency crisis, the IMF can lend it money to survive the crisis. Usually, the IMF makes such loans conditional on the country enacting some kind of reform, such as reforms of the banking system, that will prevent a recurrence of the crisis.

Some critics argue that instead of making matters better, such actions by the IMF make currency crises more likely. They cite the moral hazard problem of the IMF's role as a lender of last resort. A **lender of last resort** is usually a governmental bank or agency that can provide credit to prevent bankruptcies. The IMF in its capacity of bailing out countries threatened with a currency crisis, is therefore in a position to serve as a lender of last resort. A **moral hazard problem** occurs when agents are able to change their economic behavior after a contract has been signed. In the case of currency crises, borrowers in developing countries promise to manage their businesses safely while the local governments promise to tax and spend wisely to encourage foreigners to lend. Lenders, for their part, count on a lender of last resort, such as the IMF, to bail out the borrower if borrowers are unable to pay from their own funds.

A **lender of last resort** is usually a governmental bank or agency that can provide credit to prevent bankruptcies.

A **moral hazard problem** occurs when agents are able to change their economic behavior after a contract has been signed.

As a consequence of the IMF's role as a lender of last resort, borrowers in developing economies are encouraged to borrow beyond their resource limits and lenders are encouraged to lend to uncreditworthy borrowers. If there were no IMF to play the role of lender of last resort, both borrowers and lenders would behave more responsibly.

The Balance of Payments

A country's **balance of payments** is a summary record of its transactions with foreign residents over a year or some other period.

A country's **balance of payments** is a record of all its transactions with foreign residents. It shows the country's exports, imports, earnings by domestic residents on assets located abroad, earnings on domestic assets owned by foreign residents, capital transaction between countries, and official transactions by central banks and governments.

The balance of payments is two-sided. Each transaction is recorded on two sides of the balance-of-payments accounts: the credit side and the debit side. In the plus, or credit, column are transactions that increase the supply of foreign exchange—the payments for exports of merchandise or the income earned by selling services like transportation, insurance, and capital to foreigners. In the minus, or debit, column are transactions that increase the demand for foreign exchange—imports of merchandise and income earned by foreigners from selling transportation, insurance, or capital to U.S. resident.

The balance of payments account is divided into current and capital transactions. In Table 17.1, items 1–3 are current transactions, such as exports and imports or transfers (such as remittances of migrant workers to their home country). Capital transactions, such as U.S. purchases of foreign stocks, bonds, real estate, and other assets, are shown as item 5. Purchases of foreign assets mean an outflow of dollars (hence the negative sign). Purchases by foreign residents of U.S. assets mean an inflow of dollars (hence the positive sign). The balance of current transactions, called the *balance on current account*, is the most frequently used measure of the balance of international transactions. A positive balance shows that the country is selling more

TABLE 17.1 The U.S. Balance of Payments

Item	*Amount (billions of dollars)*
1. Exports of goods and services (total)	+ 1230
a. Exports of goods	+ 682
b. Services	+ 293
c. Income receipts on investments	+ 255
2. Imports of goods and services (total)	–1651
a. Imports of goods	–1165
b. Services	–227
c. Income payments on investments	–259
3. Net unilateral transfers abroad	–59
4. Balance on current account	–480
5. Net capital account	–528
a. U.S. capital outflow	–179
b. Foreign capital inflow	+ 707
6. Statistical discrepancy	48
7. Total of all items	0

Sources: U.S. Department of Commerce, Bureau of Economic Analysis.

goods, services, and transfers to other countries than it is buying. A negative balance shows that it is buying more than it is selling.

If a country sells to other countries more than it buys, this means that other countries "owe" them the difference. If the balance on current account is a plus $100, the country's net capital account must equal –$100. In effect, the surplus on current account results in the purchase of $100 of assets of other countries. Overall, the total (current plus capital) account must therefore be equal to zero.

Although the balance of payments always balances if all transactions are considered, specific accounts of the balance of payments need not balance. U.S. merchandise exports need not equal U.S. merchandise imports, but all the surpluses in the balance of payments, as a whole, will cancel out the deficits. Table 17.1 shows the U.S. balance of payments.

Since the balance of payments, as a whole, must balance, a deficit in one account implies a surplus in some other account. A deficit in any one account should not be treated as unfavorable or a surplus as favorable. Mercantilists, those seventeenth- and eighteenth-century writers whom Adam Smith criticized, treated a surplus of exports over imports as a good thing, even calling it a *favorable* trade balance. That such a surplus would benefit a country more than an *unfavorable* trade balance is a fallacy. If a country is importing more than it is exporting, more goods are being brought in than are being sent out and living standards are higher. A trade deficit may be a good thing yet mercantilist thinking lingers on in press reports and in the minds of most people.

Summary

1. Foreign exchange is the national currency of another country needed to carry out international transactions. The U.S. demand for foreign exchange increases when U.S. residents demand more foreign goods and services. The U.S. supply of foreign exchange increases when residents of foreign countries demand more U.S. goods and services. The demand curve for foreign exchange is downward sloping because the higher the dollar price of foreign currency, the higher the cost of foreign goods to U.S. importers. The supply curve of foreign exchange tends to be upward sloping because, as the dollar price of foreign currency rises, U.S. goods appear cheaper to foreigners.
2. Under a floating exchange-rate system, the exchange rate is allowed to float to the point where the demand for foreign exchange equals the supply. When the exchange rate reflects the relative purchasing power of the currencies of two different countries, purchasing power parity prevails between the two currencies.
3. The Bretton Woods system of fixed exchange rates was abandoned in 1971. Since then, floating exchange rates among major currencies have been used. Countries that have pegged their currencies (to the dollar) have suffered periodic currency crises.
4. The European Union has established a new currency, the euro, which has replaced national currencies.
5. A country's balance of payments provides a summary record of its economic transactions with foreign residents over a period of one year. It is a two-sided

(credit/debit) summary that must always be in accounting balance. International capital movements raise the physical capital stocks in the capital-importing countries and lower them in the capital-exporting countries.

6. Today the world is on a system of floating exchange rates, with active exchange-rate stabilization by the major central banks. The Bretton Woods system set up after World War II broke down because a currency adjustment system is fundamentally in conflict with free international capital movements. Speculation destroyed the old Bretton Woods system.

Questions and Problems

1. Suppose the euro is worth $1.20 in U.S. dollars and $1.00 is worth about 100 Japanese yen. How much would a Mercedes-Benz cost in U.S. dollars if the European price were 40,000 euros? How much would a Toyota cost in U.S. dollars if the Japanese price were 1,165,000 yen?
2. The accompanying table shows part of an actual newspaper report on the foreign-exchange market. Did the British pound rise or fall from Thursday to Friday? Did the Japanese yen rise or fall from Thursday to Friday? What happened to the dollar in terms of the pound? What happened to the dollar in terms of the yen?

	Foreign Currency in Dollars		Dollars in Foreign Currency	
	Thurs.	Fri.	Thurs.	Fri.
British pound	1.5203	1.5353	0.6578	0.6573
Japanese yen	0.009689	0.009723	103.21	102.85

3. If there were a floating exchange rate between Japan and the United States, which of the following events would cause the Japanese yen to appreciate? Which would cause it to depreciate? Explain your answers.

   a. The government of Japan orders its automobile companies to limit exports to the United States.
   b. The United States places a quota on Japanese automobiles.
   c. The United States increases its money supply relative to Japan's money supply.
   d. Interest rates in the United States rise relative to Japanese interest rates.
   e. More Japanese decide to visit the United States.

4. Indicate whether each of the following transactions represents a debit (a supply of U.S. dollars) or a credit (a demand for U.S. dollars) in the U.S. balance of payments:

   a. A U.S. commercial airline buys the European-made Airbus (an airplane competing with the Boeing 747).
   b. A European airline buys a Boeing 747.
   c. A U.S. citizen makes a trip around the world.
   d. A French company pays dividends to a U.S. investor owning its stock.

   e. A U.S. investor buys stock in a French company.
   f. A U.S. company borrows from a European investor.
   g. A Canadian oil company exports oil to Japan on a U.S. tanker.
   h. A U.S. banker makes a loan to a European manufacturer.

5. Explain the mechanism under which U.S. restrictions on imports will lead to fewer U.S. exports under a floating exchange-rate system.

6. What would happen if Mexico and the United States had a fixed exchange rate but for 20 years Mexico had significantly more inflation than the United States?

7. If you were lending money to a friend, knowing that friend had a rich grandfather, why might this situation create a moral hazard problem? Relate this problem to international lending.

8. Let us say that the country Carpathia's currency, the carp, has a fixed exchange rate whereby 1 carp equals 1 dollar. This exchange rate is fixed by Carpathia being willing to buy carps at this rate with its reserves of dollars. Carpathia's major trading partners' currencies, however, float against the dollar and are becoming every day less valuable relative to the dollar. What kinds of opportunity would you perhaps see to speculate against the carp?

9. History shows that fixed exchange rate regimes from the Bretton Woods system are unstable. Explain why this is so.

10. Country X sells \$10 worth of merchandise to other countries and buys \$5 worth of merchandise from other countries. Country X sells \$20 worth of services to other countries and buys \$25 worth of services from other countries. It receives \$5 from other countries from investments it has made in the past and pays \$7 to other countries for investments that they have made in country X in the past. These represent all of its current transactions with other countries.

   a. What is its merchandise balance?
   b. What is its balance on current account?
   c. What is its capital account balance?

11. Explain the relationship between the current account balance and the capital account balance.

GLOSSARY

Ability-to-pay principle of taxation States that those better able to pay should bear the greater burden of taxation whether or not they benefit.

Adaptive expectations Hold that people form their expectations of the future from past experience and only gradually modify their expectations as experience unfolds.

Agent Party that acts for, on behalf of, or as a representative of a principal in negotiating market transactions.

Aggregate demand curve Shows the quantities of total output economic agents are prepared to demand (buy) at different price levels.

Aggregate supply curve Shows the quantities of total output all firms in the economy are willing to supply at different price levels.

Allocation The apportionment of resources for a specific purpose or to particular persons or groups.

Annual rate of inflation Calculated by taking the annual rate of change in the Consumer Price Index or the GDP deflator.

Appreciation A currency is said to appreciate if it rises in value on the foreign-exchange market (if it buys more foreign exchange).

Arbitrage through time Buying a commodity at a time when it is cheap and reselling it at a time when it is expensive.

Automatic stabilizers Government spending or taxation actions that take place without any deliberate government control and that automatically dampen the business cycle.

Autonomous changes Taxes and government spending are changes in tax rates or government spending that do not automatically occur because of changes in income.

Average fixed cost *(AFC)* Fixed cost *(FC)* divided by output *(Q)*: $AFC = FC/Q$.

Average total cost *(ATC)* Total cost *(TC)* divided by output *(Q)*, which also equals sum of average variable cost *(AVC)* and average fixed cost *(AFC)*: $ATC = TC/Q = AVC + AFC$.

Average variable cost *(AVC)* Variable cost *(VC)* divided by output *(Q)*: $AVC = VC/Q$.

Balance of payments Summary record of a country's economic transactions with foreign residents over a year or any other period.

Balance sheet A T-shaped accounting sheet that shows the financial condition by listing assets and liabilities.

Banking The business of making loans and investments out of deposits.

Benefit principle of taxation Argues that those who benefit from a public expenditure program should pay for the program.

Bonds Bonds bind the corporation to pay a fixed sum of money (the principal) at maturity and also to pay a fixed interest payment at specified dates until the maturity date.

Bretton Woods system The system of fixed exchange rates that was used from the end of World War II until 1971.

Business cycle Pattern of upward and downward movement in the general level of real business activity.

Capitalism Economic system characterized by private ownership of the factors of production, market allocation of resources, the use of economic incentives, and decentralized decision making.

Cartel Arrangement that allows the participating firms to coordinate their output and pricing decisions to earn monopoly profits.

Cash leakage A withdrawal of currency from a bank.

Caveat emptor "Let the buyer beware." Buyer must assume liability for defective or dangerous products.

Caveat venditor "Let the seller beware." Seller must assume liability for defective or dangerous products.

Ceteris paribus "Other things being equal." The relationships identified by economic theories are defined in a ceteris paribus sense—that is, the theory describes the relationship between two factors when all other relevant factors do not change.

Circular-flow diagram Summarizes the flows of goods and services from enterprises to households and the flows of the factors of production from households to business firms.

Collective bargaining Union bargaining with management in the name of all its members.

Comparative advantage Principle that resources should be used in their relatively best (or least worst) application.

Compensating wage differentials The higher rewards that must be paid to compensate for undesirable job characteristics.

Complements Two goods are complements if the demand for one rises when the price of the other falls or when the demand for one falls when the price of the other rises.

Conglomerate corporation Corporation comprising branches that operate in different industries.

Conscious parallelism Occurs when oligopoly firms behave in the same way even though they have not agreed to act in a parallel manner.

Consumer Price Index Measures the change in consumer prices.

Consumption function Shows the relationship between real disposable income and real consumption.

Contractionary fiscal policy Lowers aggregate demand by lowering government spending and/or raising taxes.

Contractionary monetary policy Lowers aggregate demand by reducing the money supply.

Corporation Entity owned by stockholders; it has the legal status of an individual and is authorized by law to act as a legal person. The stockholders elect a board of directors, which appoints the management.

Cost/benefit analysis The comparison of the benefits and costs of any decision to determine its economic usefulness.

Credit markets Borrowers come together with lenders to determine conditions of exchange such as interest rates and the duration of a loan.

Currency appreciation Occurs when currency rises in value on the foreign-exchange market; it buys more foreign exchange.

Currency crisis Occurs when a country on a fixed exchange rate system is forced to abandon its fixed rate.

Currency depreciation Occurs when currency falls in value on the foreign-exchange market: it buys less foreign exchange.

Cyclical unemployment Unemployment associated with general downturns in the economy.

Cyclically balanced budget Is a budget whose deficits and surpluses cancel out over the business cycle.

Deficit Exists when the federal expenditures (G) exceed federal tax collections and other revenues (T)—if $G > T$.

Deflationary gap Exists if equilibrium output falls short of the natural level of output.

Demand That quantity of a good that people are actually prepared to buy with their limited income at prevailing relative prices.

Demand curve Shows the quantity of the good demanded at different prices, all other factors held constant.

Demand curve for a factor Shows the quantities of a factor that would be purchased (demanded) at different prices, *ceteris paribus.*

Demand deposits Are bank accounts on which checks can be written.

Demand, law of States that there is a negative (inverse) relationship between the price of a good and the quantity demanded, *ceteris paribus.*

Demand-side inflation Occurs when aggregate demand increases and pulls prices up. A characteristic feature of demand-side inflation is that prices rise and unemployment falls.

Deposit multiplier Ratio of the change in deposits to excess reserves.

Depreciation The value of the existing capital stock that has been consumed or used up in the process of producing output. A currency is said to depreciate if it falls in value on the foreign exchange market.

Deregulation Elimination of government controls (exercised by regulatory authorities) over a firm's prices, quantity, and quality of services.

Derived demand Results from the demand for the goods and services the factor of production helps to produce.

Devaluation Occurs when a currency's official value is lowered from one fixed exchange rate to another.

Developing country A country with a per capita income well below that of a typical advanced country.

Diminishing returns, law of States that as ever larger inputs of a variable factor are combined with fixed inputs, eventually the *MP* (marginal product) of the variable input will decline.

Discount rate Interest rate the Fed charges banks that wish to borrow reserves.

Discretionary fiscal policies Government spending and taxation actions that have been taken deliberately to achieve specified macroeconomic goals.

Discretionary policy The setting of monetary and fiscal targets by policymakers, based on their best judgments.

Dollar votes The willingness of consumers to buy at a specified price.

Double coincidence of wants Are required for barter to take place. The baker must want the shoes of the shoemaker and vice versa.

Downward-sloping curve Graph of the relationship when two variables are negatively related.

Dynamic scoring A projection of future revenues and deficits taking into account the simulative effect of lower tax rates on economic activity.

Earnings per share Equals profits divided by the number of shares.

Economic agents Engage in production, exchange, specialization, and consumption.

Economic growth The expansion of output over the long run.

Economic inefficiency When it is possible to rearrange production so that the benefits to gainers outweigh the costs to the losers.

Economic problem How to determine the use of scarce resources among competing uses. Because resources are scarce, the economy must choose *what* products to produce, *how* these products are to be produced, and *for whom.*

Economic profit Equals the firm's revenues minus its total opportunity costs (explicit plus implicit costs).

Economic system The arrangements and institutions that deal with scarcity.

Economics Study of how we use our scarce resources to specialize in production and to exchange and consume goods and services

Economic theory A coherent and plausible explanation of how certain economic facts are related. Economic theory seeks to isolate the factors that are most important in explaining an economic phenomenon. Economic theories typically yield hypotheses (or predictions) about how factors are related.

Efficient economy When no resources are unemployed and no resources are misallocated.

Elasticity Measures the degree of responsiveness to price changes of quantity demanded and supplied.

Entitlement program Requires the federal government to pay benefits to anyone who meets the eligibility requirements of the program.

Entry barriers Any conditions that put new firms at a disadvantage to old firms.

Equation of exchange ***(MV = PY)*** Used to explain the relationship between money (*M*) and prices (*P*).

Equilibrium (market-clearing) price Price at which the quantity demanded by consumers equals the quantity supplied by producers.

European Economic Community Is the core of European countries that formed the European Union.

Excess reserves An amount held in reserve that exceeds the required reserves.

Exchange Trading of goods and services produced through specialization.

Exhaustive expenditures Government purchases that divert resources from the private sector, making them no longer available for private use.

Expansionary fiscal policy Increases aggregate demand by raising government spending and/or lowering taxes.

Expansionary monetary policy Increases aggregate demand by increasing the money supply.

Explicit cost Incurred when an actual payment is made for a resource.

Extensive growth Economic growth that results from the expansion of factor inputs.

External cost An unpriced cost that is imposed on others.

Externality Unpriced marginal cost or marginal benefit. Unpriced means that the economic agent does not bear the full marginal cost or enjoy the full marginal benefit of his or her action.

External national debt Debt owed to citizens of other countries.

Factor market One in which firms purchase land, labor, or capital inputs.

Factors of production Land, labor, and capital.

Federal deficit The excess of federal government expenditures over federal government revenues.

Financial intermediaries Link lenders and borrowers.

Financial markets Are exchanges on which stocks and bonds are traded.

Fiscal policy Refers to changes in government spending or tax rates for the purpose of achieving macroeconomic goals.

Fixed costs (*FC*) Costs that do not vary with output.

Fixed exchange rate A rate set by government decree or intervention.

Fixed inputs Inputs that do not change with output.

Floating, or flexible, exchange rate A rate freely determined by the interaction of supply and demand.

Foreign exchange National currency of another country needed to carry out international transactions. Normally, foreign exchange consists of bank deposits denominated in the foreign currency but may sometimes consist of foreign money when foreign travel is involved.

Foreign-exchange rate The amount of one currency required to buy one unit of another currency.

Foreign trade effect Occurs when a rise in the domestic price level (holding foreign prices and the exchange rate constant) lowers the aggregate quantity demanded by pushing down net exports ($X - M$).

Fractional-reserve banking system Exists when the ratio of bank reserves to deposit liabilities is less than 1. Bank reserves are less than bank deposit liabilities. In modern commercial banking reserves are only a small fraction of deposit liabilities.

Free goods Goods that have a zero opportunity cost. Users can have more of the good without others having to give up some of the good.

Free rider Anyone who enjoys the benefits of a good or service without paying. A free rider does not have property rights to the good but consumes it anyway.

Frictional unemployment Unemployment associated with the changing of jobs and the entering and leaving of the labor force in a dynamic economy.

Gains from trade Occur when countries specialize and are able to purchase more by trading in goods.

GDP deflator Measures the change in the prices of all goods and services produced by the economy.

Globalization Refers to the degree to which national economic markets and international businesses are integrated and interrelated into a world economy.

Gold standard The system of international payments that pegged currencies to a fixed content of gold, used from the 1870s to 1914.

Gross domestic product (GDP) The market value of all final goods and services produced by the factors of production located in the country in one year's time.

Gross national product (GNP) Measures the production of the factors of production supplied by residents of the country whether that production took place at home or abroad.

Household production Goods that do not enter the circular flow.

Household saving What we have left over from our income after buying goods and services and paying our income taxes.

Human capital Investment in schooling, training, and health that raises productivity.

Hyperinflation Very rapid and constantly growing rate of inflation. At a minimum, prices double every year; at its worst, prices can double daily or hourly.

Implicit contract An agreement between employer and employees concerning conditions of pay, employment, and unemployment that is unwritten but understood by both parties.

Implicit cost Incurred when an alternative is sacrificed by the firm using a resource that it owns.

Import quota Limitation on the amount of a specific product that can be imported during a given period.

Income effect Increase in the purchasing power of income resulting from a decrease in price.

Inflation General increase in prices; usually expressed as an annual rate of increase.

Inflationary expectations Rates of inflation expected to prevail in the future.

Inflationary gap Exists if equilibrium output exceeds the natural level of output.

Information costs Costs in time and money of acquiring information on prices today and in the future and on product qualities.

Intensive growth Economic growth that results from increases in output per unit of factor input.

Interest rate effect Higher prices raising interest rates and thereby discouraging investment.

Interest rate spread Difference between the interest rates that banks pay their depositors and the interest rates they receive on their loans and investments.

Intermediaries Specialize in information either to bring together two parties to a transaction or to buy in order to sell again.

Intermediate goods Goods that do not enter the circular flow.

Internal national debt Debt owed to the citizens of the country.

Internet Is a network of related computers that can communicate with each other.

Investment Refers to business investment in new plants, equipment, and inventories. The rate at which society expands its capital depends on the amount of investment.

Investment cycles Show fluctuations in real investment.

Investment demand curve Shows the amount of investment desired at different interest rates.

Invisible hand States that no single person need know all prices to function efficiently in daily economic life. Economic agents need only know the prices of the things that are significant to them.

Keynesian Refers to the writings of John Maynard Keynes.

Keynesian revolution Was the notion that deliberate deficits are required during economic downturns.

Labor force Number of persons employed plus the number unemployed.

Labor market Any arrangement that brings buyers and sellers of labor services together to agree on conditions of work and pay.

Labor union Collective organization of workers and employees whose goal is to affect conditions of pay and employment.

Laissez-faire A hands-off, minimal role for government in economic affairs.

Law of comparative advantage States that it is better for people or countries to specialize in those activities at which they have the greatest advantage over other people or countries.

Law of diminishing returns States that as ever larger inputs of a variable factor are combined with fixed inputs, eventually its *MP* will decline.

Law of increasing costs States that as more of a particular commodity is produced, its opportunity cost per unit increases.

Law of scarcity States that wants always exceed our ability to meet these wants.

Lender of last resort Denotes a lender, such as a national bank, who will pay the debts of a borrower rather than let the borrower go bankrupt.

Life-cycle theory of consumption States that households base their consumption and saving decisions on the long-term income they expect to earn over their lifetimes.

Liquidity Refers to how quickly and with what risk an asset can be converted into money. The more liquid the asset the closer it substitutes.

Logrolling Permits the approval of projects by vote-trading coalitions that would be opposed by a majority if considered in isolation.

Long run A period of time long enough to vary all inputs and for firms to enter and leave the industry.

Long-run average cost (*LRAC*) Consists of the minimum average cost for each level of output when all factor inputs are variable (and when factor prices and the state of technology are fixed).

M1 Sum of currency and coins, checking account deposits held by the public (excluding the banks' own checking accounts), travelers' checks, and other deposits (such as NOW and ATS accounts) upon which checks can be written.

M2 Equals M1 plus savings deposits and small time deposits plus money-market, mutual-fund shares plus other highly liquid assets.

Maastricht Treaty The treaty that agreed to a common European currency.

Macroeconomics Studies total output and its growth, total employment and unemployment, and the general movement in prices.

Majority rule Under majority rule, the median voter determines the outcome. The median voter's preferences count most because precisely half of the remaining voters prefer less of the public good and half prefer more.

Marginal cost (*MC*) Change in total cost (*TC*) [or equivalently in variable cost (*VC*)] divided by the increase in output or, alternatively, the increase in costs per unit increase in output (Q): $MC = \Delta TC/\Delta Q = \Delta VC/\Delta Q$.

Marginal product of a factor of production (*MP*) Increase in output that results from increasing the factor by one unit, holding all other inputs and the level of technology fixed.

Marginal product of labor Increase in output that results from increasing labor input by one unit.

Marginal revenue (*MR*) Increase in revenue brought about by increasing output or sales by one unit. For a firm in perfect competition *MR* = price.

Marginal revenue product (*MRP*) A factor of production is the extra revenue generated by increasing the factor by one unit.

Marginal tax rate Ratio of the increase in taxes to the increase in income.

Market (or equilibrium) rate of interest The rate that equates the quantity of investment with the quantity of saving.

Market test Ensures that only goods whose benefits exceed their costs will be produced in the long run.

Markets Arrangements that brings buyers and sellers together for the purpose of determining conditions of exchange.

Median voter Voters whose preferences for a particular public good are such that 50 percent of the voting population desires less of the public good and 50 percent desires more of it.

Microeconomics Study of the economic decisions of the individual participants in the economy.

Minimum efficient scale The firm's lowest level of output at which long-run average costs are minimized.

Misery index The sum of the inflation and unemployment rates.

Monetary base Equals reserves on deposit at the Fed plus vault cash plus currency in circulation. It increases when the Fed buys something, decreases when the Fed sells something.

Monetary policy Refers to changes in the money supply and credit conditions for the purpose of achieving macroeconomic goals, such as a certain level of unemployment or inflation.

Monetarist Represents the conclusion that the money supply should expand at a constant rate.

Monetization of debt Creation of demand-deposit liabilities in the process of making bank loans.

Money Anything that serves as a medium of exchange, a unit of value, and a store of value.

Money illusion Could cause economic agents to think that a change in the price level is actually a change in real wages or relative prices and so change their production and employment decisions.

Money price Price expressed in monetary units (such as dollars, yen, or marks).

Monopolistic competition An industry characterized by many sellers, free entry and exit, perfect information, and a differential product.

Monopoly One seller of a good that has no close substitutes, with considerable control over price and protection from competition by barriers to entry.

Monopoly rent-seeking Is the expenditure of resources to gain monopoly rights from government.

Moral hazard problem Occurs when agents change their behavior to take advantage of principals.

Mutual interdependence Characterizes an industry where it is recognized that the actions of one firm affect other firms in the industry.

National debt Total of outstanding federal government IOUs (outstanding government bonds) on which the federal government must pay interest.

National income Equals GNP minus depreciation and indirect business (sales) taxes. National income equals the sum of factor payments made to the factors of production in the economy.

Natural level of real GDP Level of output the economy produces when it is at the natural rate of unemployment.

Natural rate of unemployment The rate at which there is an approximate balance between the number of unfilled jobs and the number of qualified job seekers.

Negative (or inverse) relationship Exists between two variables if an increase in the value of one variable is associated with a reduction in the value of the other variable.

Network externalities Apply to goods whose value increase as more units are sold.

Neutral tax system System that leaves private decision making unchanged—that is, people would make the same decisions with or without taxes.

Nominal GDP Value of final goods and services for a given year expressed in that year's prices.

Nominal interest rate The cost of borrowing expressed as an annual percentage rate unadjusted for the effects of inflation.

Nonactivism Calls for fixed monetary and fiscal policy rules.

Noncompeting groups Those groups of people that are differentiated by natural ability and education, training, and experience to the extent that they do not compete with one another for jobs.

Nontariff barriers Barriers that restrict trade other than tariffs, such as quotas.

Normal profit Earned when total revenues equal total opportunity costs. An economic profit is earned when total revenues exceed total opportunity costs.

Normative economics Study of what *ought to be* in the economy.

Oligopolist A price searcher who must consider the reactions of competitors.

Oligopoly An industry characterized by a small number of producers, barriers to entry, price searching, and mutual interdependence.

Open-market operations Purchases and sales of federal government securities (bonds and bills) on the Fed's account as directed by the Federal Open Market Committee.

Opportunistic behavior Occurs when the agent is able to fulfill formally a contract while engaging in behavior that is not in the interest of the principal.

Opportunity cost The loss of the next-best alternative through an action.

Opportunity cost of any action The value of the next-best alternative through any action of consumption, production, leisure, government spending.

Opportunity cost of any resource The payment that a resource—land, labor, capital, materials—would receive in its next-best alternative use.

Partnership Business enterprise owned by two or more people called partners who, like sole proprietors, make all the business decisions, share the profits, and bear financial responsibility jointly.

Peak The final stage of the business cycle that precedes recession. Output growth ceases after the peak is reached.

Perfect competition A market with many sellers, perfect information, a homogeneous product, and freedom of entry.

Personal disposable income Equals personal income minus personal income tax payments.

Personal income Equals the sum of all income received by persons—national income minus retained corporate profits, corporate income taxes, and social security contributions plus transfer payments received by individuals.

Phillips curve Shows a negative relationship between the unemployment rate and the inflation rate. It reveals that a reduction in the unemployment rate requires an increase in inflation.

Policy activism The deliberate manipulation of fiscal and monetary policy to iron out fluctuations in the business cycle.

Positive economics Study of *what is* in the economy.

Positive (or direct) relationship Exists between two variables if an increase in the value of one variable is associated with an increase in the value of the other variable.

Price elasticity of demand Absolute value of the percentage change in quantity demanded divided by the percentage change in price.

Price elasticity of supply Percentage change in quantity supplied divided by the percentage change in price.

Price index Shows the current year's cost of buying a particular basket of goods as a percentage of the cost of the same basket of goods in some earlier year.

Price searchers Face a downward-sloping demand curve.

Price searching firm Faces a downward-sloping demand curve. To sell more, it must lower its price.

Price system Entire set of millions of relative prices.

Price taker A buyer or seller who takes the market price as given.

Principal Engages an agent to act subject to the principal's control and instruction.

Principle of substitution States that practically no good is irreplaceable. Users are able to substitute one good for another as relative prices change.

Product markets Markets where goods and services are bought and sold to households.

Production functions Show the relationship between inputs and output. They show how much output can be produced from different amounts of labor and capital with a given state of technology.

Production possibilities frontier (PPF) Shows the combinations of goods and services available when the factors of production are utilized to their full potential. The PPF shows the economic choices open to an economy producing at full potential.

Profitable speculation Stabilizes prices and consumption by reducing fluctuations in prices and consumption over time.

Profit maximization Search by a firm for the product quantity, quality, and price that gives that firm the highest possible profit.

Progressive tax Higher-income taxpayers pay a higher percentage of their income as taxes.

Property rights Rights of the owner to use and exchange property.

Proportional tax Taxpayers earning different incomes pay the same percentage of their income as taxes.

Public good A good or service whose use by one person does not reduce its use to others and whose use by nonpayers cannot be prevented.

Purchasing power parity Holds when the exchange rate between two currencies reflects the relative purchasing power of those two currencies in their respective countries.

Pure monopoly Exists when there is one seller of a good that has no close substitutes, the seller has considerable control over price, and there is protection from competition by barriers to entry.

Pure public good Characterized by nonrival consumption among all potential users; and one that does not prevent nonpayers from using the good (nonexclusion).

Quantity supplied Amount of a good offered for sale at a particular price.

Rational expectations Assume that people use not only past experience but also their predictions about the effects of present and future policy actions.

Rational expectations economist Believe that policy can be thwarted if widely anticipated.

Rational ignorance Decision not to acquire additional information because the marginal costs exceed the marginal benefits. Rational ignorance is usually applied to the gathering of information by voters.

Real balance effect States that increases in prices cause the real value of wealth to fall. At higher price levels households will purchase less real consumption for a given income because of the decline in the purchasing power of their wealth.

Real GDP Measures the volume of real goods and services produced by the economy by removing the effects of rising prices on nominal GDP.

Real interest rate The nominal interest rate minus the anticipated rate of inflation.

Real wages Measured by money wages, *W*, divided by the price level, *P*—that is, *W/P*.

Recession Occurs when real output declines for a period of six months or more.

Recovery (expansion) Characterized by rising output, falling unemployment, rising profits, and increasing economic activity.

Regressive tax High-income taxpayers pay a smaller percentage of their income as taxes.

Relative price Price expressed in terms of other commodities.

Required-reserve ratio The amount of reserves required for each dollar of deposits.

Reservation wage The lowest wage a job hunter must be offered before accepting a job.

Reserve requirement Rule that states the amount of reserves that must be on hand to back bank deposits.

Resources Land and natural resources, labor, and capital that can be combined to produce goods and services.

Saving function Shows the relationship between real disposable income and real savings.

Say's law States that whatever aggregate output is produced will be demanded. Desired aggregate expenditures equal actual output.

Scarce goods Goods that have a positive opportunity cost. In order to have more of a scarce good, an alternative must be sacrificed. Every choice involving the allocation of scarce goods involves opportunity costs.

Scarcity Exists when the amount of the good or resource offered is less than what users would want if it were given away free.

Scarcity, law of States that wants always exceed society's ability to meet these wants because of scarce resources.

Scatter diagram Plots the values of one variable against values of another variable for a specific time interval.

Shares of stock Represent ownership shares of corporations. Once these shares have been issued, they are bought and sold (traded) on stock exchanges.

Sherman Antitrust Act of 1890 Constitutes the basic U.S. law against monopoly.

Shortage Results if the quantity demanded exceeds the quantity supplied at the prevailing price; the price is too low to equate the quantity demanded with the quantity supplied.

Short run Period of time too short for existing plant or equipment to be varied. Additional output can only be produced by increasing the variable inputs, usually labor and materials.

Short-run aggregate supply (*SRAS*) Schedule of the quantities of real output the economy is prepared to supply at different price levels, holding the expected price level and other factors constant.

Shutdown rule States that if the firm's price at all levels of output is less than average variable costs, it minimizes its losses by shutting down.

Simple arbitrage Buying in a market where a commodity is cheap and reselling it in a market where the commodity is more expensive.

Slope Exists when the straight line is the ratio of the rise (or fall) in Y over the run in X.

Socialism An economic system under which the state owns the resources and makes the economic decisions.

Sole proprietorship Most simple form of business enterprise; owned by one individual who makes all the business decisions, receives all the profits, and bears sole financial responsibility for losses.

Special-interest groups Minority voting groups with intense preferences about specific government policies.

Specialization The use of resources to their best advantage. People will produce more of a particular good than they consume and the surplus will be exchanged for the goods they want.

Speculators Those who buy or sell in the hope of profiting from market fluctuations.

Stagflation Combination of high inflation and high unemployment in a stagnant economy.

Stock Shares of stock represents the ownership of $1/n$ percent of the corporation, where n is the number of shares outstanding. Owners of shares can vote on corporate matters and receive dividends proportional to their share holdings.

Strategic behavior Occurs when rivals must anticipate the actions of other companies.

Strike Occurs when unionized employees cease work until management agrees to specific union demands.

Substitutes Two goods are substitutes if the demand for one rises when the price of the other rises or falls when the price of the other falls.

Substitution effect Tendency to buy more of a product as a result of a decrease in its relative price.

Substitution, principle of States that users are able to substitute one good for another as relative prices change.

Supply curve Quantities of a good supplied at different prices, all other factors that affect supply being held constant.

Supply curve of a factor Quantity of a factor that is offered for sale (supplied) at different factor prices, *ceteris paribus.*

Supply shock Shift in aggregate supply caused by some external factor that causes costs of production to change.

Supply-side economics Maintains that tax cuts, particularly cuts in marginal tax rates, will substantially increase output and employment by enhancing work effort and risk taking.

Supply-side inflation Occurs when aggregates supply drops and pushes the price level up. A characteristic feature of supply-side inflation is that prices and unemployment rise together.

Surplus Results when the quantity supplied exceeds the quantity demanded at the current price; the price is too high to equate the quantity demanded with the quantity supplied.

Tangent Straight line that touches the curve at only one point.

Tariff Tax levied on imports.

Technological progress Causes the production possibilities frontier to shift out. More output is produced from the same inputs.

Technology Accumulated scientific and technical knowledge about how to produce specific goods and services.

Time series A measurement of one or more variables over a designated period of time.

Time trend The tendency of variables to rise generally, or to fall generally, with the general rise in the economy.

Total costs (*TC*) Sum of fixed costs (*FC*) plus variable costs (*VC*): $TC = FC + VC$.

Trade barrier Constitutes a barrier, as tariffs or quotas, that restrict international trade.

Trade deficit Excess of imports over exports.

Transactions cost Any cost associated with bringing buyers and sellers together.

Transfer payments Payments to recipients who have not supplied goods or services in return. They are simply transfer of income from one person or organization to another.

Trough Occurs when output stops falling and the economy has reached a low point from which recovery begins.

Unemployed Person who has not worked at all during the previous week, has actively looked for work during the previous four weeks, and is currently available for work.

Unemployment rate Number of unemployed divided by the labor force (the sum of employed and unemployed persons).

Unprofitable speculation Occurs when the speculator buys at a high price and must sell at a low price.

Upward-sloping curve Graph of the relationship when two variables are positively related.

Variable costs (*VC*) Costs that vary with output.

Variable inputs Increase with output.

Velocity of circulation Measures the average number of times money changes hands in the course of a year.

Vertical merger Merger of two firms that are part of the same materials, production, or distribution network (such as a personal computer manufacturer merging with a retail computer distribution chain or a machinery manufacturer merging with a machinery parts supplier).

Virtual market Market in which goods and services are bought through electronic markets like the Internet.

Voluntary export quota Agreement between two governments in which the exporting country "voluntarily" limits the export of a certain product to the importing country.

Wants Quantities of goods and services people would wish to have if there were no costs (if the price were zero).

Wealth The total value of income-producing property or assets.

***x*-Firm concentration ratio** Percentage of industry sales (or output, labor force, or assets) accounted for by the largest *x* domestic firms in the industry.

INDEX

NOTE: Page numbers followed by *f* and *t* refer to figures and tables respectively.